CIVIL PROCEDURE 2001

Second
Cumulative Supplement
To the
2001 Edition

Up-to-date generally to October 1, 2001

LONDON
SWEET & MAXWELL
2000

Published in 2001 by Sweet & Maxwell Limited of 100 Avenue Road,
London NW3 3PF.
Reference tables typeset by Mendip Communications Ltd, Frome, Somerset. All other typesetting by Sweet & Maxwell electronic publishing system.
Printed in England by Clays Ltd, St Ives plc.

No natural forests were destroyed to make this product; only farmed timber was used and replanted.

British Library Cataloguing in Publication Data
A catalogue record for this book is available from the British Library

Civil Procedure Mainwork ISBN 0-421-720-409
Supplement 1 ISBN 0421 76320 5
Supplement 2 ISBN 0421 77200 X

All rights reserved. UK statutory material in this publication is acknowledged as Crown copyright.

No part of this publication may be reproduced or transmitted in any form or by any means, or stored in any retrieval system of any nature without prior written permission, except for permitted fair dealing under the Copyright, Designs and Patents Act 1988, or in accordance with the terms of a licence issued by the Copyright Licensing Agency in respect of photocopying and/or reprographic reproduction. Application for permission for other use of copyright material including permission to reproduce extracts in other published works shall be made to the publishers. Full acknowledgment of author, publisher and source must be given.

Such permission is hereby granted to members of the legal profession (which expression does not include individuals or organisations engaged in the supply of services to the legal profession) to reproduce, transmit and store the text of the Forms set out in Volume 1 for the purpose of enabling them to conduct proceedings on behalf of, or to provide legal advice to, their clients.

©
Sweet & Maxwell Limited
2001

Sharnjeel Ragubans

Table of Statutes

[**References in bold** type are to the paragraph at which that section, or part of that section, is set out in full.]

1925
Supreme Court of Judicature (Consolidation) Act (15 & 16 Geo. 5, c.49) ... 9A–443

1927
Landlord and Tenant Act (17 & 18 Geo. 5, c.36) ... 56PD–013
Pt. I 2BPD–011

1932
Chancel Repairs Act (22 & 23 Geo. 5, c.20)
s.2 .... 56PD–029

1948
National Assistance Act (11 & 12 Geo. 6, c.29)
s.21 .... 3A-1184.1

1954
Landlord and Tenant Act (2 & 3 Eliz. 2, c.56)
s.24 .... 2BPD–011

1960
Administration of Justice Act (8 & 9 Eliz. 2, c.65)
s.1(1) 4B–1

1962
Recorded Delivery Service Act (10 & 11 Eliz. 2, c.27) 9A–443

1968
Criminal Appeal Act (c. 19)
s.33(1) 4B–1
Courts-Martial (Appeals) Act (c. 20)
s.39(1) 4B–1

1971
Administration of Estates Act (c. 25)
s.1 .... 6B–43
s.11 .... 6B–43
Powers of Attorney Act (c. 27) 6B–334, 6B–342, 6B–370
s.3 .... 6B–361
s.5 .... 6B–340, 6B–368
Immigration Act (c. 77)
Sched. 2 para. 5 .... 3A–1015

1973
Matrimonial Causes Act (c. 18)
s.1(2) 6B–106
s.45(2) 2BPD–011
Fair Trading Act (c. 41) .. 2BPD–011

1974
Local Government Act (c. 7)
Pt. III 6B–218
Consumer Credit Act (c. 39)
s.9(4) 3B–331
Solicitors Act (c. 47) 6B–253

1976
Legitimacy Act (c. 31) ... 2BPD–011

1977
National Health Service Act (c. 49)
s.21 .... 6B–83

1978
Judicature (Northern Ireland) Act (c. 23)
s.40(1) 4B–1
s.41(1) 4B–1
s.44 .... 4B–1
Interpretation Act (c. 30)
s.7 .... 6B–388

1979
Charging Orders Act (c. 53)
s.1 .... 73.2
s.3(5) 73.9
s.5(5) 73.11, 73.16

1980
Criminal Appeal (Northern Ireland) Act (c. 47)
s.31(1) 4B–1

1981
Forgery and Counterfeiting Act (c. 45)
Pt. I 6B–215
Supreme Court Act (c. 54) . 9A–549
s.15(3) 9A–47.1
s.18 .... 6B–221
s.28(1) 9A–81.1
s.36 .... 6B–203
(1) 6B–203
s.40 .... 72.2
(3) 72.2
s.50 .... 9A–261
s.51(1) 9A–265
s.69 .... 9A–326.1
s.89 .... 6B–186
s.136 .... 9A–443

1982
Civil Jurisdiction and Judgments Act (c. 27) 70.5
Merchant Shipping (Liner Conferences) Act (c. 37) 70.5
Administration of Justice Act (c. 53) 6B–193

1983

Mental Health Act (c. 20)

Pt. II	2BPD–011, 6B–215, 6B–218
Pt. VII	6B–1, 6B–4, 6B–220, 6B–225, 6B–329
s.1(2)	6B–185
s.3	6B–1
s.7	6B–1
s.10(1)	6B–372
s.18	6B–224 — 6B–225
s.22	6B–224 — 6B–225
s.35	ccpd49–001
(7)	ccpd49–001
(8)	ccpd49–001
s.42(6)	6B–224
s.80	6B–224
s.81	6B–225
s.82	6B–225
s.86	6B–225
s.87	6B–225
s.88	6B–224 — 6B–225
s.93(1)	6B–3
(2)	6B–2
(4)	6B–213
s.94	6B–4, 6B–188, 6B–213
(1A)	6B–187
(2)	6B–2, 6B–6 — 6B–7, 6B–12, 6B–74, 6B–202, 6B–336
s.95	6B–83, 6B–147, 6B–190, 6B–194 — 6B–195
(1)	6B–84, 6B–108
(2)	6B–112
s.96	6B–195
(1)	6B–46, 6B–59, 6B–61 — 6B–63, 6B–87, 6B–100 — 6B–102, 6B–104 — 6B–106, 6B–108 — 6B–109, 6B–112 — 6B–113, 6B–115, 6B–118, 6B–124, 6B–128, 6B–134 — 6B–136, 6B–138, 6B–145 — 6B–146, 6B–190, 6B–192, 6B–210, 6B–336
(2)	6B–59, 6B–61 — 6B–62, 6B–64, 6B–70
(3)	6B–191
(4)	6B–142
s.97(1)	6B–142, 6B–192
(2)	6B–142
(3)	6B–192
(4)	6B–142
s.98	6B–12, 6B–19, 6B–74, 6B–210, 6B–214
s.99	6B–12
(3)	6B–35, 6B–41 — 6B–42, 6B–196
s.100	6B–6
s.101	6B–111, 6B–329
(1)	6B–87, 6B–111, 6B–198
(2)	6B–111, 6B–198
(3)	6B–87
(4)	6B–27
(5)	6B–198
s.103	6B–372
(2)	6B–111, 6B–201
(8)	6B–202
s.104	6B–372
(1)	6B–206, 6B–372
(2)	6B–203
(3)	6B–4
(4)	6B–224 — 6B–225, 6B–382
s.105(1)	6B–204, 6B–372
(2)	6B–9, 6B–205
s.106	6B–1, 6B–319
(4)	6B–372
(5)	6B–206
s.107	6B–1, 6B–149, 6B–319
s.108	6B–1, 6B–319
s.110	6B–6, 6B–224 — 6B–225
s.111	6B–74, 6B–78, 6B–212
(2)	6B–211
(3)	6B–211
(3A)	6B–211
s.116	6B–224
s.121(7)	6B–218
s.122	6B–224
s.126(1)	6B–215
s.128	6B–224 — 6B–225
s.129(1)	6B–217
s.131	6B–1
s.134(1)	6B–218
(2)	6B–218
(3)	6B–218 — 6B–219
s.137	6B–224 — 6B–225
s.138	6B–224 — 6B–225
s.139	6B–225
(1)	6B–224
(2)	6B–221
s.141	6B–224 — 6B–225
s.142	6B–224 — 6B–225
s.143	6B–224 — 6B–225
s.144	6B–224 — 6B–225
s.145	6B–185
Sched. 3	6B–214

Sched. 4	6B–74, 6B–78
para. 4	6B–74, 6B–78
Pt. 7	6B–224
Sched. 5	6B–224 — 6B–225
para. 45	6B–111

1984

County Courts Act (c. 28)

s.23	73.10
s.74(5A)	9A–649
s.108	72.2
(3)	72.2

Inheritance Tax Act (c. 51)

s.89	6B–132

1985

Enduring Powers of Attorney Act (c. 29) 6B–2, 6B–319, 6B–329, 6B–337, 6B–382

s.1(1)	6B–340
(2)	6B–340, 6B–375
s.2	6B–322, 6B–375, 6B–380
(2)	6B–319, 6B–340, 6B–344, 6B–375, 6B–389
(6)	6B–332
(7)	6B–344, 6B–390
(8)	6B–350
(9)	6B–390
(10)	6B–375, 6B–390 — 6B–391
(11)	6B–329, 6B–333
(13)	6B–345
s.3	6B–329
(2)	6B–348
(4)	6B–325, 6B–340, 6B–348, 6B–364
(5)	6B–329, 6B–348, 6B–364
s.4(2)	6B–351
(3)	6B–323, 6B–358, 6B–378, 6B–384
(6)	6B–344, 6B–391
(8)	6B–352
s.5	6B–375, 6B–390
s.6	6B–340, 6B–361, 6B–390
(2)	6B–358
(4)	6B–358
(5)	6B–325, 6B–358, 6B–386, 6B–390
(6)	6B–375
s.7(1)	6B–344, 6B–361, 6B–364, 6B–368
(3)	6B–361, 6B–382
s.8(1)	6B–327
(2)	6B–355, 6B–390
(3)	6B–327, 6B–361, 6B–364, 6B–368
(4)	6B–364, 6B–375, 6B–390
s.9	6B–334, 6B–353
(1)	6B–334
(2)	6B–334, 6B–368
(3)	6B–334, 6B–368, 6B–389
(4)	6B–334, 6B–389
(5)	6B–334
(6)	6B–389
(7)	6B–369
s.10	6B–380
(1)	6B–319, 6B–382
(2)	6B–372
(3)	6B–373
s.11	6B–344
(2)	6B–390
(3)	6B–390
(4)	6B–375
s.12(2)	6B–378
(3)	6B–378
s.13(1)	6B–345, 6B–349, 6B–352, 6B–356, 6B–359, 6B–363, 6B–365, 6B–369, 6B–373
Sched. 1	6B–351, 6B–354, 6B–358, 6B–378
para. 3(2)	6B–360
para. 4(2)	6B–360
Sched. 2	6B–368
Sched. 3 Pt. 1	6B–375
Pt. 2	6B–375

Local Government Act (c. 51)
Housing Act (c. 68) 6B–110

s.1	6B–12
(1)	6B–342
(3)	6B–147
s.3	6B–222
s.4	6B–222
s.5	6B–340, 6B–343, 6B–366
s.7(4)	6B–63
s.11(8)	6B–376
s.13	6B–381
(1)	6B–341, 6B–376
s.36(1)	6B–99
s.45A(10)	6B–222
s.54(2)	6B–74
s.54A	6B–222
s.65	6B–222
s.85	3A–348
s.85	3A–348
s.96	6B–147
(1)	6B–126, 6B–138
s.103(8)	6B–202
s.105	6B–9
s.106	6B–372
s.152(1)	cc49.6B

Landlord and Tenant Act (c. 70) 56PD–001

Table of Statutes

1986
- Agricultural Holdings Act (c. 5)
  - Sched. 11 .... 2BPD–011
- Company Directors Disqualification Act (c. 46) .. 9A–169
- Legal Aid (Scotland) Act (c. 47)
  - s.19 .... 4A–24, 4B–20, 4B–49
- Public Trustee and Administration of Funds Act (c. 57) 6B–188, 6B–212

1987
- Banking Act (c. 22) 72.1
- Landlord and Tenant Act (c. 31)
  - s.38 .... 2BPD–011

1988
- Legal Aid Act (c. 34) 6B–116, 6B–158
  - s.18 .... 4A–24, 4A–57, 4B–20, 4B–49
- Housing Act (c. 50)
  - s.21(4) 3A–748.1
  - s.34(1) .... 3A–776 — 3A–776.1
  - s.36(2) 3A–776.1

1989
- Law of Property (Miscellaneous Provisions) Act (c. 34)
  - s.1 .... 6B–421
- Children Act (c. 41) 6B–249

1990
- National Health Service and Community Care Act (c. 19) 6B–220
  - Sched. 9 .... 6B–221
    - para. 24(7) 6B–221
- Courts and Legal Services Act (c. 41) 6B–253
  - s.71 .... 6B–199
  - Sched. 10 .... 6B–200
    - para. 51 .... 6B–200

1991
- Criminal Justice Act (c. 53)
  - s.27 .... 6B–223

1993
- Probation Service Act (c. 47)
  - 6B–218
  - Sched. 3 .... 6B–219
    - para. 7 .... 6B–219
- Statute Law (Repeals) Act (c. 50) 6B–381

1995
- Health Authorities Act (c. 17)
  - Sched. 1 .... 6B–219, 6B–221, 6B–223
    - para. 107(10) 6B–219
    - (11) 6B–221
    - (13) 6B–223
- Private International Law (Miscellaneous Provisions) Act (c. 42)
  - s.2 .... 9A–649
- Mental Health (Patients in the Community) Act (c. 52)
  - Sched. 1 .... 6B–216
    - para. 17 .... 6B–216

1996
- Arbitration Act (c. 23)
  - s.9 .... 9A–162
- Housing Act (c. 52) cc49.6B
  - Pt. V ccpd49–001
  - Pt. VII 3A–1015
  - s.152 .... cc49.6B
  - s.155 .... cc49.6B
    - (3) cc49.6B, ccpd49–001
    - (4) cc49.6B, ccpd49–001
  - s.156(4) ccpd49–001
  - s.182 .... 3A–973
  - s.193 .... 3A–1082
    - (5) 3A–1083
  - s.202 .... 3A–1083, 3A–1135.2
  - Sched. 15 para. 2(2) cc49.6B

1997
- Civil Procedure Act (c. 12)
  - s.4 .... 9A–326.1, 9A–832
- Crime (Sentences) Act (c. 43)
  - Sched. 4 .... 6B–223
    - para. 12 .... 6B–223

1998
- Government of Wales Act (c. 38)
  - s.125 .... 6B–219
  - Sched. 12 .... 6B–219
    - para. 22 .... 6B–219
- Human Rights Act (c. 42)
  - s.6(1) 3A–302
  - Sched. 1 .... 9A–161
    - Pt. 1 .... 9A–261

1999
- Access to Justice Act (c. 22)
  - s.11 .... 4B–20, 4B–49
  - s.13 .... 9A–50
  - s.55(1) 9A–47
  - s.56 .... 9A–884.1
- Immigration and Asylum Act (c. 33)
  - Pt. VI 3A–28.10
  - s.9(1) 3A–1016.1
  - s.95 .... 3A–28.10
  - s.116 .... 3A–28.3

2000
- Postal Services Act (c. 26)
  - s.92 .... sc77.17, cc49.15

Table of Statutory Instruments

[**References in bold** type are to the paragraph at which that section, or part of that section, is set out in full.]

1977
Matrimonial Causes Rules
 (S.I. 1977 No. 344) .. 6B–115
 r. 112 .... 6B–115,
  6B–134
 (4) 6B–134

1980
Legal Aid (General) Regulations (S.I. 1980 No. 1894)
 reg. 3 .... 6B–115
 reg. 15 .... 6B–115

1981
Legal Aid, Advice and Assistance (Northern Ireland) Order (S.I. 1981 No. 228) 4B–49

1982
Court of Appeal (Civil Division) Order (S.I. 1982 No. 543) 9A–274

1984
Court of Protection Rules (S.I. 1984 No. 2035) 6B–153
 r. 17 .... 6B–139
 r. 20 .... 6B–140
 r. 27(1) 6B–202
 r. 39 .... 6B–138
 r. 47 .... 6B–202
 r. 61 .... 6B–149
 r. 65 .... 6B–149
 r. 76 .... 6B–153

1986
Enduring Powers of Attorney Act 1985 (Commencement) Order (S.I. 1986 No. 125) 6B–319, 6B–383
Enduring Powers of Attorney (Prescribed Form) Regulations (S.I. 1986 No. 126) 6B–421
 reg. 1 .... 6B–421
 reg. 3 .... 6B–421

1987
Court Funds Rules (S.I. 1987 No. 821)
 r. 7 .... 6B–24, 6B–43
 r. 43 .... 6B–43
Enduring Powers of Attorney (Prescribed Form) Regulations (S.I. 1987 No. 1612) 6B–332, 6B–421
 reg. 1 .... 6B–421

 reg. 2 .... 6B–421
  (1) 6B–332
  (2) 6B–332
 reg. 4 .... 6B–421
Enduring Powers of Attorney (Northern Ireland Consequential Amendment) Order (S.I. 1987 No. 1628) .... 6B–361 — 6B–362
Income Support (General) Regulations (S.I. 1987 No. 1967)
 reg. 51 .... 6B–128
 Sched. 9 .... 6B–126
  para. 15 .... 6B–126
 Sched. 10 para. 44 .... 6B–121
Non-Contentious Probate Rules (S.I. 1987 No. 2024)
 r. 35 .... 6B–107
  (2) 6B–107

1990
Enduring Powers of Attorney (Prescribed Form) Regulations (S.I. 1990 No. 1376) .... 6B–319 — 6B–320, 6B–421 — 6B–423
 reg. 1 .... 6B–421
 reg. 2 .... 6B–421
 reg. 3 .... 6B–322, 6B–423, 6B–427
 reg. 4 .... 6B–423
 reg. 5 .... 6B–322, 6B–421
Income Support (General) Amendment No. 3 Regulations (S.I. 1990 No. 1776) 6B–128

1992
Council Tax (Administration and Enforcement) Regulations (S.I. 1992 No. 613) 73.1, 73.3, 73.9
 reg. 50 .... 73.2 — 73.3
 reg. 51 .... 73.9
National Assistance (Assessment of Resources) Regulations (S.I. 1992 No. 2977) . 6B–120

1993
Judgment Debts (Rate of Interest) Order (S.I. 1993 No. 564) 6B–113

Table of Statutory Instruments

1994

Income-related Benefits Schemes (Miscellaneous Amendments) (No.5) Regulations (S.I. 1994 No. 2139) 6B–121

Court of Protection Rules (S.I. 1994 No. 3046) ..... 6B–9 — 6B–10, 6B–13, 6B–65, 6B–75, 6B–79, 6B–173, 6B–318

Pt. I	6B–116
Pt. II	6B–116
r. 3	6B–4
r. 7	6B–65, 6B–79
r. 8	6B–13
r. 11	6B–15
r. 15	6B–65
r. 16	6B–79
r. 17	6B–65
r. 18	6B–135
r. 19	6B–18, 6B–79
r. 26	6B–18
r. 27	6B–15
r. 29	6B–6
r. 35	6B–107
r. 42	6B–19
r. 43	6B–15, 6B–41
r. 44	6B–19
r. 46	6B–18 — 6B–19, 6B–25
r. 54	6B–9
r. 56	6B–24
r. 57	6B–24
r. 60	6B–24
r. 65	6B–33, 6B–39, 6B–41
r. 66	6B–83
r. 73	6B–27
r. 74	6B–41, 6B–43
r. 78	6B–41
r. 84	6B–41, 6B–155
r. 87	6B–15, 6B–164

Court of Protection (Enduring Powers of Attorney) Rules (S.I. 1994 No. 3047) ....

r. 3	6B–320
r. 6	6B–323
r. 8	6B–324, 6B–329
r. 9	6B–325
r. 13	6B–331
r. 14	6B–354
r. 21	6B–328
r. 23	6B–325
r. 24	6B–325
r. 27	6B–321, 6B–324
Sched. 1	6B–320, 6B–323 — 6B–324
Sched. 2	6B–321

1996

Attachment of Debts (Expenses) Order (S.I. 1996 No. 3098) 9A–719

1999

Court Funds (Amendment) Rules (S.I. 1999 No. 1021) 6B–148

r. 9	6B–12
r. 15	6B–75
r. 19	6B–36, 6B–45, 6B–52
r. 21(4)	6B–145
r. 75	6B–36

Court of Protection (Amendment) Rules (S.I. 1999 No. 2504) 6B–318

r. 57 .... 6B–3

2000

The Community Legal Service (Costs) Regulations 2000 (S.I. 2000 No. 441) 4A–24, 4A–57, 4B–49

r. 9	4B–20
r. 10	4B–20

The Homelessness (England) Regulations 2000 (S.I. 2000 No. 701) 3A–1016.1

reg. 3 .... 3A–1015

The Allocation of Housing (England) Regulations 2000 (S.I. 2000 No. 702) 3A–1016.1

The Asylum Support Regulations 2000 (S.I. 2000 No. 704)

reg. 6	3A–28.10
s.95	3A-1184.1
(1)	3A-1184.1

The Persons subject to Immigration Control (Housing Authority Accommodation and Homelessness) Order 2000 (S.I. 2000 No. 706) 3A–1016.1

The Community Legal Service (Cost Protection) Regulations 2000 (S.I. 2000 No. 824)

r. 5 .... 4A–24, 4A–57, 4B–20, 4B–49

The Court of Protection (Amendment) Rules 2000 (S.I. 2000 No. 2025) 6B–318

2001

The Civil Procedure (Amendment) Rules 2001 (S.I. 2001 No. 256) 70.0.2, 72.0.2

Table of Statutory Instruments

The Court of Protection Rules
2001 (S.I. 2001 No. 824)
.... 6B–1,
6B–139, 6B–227.1, 6B–319
r. 8 .... 6B–329
r. 40 .... 6B–138
r. 86 .... 6B–156
r. 87 .... 6B–156
r. 89 .... 6B–162

The Court of Protection
(Enduring Powers of
Attorney) Rules 2001
(S.I. 2001 No. 825) .. 6B–319
r. 21 .... 6B–140
The Civil Procedure
(Amendment No. 4)
Rules 2001 (S.I. 2001
No. 2792) 71.0.2, 73.0.2

TABLE OF CIVIL PROCEDURE RULES

References to paragraph numbers in square brackets are to Volume 2. Figures in bold type indicate where a Statutory Instrument or rule is set out in full.

1998	Civil Procedure Rules (S.I.1998 No.3132)	
	r.2.5	[9A–832]
	r.3.1(2)(e)	[2G–17]
	r.6.1(b)	6.1
	r.6.16(6)(b)(i)	6.16
	(ii)	6.16
	r.7.5(2)	sc97.6
	(3)	sc97.6
	r.14.4	[9A–634]
	r.14.14	[9A–634]
	r.16.8(a),(b)	16.8
	r.19.7	sc15.14
	r.19.9(3)(a)	19.9
	r.25.5	[9A–589A]
	r.31.17	[9A–589A]
	r.40.8	[9A–649]
	Pt 43	[6B–312]
	r.43.2(1)(c)	[6B–312]
	(d)	[6B–312]
	Pt 44	[6B–312]
	r.44.3(2)	[6B–312]
	rr44.9–44.12	[6B–312]
	r.44.12	[9A–649]
	Pt 47	[6B–312]
	r.47.8	[9A–649]
	r.47.14	[9A–649]
	Pt 48	[6B–312]
	rr48.1–48.3	[6B–312]
	r.48.1	[9A–589A]
	r.48.7	48.7
	rr48.7–48.10	[6B–312]
	r.51.1	51.1
	r.51.2	**51.2**
	Pt 54	[9A–85], [9A–138]
	Pt 55	[9B–155.1]
	Pt 55.11–55.19	[3A–748]
	r.70.1	**70.1**
	r.70.2	**70.2**
	r.70.3	**70.3**
	r.70.4	**70.4**
	r.70.5	**70.5**
	r.70.6	**70.6**
	Pts 71–73	70.1
	Pt 71	71.0.1, 71.0.2
	r.71.1	**71.1**
	r.71.2	**71.2**
	r.71.3	**71.3**
	r.71.4	**71.4**
	r.71.5	**71.5**
	r.71.6	**71.6**
	r.71.7	**71.7**
	r.71.8	**71.8**
	Pt 72	72.0.1, 72.0.2
	r.72.1	**72.1**
	r.72.2	**72.2**, 72.11
	r.72.3	**72.3**
	r.72.4	**72.4**

1998	Civil Procedure Rules—*cont.*	
	r.72.4(2)	72.2
	r.72.5	**72.5**
	r.72.6	**72.6**, 72.8
	r.72.7	**72.7**
	r.72.8	**72.8**
	r.72.9	**72.9**
	r.72.10	**72.10**, 72.11
	r.72.11	**72.11**
	Pt 73	73.0.1, 73.0.2
	r.73.1	**73.1**
	r.73.2	**73.2**
	r.73.3	**73.3**
	r.73.4	**73.4**
	r.73.5	**73.5**
	(1)	73.7
	(d)	73.6, 73.12
	r.73.6	**73.6**
	r.73.7	**73.7**
	r.73.8	**73.8**
	(2)(a)	73.4
	(3)	73.17
	r.73.9	**73.9**
	r.73.10	**73.10**
	r.73.11	**73.11**
	r.73.12	**73.12**
	r.73.13	**73.13**
	r.73.14	**73.14**
	r.73.15	**73.15**
	r.73.16	**73.16**
	r.73.17	**73.17**, 73.19
	(4)	73.18
	r.73.18	**73.18**
	r.73.19	**73.19**
	r.73.20	73.18, **73.20**
	r.73.21	73.18, **73.21**
	Sched. 1 RSC	
	RSC O.45–47, 51,52	70.1
	RSC O.45, r.3	**sc45.3**
	RSC O.51, r.A1	**sc51.A1**
	RSC O.51, r.2	sc51.2
	RSC O.53	[9A–81.1], [9A–138]
	RSC O.71	70.5
	RSC O.77, r.16(2B)	sc77.16
	RSC O.77, r.17(1)	sc77.17
	RSC O.93, r.15	sc93.15
	RSC O.93, r.20	sc93.20
	RSC O.94, r.15	[9A–112]
	RSC O.97	sc97.0.1
	RSC O.97, r.1	**sc97.1**
	RSC O.97, r.2	**sc97.2**
	RSC O.97, r.3	**sc97.3**
	RSC O.97, r.4	**sc97.4**
	RSC O.97, r.5	**sc97.5**
	RSC O.97, r.6	**sc97.6**
	RSC O.97, r.7	**sc97.7**
	RSC O.97, r.8	**sc97.8**

1998	Civil Procedure Rules—*cont.*		1998	Civil Procedure Rules—*cont.*	
	Shed. 1 RSC—*cont.*			Sched. 2 CCR	
	RSC O.97, r.9	**sc97.9**		CCR O.1, r.3	[9A–832]
	RSC O.97, r.9A	**sc97.9A**		CCR O.22, r.8(1A)(a)	**cc22.8**
	RSC O.97, r.10	**sc97.10**		CCR O.25–29	70.1
	RSC O.97, r.11	**sc97.11**		CCR O.25, r.13	70.3
	RSC O.97, r.12	**sc97.12**		CCR O.47	cc47.0.2
	RSC O.97, r.13	**sc97.13**		CCR O.49, r.6	[3A–843],
	RSC O.97, r.14	**sc97.14**			[3A–845], [3A–846]
	RSC O.97, r.16	**sc97.16**		CCR O.49, 6B	**cc49.6B**
	RSC O.97, r.17	**sc97.17**			
	RSC O.97, r.18	**sc97.18**			
	RSC O.97, r.19	**sc97.19**			

TABLE OF PRACTICE DIRECTIONS

References to paragraph numbers in square brackets are to Volume 2. Figures in bold type indicate where a Practice Direction is set out in full.

CPR Practice Directions

Pt 2 Allocation of Cases to Levels of Judiciary	**2BPD–011**
Pt 8 How to Make Claims in Schedule Rules and Other Claims	8BPD–005
Pt 12 Default Judgment	12PD–004
Pt 16 Statements of Case	16.8
Pt 35 Experts and Assessors	35PD–004
Pt 52 Appeals	52PD–015A
Pt 55 Possession Claims	55PD–001
Pt 56 Landlord and Tenant Claims	56PD–001

Other Practice Directions

Practice Direction (1968) 118 New L.J. 1097	[6B–167]
Practice Direction [1983] 1 W.L.R.922; [1983] 3 All E.R.33	[6B–141]
Practice Direction [1984] 1 W.L.R.1171; [1984] 3 All E.R.128	[6B–141]
Practice Direction, December 22, 1982 [1983] 1 W.L.R. 86; [1983] 1 All E.R. 160; (1983) 127 S.J. 40	[6B–98], [6B–166]
Practice Direction (Court of Protection) February 29, 1968; (1968) 112 S.J. 2000	[6B–80]
Practice Direction (Damages: Personal Injuries) [1984] 1 W.L.R. 1127; [1984] 3 All E.R.165	[6B–116]
Practice Direction (Estate Agents and Auctioneers Fees) (No.2) [1972] 1 W.L.R. 1431	[6B–98]
Practice Direction (Family Division: Sale of Land) [1972] 1 W.L.R. 1471	[6B–98]
Practice Direction (Housing Act 1996: Injunction)	ccpd49–001
Practice Direction (Insolvency Proceedings)	B1–001
Practice Note (1983) 133 New L.J. 6121	[6B–171]
Practice Note (Procedure for the Settlement of Personal Injury: Awards to Patients) November 15, 1996	[6B–118]
Practice Note (Transfer of Damages to Court of Protection) September 7, 1990	[6B–116]

TABLE OF INTERNATIONAL AND EUROPEAN LEGISLATION, TREATIES AND CONVENTIONS

References to paragraph numbers in square brackets are to Volume 2.

1905	Convention on Civil Procedure	
	art. 23	6.53
1954	Convention on Civil Procedure	
	art. 24	6.53
1957	Treaty establishing the European Community	6.57
1965	Hague Convention	6.52
1968	Brussels Convention	
	art. IV of the Protocol	6.52
1980	Convention on International Access to Justice	
	art. 13	6.53
1995	Directive 95/46/EC	6.54
1997	Directive 97/66/EC	6.54
1999	Decision 1999/468/EC	
	arts 3, 7	6.50
2000	Council Regulation (E.C.) No.1348/2000 Service Regulation	
	art.1	**6.33**
	art.2	**6.34**, 6.55
	art.3	**6.35**, 6.55

2000	Council Regulation (E.C.) No.1348/2000 Service Regulation—*cont.*	
	art.4	**6.36**, 6.55
	art.5	**6.37**
	art.6	**6.38**
	art.7	**6.39**
	art.8	**6.40**
	art.9	**6.41**, 6.55
	art.10	**6.42**, 6.55
	art.11	**6.43**
	art.12	**6.44**
	art.13	**6.45**, 6.55
	art.14	**6.46**, 6.55
	art.15	**6.47**, 6.55
	art.16	**6.48**
	art.17	**6.49**, 6.55
	art.18	**6.50**
	art.19	**6.51**, 6.55
	art.20	**6.52**
	art.21	**6.53**
	art.22	**6.54**
	art.23	**6.55**
	art.24	**6.56**
	art.25	**6.57**

Table of Cases

	PARA
A, Re [1904] 2 Ch. 328	6B–106
A v. A (Children: Shared Residence Order) [1994] 1 F.L.R. 669	6B–114
Adcock v. Co-operative Insurance Society Ltd, *The Times*, April 26, 2000	9A–634
Aiden Shipping Co Ltd v. Interbulk Ltd (The Vimeira) (No.2), *sub nom.* Vimeira, The (No.2) [1986] A.C. 965, HL; reversing [1985] 1 W.L.R. 1222, CA; reversing [1985] 2 Lloyd's Rep. 377	9A–265
Al-Naimi (t/a Buildmaster Construction Services) v. Islamic Press Services Inc. *See* Al Naimi (t/a Buildmaster Construction Services) v. Islamic Press Agency Inc	
Al Naimi (t/a Buildmaster Construction Services) v. Islamic Press Agency Inc, *sub nom.* Al-Naimi (t/a Buildmaster Construction Services) v. Islamic Press Services Inc [2000] 1 Lloyd's Rep. 522, CA; affirming [1999] C.L.C. 212	9A–162
Alexander v. Arts Council of Wales, *The Times* April 27, 2001, CA	9A–326.1, 9A–832
Alghile v. Westminster County Council [2001] EWCA Civ., March 2, 2001	3A–1083, 3A–1125
Alston, Re, *sub nom.* Sinclair v. Willes [1917] 2 Ch. 226	6B–111
Amand v. Secretary of State for Home Department [1943] A.C. 147	9A–55
Amoah v. Barking and Dagenham LBC, March 2001 Legal Action 27	3A–322
Ashworth Hospital Authority v. MGN Ltd. [2001] 1 W.L.R. 515	3C–27
Assheton v. Boyne. *See* King's Will Trusts, Re	
Att.-Gen. v. Ailesbury (1887) 12 L.R. App. Cas. 672	6B–111
B (CP: Notice of Proceedings), Re [1987] 1 W.L.R. 552	6B–139
Bailey v. Bailey [1942] 2 All E.R. 89	6B–134
Baker v. Baker (1860) 5 P.D. 152	6B–134
Baldwyn v. Smith [1900] Ch. 588	6B–105
Banks v. Goodfellow (1870) L.R. 5 Q.B. 549	6B–148
Barking and Dagenham LBC v. Saint, *sub nom.* Saint v. Barking and Dagenham LBC (1999) 31 H.L.R. 620	3A–32
Baron v. Lovell [1999] C.P.L.R. 630	9A–634
Beddoe, Re, *sub nom.* Downes v. Cottam [1893] 1 Ch. 547	9A–265
Belton, Re [1913] W.N. 63	6B–114
Biguzzi v. Rank Leisure Plc [1999] 1 W.L.R. 1926	9A–634
Blake, Re [1887] W.N. 173	6B–61 — 6B–62
Buckton, Re, *sub nom.* Buckton v. Buckton [1907] 2 Ch. 406	9A–265
Buckton v. Buckton. *See* Buckton, Re	
Bugdaycay v. Secretary of State for the Home Department, *sub nom.* R. v. Secretary of State for the Home Department Ex p. Bugdaycay; Nelidow Santis v. Secretary of State for the Home Department; Norman v. Secretary of State for the Home Department; Musisi v. Secretary of State for the Home Department [1987] A.C. 514, HL; affirming [1986] 1 W.L.R. 155, CA; affirming *Times*, July 11, 1985	3A–1015
Bullard &Taplin Ltd, Re [1996] B.C.C. 973	9A–560
Burris v. Azadani [1995] 1 W.L.R. 1372	9A–549
C, Re [1960] 1 W.L.R. 92	6B–135
C v. K (Inherent Powers: Exclusion Order), *sub nom.* C v. K (Ouster Order: Non-Parent) [1996] 2 F.L.R. 506	9A–549
—— v. K (Ouster Order: Non-Parent). *See* C v. K (Inherent Powers: Exclusion Order)	
CEFD, Re [1963] 1 W.L.R. 329	6B–135
CL, Re, *sub nom.* L, Re [1969] 1 Ch. 587	6B–147
C. L. v. C. F. W. [1928] P. 223	6B–7, 6B–113
CMG, Re [1970] Ch. 574	6B–145

Table of Cases

CWHT, Re [1978] Ch. 67 .... 6B–191
CWM, Re [1951] 2 K.B. 714 .... 6B–135
Cadogan Estates Ltd v. McMahon [2000] 3 WLR 1555 .... 3A–264
Caisse Nationale d'Assurance Vieillesse des Travailleurs Salaries, Region de Paris v. Jordan
    (C141/88) [1989] E.C.R. 2387 .... 6B–106
Castle Vale Housing Action v. Gallagher, February 23, 2001 .... 3A–184.1,
    3A–184.2, 3A–342 — 3A–342.2, 3A–649.1 — 3A–649.2
Cathcart, Re [1893] 1 Ch. 466 .... 6B–9,
    6B–113, 6B–155
—— [1902] W.N. 80 .... 6B–9
Charles Clarke, Re [1898] 1 Ch. 336 .... 6B–112
Charlesworth v. Relay Road Ltd [2000] 1 W.L.R. 230 .... 9A–160
Chignell Investments Ltd v. Deghdak, June 1999 .... 3A–748
Cockburn's Will Trusts, Re, *sub nom.* Cockburn v. Lewis; Cockburn, Re [1957] Ch. 438 .. 6B–76
Cockburn v. Lewis; Cockburn, Re. *See* Cockburn's Will Trusts, Re
Croydon (Unique) Ltd v. Wright [2001] Ch. 318; [1999] 4 All E.R. 257 .... 3A–291
Cumming, Re (1852) 1 De G.M. & G. 537 .... 6B–21
Curi v. Colina, *The Times*, October 14, 1998 .... 9A–581
D'Abo v. Paget (No.2),, *The Times*, August 10, 2000 .... 9A–265
D (J), Re [1982] Ch. 237 .... 6B–9,
    6B–136, 6B–145
DML, Re [1965] Ch. 1133 .... 6B–135
Davey (Deceased), Re [1981] 1 W.L.R. 164 .... 6B–145
Davies v. Thomas [1900] 2 Ch. 462 .... 6B–112
Debtor (No.1 of 1941), Re [1941] Ch. 487 .... 6B–7,
    6B–114
Didisheim v. London and Westminster Bank [1900] 2 Ch. 15 .... 6B–6
Donoghue v. Poplar HARCA (2001) April 27 .... 3A–302,
    3A–748.1
Downes v. Cottam. *See* Beddoe, Re
Du Bey v. Lord Chancellor's Department and Registry Trust, June 9, 2000, unrep. 9A–643
Duller v. South East Lines Engineers [1981] C.L.Y. 585 .... 6B–117
Ealing LBC. v. Surdonja (2000) 32 HLR 481 .... 3A–1106,
    3A–1125
Edwards, Re (1879) 10 Ch.D. 605 .... 6B–8
Enfield LBC v. B (A Minor), *sub nom.* Enfield LBC v. DB (A Child) [2000] 1 W.L.R. 2259
    .... 3A–949
—— v. DB (A Child). *See* Enfield LBC v. B (A Minor)
F (Mental Patient: Sterilisation), Re. *See* F v. West Berkshire HA
F, Re. *See* K (Enduring Powers of Attorney), Re
F v. West Berkshire HA, *sub nom.* F (Mental Patient: Sterilisation), Re [1990] 2 A.C. 1, HL;
    affirming (1989) 86(10) L.S.G. 42 .... 6B–2
Farnham, Re [1895] 2 Ch. 799 .... 6B–114
Foenander v. Bond Lewis &Co [2001] EWCA Civ 759 .... 9A–50.1
Freeman, Re [1927] 1 Ch. 479 .... 6B–135
Fuller, Re [1900] 2 Ch. 551 .... 6B–64,
    6B–106
Fulton Motors Ltd v. Toyota (GB) Ltd, July 23, 1999 .... 9A–265
Futej v. Lewandowski, 124 S.J. 777 .... 6B–117
Gilbert, ex p. (1810) 1 Ball & B. 297 .... 6B–41
Globe Equities Ltd v. Globe Legal Services Ltd, *sub nom.* Globe Equities Ltd v. Kotrie; Kot-
    rie v. Globe Equities Ltd [1999] B.L.R. 232 .... 9A–265
—— v. Kotrie; Kotrie v Globe Equities Ltd. *See* Globe Equities Ltd v. Globe Legal Services
    Ltd
Gloucestershire HA v. MA Torpy &Partners Ltd (t/a Torpy &Partners) (No.2) [1999] Lloyd's
    Rep. I.R. 203 .... 9A–265
Goodman v. Evely, April 2001 Legal Action 21, January 23, 2001 .... 3A–738

TABLE OF CASES

Goodwin v. Scott. *See* Walker, Re	
Graham, Re, *sub nom.* Graham v. Noakes [1895] 1 Ch. 66	6B–155
Graham v. Noakes. *See* Graham, Re	
Greene, Re, *sub nom.* Whitworth, Re; Wood, Re; EA, Re; Fraser, Re [1928] Ch. 528	6B–135
Greener v. Merrall. *See* Merrall, Re	
Griparion, The (No.3). *See* Tharros Shipping Co Ltd v. Bias Shipping Ltd (The Griparion) (No.3)	
Grogan v. Greenwich L.B.C.,	3A–342
H. v. H. (a child) (occupation order: power of arrest) (2001) *The Times*, January 10	3A–949
HMF (Mental Patient: Will), Re [1976] Ch. 33	6B–145
Hallam-Eames v. Merrett Syndicates Ltd [1996] 5 Re. L.R. 110, CA; reversing *The Times*, June 16, 1995	9A–319
Hamilton v. Al Fayed (No.3), *The Times*, July 25, 2001	9A–265
Hammersmith & Fulham LBC v. Clarke, March 2001, Legal Action 27	3A–322
Hansell v. Spink [1943] Ch. 396	6B–76
Harley v. McDonald [2001] UKPC 18	9A–59
Harrison's Settlement Trusts, Re, *sub nom.* Morris v. Harrison Sleap [1965] 1 W.L.R. 1492	6B–70
Henderson v. Henderson [1843-1860] All E.R. Rep. 378	9A–160
Henry Boot Construction (U.K.) Ltd v. Malmaison Hotel (Manchester) Ltd [2001] 1 All E.R. 193	9A–55
Hodgson v. Imperial Tobacco Ltd [1998] 1 W.L.R. 1056	9A–265
Horne v. Pountain (1889) 23 Q.B.D. 264	6B–113
Hounslow LBC v. McBride (1999) 31 H.L.R. 143	3A–342
Hutchings v. Islington LBC [1998] 1 W.L.R. 1629	9A–513
Imperial Tobacco Ltd v. Secretary of State for Health. *See* R. v. Secretary of State for Health Ex p. Imperial Tobacco Ltd	
Imutran Ltd v. Uncaged Campaigns Ltd [2001] 2 All E.R. 385	9A–112
Insolvency Act 1986, Re; Actual Services Ltd, Re; Abbot (John), Re. *See* Licence Holder, Re	
Jaggard v. Sawyer [1995] 1 W.L.R. 269, CA; affirming [1993] 1 E.G.L.R. 197	9A–261
James v. Dickinson. *See* Matson, Re	
Johnson v. Gore Wood & Co [1999] C.P.L.R. 155; [2001] 2 W.L.R. 72	9A–160, 9A–161
K's Settlement Trusts, Re [1969] 2 Ch. 1	6B–7
K (Enduring Powers of Attorney), Re, *sub nom.* F, Re [1988] Ch. 310	6B–322
Kaya v. Haringey LBC July, 2001 Legal Action, (2001) 1	3A–1015
Kelly v. Dawes, *The Times*, September 27, 1990	6B–117
Ketley v. Gilbert, *The Times*, January 17, 2001, CA	3B–37
King's Will Trusts, Re, *sub nom.* Assheton v. Boyne [1964] Ch. 542	6B–76
Kings Quality Homes Ltd v. AJ Paints Ltd [1998] 1 W.L.R. 124	9A–553
Kribi, The. *See* OT Africa Line Ltd v. Hijazy (The Kribi)	
L (WJG), Re, *sub nom.* WJGL, Re [1966] Ch. 135	6B–135
L, Re. *See* CL, Re	
Laimond Properties Ltd v. Raeuchle,	3A–184, 3A–342
Lambeth LBC v. Howard (2001) March 6	3A–184.2, 3A–342.2
Leather v. Kirby [1965] 1 W.L.R. 1489	6B–116
Leavesley, Re [1891] 2 Ch. 1	6B–113
Licence Holder, Re, *sub nom.* Insolvency Act 1986, Re; Actual Services Ltd, Re; Abbot (John), Re [1997] B.C.C. 666	9A–560
Locabail (U.K.) Ltd v. Bayfield Properties, *sub nom.* Locabail (U.K.) Ltd v. Waldorf Investment Corporation; Timmins v. Gorley; Williams v. H.M. Inspector of Taxes; R. v. Bristol Betting and Gaming Licensing Committee, ex p. O'Callaghan [2000] 2 W.L.R. 870	9A–44.1

Table of Cases

Locabail (U.K.) Ltd v. Waldorf Investment Corporation; Timmins v. Gorley; Williams v. H.M. Inspector of Taxes; R. v. Bristol Betting and Gaming Licensing Committee, ex p. O'Callaghan. *See* Locabail (U.K.) Ltd v. Bayfield Properties

M. v. Lester [1966] 1 W.L.R. 134	6B–116
Machin v. National Power Plc., July 31, 1998, unrep.	9A–265
Mamidoil-Jetoil Greek Petroleum SA v. Okta Crude Oil Refinery AD (No.2) [2001] 1 Lloyd's Rep. 591	9A–636
Manchester City Council v. McCann [1999] Q.B. 1214	9A–742
Marcie v. Thames Water Utilities Ltd. [2000] 3 All E.R. 698	9A–261
Marman's Trust, Re (1878) 26 W.R. 621	6B–41
Marshall v. Bradford MBC (2001) April 27	3A–348
Mason v. Mason [1972] Fam. 302	6B–106, 6B–134
Matson, Re, *sub nom.* James v. Dickinson [1897] 2 Ch. 509	6B–111
Matthews v. Rowe May, 2001 Legal Action, QBD	3A–776.1
McDonald v. Horn [1995] 1 All E.R. 961, CA; affirming *The Times*, October 12, 1993	9A–265
Merrall, Re, *sub nom.* Greener v. Merrall [1924] 1 Ch. 45	6B–84

Moir v. Wallersteiner (No.2). *See* Wallersteiner v. Moir (No.2)

Moore v. Commissioner of Police of the Metropolis, *sub nom.* Moore v. West Park Hospital, Epsom, Surrey [1968] 1 Q.B. 26	6B–9, 6B–221

—— v. West Park Hospital, Epsom, Surrey. *See* Moore v. Commissioner of Police of the Metropolis

Morris v. Harrison Sleap. *See* Harrison's Settlement Trusts, Re

Murphy v. Young & Co's Brewery Plc [1997] 1 W.L.R. 1591	9A–265
N (Deceased), Re [1977] 1 W.L.R. 676	6B–26, 6B–35, 6B–196

National Provincial Bank v. Barwell. *See* Palmer, Re

Newbegin, Re (1887) 36 Ch.D. 477	6B–83
Notting Hill Housing Trust v. Brackley (2001) April 24	3A–326, 3A–633
Nottingham C.C. v. Cutts (2001) 33 HLR 83	3A–949
O'Connor v. Old Etonians Housing Association, February 9, 2001	3A–487
OT Africa Line Ltd v. Hijazy (The Kribi), *sub nom.* Kribi, The [2001] 1 Lloyd's Rep. 76	9A–112
Palmer, Re, *sub nom.* National Provincial Bank v. Barwell [1945] Ch. 8, CA; affirming [1944] Ch. 374	6B–111
Pares, Re (1879) 12 Ch.D. 333	6B–106
Pendennis Shipyard Ltd v. Magrathea (Pendennis) Ltd, *sub nom.* Pendennis Shipyard Ltd v. Margrathea (Pendennis) Ltd (In Liquidation) [1998] 1 Lloyd's Rep. 315	9A–265

—— v. Margrathea (Pendennis) Ltd (In Liquidation). *See* Pendennis Shipyard Ltd v. Magrathea (Pendennis) Ltd

Pincke, ex p. (1817) 2 Mer. 453	6B–15
Pitt, Re (1928) 44 T.L.R. 371	6B–76
Plenderleith, Re [1893] 3 Ch. 332	6B–83, 6B–112 — 6B–113
Plumpton v. Burkinshaw [1908] 2 K.B. 572	6B–101, 6B–112
Ponder, Re, *sub nom.* Ponder v. Ponder [1921] 2 Ch. 59	6B–76

Ponder v. Ponder. *See* Ponder, Re

Portsmouth v. Portsmouth (1828) 1 Hagg. E.R. 355	6B–134
Pountain, Re (1888) 37 Ch.D. 609	6B–112
Pountney v. Griffiths, *sub nom.* R. v. Bracknell Justices Ex p. Griffiths [1976] A.C. 314, HL; affirming [1975] 2 W.L.R. 291	6B–221
Practice Direction (CA: Consolidation: Notice of Consolidation) [1999] 1 W.L.R. 1027	9A–289
Practice Direction (CP: Evidence: Documents) [1984] 1 W.L.R. 1171	6B–141
Practice Direction (CP: Title of Proceedings) [1959] 1 W.L.R. 1030	6B–76

TABLE OF CASES

Practice Direction (Fam Div: Evidence: Documents), *sub nom.* Practice Direction (Supreme Court: Documents) [1983] 1 W.L.R. 922	6B–141
Practice Direction (Supreme Court: Documents). *See* Practice Direction (Fam Div: Evidence: Documents)	
R (Enduring Power of Attorney), Re [1990] Ch. 647	6B–329
R (Sacupima) *v.* Newham LBC [2001] 1 WLR 563	3A–975.1
R. (Sezek) *v.* Secretary of State for the Home Department, *The Times*, June 20, 2001, CA	9A–47.1, 9A–59
R. (on the application of Campbell) *v.* Enfield LBC (2001) May 22	3A–1135.2
RHC, Re [1963] 1 W.L.R. 1095	6B–106, 6B–135
R. *v.* Aylesbury Vale DC Housing Benefit Review Board Ex p. England (1997) 29 H.L.R. 303, CA; reversing (1996) 28 H.L.R. 783	6B–106
—— *v.* Birmingham CC ex p. Foley, March 2001 Legal Action 29	3A–342
—— *v.* Birmingham County Council ex p. Foley, Legal Action 29 Queen's Bench Division	3A–178, 3A–184
—— *v.* Bow Street Magistrates Court Ex p. Redfearn, *sub nom.* R. v. Leeds Crown Court Ex p. Redfearn [1998] C.O.D. 437	6B–84
—— *v.* Bracknell Justices Ex p. Griffiths. *See* Pountney v. Griffiths	
—— *v.* Canterbury Crown Court, Ex p. Regentford Ltd, *The Times*, February 6, 2001	9A–81.1
—— *v.* DPP Ex p. Bull. *See* R. v. Lord Chancellor Ex p. Child Poverty Action Group	
—— *v.* Hackney London Borough Council, June 14, 1999 (unrep.)	9A–68
—— *v.* Hammersmith and Fulham LBC, Ex p. CPRE London Branch, October 26, 1999, unrep.	9A–265
—— *v.* Leeds Crown Court Ex p. Redfearn. *See* R. v. Bow Street Magistrates Court Ex p. Redfearn	
—— *v.* Leicester Crown Court, Ex p. Commissioners for Customs and Excise, *The Times*, February 23, 2001	9A–81.1
—— *v.* Lord Chancellor Ex p. Child Poverty Action Group, *sub nom.* R. v. DPP Ex p. Bull [1999] 1 W.L.R. 347	9A–265
—— *v.* Maidstone Crown Court Ex p. Harrow LBC [2000] Q.B. 719	9A–81.1
—— *v.* Merton LBC Ex p. Sembi (2000) 32 H.L.R. 439	3A–1082
—— *v.* Runighian [1977] Crim. L.R. 361	6B–221
—— *v.* Secretary of State for the Environment, Ex p. O'Byrne,	9A–265
—— *v.* Secretary of State for Health Ex p. Imperial Tobacco Ltd, *sub nom.* Imperial Tobacco Ltd v. Secretary of State for Health [2001] 1 W.L.R. 127, HL; reversing [2000] 2 W.L.R. 834, CA; reversing *The Times*, November 16, 1999	9A–68
—— *v.* Secretary of State for the Home Department Ex p. Bugdaycay; Nelidow Santis v Secretary of State for the Home Department; Norman v Secretary of State for the Home Department; Musisi v Secretary of State for the Home Department. *See* Bugdaycay v. Secretary of State for the Home Department	
—— *v.* Southwark LBC, ex p. Davies (1994) 26 H.L.R. 677	3A–1082
—— *v.* Tower Hamlets LBC Ex p. Abadie (1990) 22 H.L.R. 264	3A–672
—— *v.* Westminster County Council ex p. Abo-Ragheed, April 2001 Legal Action 22, November 27, 2001	3A–1082
Rahman *v.* Sterling Credit Limited, July 20, 2000, Case no. B3/1999/1282, CA	3B–261
Rajah *v.* Arogol Co. Ltd (2001) *The Times*, April 13	3A–776
Randall *v.* Randall [1939] P. 131	6B–134
Ray's Settled Estates, Re (1884) 25 Ch.D. 464	6B–100
Re AXA Equity and Law Life Assurance Society Plc.,	9A–265
Re B. A. S. [1898] 2 Ch. 392	6B–35
Re Brown [1900] 1 Ch. 489	6B–112 — 6B–113
Re C. A. F., transcript 62/2367	6B–12
Re Cathcart [1893] 1 Ch. 466	6B–155
Re Cedarwood Productions Ltd, *The Times*, July 12, 2001	9A–169
Re Debtors (No., 13-Misc-2000 and No. 14-Misc-2000)	9A–560

TABLE OF CASES

Re E. F. Jackson, transcript 32/401	6B–74
Re E. G. [1914] 1 Ch. 927	6B–112, 6B–155, 6B–157
Re Fletcher, *The Times*, June 12, 1984	9A–60
Re Hunt [1902] 2 Ch. 318	6B–112
Re Lee (1883) 23 Ch. D. 216	6B–114
Re Lloyd (1879) 12 Ch.D. 447	6B–15
Re Medicaments and Related Classes of Goods (No.2) [2001] 1 W.L.R. 700	9A–44.1
Re Phillips (1869) L.R. 4 Ch. App. 629	6B–108
Re Scott (1874) 22 W.R. 748	6B–6
Re Stoer (1884) 9 P.D. 120	6B–146
Re W. [1971] 1 Ch. 123	6B–2
Rice, Re (1886) 32 Ch.D. 35	6B–76
Roe v. Nix [1893] P. 55	6B–148
Royal Bank of Scotland Ltd v. Citrusdal Investments Ltd [1971] 1 W.L.R. 1469	9A–168
Royal Bank of Scotland v. Miller [2001] EWCA Civ. 344	3A–31, 3A–48
Ryder v. Bond. *See* Searle, Re	
S (FG) Re. *See* S, (FG) (Mental Health Patient), Re	
S, (FG) (Mental Health Patient), Re, *sub nom.* S (FG) Re [1973] 1 W.L.R. 178	6B–115, 6B–134
Safeway Stores Plc v. Tate [2001] 2 W.L.R. 1377	9A–326.1, 9A–832
Saint v. Barking and Dagenham LBC. *See* Barking and Dagenham LBC v. Saint	
Sanderson's Settlement Trusts, Re, *sub nom.* Sanderson (Arthur) (Great Broughton), Re [1961] 1 W.L.R. 36	6B–147
Sanderson (Arthur) (Great Broughton), Re. *See* Sanderson's Settlement Trusts, Re	
Save and Prosper Pensions Ltd v. Homebase Ltd, March 2 2000 (unreported)	9A–44.1
Scammell v. Light (1863) 32 L.J. Ch. 53	6B–41
Seager Hunt, Re [1900] 2 Ch. 54	6B–113
—— [1906] 2 Ch. 299	6B–112
Searle, Re, *sub nom.* Ryder v. Bond [1912] 2 Ch. 365	6B–111
Secretary of State for Trade and Industry v. Aurum Marketing Ltd, *The Times*, August 10, 2000	9A–265
—— v. Backhouse, *The Times*, February 23, 2001	9A–265
Shortridge, Re [1895] 1 Ch. 278	6B–64
Sinclair v. Willes. *See* Alston, Re	
Soltykoff, Re [1898] W.N. 77	6B–6
Southgate, ex p. (1751) 2 Ves.Sen. 401	6B–6
Stevens v. School of Oriental and African Studies, *The Times*, February 2, 2001	9A–161
Stewart v. Engel [2000] 1 W.L.R. 2268	9A–636
Stocznia Gdanska S.A. v. Latreefers Inc., *The Times*, March 15, 2000	9A–265
Strangwayes v. Read [1898] 2 Ch. 419	6B–41, 6B–150
Swettenham v. Swettenham (By her Guardian) [1938] P. 218	6B–7
Sykes v. Harry, *The Times*, February 27, 2001	3A–44
Symphony Group Plc v. Hodgson [1994] Q.B. 179	9A–265
Synstar Computer Service (U.K. Ltd v. I.C.L. (Sorbus) Ltd, *The Times*, May 1, 2001	9A–165
TB, Re [1967] Ch. 247	6B–135
TGA Chapman Ltd v. Christopher [1998] 1 W.L.R. 12	9A–265
TRM (A Person of Unsound Mind), Re [1939] Ch. 260	6B–83
Taj v. Ali, 97/17 L.S. Gaz., April 28, 2000	3A–184
Tharros Shipping Co Ltd v. Bias Shipping Ltd (The Griparion) (No.3), *sub nom.* Griparion, The (No.3) [1997] 1 Lloyd's Rep. 246, CA; affirming [1995] 1 Lloyd's Rep. 541	9A–265
Timins v. Timins [1938] 4 All E.R. 180	6B–134

Table of Cases

Trustees of John Black v. White,	4A–13, 4A–30, 4B–9, 4B–25
Tugwell, Re (1885) 27 Ch.D. 309	6B–111
Tye's Case [1900] 1 Ch. 249	6B–83
UYB Ltd v. British Railways Board,	9A–634
Ujima HA v. Smith, April 2001, Legal Action 22, October 16, 2000	3A–672
Ujima Housing Association v. Ansah (1998) 30 H.L.R. 831	3A–322
United Stares Government v. Montgomery [2001] UKHL/3; 1	9A–55
Uratemp Ventures Ltd v. Carrell. *See* Uratemp Ventures Ltd v. Collins	
—— v. Collins and Carrell [2000] L &TR 369	3A–89
—— v. Collins, *sub nom.* Uratemp Ventures Ltd v. Carrell (2001) 33 H.L.R. 4	3A–607
Vimeira, The (No.2). *See* Aiden Shipping Co Ltd v. Interbulk Ltd (The Vimeira) (No.2)	
W (EEM), Re, *sub nom.* W, Re [1971] Ch. 123	6B–3, 6B–115, 6B–134
W, Re. *See* W (EEM), Re	
W v. L [1974] Q.B. 711	6B–1
WJGL, Re. *See* L (WJG), Re	
WLW, Re [1972] Ch. 456	6B–196, 6B–202
Walia v. Michael Naughton Ltd [1985] 1 W.L.R. 1115	6B–350
Walker, Re [1907] 2 Ch. 120	6B–41, 6B–149
——, *sub nom.* Goodwin v. Scott [1921] 2 Ch. 63	6B–111
Wallersteiner v. Moir (No.2), *sub nom.* Moir v. Wallersteiner (No.2) [1975] Q.B. 373	9A–265
Waltham Forest CBHA v. Fanning July, 2001 Legal Action, (2001) March 12	3A–607
Watson, Re, Stamford Union v. Barlett [1899] 1 Ch. 72	6B–83
Wentworth v. Tubb (1842) 7 Jur.(o.s.) 738	6B–155
Westminster County Council v. National Asylum Support Service (2001) April 10	3A–28.10
—— v. ——, February 27, 2001	3A-1184.1
Wheater, Re [1928] 1 Ch. 223	6B–41, 6B–112
Wheeler, Re (1852) 1 De G.M. & G. 434	6B–108
Whitaker, Re (1889) 42 Ch.D. 119	6B–112
Whitworth, Re; Wood, Re; EA, Re; Fraser, Re. *See* Greene, Re	
Willson v. Ministry of Defence [1991] 1 All E.R. 638	9A–581
Wilson v. First County Trust Ltd (No. 2) [2001] 3 W.L.R. 42	3B–231
—— v. First County Trust,, *The Times*, December 6, 2000, CA	3B–21, 3B–231
Winkle, Re [1894] 2 Ch. 519	6B–7, 6B–83, 6B–112 — 6B–113
Woodgate v. Taylor (1861) L.J. P. 197	6B–134
Woodhead v. Bates [1963] 1 W.L.R. 926	6B–45
Yerburgh, Re [1928] W.N. 208	6B–76
Yonge v. Toynbee [1910] 1 K.B. 215	6B–157

VOLUME 1

CIVIL PROCEDURE RULES

SECTION A

CIVIL PROCEDURE RULES 1998

PART 2

APPLICATION AND INTERPRETATION OF THE RULES

Practice Direction—Allocation of Cases to Levels of Judiciary

Trials and Assessments of Damages

Delete text of paragraph 11.1(a)(i) – (vii) and substitute:

11.1(a) any claim which has been allocated to the small claims or fast track or which is treated as being allocated to the multi-track under rule 8.9(c) and Table 2 of the Practice Direction to Part 8, except claims:

(i) under Part I of the Landlord and Tenant Act 1927;
(ii) for a new tenancy under section 24 of the Landlord and Tenant Act 1954;
(iii) for an order under section 38 or 40 of the Landlord and Tenant Act 1987;
(iv) under paragraph 26 or 27 of Schedule 11 to or section 27 of the Agricultural Holdings Act 1986;
(v) under section 45(2) of the Matrimonial Causes Act 1973 for a declaration of legitimation by virtue of the Legitimacy Act 1976;
(vi) under section 35, 38 or 40 of the Fair Trading Act 1973; or
(vii) under Part II of the Mental Health Act 1983.

2BPD–011

PART 6

SERVICE OF DOCUMENTS

I. GENERAL RULES ABOUT SERVICE

Part 6 rules about service apply generally

In rule 6.1, delete second paragraph (b) and substitute:

6.1

(b) service in possession claims – see Part 55).

In rule 6.16(6)(b)(i), delete the cross references to O.10, O.97 and O.113. In rule 6.16(6)(b)(ii), delete the cross references to O.7, O.43 and O.49.

COUNCIL REGULATION (E.C.) NO. 1348/2000 OF 29 MAY 2000 ON THE SERVICE IN THE MEMBER STATES OF JUDICIAL AND EXTRAJUDICIAL DOCUMENTS IN CIVIL OR COMMERCIAL MATTERS

CHAPTER I — GENERAL PROVISIONS

Article 1

Scope

Add new paragraphs 6.33 to 6.57:

6.33   1. This Regulation shall apply in civil and commercial matters where a judicial or extrajudicial document has to be transmitted from one Member State to another for service there.

2. This Regulation shall not apply where the address of the person to be served with the document is not known.

Article 2

Transmitting and receiving agencies

6.34   1. Each Member State shall designate the public officers, authorities or other persons, hereinafter referred to as "transmitting agencies", competent for the transmission of judicial or extrajudicial documents to be served in another Member State.

2. Each Member State shall designate the public officers, authorities or other persons, hereinafter referred to as "receiving agencies", competent for the receipt of judicial or extrajudicial documents from another Member State.

3. A Member State may designate one transmitting agency and one receiving agency or one agency to perform both functions. A federal State, a State in which several legal systems apply or a State with autonomous territorial units shall be free to designate more than one such agency. The designation shall have effect for a period of five years and may be renewed at five-year intervals.

4. Each Member State shall provide the Commission with the following information:

(a) the names and addresses of the receiving agencies referred to in paragraphs 2 and 3;

(b) the geographical areas in which they have jurisdiction;

(c) the means of receipt of documents available to them; and

(d) the languages that may be used for the completion of the standard form in the Annex

Member States shall notify the Commission of any subsequent modification of such information.

Article 3

6.35 Central body

Each Member State shall designate a central body responsible for:

(a) supplying information to the transmitting agencies;

(b) seeking solutions to any difficulties which may arise during transmission of documents for service;

(c) forwarding, in exceptional cases, at the request of a transmitting agency, a request for service to the competent receiving agency

CHAPTER II — JUDICIAL DOCUMENTS

SECTION 1 — TRANSMISSION AND SERVICE OF JUDICIAL DOCUMENTS

Article 4

Transmission of Documents

1. Judicial documents shall be transmitted directly and as soon as possible between the agencies designated on the basis of Article 2.   **6.36**

2. The transmission of documents, requests, confirmations, receipts, certificates and any other papers between transmitting agencies and receiving agencies may be carried out by any appropriate means, provided that the content of the document received is true and faithful to that of the document forwarded and that all information in it is easily legible.

3. The document to be transmitted shall be accompanied by a request drawn up using the standard form in the Annex. The form shall be completed in the official language of the Member State addressed or, if there are several official languages in that Member State, the official language or one of the official languages of the place where service is to be effected, or in another language which that Member State has indicated it can accept. Each Member State shall indicate the official language or languages of the European Union other than its own which is or are acceptable to it for completion of the form.

4. The documents and all papers that are transmitted shall be exempted from legalisation or any equivalent formality.

5. When the transmitting agency wishes a copy of the document to be returned together with the certificate referred to in Article 10, it shall send the document in duplicate.

Article 5

Translation of documents

1. The applicant shall be advised by the transmitting agency to which he or she forwards the document for transmission that the addressee may refuse to accept it if it is not in one of the languages provided for in Article 8.   **6.37**

2. The applicant shall bear any costs of translation prior to the transmission of the document, without prejudice to any possible subsequent decision by the court or competent authority on liability for such costs.

Article 6

Receipt of documents by receiving agency

1. On receipt of a document, a receiving agency shall, as soon as possible and in any event within seven days of receipt, send a receipt to the transmitting agency by the swiftest possible means of transmission using the standard form in the Annex.   **6.38**

2. Where the request for service cannot be fulfilled on the basis of the information or documents transmitted, the receiving agency shall contact the transmitting agency by the swiftest possible means in order to secure the missing information or documents.

3. If the request for service is manifestly outside the scope of this Regulation or if non-compliance with the formal conditions required makes service impossible, the request and the documents transmitted

shall be returned, on receipt, to the transmitting agency, together with the notice of return in the standard form in the Annex.

4. A receiving agency receiving a document for service but not having territorial jurisdiction to serve it shall forward it, as well as the request, to the receiving agency having territorial jurisdiction in the same Member State if the request complies with the conditions laid down in Article 4(3) and shall inform the transmitting agency accordingly, using the standard form in the Annex. That receiving agency shall inform the transmitting agency when it receives the document, in the manner provided for in paragraph 1.

Article 7

Service of documents

6.39 1. The receiving agency shall itself serve the document or have it served, either in accordance with the law of the Member State addressed or by a particular form requested by the transmitting agency, unless such a method is incompatible with the law of that Member State.

2. All steps required for service of the document shall be effected as soon as possible. In any event, if it has not been possible to effect service within one month of receipt, the receiving agency shall inform the transmitting agency by means of the certificate in the standard form in the Annex, which shall be drawn up under the conditions referred to in Article 10(2). The period shall be calculated in accordance with the law of the Member State addressed.

Article 8

Refusal to accept documents

6.40 1. The receiving agency shall inform the addressee that he or she may refuse to accept the document to be served if it is in a language other than either of the following languages:

(a) the official language of the Member State addressed or, if there are several official languages in that Member State, the official language or one of the official languages of the place where service is to be effected; or

(b) a language of the Member State of transmission which the addressee understands.

2. Where the receiving agency is informed that the addressee refuses to accept the document in accordance with paragraph 1, it shall immediately inform the transmitting agency by means of the certificate provided for in Article 10 and return the request and the documents of which a translation is requested.

Article 9

Date of service

6.41 1. Without prejudice to Article 8, the date of service of a document pursuant to Article 7 shall be the date on which it is served in accordance with the law of the Member State addressed.

2. However, where a document shall be served within a particular period in the context of proceedings to be brought or pending in the Member State of origin, the date to be taken into account with respect to the applicant shall be that fixed by the law of that Member State.

3. A Member State shall be authorised to derogate from the provisions of paragraphs 1 and 2 for a transitional period of five years, for appropriate reasons.

This transitional period may be renewed by a Member State at five-yearly intervals due to reasons related to its legal system. That Member State shall inform the Commission of the content of such a derogation and the circumstances of the case.

Article 10

Certificate of service and copy of the document served

1. When the formalities concerning the service of the document have been completed, a certificate of completion of those formalities shall be drawn up in the standard form in the Annex and addressed to the transmitting agency, together with, where Article 4(5) applies, a copy of the document served.   **6.42**

2. The certificate shall be completed in the official language or one of the official languages of the Member State of origin or in another language which the Member State of origin has indicated that it can accept. Each Member State shall indicate the official language or languages of the European Union other than its own which is or are acceptable to it for completion of the form.

Article 11

Costs of service

1. The service of judicial documents coming from a Member State shall not give rise to any payment or reimbursement of taxes or costs for services rendered by the Member State addressed.   **6.43**

2. The applicant shall pay or reimburse the costs occasioned by:

(a) the employment of a judicial officer or of a person competent under the law of the Member State addressed;

(b) the use of a particular method of service.

SECTION 2 — OTHER MEANS OF TRANSMISSION AND SERVICE OF JUDICIAL DOCUMENTS

Article 12

Transmission by consular or diplomatic channels   **6.44**

Each Member State shall be free, in exceptional circumstances, to use consular or diplomatic channels to forward judicial documents, for the purpose of service, to those agencies of another Member State which are designated pursuant to Article 2 or 3.

Article 13

Service by diplomatic or consular agents

1. Each Member State shall be free to effect service of judicial documents on persons residing in another Member State, without application of any compulsion, directly through its diplomatic or consular agents.   **6.45**

2. Any Member State may make it known, in accordance with Article 23(1), that it is opposed to such service within its territory, unless the documents are to be served on nationals of the Member State in which the documents originate.

Article 14

Service by post

1. Each Member State shall be free to effect service of judicial documents directly by post to persons residing in another Member State.   **6.46**

2. Any Member State may specify, in accordance with Article 23(1), the conditions under which it will accept service of judicial documents by post.

Article 15

Direct service

6.47 1. This Regulation shall not interfere with the freedom of any person interested in a judicial proceeding to effect service of judicial documents directly through the judicial officers, officials or other competent persons of the Member State addressed.

2. Any Member State may make it known, in accordance with Article 23(1), that it is opposed to the service of judicial documents in its territory pursuant to paragraph 1.

CHAPTER III — EXTRAJUDICIAL DOCUMENTS

Article 16

6.48 Transmission

Extrajudicial documents may be transmitted for service in another Member State in accordance with the provisions of this Regulation.

CHAPTER IV — FINAL PROVISIONS

Article 17

6.49 Implementing rules

The measures necessary for the implementation of this Regulation relating to the matters referred to below shall be adopted in accordance with the advisory procedure referred to in Article 18(2):

(a) drawing up and annually updating a manual containing the information provided by Member States in accordance with Article 2(4);

(b) drawing up a glossary in the official languages of the European Union of documents which may be served under this Regulation;

(c) updating or making technical amendments to the standard form set out in the Annex

Article 18

Committee

6.50 1. The Commission shall be assisted by a committee.

2. Where reference is made to this paragraph, Articles 3 and 7 of Decision 1999/468/EC shall apply.

3. The Committee shall adopt its rules of procedure.

Article 19

Defendant not entering an appearance

6.51 1. Where a writ of summons or an equivalent document has had to be transmitted to another Member State for the purpose of service, under the provisions of this Regulation, and the defendant has not appeared, judgment shall not be given until it is established that:

(a) the document was served by a method prescribed by the internal law of the Member State addressed for the service of documents in domestic actions upon persons who are within its territory; or

(b) the document was actually delivered to the defendant or to his residence by another method provided for by this Regulation;

and that in either of these cases the service or the delivery was effected in sufficient time to enable the defendant to defend.

2. Each Member State shall be free to make it known, in accordance with Article 23(1), that the judge, notwithstanding the provisions of paragraph 1, may give judgment even if no certificate of service or delivery has been received, if all the following conditions are fulfilled:

(a) the document was transmitted by one of the methods provided for in this Regulation;

(b) a period of time of not less than six months, considered adequate by the judge in the particular case, has elapsed since the date of the transmission of the document;

(c) no certificate of any kind has been received, even though every reasonable effort has been made to obtain it through the competent authorities or bodies of the Member State addressed.

3. Notwithstanding paragraphs 1 and 2, the judge may order, in case of urgency, any provisional or protective measures.

4. When a writ of summons or an equivalent document has had to be transmitted to another Member State for the purpose of service, under the provisions of this Regulation, and a judgment has been entered against a defendant who has not appeared, the judge shall have the power to relieve the defendant from the effects of the expiration of the time for appeal from the judgment if the following conditions are fulfilled:

(a) the defendant, without any fault on his part, did not have knowledge of the document in sufficient time to defend, or knowledge of the judgment in sufficient time to appeal; and

(b) the defendant has disclosed a prima facie defence to the action on the merits.

An application for relief may be filed only within a reasonable time after the defendant has knowledge of the judgment.

Each Member State may make it known, in accordance with Article 23(1), that such application will not be entertained if it is filed after the expiration of a time to be stated by it in that communication, but which shall in no case be less than one year following the date of the judgment.

5. Paragraph 4 shall not apply to judgments concerning status or capacity of persons.

Article 20

Relationship with agreements or arrangements to which Member States are Parties

1. This Regulation shall, in relation to matters to which it applies, prevail over other provisions contained in bilateral or multilateral agreements or arrangements concluded by the Member States, and in particular Article IV of the Protocol to the Brussels Convention of 1968 and the Hague Convention of 15 November 1965.

2. This Regulation shall not preclude individual Member States from maintaining or concluding agreements or arrangements to expedite further or simplify the transmission of documents, provided that they are compatible with this Regulation.

3. Member States shall send to the Commission:

(a) a copy of the agreements or arrangements referred to in paragraph

2 concluded between the Member States as well as drafts of such agreements or arrangements which they intend to adopt; and

(b) any denunciation of, or amendments to, these agreements or arrangements.

Article 21

6.53 Legal aid

This Regulation shall not affect the application of Article 23 of the Convention on Civil Procedure of 17 July 1905, Article 24 of the Convention on Civil Procedure of 1 March 1954 or Article 13 of the Convention on International Access to Justice of 25 October 1980 between the Member States Parties to these Conventions.

Article 22

Protection of information transmitted

6.54 1. Information, including in particular personal data, transmitted under this Regulation shall be used by the receiving agency only for the purpose for which it was transmitted.

2. Receiving agencies shall ensure the confidentiality of such information, in accordance with their national law.

3. Paragraphs 1 and 2 shall not affect national laws enabling data subjects to be informed of the use made of information transmitted under this Regulation.

4. This Regulation shall be without prejudice to Directives 95/46/EC and 97/66/EC.

Article 23

Communication and publication

6.55 1. Member States shall communicate to the Commission the information referred to in Articles 2, 3, 4, 9, 10, 13, 14, 15, 17(a) and 19.

2. The Commission shall publish in the Official Journal of the European Communities the information referred to in paragraph 1.

Article 24

6.56 Review

No later than 1 June 2004, and every five years thereafter, the Commission shall present to the European Parliament, the Council and the Economic and Social Committee a report on the application of this Regulation, paying special attention to the effectiveness of the bodies designated pursuant to Article 2 and to the practical application of point (c) of Article 3 and Article 9. The report shall be accompanied if need be by proposals for adaptations of this Regulation in line with the evolution of notification systems.

Article 25

6.57 Entry into force

This Regulation shall enter into force on 31 May 2001. This Regulation shall be binding in its entirety and directly applicable in the Member States in accordance with the Treaty establishing the European Community. Done at Brussels, 29 May 2000. For the Council.

PART 8

ALTERNATIVE PROCEDURE FOR CLAIMS

Practice Direction—How to Make Claims in Schedule Rules and Other Claims

In paragraph A.2(1), delete "Schedule". **8BPD–005**

Delete the references to RSC O. 88, r.3; RSC O.97 (all references) and O. 113, r.1 in Table 1. **8BPD–006**

SECTION B

Application

For paragraph B.1(2) and sub-paragraphs (a) and (b) substitute:

B.1(2) in the county court is for, or includes a claim for damages for harassment under Section 3 of the Protection from Harassment Act 1997; **8BPD–007**

In paragraph B.1(3)(b)(ii), delete "Schedule"

Delete the references to CCR O.24, r.1(1); CCR O.43 (all references); CCR O.49, r.1(2), r.4(5), r.4(9), r.4(14), r.4(15), r.6(5), r.6A(5), r.9(3) and r.13(1) in Table 2.

Special provisions take precedence

In paragraph B.2, delete reference to CCR, O.7. **8BPD–010**

Restrictions on where to start the claim

In paragraph B.7, delete sub-paragraphs (1) and (2), then renumber sub-paragraphs (3) and (4) **8BPD–011**

Claim form

In paragraph B.8, delete sub-paragraph (2), then renumber sub-paragraph (3). **8BPD–012**

PART 12

DEFAULT JUDGMENT

Practice Direction—Default Judgment

Evidence

In paragraph 4.4(3), for "(unless the State agreed to a different form of service), and" substitute:

4.4(3) Or, where the State has agreed to another form of service, that the claim was served in the manner agreed; and **12PD–004**

For text of paragraph 4.4(4) substitute:

(4) establish that the time for acknowledging service, (which is extended to two months by section 12(2) of the Act when the claim is sent through the Foreign and Commonwealth Office to the Ministry of Foreign Affairs for the State) has expired.

PART 16

STATEMENTS OF CASE

In the second paragraph (a) of rule 16.8, delete references to O.88 and O.97.

In the second paragraph (b) of rule 16.8, delete references to O.6 and O.43. **16.8**

Practice Direction—Statements of Case

Delete paragraph 6(6) – Recovery of Land and renumber subsequent paragraphs accordingly. **16PD–006**

PART 19

PARTIES AND GROUP LITIGATION

II. REPRESENTATIVE PARTIES

19.9 *In rule 19.9(3)(a) delete "except".*

PART 35

EXPERTS AND ASSESSORS

Practice Direction—Experts and Assessors

Questions to experts

Delete text of paragraph 4.2 and substitute:

35PD–004   4.2 Where a party sends a written question or questions direct to an expert, a copy of the questions should, at the same time, be sent to the other party or parties.

PART 48

COSTS—SPECIAL CASES

II. COSTS RELATING TO SOLICITORS AND OTHER LEGAL REPRESENTATIVES

48.7 *In rule 48.7, delete sub-paragraph (3) and renumber subsequent paragraphs accordingly.*

PART 51

TRANSITIONAL ARRANGEMENTS AND PILOT SCHEMES

The heading for CPR Part 51 should be amended to read "Transitional Arrangements and Pilot Schemes".

Add new rule 51.2 after rule 51.1:

51.2   51.2 Practice directions may modify or disapply any provision of these rules –
  (a) for specified periods; and
  (b) in relation to proceedings in specified courts,
during the operation of pilot schemes for assessing the use of new practices and procedures in connection with proceedings.

PART 52

APPEALS

Small Claims

Add new paragraphs after 5.8B:

52PD–015A   5.8C The appellant need not file a record of the reasons for judgment of the lower court with his appellant's notice unless paragraph 5.8D applies.

5.8D The court may order a suitable record of the reasons for judgment of the lower court (see paragraph 5.12) to be filed –
   (a)   to enable it to decide if permission should be granted; or
   (b)   if permission is granted to enable it to decide the appeal.

Appeals to the High Court
For "Midland and Oxford Circuit" substitute:

Midland Circuit			**52PD–038**

Delete "Oxford" from the Hearing Only Centres for the Midland Circuit.

Delete "Chelmsford" from the Hearing Only Centres for the South Eastern Circuit.

In paragraphs 8.9 and 8.10, for "section 9(1)" substitute:
8.9 section 9

PART 55

Possession Claims

PRACTICE DIRECTION — POSSESSION CLAIMS

Section 1

GENERAL RULES

55.3 Starting the claim

Add new paragraph after 1.5:
1.6 High Court claims for the possession of land and subject to a mortgage will be assigned to the Chancery Division.   **55PD–001**

PART 56

Landlord and Tenant Claims and Miscellaneous Provisions About Land

PRACTICE DIRECTION — LANDLORD AND TENANT CLAIMS AND MISCELLANEOUS PROVISIONS ABOUT LAND

Section I

LANDLORD AND TENANT CLAIMS

Renumber paragraph (3) as paragraph (4), then add new text to new paragraph (3):
1.1(3)   "the 1985 Act" means the Landlord and Tenant Act 1985.   **56PD–001**

Evidence

Add new paragraph after 3.7:

56PD–007 3.8 The evidence required to be served under rule 56.3(10) or (11) is that supporting the parties' positions so that the court can identify the issues and give appropriate further directions which may include directions about –
- (1) the trial of any preliminary issues;
- (2) the service of –
  - (a) further witness statements; and
  - (b) any further evidence.

Other claims under Part II of the 1954 Act

In paragraph 4.2, for "section 47(5)" substitute:

56PD–008 4.2 section 37(5)

Add after "The defendant must":

56PD–011 5.5 immediately

Compensation under section 1 or 8 of the 1927 Act

Add new paragraphs after 5.7:

56PD–013 5.8 A claim under section 1(1) or 8(1) of the 1927 Act must be in writing, signed by the claimant, his solicitor or agent and include details of –
- (1) the name and address of the claimant and of the landlord against whom the claim is made;
- (2) the property to which the claim relates;
- (3) the nature of the business carried on at the property;
- (4) a concise statement of the nature of the claim;
- (5) particulars of the improvement, including the date when it was completed and costs; and
- (6) the amount claimed.

5.9 A mesne landlord must immediately serve a copy of the claim on his immediate superior landlord. If the person so served is not the freeholder, he must serve a copy of the document on his landlord and so on from landlord to landlord.

(Paragraphs 5.8 and 5.9 provide the procedure for making claims under section 1(1) and 8(1) of the 1927 Act – "claims" do not, at this stage, relate to proceedings before the court).

Chancel Repairs Act 1932

Add new paragraphs after 12.1:

56PD–029 12.2 A notice to repair under section 2 of the Chancel Repairs Act 1932 must –
- (1) state –
  - (a) the responsible authority by whom the notice is given;
  - (b) the chancel alleged to be in need of repair;
  - (c) the repairs alleged to be necessary; and
  - (d) the grounds on which the person to whom the notice is addressed is alleged to be liable to repair the chancel; and
- (2) call upon the person to whom the notice is addressed to put the chancel in proper repair.

12.3 The notice must be served in accordance with Part 6.

PART 70

GENERAL RULES ABOUT ENFORCEMENT OF JUDGMENTS AND ORDERS
(THIS PART DOES NOT COME INTO FORCE UNTIL MARCH 25, 2002)

Contents   70.0.1

70.1	Scope of this Part and interpretation	para. 70.1
70.2	Methods of enforcing judgments or orders	para. 70.2
70.3	Transfer of proceedings for enforcement	para. 70.3
70.4	Transfer of proceedings for enforcement	para. 70.4
70.5	Enforcement of awards of bodies other than the High Court and county courts	para. 70.5
70.6	Effect of setting aside judgment ot order	para. 70.6

Editorial Introduction

Add new Parts 70, 71, 72 and 73 after Part 57.

Part 70 is added to the CPR by the Civil Procedure Amendment Rules 2001 (S.I. 2001 No. 2792) and comes into force on March 25, 2002   **70.0.2**

Scope of this Part and interpretation

70.1—(1) This Part contains general rules about enforcement of judgments and orders.   **70.1**

(Rules about specific methods of enforcement are contained in Parts 71 to 73, Schedule 1, RSC Orders 45 to 47, 51 and 52 and Schedule 2, CCR Orders 25 to 29)

(2) In this Part and in Parts 71 to 73—
    (a) "judgment creditor" means a person who has obtained or is entitled to enforce a judgment or order;
    (b) "judgment debtor" means a person against whom a judgment or order was given or made;
    (c) "judgment or order" includes an award which the court has—
        (i) registered for enforcement;
        (ii) ordered to be enforced; or
        (iii) given permission to enforce as if it were a judgment or order of the court, and in relation to such an award, "the court which made the judgment or order" means the court which registered the award or made such an order; and
    (d) "judgment or order for the payment of money" includes a judgment or order for the payment of costs, but does not include a judgment or order for the layment of money into court.

Methods of enforcing judgments or orders

70.2—(1) The relevant practice direction sets out methods of enforcing judgments or orders for the payment of money.   **70.2**

(2) A judgment creditor may, except where an enactment, rule or practice direction provides otherwise—
    (a) use any method of enforcement which is available; and
    (b) use more than one method of enforcement, either at the same time or one after another.

Transfer of proceedings for enforcement

70.3 70.3—(1) A judgment creditor wishing to enforce a High Court judgment or order in a county court must apply to the High Court for an order transferring the proceedings to that county court.

(2) A practice direction may make provisions about the transfer of proceedings for enforcement.

(CCR Order 25, rule 13 contains provisions about the transfer of county court proceedings to the High Court for enforcement.)

Transfer of proceedings for enforcement

70.4 70.4 If a judgment or order is given or made in favour of or against a person who is not a party to proceedings, it may be enforced by or against that person by the same methods as if he were a party.

Enforcement of awards of bodies other than the High Court and county courts

70.5 70.5—(1) This rule applies, subject to paragraph (2), if—
   (a) an award of a sum of money is made by any court, tribunal, body or person other than the High Court or a county court; and
   (b) an enactment provides that the award may be enforced as if payable under a court order.

(2) This rule does not apply to—
   (a) any judgment or recommendation to which RSC Order 71 applies; or
   (b) arbitration awards.
      (RSC Order 71 provides for the registration in the High Court for the purpose of enforcement of—
         (i) foreign judgments;
         (ii) European Community judgments;
         (iii) judgments to which the Civil Jurisdiction and Judgments Act 1982 applies;
         (iv) recommendations under the Merchant Shipping (Liner Conferences) Act 1982.)

(3) If the enactment provides that the award is enforceable if a court so orders, an application for such an order must be made in accordance with paragraphs (4) to (7) of this rule.

(4) An application for an order that an award may be enforced as if payable under a court order—
   (a) may be made without notice; and
   (b) must be made to the court for the district where the person against whom the award was made resides or carries on business, unless the court otherwise orders.

(5) The application notice must—
   (a) be in the form; and
   (b) contain the information
      required by the relevant practice direction.

(6) A copy of the award must be filed with the application notice.

(7) The application may be dealt with by a court officer without a hearing.

(8) An application to the High Court to register a decision of a Value Added Tax Tribunal for enforcement must be made in accordance with the relevant practice direction.

Effect of setting aside judgment ot order
70.6 If a judgment or order is set aside, any enforcement of the judgment or order shall cease to have effect unless the court otherwise orders.

PART 71

ORDERS TO OBTAIN INFORMATION FROM JUDGMENT DEBTORS (THIS PART DOES NOT COME INTO FORCE UNTIL MARCH 25, 2002)

Contents   **71.0.1**

71.1	Scope of this Part	para. 71.1
71.2	Order to attend court	para. 71.2
71.3	Service of order	para. 71.3
71.4	Travelling expenses	para. 71.4
71.5	Judgment creditor's affidavit	para. 71.5
71.6	Conduct of the hearing	para. 71.6
71.7	Adjournment of the hearing	para. 71.7
71.8	Failure to comply with order	para. 71.8

Editorial introduction
Part 71 is added to the CPR by the The Civil Procedure 2001 (S.I. 2001 No. 2792) and comes into force on March 25, 2002.   **71.0.2**

Scope of this part
71.1 This Part contains rules which provide for a judgment debtor to be required to attend court to provide information, for the purpose of enabling a judgment creditor to enforce a judgment or order against him.

Order to attend court
71.2—(1) A judgment creditor may apply for an order requiring –
    (a) a judgment debtor; or
    (b) if a judgment debtor is a company or other corporation, an officer of that body,
        (i) the judgment debtor's means; or
        (ii) any other matter about which information is needed to enforce a judgment or order.
(2) An application under paragraph (1) –
    (a) may be made without notice; and
    (b) (i) must be issued in the court which made the judgment or order which it is sought to enforce, except that
        (ii) if the proceedings have since been transferred to a different court , it must be issued in that court.
(3) The application notice must –

(a) be in the form; and
(b) contain the information
required by the relevant practice direction.

(4) An application under paragraph (1) may be dealt with by a court officer without a hearing.

(5) If the application notice complies with paragraph (3), an order to attend court will be issued in the terms of paragraph (6).

(6) A person served with an order issued under this rule must –
    (a) attend court at the time and place specified in the order;
    (b) when he does so, produce at court documents in his control which are described in the order; and
    (c) answer on oath such questions as the court may require.

(7) An order under this rule will contain a notice in the following terms –
"You must obey this order. If you do not, you may be sent to prison for contempt of court."

Service of order

71.3 71.3—(1) An order to attend court must, unless the court otherwise orders, be served personally on the person ordered to attend the court not less than 14 days before the hearing.

(2) If the order is to be served by the judgment creditor, he must inform the court not less than 7 days before the date of the hearing if he has been unable to serve it.

Travelling expenses

71.4 71.4—(1) A person ordered to attend may, within 7 days of being served with the order, ask the judgment creditor to pay him a sum reasonably sufficient to cover his travelling expenses to and from court.

(2) The judgment creditor must pay a sum if requested.

Judgment creditor's affidavit

71.5 71.5—(1) The judgment creditor must file an affidavit^{GL} or affidavits –
    (a) by the person who served the order (unless it was served by the court) giving the details of how and when it was served;
    (b) stating either that –
        (i) the person ordered to attend court has not requested payment of his travelling expenses
        (ii) the judgment creditor has paid a sum in accordance with suxh a request; and

(2) The judgment creditor must either –
    (a) file the affidavit^{GL} or affidavits not less than 2 days before the hearing; or
    (b) produce it or them at the hearing.

Conduct of the hearing

71.6 71.6—(1) The person ordered to attend court will be questioned on oath.

(2) The questioning will be carried out by a court officer unless the court has ordered that the hearing shall be before a judge.
(3) The judgment creditor or his representative –
   (a) may attend and ask questions where the questioning takes place before a court officer; and
   (b) must attend and conduct the questioning if the hearing is before a judge.

Adjournment of the hearing

71.7 If the hearing is adjourned, the court will give directions as to the manner in which notice of the new hearing is to be served on the judgment debtor.

Failure to comply with order

71.8—(1) If a person against whom an order has been made under rule 71.2 –
   (a) fails to attend court;
   (b) refuses at the hearing to take the oath or to answer any question; or
   (c) otherwise fails to comply with the order,
the court will refer the matter to a High Court judge or circuit judge.
(4)
   (a) the order shall be suspended provided that the person –
   (b) if the person fails to attend court at that time and place, he shall be brought before a judge to consider whether the committal order should be discharged.

PART 72

Third Party Debt Orders (This Part does not come into force until March 25, 2002)

Contents

72.1	Scope of this Part and interpretation	para. 72.1
72.2	Third party debt order	para. 72.2
72.3	Application for third party debt order	para. 72.3
72.4	Interim third party debt order	para. 72.4
72.5	Service of interim order	para. 72.5
72.6	Obligations of third parties served with interim order	para. 72.6
72.7	Arrangements for debtors in hardship	para. 72.7
72.8	Further consideration of the application	para. 72.8
72.9	Effect of final third party debt order	para. 72.9
72.10	Money in court	para. 72.10
72.11	Costs	para. 72.11

Editorial Introduction
Part 72 is added to the CPR by the Civil Procedure Amendment Rules 2001 (S.I. 2001 No. 2792) and comes into force on March 25, 2002

Scope of this Part and interpretation

72.1 72.1—(1) This Part contains rules which provide for a judgment creditor to obtain an order for the payment to him of money which a third party who is within the jurisdiction owes to the judgment debtor.

(2) In this Part "bank or building society" includes any person carrying on a business which is a deposit-taking business for the purposes of the Banking Act 1987.

Third party debt order

72.2 72.2—(1) Upon the application of a judgment creditor, the court may make an order (a "final third party debt order") requiring a third party to pay to the judgment creditor—

  (a) the amount of any debt due or accruing due to the judgment debtor from the third party; or

  (b) so much of that debt as is sufficient to satisfy the judgment debt and the judgment creditor's costs of the application.

(2) The court will not make an order under paragraph 1 without first making an order (an "interim third party debt order") as provided by rule 72.4(2).

(3) in deciding whether money standing to the credit of the judgment debtor in an account to which section 40 of the Supreme Court Act 1981 or section 108 of the County Courts Act 1984 relates may be made the subject of a third party debt order, any condition applying to the account that a receipt for money deposited in the account must be produced before any money is withdrawn will be disregarded.

(Section 40(3) of the Supreme Court Act 1981 and section 108(3)of the County Courts Act 1984 contain a list of other conditions applying to accounts that will also be disregarded.)

Application for third party debt order

72.3 72.3—(1) An application for a third party debt order –

  (a) may be made without notice; and

  (b) (i) must be issued in the court which made the judgment or order which it is sought to enforce except that

   (ii) if the proceedings have since been transferred to a different court, it must be issued in that court.

(2) The application notice must –

  (a) (i) be in the form; and

   (ii) contain the information required by the relevant practice direction; and

  (b) be verified by a statement of truth.

Interim third party debt order

72.4 72.4—(1) An application for a third party debt order will initially be dealt with by a judge without a hearing.

(2) The judge may make an interim third party debt order –

  (a) fixing a hearing to consider whether to make a final third party debt order; and

(b) directing that until that hearing the third party must not make any payment which reduces the amount he owes the judgment debtor to less than the amount specified in the order.

(3) An interim third party debt order will specify the amount of money which the third party must retain, which will be the total of –
   (a) the amount of money remaining due to the judgment creditor under the judgment or order; or
   (b) an amount for the judgment creditor's fixed costs of the application, as specified in the relevant practice direction.

(4) An interim third party debt order becomes binding on a third party when it is served on him.

(5) The date of the hearing to consider the application shall be not less than 28 days after the interim third party debt order is made.

Service of interim order

72.5—(1) Copies of an interim third party debt order, the application notice and any documents filed in support of it must be served –
   (a) on the third party, not less than 21 days before the date fixed for the hearing; and
   (b) on the judgment debtor not less than –
      (i) 7 days after a copy has been served on the third party; and
      (ii) 7 days before the date fixed for the hearing.

(2) If the judgment creditor serves the order, he must either –
   (a) file a certificate of service not less than 2 days before the hearing; or
   (b) produce a certificate of service at the hearing.

Obligations of third parties served with interim order

72.6—(1) A bank or building society served with an interim third party debt order must carry out a search to identify all accounts held with it by the judgment debtor.

(2) The bank or building society must disclose to the court and the creditor within 7 days of being served with the order, in respect of each account held by the judgment debtor –
   (a) the number of the account;
   (b) whether the account is in credit; and
   (c) if the account is in credit –
      (i) whether the balance of the account is sufficient to cover the amount specified in the order; and
      (ii) the amount of the balance at the date it was served with the order, if it is less than the amount specified in the order.

(3) If –
   (a) the judgment debtor does not hold an account with the bank or building society; or
   (b) the bank or building society is unable to comply with the order for any other reason (for example, because it has more than one account holder whose details match the information contained in the order, and cannot identify which account the order applies to),

the bank or building society must inform the court and the judgment creditor of that fact within 7 days of being served with the order.

(4) Any third party other than a bank or building society served with an interim third party debt order must notify the court and the judgment creditor in writing within 7 days of being served with the order, if he claims –
- (a) not to owe any money to the judgment debtor; or
- (b) to owe less than the amount specified in the order.

72.7 72.7—(1) If –
- (a) a judgment debtor is an individual;
- (b) he is prevented from withdrawing money from his account with a bank or building society as a result of an interim third party debt order; and
- (c) he or his family is suffering hardship in meeting ordinary living expenses as a result,

the court may, on an application by the judgment debtor, make an order permitting the bank or building society to make a payment or payments out of the account ("a hardship payment order").

(2) An application for a hardship payment order may be made –
- (a) in High Court proceedings, at the Royal Courts of Justice or to any district registry; and
- (b) in county court proceedings, to any county court.

(3) A judgment debtor may only apply to one court for a hradship payment order.

(4) An application notice seeking a hardship payment order must –
- (a) include detailed evidence explaining why the judgment debtor needs a payment of the amount requested; and
- (b) be verified by a statement of truth.

(5) Unless the court orders otherwise, the application notice –
- (a) must be served on the judgment creditor at least 2 days before the hearing; but
- (b) does not need to be served on the third party.

(6) A hardship payment order may –
- (a) permit the third party to make one or more payments out of the account; and
- (b) specify to whom the payments may be made.

Further consideration of the application

72.8 72.8—(1) If the judgment debtor or the third party objects to the court making a final third party debt order, he must file and serve written evidence stating the grounds for his objections.

(2) If the judgment debtor or the third party knows or believes that a person other than the judgment debtor has any claim to the money specified in the interim order, he must file and serve written evidence stating his knowledge of that matter.

(3) If –
- (a) the third party has given notice under rule 72.6 that he does not owe any money to the judgment debtor, or that the

amount which he owes is less than the amount specified in the interim order; and
(b) the judgment creditor wishes to dispute this,
the judgment creditor must file and serve written evidence setting out the grounds on which he disputes the third party's case.

(4) Written evidence under paragraphs (1), (2) or (3) must be filed and served on each other party as soon as possible, and in any event not less than 3 days before the hearing.

(5) If the court is notified that some person other than the judgment debtor may have a claim to the money specified in the interim order, it will serve on that person notice of the application and the hearing.

(6) At the hearing the court may –
(a) make a final third party debt order;
(b) discharge the interim third party debt order and dismiss the application;
(c) decide any issues in dispute between the parties, or between any of the parties and any other person who has a claim to the money specified in the interim order; or
(d) direct a trial of any such issues, and if necessary give directions.

Effect of final third party order

72.9—(1) A final third party debt order shall be enforceable as an order to pay money.
(2) If –
(a) the third party pays money to the judgment creditor in compliance with a third party debt order; or
(b) the order is enforced against him,
the third party shall, to the extent of the amount paid by him or realised by enforcement against him, be discharged from his debt to the judgment debtor.
(3) Paragraph (2) applies even if the third party debt order, or the original judgment or order against the judgment debtor, is later set aside.

Money in court

72.10—(1) If money is standing to the credit of the judgment debtor in court –
(a) the judgment creditor may not apply for a third party debt order in respect of that money; but
(b) he may apply for an order that the money in court, or so much of it as is sufficient to satisfy the judgment or order and the costs of the application, be paid to him.
(2) An application notice seeking an order under this rule must be served on –
(a) the judgment debtor; and
(b) the Accountant General at the Court Funds Office.
(3) If an application notice has been issued under this rule, the money in court must not be paid out until the application has been disposed of.

Costs

72.11 72.11 If the judgment creditor is awarded costs on an application for an order under rule 72.2 or 72.10 –

(a) he shall, unless the court otherwise directs, retain those costs out of the money recovered by him under the order; and

(b) the costs shall be deemed to be paid first out of the money he recovers, in priority to judgment debt.

PART 73

CHARGING ORDERS, STOP ORDERS AND STOP NOTICES (THIS PART DOES NOT COME INTO FORCE UNTIL MARCH 25, 2002)

73.0.1 Contents

73.1	Scope of this Part and interpretation	para. 73.1

SECTION I - CHARGING ORDERS

73.2	Scope of this Section	para. 73.2
73.3	Application for charging order	para. 73.3
73.4	Interim charging order	para. 73.4
73.5	Service of interim order	para. 73.5
73.6	Effect of interim order in relation to securities	para. 73.6
73.7	Effect of interim order in relation to funds in court	para. 73.7
73.8	Further consideration of the application	para. 73.8
73.9	Discharge or variation of order	para. 73.9
73.10	Enforcement of charging order by sale	para. 73.10

SECTION II - STOP ORDERS

73.11	Interpretation	para. 73.11
73.12	Application for stop order	para. 73.12
73.13	Stop order relating to funds in court	para. 73.13
73.14	Stop order relating to securities	para. 73.14
73.15	Discharge or variation of order	para. 73.15

SECTION III - STOP NOTICES

73.16	General	para. 73.16
73.17	Request for stop notice	para. 73.17
73.18	Effect of stop notice	para. 73.18
73.19	Amendment of stop notice	para. 73.19
73.20	Withdrawal of stop notice	para. 73.20
73.21	Discharge or variation of stop notice	para. 73.21

Editorial Introduction

73.0.2 Part 73 is added to the CPR by the The Civil Procedure Rules 2001 (S.I. 2001 No. 2792), and comes into force on March 25, 2002.

Scope of this part and interpretation

73.1—(1) This Part contains rules which provide for a judgment creditor to enforce a judgment by obtaining –
- (a) a charging order (Section I)
- (b) a stop order (Section II)
- (c) a stop notice (Section III)

over or against the judgment debtor's interest in an asset.

(2) In this Part –
- (a) "the 1979 Act"means the Charging Orders Act 1979;
- (b) "the 1992 Regulations"means the Council Tax (Administration and Enforcement) Regulations 1992;
- (c) "funds in court" includes securities held in court;
- (d) "securities "means securities of any kinds specified in section 2(2)(b) of the 1979 Act;

Section I - Charging Orders

Scope of this section

73.2 This Section applies to an application by a judgment creditor for a charging order under –
- (a) section 1 of the 1979 Act; or
- (b) regulation 50 of the 1992 Regulations.

Application for charging order

73.3—(1) An application for a charging order may be made without notice.

(2) An application for a charging order must be issued in the court which made the judgment or order which it is sought to enforce, unless –
- (a) the proceedings have since been transferred to a different court, in which case the application must be issued in that court;
- (b) the application is made under the 1992 Regulations, in which case it must be issued in the county court for the district in which the relevant dwelling (as defined in regulation 50(3)(b) of those Regulations) is situated;
- (c) the application is for a charging order over an interest in a fund in court, in which case it must be issued in the court in which the claim relating to that fund is or was proceeding; or
- (d) the application is to enforce a judgment or order of the High Court and it is required by section 1(2) of the 1979 Act to be made to a county court.

(3) Subject to paragraph (2), a judgment creditor may apply for a single charging order in respect of more than one judgment or order against the same debtor.

(4) The application notice must –
- (a) (i) be in the form; and
    - (ii) contain the information,
    required by the relevant practice direction; and
- (b) be verified by a statement of truth.

Interim charging order

73.4—(1) An application for a charging order will initially be dealt with by a judge without a hearing.

(2) The judge may make an order (an "interim charging order") –
    (a) imposing a charge over the judgment debtor's interest in the asset to which the application relates; and
    (b) fixing a hearing to consider whether to make a final charging order as provided by rule 73.8(2)(a).

Service of interim order

73.5   73.5—(1) Copies of the interim charging order, the application notice and any documents filed in support of it must, not less than 21 days before the hearing, be served on the following persons –
    (a) the judgment debtor;
    (b) such other creditors as the court directs;
    (c) if the order relates to an interest under a trsut, on such of the trustees as the court directs;
    (d) if the interest charged is in securities other than the securities held in court, then –
        (i) in the case of stock for which the Bank of England keeps the register, the Bank of England;
        (ii) in the case of the government stock to which (i) does not apply, the keeper of the register;
        (iii) in the case of stock of any body incorporated within England and Wales, that body;
        (iv) in the case of stock of any body incorporated outside England and Wales or of any state or territory outside the United Kingdom, which is registered in a register kept in England and Wales, the keeper of that register;
        (v) in the case of units of any unit trust in respect of which a register of the unit holders is kept in England and Wales, the keeper of that register; and
    (e) if the interest charged is in funds in court, the Accountant General at the Courts Funds Office.
(2) If the judgment creditor serves the order, he must either –
    (a) file a certificate of service not less than 2 days before the hearing; or
    (b) produce a certificate of service at the hearing.

Effect of interim order in relation to securities

73.6   73.6—(1) If a judgment debtor disposes of his interest in any securities, while they are subject to interim charging order which has been served on him, that disposition shall not, so long as that order remains in force, be valid as against the judgment creditor.
(2) A person served under rule 73.5(1)(d) with an interim charging order relating to securities must not, unless the court gives permission –
    (a) permit any transfer of any of the securities; or
    (b) pay any dividend, interest or redemption payment relating to them.
(3) If a person acts in breach of paragraph (2), he will be liable to pay to the judgment creditor –
    (a) the value of the securities transferred or the amount of the payment made (as the case may be); or

(b) if less, the amount necessary to satisfy the debt in relation to which the interim charging order was made.

Effect of interim order in relation to funds in court
73.7 If a judgment debtor disposes of his interest in funds in court while they are subject to an interim charging order which has been served on him and on the Accountant General in accordance with rule 73.5(1), that disposition shall not, so long as that order remains in force, be valid as against the judgment creditor.

Further consideration of the application
73.8—(1) If any person objects to the court making a final charging order, he must –
    (a) file; and
    (b) serve on the applicant;
        written evidence stating the grounds of his objections, not less than 7 days before the hearing.
(2) At the hearing the court may –
    (a) make a final charging order confirming that the charge imposed by the interim charging order shall continue, with or without modification;
    (b) discharge the interim charging order and dismiss the application;
    (c) decide any issues in dispute between the parties, or between any of the parties and any other person who objects to the court making a final charging order; or
    (d) direct a trial of any such issues, and if necessary give directions.
(3) If the court makes a final charging order which charges securities other than securities held in court, the order will include a stop notice unless the court otherwise orders.
(Section III of this Part contains provisions about stop notices.)
(4) Any order made at the hearing must be served on all the persons on whom the interim charging order was required to be served.

Discharge or variation of order
73.9—(1) Any application to discharge or vary a charging order must be made to the court which made the charging order.
(Section 3(5) of the 1979 Act and regulation 51(4) of the 1992 Regulations provide that the court may at any time, on the application of the debtor, or of any person interested in any property to which the order relates, or (where the 1992 Regulations apply) of the authority, make an order discharging or varying the charging order).
(2) The court may direct that –
    (a) any interested person should be joined as a party to such an application; or
    (b) the application should be served on any such person.
(3) An order discharging or varying a charging order must be served on all the persons whom the charging order was required to be served.

Enforcement of charging order by sale

73.10 73.10—(1) Subject to the provisions of any enactment, the court may, upon a claim by a person who has obtained a charging order over an interest in property, order the sale of the property to enforce the charging order.

(2) A claim for an order for sale under this rule should be made to the court which made the charging order, unless that court does not have jurisdiction to make an order for sale.

(A claim under this rule is a proceeding for the enforcement of a charge, and section 23(c) of the County Courts Act 1984 provides the extent of the county court's jurisdiction to hear and determine such proceedings).

(3) The claimant must use the Part 8 procedure.

(4) A copy of the charging order must be filed with the claim form.

(5) The claimant's written evidence must include the information required by the relevant practice direction.

Section II – Stop Orders

Interpretation

73.11 73.11 In this Section, "stop order" means an order of the High Court not to take, in relation to funds in court or securities specified in the order, any of the steps listed in section 5(5) of the 1979 Act.

Application for stop order

73.12 73.12—(1) The High Court may make –
  (a) a stop order relating to in court, on the application of any person –
    (i) who has a mortgage or charge on the interest of any person in the funds; or
    (ii) to whom that interest has been assigned; or
    (iii) who is a judgment creditor of the person entitled to that interest; or
  (b) a stop order relating to securities other than securities held in court, on the application of any person claiming to be beneficially entitled to an interest in the securities.

(2) An application for a stop order must be made –
  (a) by application notice in existing proceedings; or
  (b) by Part 8 claim form if there are no exisitng proceedings in the High Court.

(3) The application notice or claim form must be served on –
  (a) every person whose interest may be affected by the order applied for; and
  (b) either ;
    (i) the Accountant General at the Court Funds Office, if the application relates to funds in court; or
    (ii) the person specified in rule 73.5(1)(d), if the application relates to securities other than securities held in court.

Stop order relating to funds in court

73.13 A stop order relating to funds in court shall prohibit the transfer, sale and delivery out, payment or other dealing with –
   (a) the funds or any part of them; or
   (b) any income on the funds.

Stop order relating to securities

73.14—(1) A stop order relating to securities other than securities held in court may prohibit all or any of the following steps –
   (a) the registration of any transfer of the securities;
   (b) the making of any payment by way of dividend, interest or otherwise in respect of the securities; and
   (c) in the case of units of a unit trust, any acquisition of or other dealing with the units by any person or body exercising functions under the trust.
(2) The order shall specify –
   (a) the securities to which it relates;
   (b) the name in which the securities stand;
   (c) the steps which may not be taken; and
   (d) whether the prohibition applies to the securities only or to the dividends or interest as well.

Variation or discharge of order

73.15—(1) The court may, on the application of any person claiming to have a beneficial interest in the funds or securities to which a stop order relates, make an order discharging or varying the order.
(2) An application notice seeking the variation or discharge of a stop order must be served on the person who obtained the order.

Section III – Stop Notices

General

73.16 In this Section –
   (a) "stop notice" means a notice issued by the court which requires a person or body not to take, in relation to securities specified in the notice, any of the steps listed in section 5(5) of the 1979 Act, without first giving notice to the person who obtained the notice; and
   (b) "securities" does not include securities held in court.

Request for stop notice

73.17—(1) The High Court may, on the request of any person claiming to be benficially entitled to an interest in securities, issue a stop notice.
(A stop notice may also be included in a final charging order, by either the High Court or a county court, under rule 73.8(3)).
(2) A request for a stop notice must be made by filing –
   (a) a draft stop notice; and
   (b) written evidence which –
      (i) identifies the securities in question;

(ii) describes the applicant's interest in the securities; and
(iii) gives an address for service for the applicant.
(A sample form of stop notice is annexed to the relevant practice direction.)
(3) If a court officer considers that the request complies with paragraph (2), he will issue a stop notice.
(4) The applicant must serve copies of the stop notice and his written evidence on the person to whom the stop notice is addressed.

Effect of stop notice
73.18 73.18—(1) A stop notice –
  (a) takes effect when it is served in accordance with rule 73.17(4); and
  (b) remains in force unless it is withdrawn or discharged in accordance with rule 73.20 or 73.21
(2) While a stop notice is in force, the person on whom it is served –
  (a) must not –
    (i) register a transfer of the securities described in the notice; or
    (ii) take any other step restrained by the notice,
    without first giving 14 days' notice to the person who obtained the stop notice; but
  (b) must not, by reason only of the notice, refuse to register a transfer or to take any other step, after he has given 14 days' notice under paragraph (2)(a) and that period has expired.

Amendment to stop notice
73.19 73.19—(1) If any securities are incorrectly described in a stop notice which has been obtained and served in accordance with rule 73.17, the applicant may request an amended stop notice in accordance with that rule.
(2) The amended stop notice takes effect when it is served.

Withdrawal of stop notice
73.20 73.20—(1) A person who has obtained a stop notice may withdraw it by serving a request for its withdrawal on –
  (a) the person or body on whom the stop notice was served; and
  (b) the court which issued the stop notice.
(2) The request must be signed by the person who obtained the stop notice, and his signature must be witnessed by a practising solicitor.

Discharge or variation of stop notice
73.21 73.21—(1) The court may, on the application of any person claiming to be beneficially entitled to an interest in the securities to which a stop notice relates, make an order discharging or varying the notice.
(2) An application to discharge or vary a stop notice must be made to the court which issued the notice.
(3) The application to discharge or vary a stop notice must be made to the court which issued the notice.

Schedule 1

RSC ORDER 15 - CAUSES OF ACTION, COUNTERCLAIMS AND PARTIES
Representation of beneficiaries by trustees, etc.

In paragraph 14(2), for "under rule 13" substitute:
 14.—(2) under CPR Rule 19.7   sc15.14

RSC ORDER 45 - ENFORCEMENT OF JUDGMENTS AND ORDERS: GENERAL
Enforcement of judgment for possession of land

In paragraph 3(2), for "mortgage proceedings to which Order 88 applies" substitute:
 3.—(2) proceedings by a mortgagee or mortgagor or by any person having the right to foreclose or redeem any mortgage, being proceedings in which there is a claim for –   sc45.3
  (a) payment of moneys secured by the mortgage;
  (b) sale of the mortgaged property;
  (c) foreclosure;
  (d) delivery of possession (whether before or after foreclosure or without foreclosure) to the mortgagee by the mortgagor or by any person who is alleged to be in possession of the property;
  (e) redemption;
  (f) reconveyance of the land or its release from the security; or
  (g) delivery of possession by the mortgagee.

Add new paragraph after 3(2):
 (2A) In paragraph (2) "mortgage" includes a legal or equitable mortgage and a legal or equitable charge, and reference to a mortgagor, a mortgagee and mortgaged land is to be interpreted accordingly.

In paragraph 3(3), add after "permission":
 (3) as is referred to in paragraph (2)

RSC ORDER 51 - RECEIVERS: EQUITABLE EXECUTION
Order to apply to High Court and County Court

Add new rule A1 before existing rule 1:
 A1. This order applies to proceedings both in the High Court and in county courts.   sc51.A1

Appointment of receiver by way of equitable execution

 1. Where an application is made for the appointment of a receiver by way of equitable execution, the court in determining whether it is just or convenient that the appointment should be made shall have regard to the amount claimed by the judgment creditor, to the amount likely to be obtained by the receiver and to the probable costs of his appointment and may direct an inquiry on any of these matters or any other matter before making the appointment.   sc51.1

Masters etc. may appoint receiver

In rule 2, add after "Family Division":
 2. and a district judge   sc51.2

RSC ORDER 77 - PROCEEDINGS BY AND AGAINST THE CROWN
Attachment of debts, etc.

In rule 16(2B), delete "of the Post Office".
 16.—(2B)   sc77.16

Second Cumulative Supplement

Proceedings relating to postal packets

In rule 17(1), for "section 30(5) of the Post Office Act 1969" substitute:

sc77.17 17.—(1) section 92 of the Postal Services Act 2000

RSC ORDER 88 - MORTGAGE CLAIMS

Order 88, rules 1, 2, 3, 4, 5 and 7 revoked from October 15, 2001.

RSC ORDER 93 - APPLICATIONS AND APPEALS TO HIGH COURT UNDER VARIOUS ACTS: CHANCERY DIVISION

Rule 15 revoked from October 15, 2001

Rule 20 revoked from October 15, 2001.

RSC ORDER 97 - THE LANDLORD AND TENANT ACTS 1927, 1954 AND 1987

Order 97 revoked from October 15, 2001.

RSC ORDER 113 - SUMMARY PROCEEDINGS FOR POSSESSION OF LAND

Order 113, rules 1, 1A, 2, 3, 4, 5, 6 and 8 revoked from October 15, 2001.

SCHEDULE 2

CCR ORDER 4 - VENUE FOR BRINGING PROCEEDINGS

cc4.3 *Rule 3(a) revoked from October 15, 2001. Paragraphs 3(b) and (c) should be renumbered accordingly.*

CCR ORDER 6 - PARTICULARS OF CLAIM

Order 6, rules 3, 5 and 5A revoked from October 15, 2001.

CCR ORDER 7 - SERVICE OF DOCUMENTS

Order 7 revoked from October 15, 2001.

CCR ORDER 22 - JUDGMENTS AND ORDERS

Certificate of judgment

For text of rule 8(1A)(a) substitute:

cc22.8 8.—(1A)
  (a) state that –
    (i) it is intended to enforce the judgment or order by execution against goods; or
    (ii) the judgment or order to be enforced is an order for possession of land made in a possession claim against trespassers; or

CCR ORDER 24 - SUMMARY PROCEEDINGS FOR THE RECOVERY OF LAND

Order 24, rules 1, 2, 3, 4, 5 and 7 revoked from October 15, 2001.

CCR ORDER 43 - THE LANDLORD AND TENANT ACTS 1927, 1954, 1985 AND 1987

Order 43 revoked from October 15, 2001.

CCR ORDER 47 - DOMESTIC AND MATRIMONIAL PROCEEDINGS

Editorial Introduction

For "blood tests" substitute:
   scientific tests   **cc47.0.2**

For "blood test" substitute:
scientific test

Family Law Reform Act 1969

For "blood tests" substitute:
   scientific tests   **cc47.5**

CCR ORDER 49 - MISCELLANEOUS STATUTES

Order 49, rules 1, 1A, 2, 4, 6A, 8, 9, 13 and 16 revoked from October 25, 2001.

In rule 6B, delete "and powers of arrest" from the heading.

Housing Act 1996: injunctions

Add new paragraph after 7(b):

6B.—(7A) An application for a warrant of arrest under section 155(3) **cc49.6B** of the Housing Act 1996 must be made in accordance with Part 23 and may be made without notice.

(Section 155(4) of the Housing Act 1996 provides that a warrant shall not be issued unless the application is substantiated on oath.)

For text of paragraphs 8 (a) and (b) substitute:

(8) The judge before whom a person is brought following his arrest may –
      (a) deal with the matter; or
      (b) adjourn the proceedings.

Add new paragraphs after 8(b):

(8A) Where the proceedings are adjourned the judge may remand the arrested in accordance with section 155(2)(b) or (5) of the Housing Act 1996.

(8B) Where the proceedings are adjourned and the arrested person is released –
      (a) the matter must be dealt with (whether by the same or another judge) within 14 days of the day on which he was arrested; and
      (b) the arrested person must be given not less than 2 days' notice of the hearing.

(8C) An application notice under Order 29, rule 1(4) may be issued even if the arrested person is not dealt with within the period mentioned in paragraph (8B)(a).

Delete text in paragraphs (9), (10), (11) and substitute:

(9) Order 29, rule 1 shall apply where an application is made to commit a person for breach of an injunction as if references in that rule to the judge included references to a district judge.

(10) A person against whom a committal order has been made may apply to the court under Order 29, rule 3 for his discharge and, if he does so, must, not less than 1 day before the hearing, serve the application notice on the person who made the application for committal.

(11) Where, in accordance with paragraph 2(2)(b) of Schedule 15 to the Housing Act 1996, the court fixes the amount of any recognizance

with a view to it being taken subsequently, the recognizance may be taken by –
- (a) a judge;
- (b) a justice of the peace;
- (c) a justices' clerk;
- (d) a police officer of the rank of inspector or above or in charge of a police station; or
- (e) where the arrested person is in his custody, the governor or keeper of a prison, with the same consequences as if it had been entered into before the court.

Add new paragraphs after 11(e):

(11A) The person having custody of an applicant for bail must release him if satisfied that the required recognizances have been taken.

(11B) In paragraph (8) "arrest" means the arrest of a person pursuant to –
- (a) a power of arrest which, in exercise of the powers conferred by section 152(6) or 153(1) of the Housing Act 1996, has been attached to an injunction; and
- (b) a warrant of arrest issued under section 155 of that Act.

Postal Services Act 2000

For heading "Post Office Act 1969" substitute:

cc49.15 15. Postal Services Act 2000

In paragraph 15(1), for "section 30(5) of the Post Office Act 1969" substitute:

(1) section 92 of the Postal Services Act 2000

In paragraph 15(2), for "Post Office" substitute:

(2) universal service provider

PRACTICE DIRECTION – HOUSING ACT 1996: INJUNCTION

Add new Practice Direction after cc49.20.1.

ccpd49–001 This Practice Direction supplements CCR Order 49 (Schedule 2 to the CPR).

Application for Warrant of Arrest

1.1 An applicant for a warrant of arrest under section 155(3) of the Housing Act 1996 ("the Act") must –
- (1) file an affidavit setting out grounds for the application with the application notice; or
- (2) give oral evidence as to the grounds for the application at the hearing. (Section 155(4) of the Act provides that an application for a warrant of arrest under section 155(3) must be substained on oath.)

ccpd49–002 application for bail

2.1 An application for bail made by a person arrested under –
- (1) a power of arrest attached to an injunction under Chapter III of Part V of the Housing Act 1996; or
- (2) a warrant of arrest issued on an applicant under section 155(3) of that Act,

may be either orally or in an application notice.

2.2 An application notice seeking bail must contain –

(1) the full name of the person making the application;
(2) the address of the place where the person making the application is detained at the time when the application is made;
(3) the address where the person making the application would reside if he were to be granted bail;
(4) the amount of the recognizance in which he would agree to be bound; and
(5) the grounds on which the application is made and, where previous application has been refused, full details of any change in circumstances which has occurred since that refusal.

2.3 A copy of the application notice must be served on the person who sought the injunction.

Remand for Medical Examination and Report

ccpd49–003

3.1 Section 156(4) of the Act provides that the judge has power to make an order under section 35 of the Mental Health Act 1983 in certain circumstances. If he does so attention is drawn to section 35(8) of that Act which provides that a person remanded to hospital under that section may obtain at his own expense an independent report on his mental condition from a registered medical practitioner chosen by him and apply to the court on the basis of it for his remand to be terminated under section 35(7).

SECTION B

MISCELLANEOUS PRACTICE DIRECTIONS

PRACTICE DIRECTION INSOLVENCY PROCEEDINGS

PART ONE

1. General

Add at end:

1.6

B1–001

(1) This paragraph applies where an insolvency practitioner ("the outgoing office holder") holds office as a liquidator, administrator, trustee or supervisor in more than one case and dies, retires from practice as an insolvency practitioner or is otherwise unable or unwilling to continue in office.

(2) A single application may be made to a Judge of the Chancery Division of the High Court by way of ordinary application in Form 7.2 for the appointment of a substitute office holder or office holders in all cases in which the outgoing office holder holds office, and for the transfer of each such case to the High Court for the purpose only of making such an order.

(3) The application may be made by any of the following:
 (i) the outgoing office holder (if he is able and willing to do so);
 (ii) any person who holds office jointly with the outgoing office holder;
 (iii) any person who is proposed to be appointed as a substitute for the outgoing office holder; or

Second Cumulative Supplement

        (iv) any creditor in the cases where the substitution is proposed to be made.

(4) The outgoing office holder (if he is not the applicant) and every person who holds office jointly with the office holder must be made a respondent to the application, but it is not necessary to join any other person as a respondent or to serve the application upon any other person unless the Judge or Registrar in the High Court so directs.

(5) The application should contain schedules setting out the nature of the office held, the identity of the Court currently having jurisdiction over each case and its name and number.

(6) The application must be supported by evidence setting out the circumstances which have given rise to the need to make a substitution and exhibiting the written consent to act of each person who is proposed to be appointed in place of the outgoing office holder.

(7) The Judge will in the first instance consider the application on paper and make such order as he thinks fit. In particular he may do any of the following:
    (i) make an order directing the transfer to the High Court of those cases not already within its jurisdiction for the purpose only of the substantive application;
    (ii) if he considers that the papers are in order and that the matter is straightforward, make an order on the substantive application;
    (iii) give any directions which he considers to be necessary including (if appropriate) directions for the joinder of any additional respondents or requiring the service of the application on any person or requiring additional evidence to be provided;
    (iv) if he does not himself make an order on the substantive application when the matter is first before him, give directions for the further consideration of the substantive application by himself or another Judge of the Chancery Division or adjourn the substantive application to the Registrar for him to make such order upon it as is appropriate.

(8) An order of the kind referred to in sub-paragraph (6)(i) shall follow the draft order in Form PDIP 3 set out in the Schedule hereto and an order granting the substantive application shall follow the draft order in Form PDIP 4 set out in the schedule hereto (subject in each case to such modifications as may be necessary or appropriate).

(9) It is the duty of the applicant to ensure that a sealed copy of every order transferring any case to the High Court and of every order which is made on a substantive application is lodged with the court having jurisdiction over each case affected by such order for filing on the court file relating to that case.

(10) It will not be necessary for the file relating to any case which is transferred to the High Court in accordance with this paragraph to be sent to the High Court unless a Judge or Registrar so directs.

VOLUME 2

CIVIL PROCEDURE RULES

SECTION 2

SPECIALIST PROCEEDINGS UNDER PART 49 OF THE CIVIL PROCEDURE RULES

2A ADMIRALTY JURISDICTION AND PROCEEDINGS

General

In Rule 1.11, delete "Rule CPR".   **2A–5**

Claim in rem

In the fifth paragraph, after "Republic of India v. India Steamship Co. Ltd", for "[1977]" substitute:
[1997]   **2A–8**

Scale of valuation fees as from May 25, 2001

Note new heading added to paragraph 2A–123.
   Not exceeding £20,000: £200   **2A–123**
   Exceeding £20,000: £400

Where the condition of the ship and/or the state of the market make it advisable that there should be a dual valuation for both trading and demolition purposes the full fee will apply in respect of the valuation for trading and in addition a fee at half the above rates will apply in respect of the valuation for demolition.

Note

Add at end:
   See too "Nore Challenger" and "Nore Commander" [2001] 2 Lloyd's Rep. 103.   **2A–162**

2B ARBITRATION PROCEEDINGS

Meaning of arbitration application

In rule 2.1, for "paragraph 22.2" substitute:
   2.1 paragraph 2.2   **2B–17**

Registration of awards under the Arbitration (International Investment Disputes) Act 1966

In Rule 34.4(2) for "paragraph 3(1)(c)(i) and (ii)" substitute: **2B–67**
paragraph (1)(c)(i) and (ii)

FIRST SCHEDULE

PROTOCOL ON ARBITRATION CLAUSES SIGNED ON BEHALF OF HIS MAJESTY AT A MEETING OF THE ASSEMBLY OF THE LEAGUE OF NATIONS HELD ON THE TWENTY-FOURTH DAY OF SEPTEMBER, NINETEEN HUNDRED AND TWENTY-THREE

2B–84
In paragraph 4, for "States" substitute:
4. case the agreement or the arbitration cannot proceed or become inoperative

In paragraph 8, delete:
8. [1924, Sched.]

Appeals to the Court of Appeal

2B–256
In the final paragraph, for "[2000] 3 W.L.R. 1854; [2001] 1 All E.R. 193" substitute:
[2001] Q.B. 388; [2001] 1 All E.R. 257 CA

2C COMMERCIAL AND MERCANTILE COURTS AND BUSINESS LISTS

B6 Service of the claim form out of the jurisdiction

2C–46
In B6.1, for "[CPR 6 and 17 et seq.]" substitute:
B6.1 [CPR 6.17]

In B6.2, for "[CPR 6 and 17 et seq.]" substitute:
B6.2 [CPR 6.17]

The Practice Direction supplementing [CPR r. 6 Part III]

2C–265
In the final sentence of paragraph 7, for "Same" substitute:
7 former

Service out of the jurisdiction

2C–399
Add at end of paragraph 3:
3. [See too editor's note at para. 2C–265].

2F APPLICATIONS UNDER THE COMPANIES ACT 1985 AND THE INSURANCE COMPANIES ACT 1982

PRACTICE DIRECTION—APPLICATIONS UNDER THE COMPANIES ACT 1985 AND THE INSURANCE COMPANIES ACT 1982

General

2F–1
Add to paragraph 1(1) after "Companies Act 1985.":
And includes the Act as applied to limited liability partnerships by the Limited Liability Partnerships Regulations 2001

2G CONTENTIOUS PROBATE PROCEEDINGS

Editorial Introduction

2G–1
For paragraph which begins "RSC, O.76 has not been..." substitute:
By virtue of the Civil Procedure (Amendment No. 2) Rules 2001 this Practice Direction is due to be replaced on October 15, 2001 with a new Part 57 (Probate Claims, Rectification

of Wills and Substitution and Removal of Personal Representatives), supplemented by a new Practice Direction.

It is worth noting even now that one important new feature of Part 57 will be a requirement for the claimant to file his affidavit of testamentary scripts and lodge the scripts when he issues his claim form, and for the defendant to file his affidavit of testamentary scripts and lodge the scripts when he acknowledges service (the time for which will be 28 days).

Meanwhile this current Practice Direction applies, and it will continue to apply to cases in which the claim form was issued before October 15, 2001. The following comments relate to the current Practice Direction.

Probate counterclaim in other proceedings

In paragraph 16.4, for "CPR 3.2(e)" substitute:

16.4 CPR 3.1(2)(e)   2G–17

SECTION 3

OTHER PROCEEDINGS

3A HOUSING

Editorial Introduction

In the first paragraph, for "Note that the s.21 was amended by Immigration and Asylum Act 1999, s.116" substitute:
Note that s.21 was amended by Immigration and Asylum Act 1999, s.116   **3A–28.3**

In the second paragraph, for "destitute" substitute:
be destitute

accommodation

For "reading" substitute:
renting   **3A–28.7**

Asylum Seekers

In the first paragraph, for "[2000] 4 All E.R. 590" substitute:
[2000] 1 W.L.R. 2539, [2000] 4 All E.R. 590, [2000] 4 LG.R. 591   **3A–28.8.1**

In the last paragraph, for "Legal Action (June 22, 2000, CA)" substitute:
[2000] 1 W.L.R. 2539, [2000] 4 All E.R. 590, [2000] 4 LG.R. 591

Add after 3A–28.9:

See Immigration and Asylum Act 1999 Part VI (see 3A–1175 below). The duty of central government to provide support to asylum seekers under Immigration and Asylum Act 1999, s.95 applies only where need arises solely from destitution rather than sickness, age or disability. Otherwise local authorities are obliged to provide accommodation under s.21. Regulation 6(4) of the Asylum Support Regulations 2000 S.I. No. 704 requires the secretary of state to take into account any other support available to an asylum seeker when determining whether that asylum seeker is destitute for the purposes of s.95(1).That   **3A–28.10** regulation includes accomodation that the local authority is obliged to provide by s.21. *Westminster City Council v. National Asylum Support Service*, (2001) April 10, CA.

"Additional powers of court ..."

Add after third paragraph:

3A–31   In *Royal Bank of Scotland v. Miller* [2001] EWCA Civ. 344, (2001) February 27, CA it was held that (1) the relevant time for determining whether land consists of or includes a dwelling-house within the meaning of s.36 is the time when the mortgagee claims possession, not the date when the legal charge is entered into; and (2) breach of a term of the mortgage (*e.g.* occupation by a third party without consent) does not prevent s.36 from applying.

"a reasonable period"

In the first paragraph, delete "for sale".

3A–32   *In the fourth paragraph, delete the following text and replace with a full stop.*

; *cf. Saint v. Barking and Dagenham LBC* (1999) 31 H.L.R. 620; November 1998, *Legal Action* 25, CA (oppression where warrant executed without prior notification to tenant who was in prison and without inviting him to renew his application for housing benefit).

"Landlord's duty of care ..."

Add after first paragraph:

3A–44   A tenant relying upon s.4 merely has to show a failure on the part of the landlord to take such care as is reasonable in the circumstances to see that the tenant is reasonably safe from personal injury. That duty is owed if the landlord "ought in all circumstances" to have known of the relevant defect. That is a general test of negligence. There is no express or implied exclusion of the tenant from the category of persons who might be affected. The burden of a tenant in establishing a breach of duty under s.4 should not be equated with the need under Landlord and Tenant Act 1987, s.11 to demonstrate notice (actual or constructive) of the actual defect giving rise to injury (*Sykes v. Harry* [2001] 17 E.G. 221, *The Times*, February 27, 2001, CA).

"Extension of powers of court ..."

Add after "Bank of Scotland v. Grimes [1985] 2 All E.R. 254, CA":

3A–48   and *Royal Bank of Scotland v. Miller* [2001] EWCA Civ. 344, (2001) February 27, CA

"as a separate dwelling"

For "Uratemp Ventures Ltd v. Collins and Carrell, [2000] L & TR 369, CA; The Times, December 10, 1999, CA" substitute:

3A–89   *Uratemp Ventures Ltd v. Collins and Carrell*, [2000] L. & T.R. 369; *The Times*, December 10, 1999; (2001) 33 H.L.R. 37, CA

Grounds for possession of certain dwelling-houses

For "CA." substitute:

3A–178   CA and *R. v. Birmingham County Council, ex p. Foley*, March 2001, Legal Action 29, Queen's Bench Division.

Reasonable

For "Laimond Properties Ltd v. Raeuchle, April 2000, Legal Action 31, CA" substitute:

3A–184   *Laimond Properties Ltd v. Raeuchle*, April 2000, Legal Action 31; (2001) 33 H.L.R. 113, CA

For "Taj v. Ali, 97/17 L.S. Gaz., April 28, 2000, p36, CA" substitute:

Taj v. Ali, 97/17 L.S. Gaz., April 28, 2000, p.36, [2000] 43 EG 183; (2001) 33 H.L.R. 37, CA

Add after "143, CA":

and *R. v. Birmingham County Council, ex p. Foley*, March 2001, Legal Action 29, Queen's Bench Division.

Appeals on questions of reasonableness

Add after 3A–184:

Although County Courts Act 1984 s.77(6) excludes appeals against judges' findings of fact, it does not exclude, in a proper case, the possibility of an appeal against a finding of reasonableness (*Castle Vale Housing Action v. Gallagher*, February 23, 2001, CA).

3A–184.1

ECHR Art 8 and reasonableness

The Court of Appeal has doubted whether Article 8 makes any difference to the way in which courts have approached questions of the reasonableness of making possessions order. Article 8 does, however, reinforce the importance of only making an order depriving someone of his or her home in circumstances where a clear case is made out (*Castle Vale Housing Action Trust v. Gallagher*, February 23, 2001, CA). There is a need to find a fair balance and to protect the rights of the neighbours and other members of the public (*Lambeth LBC v. Howard* (2001) March 6, CA).

3A–184.2

member of the original tenant's family

Add after "705, HL":

; [2001] 1 A.C. 27.

3A–232

SCHEDULE 15 - GROUNDS FOR POSSESSION OF DWELLING-HOUSES LET ON OR SUBJECT TO PROTECTED OR STATUTORY TENANCIES

Breach of any other tenancy obligation

For "Cadogan Estates Ltd v. McMahon [2000] 3 WLR 1555; [2000] 4 All E.R. 897; (2000) The Times, November 1, HL" substitute:

Cadogan Estates Ltd v. McMahon [2000] 3 W.L.R. 1555; [2000] 4 All E.R. 897; (2000) *The Times*, November 1; [2001] A.C. 378, HL

3A–264

Forms of order

Delete "N27 (Judgment for claimant in Action of Forfeiture for non-payment of rent), N27(1) (Judgment for claimant—for Non Payment of Rent where order refused under Rent Acts) and N27(2) (Judgment for claimant—for Non Payment of rent where order suspended under Rent Acts)".

3A–290

"person with an interest"

For "Croydon (Unique) Ltd v. Wright [2000] 2 W.L.R. 683, [2000] L.&T.R. 20, CA [1999] 4 All E.R. 257; [1999] 40 E.G. 189, The Times, August 24, 1999, CA" substitute:

Croydon (Unique) Ltd v. Wright [2000] 2 W.L.R. 683, [2000] L. & T.R. 20, CA [1999] 4 All E.R. 257; [1999] 40 E.G. 189; *The Times*, August 24, 1999; [2001] Ch.D. 318, CA

3A–291

Housing associations and the Human Rights Act 1998

Add at end:

Whilst the activities of a housing association need not involve the performance of public functions, in taking over the responsibilities of a local housing authority as landlord of a tenant who had been granted a non-secure tenancy pending the determination of her application as a homeless person and in deciding to bring possession proceedings, the functions of a housing association were so closely assimilated to the council that it was properly to be regarded as a functional public authority within the meaning of the Human Rights Act 1998 s.6(1) (*Donoghue v. Poplar HARCA* [2001] 19 E.G. 141 (CS); (2001) April 27, CA).

3A–302

The tenant condition

Add after second paragraph:

Temporary absence may be lengthy. In *Amoah v. Barking and Dagenham LBC*, March 2001 Legal Action 27, Ch.D. a secure tenant was sentenced to 12 years' imprisonment. He left items of furniture in the property and appointed a relative to act as "caretaker" in his absence and intended to return on his release. Etherton J. held that he had retained his secure status.

The court should consider whether the tenant has an intention to return at the date of expiry of the notice to quit. It should focus on "the enduring intention" of the tenant and not on "fleeting changes of mind". This is particularly true of an elderly tenant in poor health whose intentions "may well have fluctuated from time to time and even from day to day". *Hammersmith & Fulham LBC v. Clarke*, March 2001, Legal Action 27, CA.

3A–322

Add after "30 H.L.R 43, CA":
   Ujima Housing Association v. Asnah (1998) 30 H.L.R. 831, CA (assured tenancy)

Security of tenure

Add at end of first paragraph:

3A–326   and *Notting Hill Housing Trust v. Brackley* (2001) April 24, CA

"the court considers it just and equitable to do dispense with the requirement of such a notice" (s.83(1)(b))

3A–331 For "There have been no Court of Appeal decisions involving cases where landlords have completely failed to serve any notice under s.83 or Housing Act 1988, s.8. However in" substitute:
   In

"reasonable"

In the third paragraph, for "Laimond Properties Ltd v. Raeuchle, April 2000 Legal Action 31, CA" substitute:

3A–342   *Laimond Properties Ltd v. Raeuchle*, April 2000 Legal Action 31; (2001) 33 H.L.R. 113, CA.

Add after "the warrant should be set aside":
   After *Hounslow LBC v. McBride* (1999) 31 H.L.R. 143 CA. See too *R. v. Birmingham CC, ex p. Foley*, March 2001, Legal Action 29, Queen's Bench Division.

In the eleventh paragraph, for "Grogan v. Greenwich L.B.C., The Times, March 28, 2000, Gazette 97/09, March 2, 2000, p.40, CA" substitute:
   Grogan v. Greenwich LBC, The Times, March 28, 2000, (2000) 97(9) L.S.G. 40, March 2, 2000; p.40; (2001) 33 H.L.R. 140, CA

Add after "in favour of suspending order).":
   An outright possession order may not be appropriate where the anti-social behaviour was not caused by the tenant, but by a member of the tenant's family who has since left the premises, with the result that the chances of recurrence are reduced. (*Castle Vale Housing Action Trust v. Gallagher*, February 23, 2001, CA).

appeals on questions of reasonableness

Add new paragraphs after 3A–342:

3A–342.1   Although County Courts Act 1984 s.77(6) excludes appeals against judges' findings of fact, it does not exclude, in a proper case, the possibility of an appeal against a finding of reasonableness. (*Castle Vale Housing Action Trust v. Gallagher* February 23, 2001 CA).

ECHR Art 8 and reasonableness

3A–342.2   The Court of Appeal has doubted whether Article 8 makes any difference to the way in which courts have always approached questions of the reasonableness of making possessions order. Article 8 does, however, reinforce the importance of only making an order depriving someone of his or her home in circumstances where a clear case is made out. (*Castle Vale Housing Action Trust v. Gallagher* February 23, 2001, CA). There is a need to find a fair balance and to protect the rights of the neighbours and other members of the public (*Lambeth LBC v. Howard*, (2001) March 6, CA).

Forms of order

For "Forms N26A (Order that claimant have Possession (Assured tenancies)" substitute:

3A–343   Forms N26 (Order for possession)

Extended discretion of court in certain proceedings for possession

For "see the commentary to s.84" substitute:

3A–348   see the commentary to s.85

For "exceptional hardship s.843" substitute:
exceptional hardship (s.85(3

Add to fourth paragraph after "—possession order granted)":
   and *Marshall v. Bradford MBC* [2001] 19 E.G. 140 (CS); (2001) April 27, CA (claim for breach of repairing obligations struck out)

Add to fifth paragraph after"(1997) 29 H.L.R., HL;":
Marshall v. Bradford MBC (2001) April 27, CA

Add at end of fifth paragraph, after "[1997] E.G.C.S. 11, CA)":
and *Marshall v. Bradford MBC* (2001) April 27, CA. When considering an application to revive retrospectively a tenancy, the court should bear in mind: (i) the tenant's previous payment record; (ii) whether all parties were before the court; and (iii) whether the tenant was seeking merely the execution of works of repair or also damages for past disrepair (*Marshall v. Bradford MBC*)

Add after "27 H.L.R. 368":
[2001] L. & T.R 423, CA.

Persons qualified to succeed tenant

In the seventh paragraph, add after "3 W.L.R. 1113":
[2001] 1 A.C. 27

3A–357

Assignments by way of exchange

In the third paragraph, delete "noted in New Law Property".

3A–381

"repair"

Add at end:
In *O'Connor v. Old Etonians Housing Association*, February 9, 2001, Ch D it was held that the obligation under s.11 is a continuing one. A landlord's obligation is to ensure that installations for the supply of water are in proper working order in the sense of keeping them physically and mechanically capable of supplying water at an adequate pressure.

3A–487

"fully mutual housing association"
(a)

In the third paragraph, for "Uratemp Ventures Ltd v. Collins and Carell [2000] L & TR 369, CA; The Times, December 10, 1999, CA" substitute:
Uratemp Ventures Ltd v. Collins and Carell, [2000] L & TR 369, CA; *The Times*, December 10, 1999, (2001) 33 H.L.R. 37, CA, Peter Gibson L.J.
(c)

3A–607

Add to tenth paragraph after "Brent L.B.C. v. Cronin (1997) 30 H.L.R. 43, CA, cf.":
Waltham Forest CBHA v. Fanning July 2001 Legal Action 33, (2001) March 12, QBD and

Security of tenure

Add to end of first paragraph, after "Greenwich L.B.C. v. McGrady, (1982) 81 L.G.R. 288; (1982) 46 P. & C.R. 223; (1983) 6 H.L.R. 361; (1982) 267 E.G. 515, CA":
and *Notting Hill Housing Trust v. Brackley*, (2001) April 24, CA

3A–633

appeals on questions of reasonableness

Add new paragraphs after 3A–649:
Although County Courts Act 1984 s.77(6) excludes appeals against judges' findings of fact, it does not exclude, in a proper case, the possibility of an appeal against a finding of reasonableness *Castle Vale Housing Action Trust v. Gallagher*, February 23, 2001, CA.

3A–649.1

ECHR art 8 and reasonableness

The Court of Appeal has doubted whether Article 8 makes any difference to the way in which courts have always approached questions of the reasonableness of making possession orders. Article 8 does, however, reinforce the importance of only making an order depriving someone of his or her home in circumstances where a clear case is made out. (*Castle Vale Housing Action Trust v. Gallagher*, February 23, 2001, CA). There is a need to find a fair balance and to protect the rights of the neighbours and other members of the public (*Lambeth LBC v. Howard* (2001) March 6, CA).

3A–649.2

Extended discretion of court in possession claims

Add after "H.L.R. 539, QBD":
Section 9 "gives a wide power to stay or suspend an order for possession which is applicable to all cases except those where it is expressly excluded by statute." The power may

3A–672

be exercised where circumstances have changed since the original hearing, even where an outright order was made by a different judge, (*Ujima HA v. Smith*, April 2001, Legal Action 22, October 16, 2000, Ch D, where the defendant was by the time of the application to suspend accepting her legal responsibility for serious damage to a shared kitchen and offering to pay £150 in compensation)

For "*it only applies*" substitute:
the power only applies

In the fourth paragraph, for "*Tower Hamlets L.B.C. v. Abdul Jolil* October 1998, Legal Action 22, CA" substitute:
Tower Hamlets LBC v. Abadie (1990) 22 H.L.R. 264, CA

Succession to assured periodic tenancy by spouse

3A-719 Add after "*4 All E.R. 705, HL*":
[2001] 1 A.C. 27

Assured shorthold tenancies: pre-Housing Act 1996 tenancies
(a)

3A-738 Add after "*a fixed term of not less than six months*":
(A tenancy granted for "a term certain of one year ... and ... thereafter from month to month" is a tenancy granted for a term certain within the meaning of s.20(1)(a) which was capable of being an assured shorthold tenancy. (*Goodman v. Evely*, April 2001, Legal Action 21, January 23, 2001, CA))

Recovery of possession on expiry or termination of assured shorthold tenancy

In the fourth paragraph, for "and *Chignell Investments Ltd v. Deghdak*, June 1999, Legal Action 23, Central London County Court" substitute:

3A-748 , *Chignell Investments Ltd v. Deghdak*, June 1999, Legal Action 23, Central London County Court

In the last paragraph, for "*CCR, O.49, r.6A*" substitute:
CPR, Part 55.11 to 55.19

Section 21 and ECHR Article 8

Add new paragraph after 3A–748:

3A-748.1 Notwithstanding its mandatory terms, the right to possession contained in s.21(4) does not conflict with the tenant's right to family life under ECHR Article 8. The section is clearly necessary in a democratic society insofar as there has to be a procedure for recovering possession of property at the end of a tenancy. The court would defer to Parliament as to whether the restricted power of the court under that section was legitimate and proportionate (*Donoghue v. Poplar HARCA* [2001] 19 E.G. 141 (CS); (2001) April 27, CA).

New protected tenancies and agricultural occupancies restricted to special cases
(2)

3A-776 Add to end of paragraph (2) after "*granted by the same landlords.*":
See too *Rajah v. Arogol Co Ltd*, (2001) *The Times*, April 13, CA. It is the identity of the landlord and tenant that matters, not the identity of the premises. Further, the fact that the landlord has changed between the grant of the two tenancies does not affect the position. Section 34(1)(b) clearly refers to a grant at a later date by the person who was the landlord at the time of the later grant.

restricted contracts

Add new paragraph after 3A–776:

3A-776.1 For the effect of Housing Act 1988 ss.34(1) and 36(2)(a) on restricted contracts, see *Matthews v. Rowe* May 2001 Legal Action 24, QBD.

"restricted contract"

Add at end:

3A-783.1 For the effect of Housing Act 1988 ss.34(1) and 36(2)(a) on restricted contracts, see *Matthews v. Rowe*, June 2001 Legal Action, QBD.

Mandatory Grounds

Ground 1

Delete the last paragraph which begins "A landlord relying upon this ground..." to end. **3A–841**

Ground 2
(a)

In point (a), for "a mortgage" substitute: **3A–842**

a mortgagee

Ground 3

Delete "A landlord relying upon this ground may use the Accelerated Possession Procedure (see CCR, O.49, r.6).". **3A–843**

"specified educational institution"

Delete "A landlord relying upon this ground may use the Accelerated Possession Procedure (see CCR, O.49, r.6).". **3A–845**

Ground 5

Delete "A landlord relying upon this ground may use the Accelerated Possession Procedure (see CCR, O.49, r.6).". **3A–846**

Ground 7

For "Shepping v. Osada, The Times, March 23, 2000, CA" substitute:
Shepping v. Osada, The Times, March 23, 2000; [2000] 30 E.G. 125; [2001] L & TR 489; (2001) 33 H.L.R. 146, CA **3A–848**

Power to grant injunctions against anti-social behaviour

In the third paragraph, for "Enfield L.B.C. v. B (a minor), The Times, September 7, 1999, CA" substitute:
Enfield LBC v. B (a minor), [2001] 1 All E.R. 255; [2000] 1 W.L.R. 2259, *The Times,* September 7, 1999, CA—but see *H. v. H. (a child) (occupation order: power of arrest)* (2001), *The Times,* January 10, CA where it was held that the court has the power to attach a power of arrest to an occupation order made against a minor under the similar provision in Family Law Act 1996 s.47(2). **3A–949**

In the fourth paragraph, for "Enfield L.B.C. v. B (a minor) [2000] 1 All E.R. 255, The Times, September 7, 1999, CA" substitute:
Enfield LBC v. B (a minor) [2000] 1 All E.R. 255; [2000] 1 W.L.R. 2259, *The Times,* September 7, 1999, CA

In the last paragraph, for "Nottingham C.C. v. Cutts, May 2000 Legal Action 29, CA" substitute:
Nottingham CC v. Cutts, (2001) 33 H.L.R. 83, CA

Housing Act 1996—Pt VII

In the first sentence of the fourth paragraph, delete "new" before "Code of Guidance":
In the second sentence of the fourth paragraph, for "new Code of Guidance" substitute: **3A–973**
current Code of Guidance

"any enactment or rule of law"

For "(R v. Newham LBC ex p. Sacupima (2000) November 23, CA" substitute:
(R (Sacupima) v. Newham LBC [2001] 1 W.L.R. 563; (2001) 33 H.L.R. 18; (2000), *The Times* January 12, QBD **3A–975.1**

Guidance by the Secretary of State

In the first sentence, delete "new" before "Code of Guidance".

3A–995 In the second sentence, for "new Code of Guidance" substitute:
current Code of Guidance

Persons from abroad not eligible for housing assistance

3A–1015 Add at end of "Class E—people who have been granted exceptional leave to enter and remain and whose leave is not conditional on them accommodating themselves without recourse to public funds":
. A post-April 2000 port entry asylum seeker who has been granted temporary admission under Immigration Act 1971 Sched. 2, para. 5, pending determination of her asylum application is not "lawfully present" in the U.K. (*R v. Home Department, ex p. Bugdaycay* [1987] A.C. 514, HL). Accordingly, such a person does not fulfil the three criteria of Class E of the Homelessness (England) Regulations 2000 (S.I. No. 701), reg. 3 and so is not owed the full duty under Housing Act 1996, Part VII (*Kaya v. Haringey LBC*, June 2001 2001 Legal Action 26; (2001) 1 May, CA)

Note

Replace text of existing 3A–1016.1 with text of 3A–1061.1; 3A–1061.1 is then deleted.

3A–1016.1 This section was repealed by Immigration and Asylum Act 1999, s.117(5) and Sched 16. Any accommodation which is to be made available for asylum seekers and their dependents should now be provided by via the National Asylum Support Service. See the Immigration and Asylum Act 1999, ss.94–100 at paras 3A–1177 *et seq.* below and the Homelessness (England) Regulations 2000 (S.I. 2000 No. 701), the Allocation of Housing (England) Regulations 2000 (S.I. 2000 No. 702) and the Persons Subject to Immigration Control (Housing Authority Accommodation and Homelessness) Order 2000 (S.I. 2000 No. 706) came into force on April 3, 2000. They:

- close access to homelessness legislation for asylum seekers who claim asylum after April 2, 2000;
- change the rules on access to the housing register and eligibility for homelessness assistance for nationals of signatory countries to the European Convention on Social and Medical Assistance or the European Social Charter;
- enable authorities to grant non-secure tenancies of hard to let accommodation directly to overseas students; and
- consolidate existing orders under Asylum and Immigration Act 1996, s.9(1) and existing regulations under Housing Act 1996, Parts VI and VII.

Suitability of interim accommodation

For "R. v. Ealing L.B.C., ex p. Surdonja (2000) 32 H.L.R. 481, (1999) 31 H.L.R. 686; The Times, October 1998, QBD affirmed on appeal, [2000] 2 All E.R. 597, CA" substitute:

3A–1036 Ealing LBC. v. Surdonja (2000) 32 H.L.R. 481; (1999) 31 H.L.R. 686; *The Times*, October 1998, QBD affirmed on appeal, [2000] 2 All E.R. 597; [2001] Q.B. 97, CA

Add new paragraph after 3A–1038:

3A–1038.1 The provisions of s.189 do not breach ECHR Art. 8(1) in enacting a scheme of priorities whereby applications for accommodation by homeless persons are to be determined by local housing authorities. In assessing priorities, Parliament was entitled to take into account considerations such as vulnerability, which might or might not have an impact on family life, as well as those that inevitably did. Specifically Art. 8(1) does not require applicants with child spouses to be given priority over applicants with adult spouses or over other categories of applicant. (*Hackney LBC v. Ekinci* (2001) May 24, CA.)

dependent children

Immediately after the heading "dependent children", add new paragraph:

3A–1039 The term "dependent child" in s.189(1) does not include a wife under the age of 18 who is in full-time education and dependent upon her husband (*Hackney LBC v. Ekinci* (2001) May 24, CA).

Note

3A–1061.1 *Delete paragraph 3A-1061.1.*

Duty to persons with priority need who are not homeless intentionally
(b)

3A–1082 *Add after "accommodation should be suitable":*
not only for the applicant, but also for his or her family. (*R. v. Westminster County Council ex p. Abo-Ragheed*, April 2001, Legal Action 22, November 27, 2001, QBD Admin Ct)

In the fifth paragraph, for "(2000) 32 H.L.R. 470, The Times, June 9, 1999" substitute:
under s.193

Reviews

Add at end:

It is not open to an applicant for housing to accept an offer of accommodation made under s.193(5) but at the same time to challenge the suitability of the accommodation by requesting a review under s.202. (*Alghile v. Westminster County Council* [2001] EWCA Civ., March 2, 2001, CA).

3A–1083

Referral of case to another local housing authority

In the third paragraph, for "R. v. Ealing L.B.C., ex p. Surdonja, [2000] 2 All E.R. 587; The Times, February 11, 2000, CA" substitute:

Ealing LBC. v. Surdonja (2000) 32 H.L.R. 481, (1999) 31 H.L.R. 686; *The Times*, October 1998, QBD, affirmed on appeal, [2000] 2 All E.R. 597; [2001] Q.B. 97, CA

3A–1106

Reviews

For "Ealing L.B.C. v. Surdonja [2000] 2 All E.R. 597; The Times, February 11, 2000, CA" substitute:

Ealing LBC. v. Surdonja (2000) 32 H.L.R. 481, (1999) 31 H.L.R. 686; *The Times*, October 1998, QBD affirmed on appeal, [2000] 2 All E.R. 597; [2001] Q.B. 97, CA

3A–1125

Add at end:

It is not open to an applicant for housing to accept an offer of accommodation made under s.193(5)but at the same time to challenge the suitability of the accommodation by requesting a review under s.202. (*Alghile v. Westminster County Council* [2001] EWCA, March 2, 2001, CA).

Judicial review

Add new paragraph:

An application for judicial review is an abuse of the process, and not available, where a homeless person does not exhaust the right to a statutory review and appeal to the county court under ss.202 and 204 (*R. (on the application of Campbell) v. Enfield LBC* (2001) May 22, QBD Admin Ct).

3A–1135.2

In the first paragraph, for "will take" substitute:
has taken

3A–1176

Duties of central and local government

Add new paragraph after 3A-1184:

The duty of central government to provide support to asylum seekers under s.95 applies only where need arises solely from destitution rather than sickness, age or disability. Otherwise local authorities are obliged to provide accomodation under National Assistance Act 1948, s.21 (see 3A–28.1 above). Regulation 6(4)of the Asylum Support Regulations 2000, SI 2000 No. 704 requires the secretary of state to take into account any other support available to an asylum seeker when determining whether that asylum seeker is destitute for the purposes of s.95(1). That regulation includes accomodation that the local authority is obliged to provide by s.21(*Westminster County Council v. National Asylum Support Service*, February 27, 2001, QBD Admin Ct).

3A-1184.1

3B CONSUMER CREDIT AND CONSUMER LAW

Subs. (4)

For "Wilson v. First County Trust, The Times, December 6, 2000, CA. The latter is" substitute:

Watchtower Investments Ltd. v. Payne [2001] EWCA Civ. 1159; The Times, August 22, 2001 – both explained at para. 3B–331 below. See also *Wilson v. First County Trust* [2001] 2 W.L.R. 302 –

3B–21

Exempt agreements

3B–37 For ", *The Times*, January 17, 2001" substitute:
[2001] 1 W.L.R. 986

No enforcement order possible

3B–231 For "*Wilson v. First County Trust, The Times,* December 6, 2000, *CA*" substitute:
Wilson v. First County Trust [2001] 2 W.L.R. 30

For "—*see also*" substitute:
. In its judgment (2 May 2001) following that hearing, the court held that it was right to make such a declaration of incompatibility: *Wilson v. First County Trust Ltd. (No. 2)* [2001] 3 W.L.R. 42. This does not, however, alter the law as created by s. 127(3). See

EXTORTIONATE CREDIT BARGAINS

Reopening of extortionate agreements

Restrictions on court's ability to re-open agreement

3B–261 For "*Rahman v. Sterling Credit Limited, The Times,* October 17, 2000; [2000] N.P.C. 84" substitute:
Rahman v. Sterling Credit Limited, The Times, October 17, 2000, [2001] 1 W.L.R. 496

Regulation 4

Add at end:

3B–331 Reg. 4 does not define what it means by "charges". However, two things are mutually exclusive, namely the "credit" and anything entering into the "total charge for credit": s. 9(4)of the Consumer Credit Act 1974. It would be absurd for anything to fall within the concept of a "charge" under reg. 4 which is in reality a part of the "credit". Thus where a debtor buys goods or services on credit, clearly the cash price of the goods or services is not one of the charges, even though payment of that price may well be a condition or term of the credit agreement. Equally, where the purpose (or one of the purposes) of a loan is to enable the debtor to pay off an existing debt, the amount advanced in order to pay off that debt is part of the credit and is not a *charge* for the credit – and that is so even if paying off that debt is a condition of the loan: *Watchtower Investments Ltd v. Payne* [2001] EWCA Civ. 1159; *The Times,* August 22, 2001.

Enforcement bodies

Add after "the Consumers' Association":

3B–455 Now that the Injunctions Directive has been implemented by the Stop Now Orders (EC Directive) Regulations 2001, the form of the injunction for which the enforcement body applies to the court is likely to be a Stop Now Order under those regulations.

3C CONTEMPT OF COURT ACT 1981

Publication of matters exempted from disclosure in court

Add at end of Section 11:

3C–27 11. The jurisdiction to order disclosure of the identity of a wrongdoer is one of general application, exisiting in equity. The "interests of justice" in s.10 means interests which were justifiable, and was not confined to the technical sense of the administration of justice in the course of legal proceedings in a court of law. *Ashworth Hospital Authority v. MGN Ltd* [2001] 1 W.L.R. 515, (Lord Phillips of Worth Matravers M.R., May and Laws L.JJ.).

SECTION 4

HOUSE OF LORDS APPEALS

4A CIVIL APPEALS

Admissibility of petitions

Delete 1.6(b).   **4A–5**

[Practice Direction 1.6(b) is repealed]

Title

Add after the second sentence of paragraph 3.3:   **4A–13**

3.3 Causes in which trustees, executors, etc. are parties are to be titled in the short form, for example, *Trustees of John Black's Charity v. White.*

Delete text of paragraphs 4.5, 4.6 and 4.7 and substitute:

Consideration on the papers

4.5 If a petition is admissible, the Appeal Committee will consider whether leave to appeal should be given. The Appeal Committee do not give reasons for their decisions. Leave to appeal is granted to petitions which raise an arguable point of law of general public importance which ought to be considered by the House at that time, bearing in mind that the cause will have already been the subject of judicial decision. A petition which, in the opinion of the Appeal Committee, does not raise such a point will be refused for that reason.   **4A–19**

4.6 If the Appeal Committee are satisfied that leave to appeal should be given, the House may give leave either outright or on terms. If the Committee are minded to impose terms, the parties will be given two weeks to lodge observations on the proposed terms. Any such observation must be served on the other parties.

Respondents' objections

4.7 If the Appeal Committee take the provisional view that leave to appeal should be given, the respondents will be invited to lodge objections to the petition within two weeks, briefly setting out the reasons why the petition should not be allowed or making other submissions as to the terms upon which leave should be granted. Any such objections must be served on the other parties.   **4A–20**

5.
COSTS

(c)

For text of paragraph 5.1(c) substitute: **4A–24**

to an unassisted respondent where the petitioner is publicly funded or legally aided, payment out of the Community Legal Service Fund (pursuant to s.11 of the Access to Justice Act 1999 [1]) [2] of costs as specified at (b) above;

Title

Add at end of paragraph 9.3:   **4A–30**

9.3 Causes in which trustees, executors, etc. are parties are to be titled in the short form, for example, *Trustees of John Black's Charity v. White.*

---

[1] Also pursuant to r.5(2) Community Legal Service (Cost Protection) Regulations 2000 and in accordance with the procedural requirements of rr.9, 10 Community Legal Service (Costs) Regulations (2000) as amended.

[2] Or s.18 Legal Aid Act 1988; or, in Scotland, pursuant to s.19 Legal Aid (Scotland) Act 1986; or, in Northern Ireland, pursuant to Article 16 Legal Aid Advice and Assistance (N.I.) Order 1981.

Second Cumulative Supplement

Human Rights Act 1998

Add at end of paragraph 9.5:

4A–31.1 In any cause where the House is to be asked to consider whether to make, uphold or reverse a declaration that a provision of primary or subordinate legislation is incompatible with a declaration that a provision of primary or subordinate legislation is incompatible with a Convention right [1] or to consider any issue which may lead the House to make such a declaration, or where such an issue is or may be raised in respect of a judicial act, the appellants must, by letter to the Principal Clerk, draw this to the attention of the Judicial Office at the time of lodgment of the petition. [2]

11.

Statement of Facts and Issues

Add at end of 11.2:

4A–38 11.2 In accordance with Practice Direction 31, it must draw attention to any possibility of a declaration of incompatability.

15.

Appellants' and Respondents' Cases

Add before paragraph 15.1:

4A–49 In cases where the House has granted leave to appeal, it should not be assumed that those who will hear the appeal will be familiar with the arguements set out in the petition for leave to appeal.

Lodgment and exchange of cases

Delete text of paragraph 15.12 and substitute:

4A–52 15.12 No later than **five weeks** before the proposed date of the hearing, the appellants must lodge in the Judicial Office eight copies of their case and serve it on the respondents. No later than **three weeks** before the proposed date of the hearing, the respondents must lodge in the Judicial Office eight copies of their case in response, as must any other party lodging a case. The number of copies of cases exchanged should be sufficient to meet the requirements of counsel and agents but should not usually exceed eight. To enable the appellants to lodge the bound volumes, the respondents and any other party who has lodged a case must provide the appellants with fifteen further copies of their case. Following the exchange of cases, further arguments, by either side, may not be submitted in advance of the hearing without leave.

19.

Costs

Delete text of paragraph 19.2 and substitute:

4A–57 19.2 Where one party is publicly funded or legally aided and where, in the event of proceedings being decided in favour of the unassisted party, the unassisted party would seek an order for costs under s.11 of the Access to Justice Act 1999, [3] a submission to that effect should be made and the Legal Services Commission should be informed (the procedure is set out in regulations 9 and 10 of the Community Legal Service (Costs) Regulations 2000 as amended).In these circumstances, it is the responsibility of the parties to bring to the attention of the Judicial Office any factor which might affect the making of such an order by the House. [4]

---

[1] Under the Human Rights Act 1998, which gives further effect in domestic law to much of the Convention for the Protection of Human Rights and Fundamental Freedoms agreed by the Council of Europe at Rome on November 4, 1950.

[2] See Directions 9.7 and 31. See also *Appeal Committee, 31st Report (2000-2001), Regina v. A (Respondent)* (HL 44).

[3] Also pursuant to r.5(2) Community Legal Service (Cost Protection) Regulations 2000.

[4] This Direction also applies to unassisted parties who, if successful, would seek an order for costs under s.18 Legal Aid Act 1988, s.19 Legal Aid (Scotland) Act 1986 or Article 16 Legal Aid, Advice and Assistance (Northern Ireland) Order 1981; such parties should inform the Scottish Legal Aid Board or the Legal Aid Committeerespectively.

31.

EUROPEAN CONVENTION ON HUMAN RIGHTS

For "who will represent the Crown" substitute:
31.4 the identity of the Minister or other person who is to be joined as a party to the appeal **4A–75**

For "Crown" substitute:
31.5 Minister or other person

4B CRIMINAL APPEALS

Application for extension of time

Add after "not the prosecutor":
3.3 See Appeal Committee, 28th Report (2000-2001), *Regina v. Weir (Respondent)* (HL 28). **4B–6**

Title and designation of prosecutor

Add after "used in the court below,":
4.4 Causes in which trustees, executors, etc. are parties are to be titled in the short form, for example, *Trustees of John Black's Charity v. White*. **4B–9**

Preliminary procedure

Delete text of paragraphs 5.5, 5.6 and 5.7 and substitute:
5.5 If a petition is admissible, the Appeal Committee will consider whether leave to appeal should be given. The Appeal Committee do not give reasons for their decisions. Leave to appeal is granted to petitions which raise an arguable point of law of general public importance which ought to be considered by the House at that time, bearing in mind that the cause will have already been the subject of judicial decision. A petition which, in the opinion of the Appeal Committee, does not raise such a point will be refused for that reason. **4B–15**

5.6 If the Appeal Committee are satisfied that leave to appeal should be given, the House may give leave either outright or on terms. If the Committee are minded to impose terms, the parties will be given two weeks to lodge observations on the proposed terms. Any such observation must be served on the other parties.

Provisional leave

5.7 If the Appeal Committee take the provisional view that leave to appeal should be given, the respondents will be invited to lodge objections to the petition within two weeks, briefly setting out the reasons why the petition should not be allowed or making other submissions as to the terms upon which leave should be granted. Any such objections must be served on the other parties. **4B–16**

6.

COSTS

(c)

For text of paragraph 6.1(c) substitute: **4B–20**
to an unassisted respondent where the petitioner is publicly funded or legally aided, payment out of the Community Legal Service Fund (pursuant to s.11 of the Access to Justice Act 1999 [1]) [2] of costs as specified at (b) above;

Title and designation of prosecutor

Add after "included in the title":
10.3 Causes in which trustees, executors, etc. are parties are to be titled in the short form, for example, *Trustees of John Black's Charity v. White*. **4B–25**

---

[1] Also pursuant to r.5(2) Community Legal Service (Cost Protection) Regulations 2000 and in accordance with the procedural requirements of rr.9, 10 Community Legal Service (Costs) Regulations (2000) as amended.
[2] Or s.18 Legal Aid Act 1988; or, in Scotland, pursuant to s.19 Legal Aid (Scotland) Act 1986; or, in Northern Ireland, pursuant to Article 16 Legal Aid Advice and Assistance (N.I.) Order 1981.

Second Cumulative Supplement

Human Rights Act 1998

Add after paragraph 10.3:

4B–26.1 In any cause where the House is to be asked to consider whether to make, uphold or reverse a declaration that a provision of primary or subordinate legislation is incompatible with a declaration that a provision of primary or subordinate legislation is incompatible with a Convention right [1] or to consider any issue which may lead the House to make such a declaration, or where such an issue is or may be raised in respect of a judicial act, the appellants must, by letter to the Principal Clerk, draw this to the attention of the Judicial Office at the time of lodgment of the petition. [2]

12.

Statement of Facts and Issues

Add at end of paragraph 12.2:

4B–32 12.2 In accordance with practice direction 30, it must draw attention to any possibility of a declaration of incompatability.

16.

Appellants' and Respondents' Cases

Add before paragraph 16.1:

4B–41 In cases where the House has granted leave to appeal, it should not be assumed that those who will hear the appeal will be familiar with the arguements set out in the petition for leave to appeal.

Lodgment and exchange of cases

Delete text of paragraph 16.13 and substitute:

4B–44 16.13 No later than **five weeks** before the proposed date of the hearing, the appellants must lodge in the Judicial Office eight copies of their case and serve it on the respondents. No later than **three weeks** before the proposed date of the hearing, the respondents must lodge in the Judicial Office eight copies of their case in response, as must any other party lodging a case. The number of copies of cases exchanged should be sufficient to meet the requirements of counsel and agents but should not usually exceed eight. To enable the appellants to lodge the bound volumes, the respondents and any other party who has lodged a case must provide the appellants with fifteen further copies of their case. Following the exchange of cases, further arguments, by either side, may not be submitted in advance of the hearing without leave.

20.

Costs

Delete text of paragraph 20.2 and substitute:

4B–49 20.2 Where one party is publicly funded or legally aided and where, in the event of proceedings being decided in favour of the unassisted party, the unassisted party would seek an order for costs under s.11 of the Access to Justice Act 1999, [3] a submission to that effect should be made and the Legal Services Commission should be informed (the procedure is set out in regulations 9 and 10 of the Community Legal Service (Costs) Regulations 2000 as amended). In these circumstances, it is the responsibility of the parties to bring to the attention of the Judicial Office any factor which might affect the making of such an order by the House. [4]

---

[1] Under the Human Rights Act 1998, which gives further effect in domestic law to much of the Convention for the Protection of Human Rights and Fundamental Freedoms agreed by the Council of Europe at Rome on November 4, 1950.

[2] See Directions 9.7 and 31. See also *Appeal Committee, 31st Report (2000-2001)*, *Regina v. A (Respondent)* (HL 44).

[3] Also pursuant to r.5(2) Community Legal Service (Cost Protection) Regulations 2000.

[4] This Direction also applies to unassisted parties who, if successful, would seek an order for costs under s.18 Legal Aid Act 1988, s.19 Legal Aid (Scotland) Act 1986 or Article 16 Legal Aid, Advice

Form of appendix

In paragraph 29.10, for "blue" substitute:
29.10 red   4B–62

30.
EUROPEAN CONVENTION ON HUMAN RIGHTS

In paragraph 30.4, for "Direction 31.2 or 31.3" substitute:
30.4 Direction 30.2 or 30.3   4B–65

In paragraph 30.4, for "who will represent the Crown" substitute:
the identity of the Minister or other person who is to be joined as a party to the appeal[1]

In paragraph 30.5, for "Crown" substitute:
30.5 Minister or other person

SECTION 5

EUROPEAN JURISDICTION

GENERAL

Civil Jurisdiction and Judgments Act 1982

For paragraph which begins "The Civil Procedure Rules, the Rules of the Supreme Court..." substitute:
 The Civil Procedure Rules and the relevant Practice Directions give procedural effect to   5–3
the provisions of the Act and the Conventions. The principal rules are CPR Part 6 section 6.19 (service of Claim Form where the permission of the Court is not required), and Practice Direction 6B, paras 1.1 to 1.3 (form of certificates on claim form when service abroad is to be effected without permission). See also Schedule 1 and RSC O.71 (reciprocal enforcement of judgments under the Conventions) and the Practice Direction supplementing O.71. For applications under RSC O.71 the appropriate Practice Forms should be used: see PF157 QB to 165 QB.

SECTION 6

ADMINISTRATION OF FUNDS, PROPERTY AND AFFAIRS

6A   COURT FUNDS

Court Funds Rules 1987

(S.I. 1987 No. 821)

For "and S.I. 2000 No. 2918" substitute:

, S.I. 2000 No. 2918 and S.I. 2001 No. 703.   6A–18

For "Court Funds Office" means the Court Funds Division of the Public Trust Office;" substitute:

Interpretation

 "Court Funds Office" means the Court Funds Division of the Court   6A–22
  Service;

---

and Assistance (Northern Ireland) Order 1981; such parties should inform the Scottish Legal Aid Board or the Legal Aid Committee respectively.
 [1] ss. 5(2) and 9(5) Human Rights Act 1998.

Note

6A–23 For "and S.I. 1999 No. 1021," substitute:
; S.I. 1999 No. 1021; S.I. 2000 No. 2918 and S.I. 2001 No. 703.

6B COURT OF PROTECTION

GENERAL

The Mental Health Act 1983

Delete existing 6B and substitute the following re-paragraphed section, incorporating two new Statutory Instruments; The Court of Protection Rules 2001 and The Court of Protection (Enduring Powers of Attorney) Rules 2001

6B–1 The Mental Health Act 1983, came into operation on September 30, 1983, and has effect with respect to the reception care and treatment of mentally disordered patients, the management of their property and other related matters. "Mental disorder" is a generic term, statutorily defined in s.1(2), embracing all forms of unsoundness of mind to which previous Acts applied. See para. 6B–185.

The terms "lunatic", "persons of unsound mind" and "defectives" are obsolete; they all fall into one class of "persons suffering from mental disorder".

So far as rendering a person liable to compulsory detention or guardianship is concerned, the Act recognises four forms of mental disorder, namely, mental illness, severe mental impairment, psychopathic disorder and mental impairment (see Mental Health Act 1983, ss.3(2) and 7(2)) but the particular form of mental disorder has no special significance when the question of ability to manage one's affairs is concerned.

The Act contains no definition of "mental illness". The words have to be construed in the way that ordinary sensible people would construe them (see *W. v. L. (Mental Health Patient)* [1974] Q.B. 711; [1973] 3 All E.R. 884).

Wherever possible patients are now admitted voluntarily for treatment with absence of formality (s.131). A magistrate's order is no longer necessary to secure the admission and detention of a patient against his will, this normally being secured by an application, duly supported by medical evidence, to the managers of the hospital or mental nursing home concerned (ss.3–6). Provision is also made for guardianship in suitable cases (ss.7–8).

For "Court of Protection Rules 1994" substitute: Court of Protection Rules 2001

Part VII of the Act (set out at paras 6B–186 *et seq.*) deals with the management of the property and affairs of mental patients and the jurisdiction of the Court of Protection. The rules are the Court of Protection Rules 2001 made pursuant to ss.106, 107 and 108 of the Mental Health Act 1983 and s.54(2) of the Trustee Act 1925.

The Court of Protection

For "Public Trust Office (PTO)" substitute: Public Guardianship Office (PGO)

6B–2 The Court of Protection and the Protection Division of the Public Guardianship Office (PGO) are situated at Stewart House, 24 Kingsway, London WC2B 6JX. Tel: 020 7664 7000, DX: 37965 Kingsway, Fax: 020 7664 7705. The purpose of the jurisdiction of the court is to protect and administer the property and affairs of persons who are incapable by reason of mental disorder of managing and administering their own property and affairs (Mental Health Act 1983, ss.93(2) and 94(2)). The court also has jurisdiction in relation to the Enduring Powers of Attorney Act 1985 (see paras 6B–358 *et seq.*) It has no jurisdiction over the management or care of the patient's person (*Re W.* [1971] 1 Ch. 123) or whether the patient should undergo a surgical operation, including an operation for sterilisation (*F. v. West Berkshire Health Authority, sub nom. Re F.* [1989] 2 W.L.R. 1025).

The offices are open to the public between the hours of 10 a.m. and 4.30 p.m. on working days, which are as prescribed for the Supreme Court offices (O.64, r.7).

All correspondence should be sent to the above address and the case number and any court reference on correspondence should be quoted.

Delete paragraph which begins "With the coming into effect..." to end.

The Judge

6B–3 Pursuant to s.93(1) of the Act, the Lord Chancellor has nominated all the judges for the time being of the Chancery Division to act for the purposes of Pt VII of the Mental Health Act 1983 (Court of Protection matters).

Any matters dealt with by the judge are taken at the Royal Courts of Justice. Sometimes this will be in the judge's private room, though more frequently in court as chambers; if the matter is to be heard in court, the usual practice is for it to be *in camera* but subject to the safeguard of anonymity, matters of principle, and particularly the judgments, should be dealt with in public (see *Re W. (E.E.M.)* [1971] Ch. 123).

For "r.57(3)" substitute: r.55(3)

The Court of Protection Registrar, subject to the provisions of r.55(3) arranges for parties to be notified of the time fixed for the hearing and draws and settles the order at the Court of Protection.

The Master

Delete "the Assistant Masters"

Generally speaking the jurisdiction of the judge under Pt VII of the Act and other enactments is exercised by the master, (and other nominated officers—see r.3 of the Court of Protection Rules and s.94), though certain matters are reserved to the Lord Chancellor or a nominated judge (see s.104(3)). Unless the contrary is stated or the context otherwise requires, the term "master" in these notes includes the Assistant masters or other nominated officer. In practice the master deals with applications for statutory wills, large gifts and complex disputes and the Assistant masters deal mainly with contentious receivership work.

All applications are returnable before the master who will usually deal with the matter although there is power to refer any matter to the nominated judge.

6B–4

Delete paragraph which begins "In construing other enactments...".

Consideration of applications

It is primarily a matter for country solicitors whether or not London agents are instructed in matters relating to the Court of Protection. All first applications for the appointment of a receiver and formal applications, save those mentioned below, are stamped on issue "Attendance not required unless notified." Attendance will therefore be required only when the master so directs or the persons concerned wish to attend.

If the master requires the attendance of solicitors in connection with applications, country solicitors are at liberty either to instruct London agents or to attend themselves.

6B–5

Patient or property outside England and Wales

A receiver will be appointed in respect of a patient resident abroad but only where there is property within the jurisdiction, *i.e.* England and Wales (*Ex p. Southgate* (1751) 2 Ves. Sen. 401; *Re Scott* (1874) 22 W.R. 748; *Re Soltykoff* [1898] W.N. 77). As to reciprocal jurisdiction between Scotland and Northern Ireland and this country, see s.110 of the Mental Health Act 1983. Briefly, the effect is that, as between Scotland and Northern Ireland on the one hand and England and Wales on the other hand, so long as jurisdiction has been invoked in one country only (treating England and Wales as one country) that jurisdiction is effective to deal with property, other than land or interests in land, in the other country. As to the power of a foreign curator in respect of movable property in this country, see *Didisheim v. London and Westminster Bank* [1900] 2 Ch.15.

6B–6

Section 100 of the Mental Health Act 1983 (see para. 6B–197) provides a convenient procedure where:

(a) stock, or the proceeds thereof is or are to be remitted to a foreign curator; or
(b) dividends only are to be remitted and the stock consists of gilt-edged or other securities suitable to be retained indefinitely; or
(c) although dividends only are to be remitted and although the stock consists of equities unsuitable for permanent retention, it is proposed that the stock be sold and reinvested in securities suitable to be retained indefinitely.

The procedure is *not* suitable where the stock is to be retained in this country and consists of or comprises equities or short-term gilts. In such cases a receiver will usually be required.

Where stock is to be retained and an order is made under s.100, it is usually convenient to lodge the securities in court. This has the advantages of safeguarding the stock certificates and providing for the court's fees.

It should be noted that s.100 of the Mental Health Act 1983, relates exclusively to stock, as defined by the section, *standing in the name of a patient* beneficially, so that stock vested in a foreign curator on behalf of a patient, the subject of foreign jurisdiction, would not fall to be dealt with thereunder. Further, the section should not be invoked if a receiver has already been appointed by the Court of Protection or where the stock in question stands in the name of the patient as trustee.

After "jurisdiction of the court" for "(see r. 29" substitute: (see r.27

Where a receiver is to be appointed, it is usually convenient to appoint as receiver a nominee of the foreign curator residing in this country. A receiver can only be appointed if there is medical evidence before the court to satisfy the requirements of s.94(2) of the Mental Health Act 1983. There is no reason why an office copy of a medical affidavit sworn in the foreign proceedings should not, in suitable cases, be accepted as establishing the jurisdiction of the court (see r.27 of the Court of Protection Rules).

Generally as regards practice, see Heywood and Massey, *Court of Protection Practice* (12th ed., 1991) Chap. 3.

As to court fees payable on any application and order made, see paras 6B–316 and 6B–337.

Jurisdiction of Chancery Division

6B–7 The question of the jurisdiction of the Chancery Division to deal with property of persons of unsound mind has for long been the subject of many decisions, often conflicting. The whole subject and the authorities were exhaustively reviewed by Megarry J. in *Re K.'s Settlement Trusts* [1969] 2 Ch. 1, and he decided that the Chancery Division would exercise jurisdiction, assuming it existed at all, only if the property in question were small, the income therefrom would plainly all be used up in the patient's maintenance (so that there would be no likelihood of surplus income to be dealt with) and the Chancery Division already had some control of the property by reason of some pending proceedings, thus having "seisin". Further, such jurisdiction is at most discretionary and it is better that the Chancery Division "should leave to the Court of Protection that specialist jurisdiction which it exercises with such experience and understanding and not to attempt, with less adequate tools, to exercise an overlapping jurisdiction in a limited and ill-defined category of cases" (*Re K.'s Settlement Trusts*, above, p. 7).

In the course of the judgment the further condition of its not being possible for an application to be made to the Court of Protection was also mentioned but, assuming evidence to satisfy s.94(2) of the Act were available, it is not readily seen how this situation could arise. In any event, where the patient's affairs are being dealt with by the Court of Protection, it would seem the Chancery Division would not exercise jurisdiction as this would be an interference with the control of the patient's affairs by the Court of Protection (see *Re Winkle* [1894] 2 Ch. 519; *C.L. v. C.F.W.* [1928] P. 223; *Swettenham v. Swettenham (By her Guardian)* [1938] P. 218 and *Re A Debtor (No. 1 of 1941)* [1941] Ch. 487).

Minor (Infant) under mental disability

6B–8 The jurisdiction of the Family Division over a minor ward is not ousted by his being in such a state as would, if he were adult, attract the jurisdiction of the Court of Protection (*Re Edwards* (1879) 10 Ch.D. 605). The Court of Protection has jurisdiction to deal with the affairs of a minor patient, and will do so in a proper case. See Heywood and Massey, *Court of Protection Practice* (12th ed., 1991) pp. 17–18. Where damages are recovered on behalf of a minor patient, the Court of Protection will now usually accept jurisdiction to administer such damages if the minor patient is likely to survive until attaining his majority and is not likely to recover before then.

Where judicial relief is only required to enable a minor's property to be applied for his maintenance and there are no family disputes as to what should be done, the jurisdiction of the Court of Protection is usually to be preferred to that of the Family Division, particularly when the minor is approaching his majority; where, however, questions of maintenance are mixed up with family disputes as to where he shall live, and under whose custody, the matter is one for the Family Division.

As to administration of damages by the court of Protection, see para. 6B–115.

As, with few exceptions, transfers in favour of a minor of stocks and shares cannot be registered, any investments on behalf of minors (including the purchase of equities) are usually made in the name of the Accountant General in court. Exceptionally, investment might be made in the name of the receiver or in the names of trustees.

Appeals

For "rr. 56 and 57" substitute: rr. 54 and 55

See s.105 and rr.54 and 55. On an appeal from the master to the judge, the notice of appeal is lodged in the Protection Division and is then forwarded to the appropriate nominated judge. The Court of Protection Registrar sits as Registrar not only on appeals to the judge but on appeals to the Court of Appeal (see "The Judge", para. 6B–3).

An appeal from the judge in a Court of Protection matter under s.105(2) of the Mental Health Act 1983 lies to the Court of Appeal without leave (*Re Cathcart* [1893] 1 Ch. 466; *Re Cathcart* [1902] W.N. 80; see also *Moore v. Commissioner of Metropolitan Police* [1968] 1 Q.B. 26; [1967] 2 All E.R. 827). Generally as to Court of Protection appeals, see Heywood and Massey, *Court of Protection Practice* (12th ed., 1991) pp. 48 *et seq.*

See *Re D. (J.)* [1982] Ch. 237; [1982] 2 All E.R. 37 as to the discretion of the nominated judge in an appeal from the master against the contents of a statutory will.

Forms

For "r. 2(3)" substitute:

See r. 2(2)(c) and the Schedule to the Rules. The following forms may be obtained (free) from the Protection Division:

In 6B-10 table delete first two entries; in third entry delete "and C.P. 3 (P.T.)" and then in the fourth entry delete C.P. 5 (P.T.)

Fees

For "rr. 78-86" substitute: rr. 76 to 83

See rr.78–86 and the Appendix to the Rules. Payment of fees may be made as follows:
   (i) in cash at the Protection Division, 24, Kingsway, London, WC2B 6JX;
   (ii) by cheque or postal order made payable to the

For "Public Trust Office" substitute: Public Guardianship Office

Public Guardianship Office and crossed and sent by post to the Protection Division.

APPOINTMENT AND DISCHARGE OF RECEIVER

(a) First Application

General note

The jurisdiction to appoint a receiver stems from ss.94(2) and 99 of the Mental Health Act 1983. In particular it must be noted that the jurisdiction is, normally, only exercisable where, after considering medical evidence, the court is satisfied that the person in question is incapable, by reason of mental disorder (see s.1) of managing and administering his property and affairs, though under s.98 there is jurisdiction to deal with cases of emergency without conclusive evidence of incapacity.

The question of the degree of incapability of managing and administering a patient's property and affairs must be related to the circumstances, including the state in which he lives and the complexity and importance of the property and affairs which he has to administer, and the court has a discretion of deciding whether in these circumstances and upon the facts it is right for a receiver to be appointed (*Re C. A. F.*, March 23, 1962; unrep., C.A. transcript 62/2367, *per* Wilberforce J.).

For "PTO" substitute: PGO

If the property of the patient does not exceed £10,000 in value, the facts should be brought to the notice of the PGO by letter in the first instance as the PGO court may be willing to give a direction pursuant to

For "r. 9" substitute: r. 8

r.8 (see para.). This simple and inexpensive procedure (called a

For "Direction of the Public Trustee" substitute: Short Order

Short Order) is often used to enable a patient's share in an estate to be invested and the income thereof applied for his benefit. A commencement fee of £230 is payable (see paras 6B–312 and 6B–337).

Mode of application

For "r. 8) entitled" substitute: r. 7) usually in the form of a letter unless the court directs that it should be formed in which case it shall be made

SECOND CUMULATIVE SUPPLEMENT

6B–13 Proceedings are by way of application (r.7) usually in the form of a letter unless the court directs that it should be formed in which case it shall be made as in Form A in the Schedule to the Rules.

The application is issued in the Protection Division. A commencement fee of £230 is payable (see para. 6B–337).

Withdrawal of application

6B–14 An application can only be withdrawn with the consent of the court. It is a matter for the master's discretion whether the master allows an application to be disposed of by withdrawal, dismissal or staying further proceedings, or whether the master appoints as receiver a person, willing to be so appointed, notwithstanding that the applicant or any other person objects.

Applicants and receivers

For "r.27" substitute: r. 25

6B–15 The spouse or other nearest relative is normally the applicant and where the application is not so made the reason should be stated in the evidence. Relatives of a degree nearer than, or equal to, that of the applicant to the patient, should be notified and the court should be informed that this has been done (r.25). The Rules, however, do not lay down who is to apply and, accordingly, when the circumstances so require the application could be made by any person interested, *e.g.* the patient's solicitor, a trustee, a creditor or a friend.

For "r.90" substitute: r. 87

It is usual to appoint a near relative as receiver. Until recent times it was not the normal practice to appoint the solicitor in the matter (see *Ex p. Pincke* (1817) 2 Mer. 453; *Re Lloyd* (1879) 12 Ch.D. 447), but in the absence of any other suitable person the court now often considers favourably such an appointment. In suitable cases the court will authorise the solicitor so appointed to charge profit costs for work not usually requiring professional assistance (see r.87). Where the appointment of some other professional person with remuneration is sought, *e.g.* an accountant or estate agent, directions as to remuneration should be asked for in the evidence of family and property and the suggested amount specified. The general practice is to direct remuneration (when granted) to be fixed subsequently, normally on the passing of the receiver's accounts. Generally as to remuneration see

For "r.45" substitute: r. 43

r.43.

An accounting party will not be appointed unless and until his accounts are clear. Joint receivers are not usually favoured.

Normally the court requires that the proposed receiver should be resident in England or Wales.

For "the Public Trustee" substitute:

The court has power to direct that the application be made by an officer of the courtan officer of the court or (if he consents) by the Official Solicitor (see

For "r.12" substitute: r. 11

r.11). In the absence of any suitable relative or other person the court may appoint an officer of the court to act as receiver.

Death of applicant

6B–16 If the applicant dies before the application is considered or the entry of the order, the application cannot proceed until a new applicant is substituted, for which purpose the master's direction is required. The solicitor should file a statement giving the following information:
  (i) The date of death of the applicant;
  (ii) The name, address, occupation and relationship to the patient of the proposed new applicant;
  (iii) The name, address, occupation and relationship to the patient of the proposed receiver (if other than originally proposed) together with the name, address and occupation of a referee;
  (iv) Details of any change of the patient's circumstances caused by applicant's death;
  (v) Whether service of notification has been effected on the patient and when.

Add after "copy of the application": (if any)

The statement should be accompanied by a certificate of death of the applicant, and what is said above as to an original applicant and notification of relatives applies. The master's direction for substitution will be endorsed on the court's copy of the application (if any) and on the original and the application is then amended and sealed in the usual way. If service had been effected before the applicant's death no further service is required but, if not, the notification should be served on the patient showing, if necessary, the substituted receiver.

If the proposed receiver (not being the applicant) dies before the hearing or the entry of the order, some other person can be appointed without amendment of the proceedings.

Documents and evidence

The printed forms required for the application are obtainable free of charge (in sets) from the Protection Division. The following are necessary:

    (i)

6B–17

Delete the whole of part (i) and renumber the rest.

    (ii) Certificate of family and property (Form C.P. 5).

Add at end: The certificate includes provision for details of the applicant and the proposed receiver.

The certificate includes provision for details of the applicant and the proposed receiver.

Service of notice

Delete ", unless service is dispensed with,".

The application itself is not served on the patient but notification of the application (Form C.P.6) is served on him personally (see

6B–18

For "r. 26" substitute: r. 24

r.24). The necessary forms are provided without request on the issue of the application.

For "r. 21" substitute: r. 19

Service of the notice (which is left with the patient) should be effected as soon as possible after the issue of the application, and at least 10 clear days before the return date (r.19). Otherwise service is bad and the case will have to be adjourned to another date to enable service to be effected in due time

Delete ", unless the court decides to dispense with service pursuant to r.26(2) (see para. 6B–259)".

In any event the order may not be entered until the expiration of 10 clear days from service (

For "r. 48(1)" substitute: r. 46(1)

r.46(1)). The patient is, of course, at liberty, if he is able, to instruct solicitors on his behalf or if he so wishes may communicate with the court by post, addressing his letter to "The Court of Protection, 24, Kingsway, London, WC2B 6JX."

Delete paragraph which begins "Where it is desired...".

Interim order and direction

For "r. 44(1)(b)" substitute: r. 42(1)(b)

In any case where the circumstances necessitate that immediate steps be taken a receiver *ad interim* may be appointed forthwith (r.42(1)(b)) before comliance with the requirements as to notification (

6B–19

For "r. 48(2)" substitute: r. 46(2)

r.46(2)). The solicitor should file the normal appropriate medical evidence unless, in an exceptional case, under the provision of s.98 of the Mental Health Act 1983, it is intended to endeavour to persuade the court to make the order on lay evidence only. The master may require the solicitors to attend before her/him at the time of the issue of the application or as soon thereafter as can be arranged.

For "r. 44(2)" substitute: r. 42(2)

The order is drafted immediately, and settled and engrossed without delay. It is usual for the receiver *ad interim* to be authorised to act at once before giving security and for him to be directed in the order to give security in the sum fixed as soon as he reasonably can. The order also states that a copy of the order is to be served upon the patient within a certain specified time (usually 14 days) and that he may apply within (usually) 14 days for reconsideration of the order (r.44(2)).

Delete sentence which begins "Where notification to the patient".

The usual practice as to the issue of orders applies (see "Entry and sealing of order," para. 6B–25). Evidence of service (which may be in certificate form unless the court otherwise directs) of the copy order *ad interim* should be filed before the date the formal application is due to be considered. Generally, see Heywood and Massey, *Court of Protection Practice* (12th ed., 1991) pp. 39 *et seq.*

For "r. 44(1)(a)" substitute: r. 42(1)(a)

If money is required for maintenance or other necessary requirements before the order appointing a receiver can be drawn up, or any other urgent matter arises but the circumstances of the case do not warrant the appointment of a receiver *ad interim*, it may well be possible to deal with the matter by an interim certificate or direction under r.42(1)(a). An *interim* sale of land will be authorised by order not by certificate.

A commencement fee of £230 is payable—see paras and 6B–337.

Where the court makes an interim order for sale, the order will, if thought fit, contain directions for service on the patient as if it were an order appointing a receiver *ad interim* in accordance with the provisions of r.42(2).

The order

6B–20 As indicated in para. 6B–5 attendance on the consideration of the application will seldom be necessary. Where an attendance is required the persons concerned should first ask to see the appropriate Branch Officer who will then take them to the master concerned.

In making the appropriate order the master has to consider the case as a whole. The following are some of the more important points upon which it is usual to give directions on a first application:

    (i) The person to be appointed receiver.
    (ii) Amount of receiver's security (if any) (see para. 6B–24, "Security").
    (iii) Directions as to maintenance of the patient and, if necessary, any dependant; upkeep of establishment, etc., if the patient is living at home.
    (iv) Payment of debts.
    (v) Retention or sale of property, including, in the case of house property or land, letting powers for periods not exceeding three years.
    (vi) Carrying on or closing down of a patient's business.
    (vii) Deposit of securities and deeds and perhaps jewellery at a bank for safe custody. Patient's wills are usually allowed to remain deposited with the solicitor who prepared them—but otherwise they are deposited at a bank.
    (viii) Lodgment in court of securities or cash.
    (ix) Costs (see paras 6B–155 *et seq.*).

Objection by alleged patient

6B–21 It is the right of a person to require that the free use of his property, and personal freedom, shall not be taken away from him on the ground of alleged incapability without his being allowed the opportunity of establishing his capacity or denying his mental disorder (previously before a jury) not merely as a subject of inquiry (*Re Cumming* (1852) 1 De G.M. & G. 537 at 545). See also Heywood and Massey, *Court of Protection Practice* (12th ed., 1991) pp. 25–26 and para. 6B–159.

Draft order and settlement

6B–22 Only in exceptional circumstances are draft orders now sent out for approval. The order is drafted and any additional information called for. It is then engrossed and dispatched to the solicitors having carriage of the order.

Normally five copies of the engrossment are prepared by the court for use as follows:

    (i) The original retained by the court.
    (ii) The file copy also retained by the court.
    (iii) The receiver's plain copy specially noted on the indorsement "This copy to be retained in the personal custody of the receiver."
    (iv) Two office copies. It is, however, open to solicitors to request further copies, if required.

Where there is a lodgment and payment schedule to the order an additional copy of such schedule alone is prepared for the use of the Court Funds Office and is transmitted direct.

Note

If the order entails the execution of a deed, *e.g.* on a sale of land, an additional copy for placing with the title deeds should be requested.

6B–23

Security

For "r. 58" substitute: r. 56

Where the court directs that security be given (r.56) it is usually in such a sum as will with a reasonable margin cover the annual amount passing through the receiver's hands; and where at any time the receiver is directed to receive capital money temporary increase of such security may, in some cases, be directed. Security can be effected by one of the four following methods (

6B–24

For "r. 59" substitute: r. 57

r.57):

   (a) *By a Bond with a Guarantee Society* in which case the proposal form must be fully completed by the receiver and forwarded to the company selected. The annual premium will be payable out of the Patient's estate. A list of the companies approved by the court is made available.

   (b) *By use of a simplified arrangement with HSBC Gibbs Ltd (formerly Gibbs Hartley Cooper Ltd and Frizzell U.K. Ltd)* in which case an endorsement supplied by the

For "Public Trust Office" substitute: Public Guardianship Office

Public Trust Office should be signed, witnessed and sent to HSBC Gibbs Ltd together with the premium.

   (c) *By the lodgment in Court by the Receiver of cash* to the amount of the security directed. The cash will be invested in accordance with directions to be given by the court (usually in an appropriate Government stock). The interest will be paid to the Receiver.

   (d) *By the transfer into court of stock* approved by the court to the value of the amount of the security directed. The interest on the stock will be paid to the Receiver.

If the receiver decides to adopt method (c) or (d) he should notify the Public Guardianship Office stating either the stock in which he would like the cash invested (see (c) above) or give the nominal amount and full description of the stock proposed to be transferred into ourt (see (d) above). A form of request for leave to give security by one of these methods will then be sent for completion.

Methods (c) and (d), although still available, have virtually fallen into disuse.

   (e) *By a Bond given by Personal Sureties*. This method is not advocated for many reasons, *e.g.* the expense incurred in the execution of a new bond on the death or bankruptcy of one of the sureties.

      The bond is prepared as in (a) above, but the court's sanction is required; the solicitor prepares the affidavits of sufficiency and due execution.

      The bond and the affidavits, when complete, are filed with the Public Guardianship Office. See

For "r. 62" substitute: r.60

as to maintenance of security by bond.

      When it is directed that the security be increased, in a case where security has been given by bond with a guarantee society, a memorandum will be prepared by the

For "PTO" substitute : PGO

PGO and sent to the solicitor. This document when duly executed is filed in the PGO and attached to the original bond. In the case of a bond with private sureties, a new bond will be required. To increase security where it has been effected by lodgment in court of cash or securities, the necessary lodgment direction will issue for the additional cash or securities to be lodged.

      Where security is to be reduced the bond will be indorsed accordingly and the guarantee society will be notified by the PGO. Reduction of penalty in the case of private sureties is not likely to be sanctioned. Where security has been effected by lodgment in court, reduction will be effected by a direction under the Court Funds Rules 1987, r.7.

      For vacation of security, see paras 6B–33, 6B–39, 6B–47 and 6B–57. Should default be made in a case where security has been effected by bond, a certificate of default will issue which, under the term of the bond, is conclusive evidence against the receiver and the sureties. Generally as to liability of sureties, etc., see Heywood and Massey, *Court of Protection Practice* (12th ed., 1991) pp. 54–55.

Entry and sealing of order

For "r. 48" substitute: r. 46

6B–25 All orders are sealed and entered in the Sealing Room. Office copies are sent to the solicitors as soon as the engrossments are ready, but where security has been directed the order cannot normally be issued until security has been completed. See also r.46.

Carrying first order into effect

6B–26 An office copy of the order should be registered with all sources of income including those companies in which the patient has securities (or with banks at which any of the securities are domiciled) other than in respect of those securities which are to be lodged in court. Not to do so would amount to an irregularity and conversion; see *Re N. (decd.)* [1977] 1 W.L.R. 676; [1977] 2 All E.R. 687, CA.

Any necessary undertaking and inventory as to furniture and household effects or bankers' receipt and undertaking (Form C.P.12) should be filed as soon as possible.

In the case of the court directing any investigation, inquiry or report every effort should be made to ensure that the direction is complied with within the period limited by the order, or, if no time limited, as soon as possible.

Special consideration should be given to the detailed directions which are usually incorporated in an order directing the carrying on of a business. See "Business," para. 6B–101.

If a patient holds a driving licence, the licensing authority (Driver's Medical Branch, Driver and Vehicle Licensing Agency, Swansea SA99 1AB) should be notified by the Receiver by reference to the name, address, date of birth and sex of the patient. See Heywood and Massey, *Court of Protection Practice* (12th ed., 1991), pp. 108n–109n.

Lodgments in Court

For "r. 75" substitute: r. 73

6B–27 Where stock or shares to be lodged stand in the name of a patient the lodgment is made by the proper officer of the company (r.73) and where they stand in the joint names of a patient and another the lodgment is made by the proper officer of the company and that other; the lodgment will, usually, only be directed where the patient is solely entitled thereto. In cases where the patient holds securities either solely or jointly as trustee the question of appointing a new trustee in place of the patient and obtaining any necessary vesting order would have to be considered. See paras 6B–59 *et seq.*

Funds to be lodged are transferred into the name of the Accountant General, usually to the general credit of the patient, but where any income is not required for maintenance or other necessary expenditure an "accumulating fund" is sometimes created, the Accountant General of the Supreme Court being directed to invest and accumulate the income. Accumulations are placed on Special Account pending investment.

On the sale of or realisation of specifically bequeathed or nominated property the proceeds may be directed to be lodged to a special credit or otherwise earmarked in accordance with s.101(4) of the Mental Health Act 1983. See also para. 6B–111.

(b) Appointment of New Receiver

When and by whom made

6B–28 Somewhat the same considerations arise as upon the first application, but where a receiver is retiring he should usually be the applicant. The appointment of a new receiver may become necessary for one of many reasons, *e.g.* the death or illness of the existing receiver, the default or other misdemeanour of the receiver, his permanent residence abroad, his desire to retire or perhaps his bankruptcy.

Whenever it becomes necessary to appoint a new receiver the application should be made without undue delay, as it is obviously imperative to have someone through whom the court can give directions and who will take an active and personal interest in the patient, his condition, welfare and estate.

If money is required for maintenance or other necessary requirements before the order appointing a new receiver can be drawn up, or any other urgent matter arises, it may well be possible to deal with the matter by interim order or direction, see para. 6B–19.

Proceedings are by way of format application.

Documents and evidence

6B-29 The application should ask that "A. B." (name, address and occupation of proposed new receiver and relationship to patient—if any) "be appointed receiver in place of C.D., the receiver appointed by order dated—and that such other necessary directions be given." The address of the patient should be indorsed on the back of the application (court's copy) as should also the name, address and occupation of a referee with whom the court can communicate as to the proposed receiver's fitness to act.

The following are necessary:
(i) Two copies of the formal application (Form C.P.9).
(ii) On the death of the receiver—a certificate of death or production of the grant of representation (or office copy) to the deceased receiver's estate.
(iii) A statement of facts showing the grounds of the application giving particulars of any change in the circumstances or property of the patient, *e.g.* any benefit to which the patient may be entitled under the will or intestacy of the late receiver.
(iv) Certificate of the fund in court (if any). (*Note*—If there is none, a statement to this effect should be indorsed on the court's copy of the application.)

The formal application is not served on the patient but he is notified in the same way as on the issue of a first application for the appointment of a receiver (see para. 6B–18). A Transaction fee of £175 is payable — see paras 6B–316 and 6B–337.

The order

6B-30 The following are some of the more important points in regard to which directions are usually given:
(i) The person appointed new receiver.
(ii) Receiver's security (if any).
(iii) The discharge of the old receiver (if alive) and, in any case, directions as to the passing of, or dispensing with, his final account and discharge of his security (if any).
(iv) Directions as to maintenance of the patient and, if necessary, any dependants; upkeep of establishment, etc.
(v) The repetition of any previous authority or direction which is either of such a nature as to require continuance or has not yet been complied with.

Order, settlement, entry and sealing

6B-31 As on first application (see paras 6B–22, 6B–23 and 6B–25).

Security

6B-32 As on first application (see para. 6B–24).

Vacation of receiver's security

6B-33 Where the court dispenses with a final account of the former receiver and discharges his security the security may be vacated forthwith and the bond will be returned duly vacated direct to the guarantee society (or to the solicitor when there are private sureties) and the solicitor informed accordingly. Where, however, security has been effected by lodgment in court a direction to the Accountant General of the Supreme court to transfer the fund standing to the "Receiver's Security Account" to the former receiver, or his personal representatives, will be included in the order.

For "r. 67" substitute: r. 65

If, as is more usually the case, the court directs that a final account of the former receiver be passed, either by that receiver or his personal representatives, the security cannot be vacated until such account is passed and the balance found due thereon paid over to the new receiver and (unless the new receiver is the personal representative of the late receiver) his receipt obtained and produced to the court. Where the security has been effected by lodgment in court a separate direction to the Accountant General of the Supreme court will be prepared by the court. See r.65.

Passing final account of former receiver

6B-34 (See "Accounts", paras 6B–149 *et seq.*).

(c) Application on Recovery of Patient

Recovery of patient

6B–35   Under s.99(3) of the Mental Health Act 1983, a receiver must be discharged by order on the court being satisfied that the patient has become capable of managing and administering his property and affairs. The question must be divorced from such considerations as whether or not he remains in an institution, or whether or not he continues to be liable to be detained under any compulsory powers (see *Re B. A. S.* [1898] 2 Ch. 392, where, under the Lunacy Act 1890, it was held that discharge of a reception order did not of itself determine the receivership). The test is, "Is the patient now capable of managing and administering his property and affairs?"

Proceedings are by way of formal application.

If the court is not satisfied that the patient is capable of managing and administering the whole of his affairs so as to satisfy the first part of the section, it may consider discharging the receiver on the grounds that it is "expedient to do so", *e.g.* if a settlement of the patient's property were first executed under an order of the court, see para. 6B–135. It must be noted, however, that "expedient" means "expedient for the patient" and not for any other purpose, see *Re N. (decd.)* [1977] 1 W.L.R. 676; [1977] 2 All E.R. 687, CA.

Documents and evidence

For "para. 6B-188" substitute: para. 6B–187

6B–36   A precedent for a medical certificate in support is given in para. 6B–187 . If the certificate is to be made by the doctor who gave the medical evidence in support of the first application, the deponent should traverse his former evidence; if not, the deponent should state that he has read a copy of such former evidence. In either case the deponent must give the reasons upon which he bases his conclusions as to recovery, and must state that in his opinion the patient is capable of managing and administering his property and affairs. If not satisfied with such evidence the master may request one of the Lord Chancellor's Medical Visitors to visit the patient and report. See paras 6B–199 and 6B–206.

For "r. 77" substitute: r. 75

Where the same solicitors are acting on the application for the order determining proceedings as acted on the first application, no doubt (except in cases where the evidence was obtained direct by the court) they will have their completed draft of the original medical evidence from which to prepare a copy for the deponent as above, but if necessary an office copy should be bespoken. Where different solicitors are acting they should first apply to the solicitors who filed the original medical evidence who should, if necessary, bespeak an office copy (r.75). Such copies of medical evidence are for the use of the patient's medical and legal advisers and should not in any circumstances be disclosed to the patient or anyone else without the leave of the court.

For "r. 21" substitute: r. 19

The patient makes the application, and, if acting by the same solicitors, the receiver should be joined as an applicant, but if not the receiver should be notified and a copy of the application served on him at least two clear days before the hearing date (r.19). If the receiver is dead, a certificate of death or the grant of representation to his estate should be produced; but his personal representatives need not be notified unless the court so directs.

The application should ask that:

(1) The patient be restored to the management of his property and that the powers of the receiver be determined.

In (2) delete "(as the patient may require)".

(2) The final account of the receiver be dispensed with, or passed and that his security (if any) may be discharged.

(3) The will, deeds, securities and other documents (if any) deposited with   Bank (or elsewhere) subject to the directions of the court may be delivered to the patient. The application should also ask for the release from restriction of any other assets, e.g. furniture and effects, building society or bank accounts (N.B. not receivership bank account) held subject to the directions of the court.

(4) The funds in court (if any) be transferred to the patient.

(5) The costs of the application (and the costs directed to be taxed or assessed by any previous order which may not yet have been taxed and paid) and any outstanding costs of general management may be assessed (unless agreed) and paid out of the fund in court (or paid by the patient). See also "Costs," paras 6B–155 to 6B–162. The following are necessary:

(i) Two copies of the formal application (Form C.P. 9).

(ii) Medical certificate in support (para. 6B–187).
(iii) Certificate of the fund in court (if any).

Order, settlement, entry and sealing

As on first application, except that no "receiver's copy" of the order is issued (see paras 6B–22, 6B–23 and 6B–25).

6B–37

Transfer out of fund in Court

Subject to compliance with the procedure of the Court Funds Office the balance of the fund in court can be transferred to the patient immediately under the terms of the order unless:
(i) A final account is to be passed and any administration fees certified due upon the passing thereof paid out of the fund in court, or
(ii) The costs are to be assessed (unless agreed) and paid out of the fund in court.

6B–38

Pending the disposal of such questions (if any) the whole fund cannot be transferred, but it is not unusual for the order to provide for the transfer of the greater part at once and the reservation of such a part only of the fund as is considered will be adequate to meet the above-mentioned payments. Any ultimate surplus is finally transferred as directed by the order after the two above-mentioned payments have been made.

Where the direction is for the costs to be assessed (unless agreed) and paid out of the fund in court, the Accountant General of the Supreme Court will accept a letter from the solicitors that such costs have been or will be agreed. As to realisation of Common Investment Fund units, see para. .

Vacation of security

Where the court dispenses with a final account of the receiver and discharges his security the security may normally be vacated forthwith and the bond will be returned duly vacated to the guarantee society (or to the solicitor when private sureties) and the solicitor informed accordingly. Where, however, security has been effected by lodgment in court a direction to the Accountant General of the Supreme Court to transfer the "Receiver's Security Account" to the receiver will be included in the order.

6B–39

For "r. 67" substitute: r. 65

If a final account is to be passed the security will not be vacated until such account has been passed and any balance found due thereon paid to the recovered patient and his receipt therefor obtained and produced to the court when bespeaking the bond as above. Where security has been effected by lodgment in court a separate direction to the Accountant General of the Supreme Court will be prepared. See r.65.

Passing final account of former receiver

See "Accounts," paras 6B–149 *et seq.*

6B–40

(d) Final Order or Direction on Death of Patient

Death of patient

The court should be notified immediately of the death of the patient.

6B–41

For "r. 87(3)" substitute: r. 84(3)

The jurisdiction of the Court of Protection ceases on the death of the patient (*Re Walker* [1907] 2 Ch. 120; *Re Wheater* [1928] 1 Ch. 223; and the powers of the receiver are automatically determined (*Re Walker*) and he is discharged from the office (without an order) by the death (Mental Health Act 1983, s.99(3)). Certain jurisdiction, incidental to the winding up of the proceedings, however, survives; as to costs, see r.84(3); as to remuneration, see

For "r. 45(2)" substitute: r. 43(2)

r.43(2); as to administration fees, see

For "r. 80(4)" substitute: r. 78(4)

r.78(4); as to final accounts, see

In 6B-41 for "r. 67" substitute: r. 65

r.65; as to transfer and delivery of funds, see

For "r. 76" substitute: r. 74

r.74.

The Court of Protection will not administer the estate nor decide who is entitled to any fund in court or other property (*Ex p. Gilbert* (1810) 1 Ball & B. 297) nor order payment of debts (*Re Marman's Trusts* (1878) 26 W.R. 621) nor make the receiver or any one else account for any thing received after the death (*Re Walker*; but the Chancery Division may (*Scammell v. Light* (1863) 32 L.J.Ch. 53). In *Strangwayes v. Read* [1898] 2 Ch. 419, the committee of the person was made to account for money paid to him in advance for maintenance of the patient, who died within a short time after the receipt of the money.

Where since the death an order had been made in the Chancery Division for the administration of the patient's estate, the fund in court to the credit of the patient was by consent ordered to be carried over to the credit of the administrator's action, and an order of the Court of Protection for payment to creditors gives them no equitable charge on the fund (*Re Wheater*).

When order necessary

6B–42 Should a patient die between the date of the first application and the entering of the order, the court requires proof of death, usually by production of a death certificate.

A receiver is automatically discharged on the death of a patient (Mental Health Act 1983, s.99(3); see para. 6B–195) but a final order or directions will be necessary to wind up the proceedings in the court. No order is usually required: a direction of the court is sufficient as to the passing or dispensing with the receiver's final account and discharging his security, the release of the funds in court (if any) and the release by formal authority under the seal of the court of any documents or assets held subject to the directions of the court where the restriction is not limited to "the lifetime of the patient". The majority of cases can be dealt with by a letter, accompanied by a statement of facts, asking for the required directions. Formal proceedings for a final order are only now required where it is anticipated that an order of the court will be necessary to enforce payment of costs in the proceedings.

Where there is a charge on the fund in court, it may be convenient to let the chargees make their own application to enforce their charge. If any surplus remains of the fund after payment of the charge, the order or directions would then provide for payment of the residue to the personal representatives of the patient.

For "the Public Trustee" substitute: an officer of the court

A Transaction fee of £1015 is payable where an officer of the court has been appointed receiver or £125 otherwise — see paras 6B–316 and 6B–337.

Representation to patient's estate

For "r. 76(3)" substitute: r. 74(3)

6B–43 Before application can be made for a final order, or final directions given, the appropriate grant of representation must, normally, be obtained. Where, however, the net estate is under £5,000 in value there is usually no need to obtain a grant and the matter can be dealt with under the provisions of r.74(3). If there is a fund in court directions can be given either for it to be transferred to the personal representatives of the patient (when constituted) under the Court Funds Rules 1987, r.43, or to a named payee, under the Court Funds Rules 1987, r.7, as may be appropriate.

To enable payment, transfer, delivery or release to be directed under r.74(3) a certificate of death and the will (if any) should be lodged together with a statement showing (a) the total assets of the deceased and their value (b) the debts and whether paid or not and in the case of funeral expenses forward the undertaker's account and if paid say who paid them and (c) the names, addresses and relationship of the persons entitled and where the person applying is neither the executor nor the only person entitled a statement should be filed signed by the persons entitled nominating one of their number to collect the assets. If there is any minority interest a grant may be necessary.

A Scottish confirmation or Northern Irish grant of representation in respect of a patient who dies domiciled in Scotland or Northern Ireland, as the case may be, will be recognised without resealing in the Principal Probate Registry provided it contains a statement as to such domicile (see the Administration of Estates Act 1971, s.1). A Colonial grant which is to be acted upon in respect of estate of a patient in England and Wales will, however, require to be resealed before production to the Court of Protection (see *ibid.*, s.11).

How application is made

6B–44 Where (as is rarely the case) an order is necessary, application is made by way of formal application.

Documents and evidence

The application is made by the personal representatives of the deceased patient, and where the receiver is also a personal representative, such an applicant should be described in both capacities, but in the capacity of executor or administrator first. **6B–45**

For "r. 21" substitute: r. 19

The receiver, if he is not also a personal representative, should, where he is acting by the same solicitors, be joined as an applicant, but if not he should be notified and a copy of the application should be served on him at least two clear days before the return day (r.19). If the receiver is also dead, a certificate of death or the grant of representation (or a sealed office copy) to his estate should be produced; but his personal representatives need not be notified unless the court so directs.

The formal application should ask that:

(1) The receiver's final account be dispensed with or passed.

In (1) delete "(as the personal representatives may require)".

and that the security (if any) be discharged.

(2) The deeds, securities or other documents (if any) deposited with the Bank (or elsewhere) be delivered to the executor or administrator. The application should also ask for the release from restriction of any other assets, *e.g.* furniture and effects, building society or bank accounts (*N.B.* not receivership bank account) held subject to the directions of the court. Present-day orders provide for documents and items to be held subject to the directions of the court only *during the lifetime of the patient* and in those cases the documents, etc., can be released without further authority on the death of the patient.

(3) The fund in court be transferred to the executor or administrator or that the fund in court be sold and that after discharge of the charge thereon (if any) the balance of the proceeds be paid, etc. (as the case may require).

(4) The costs of the application (and the costs directed to be taxed or assessed by any previous order which may not yet have been assessed and paid) and any outstanding costs of general management be assessed (unless agreed) and paid out of the patient's estate or fund in court (as the case may require).

The grant of representation (or a sealed office copy), which will normally be accepted as sufficient evidence of death and identity, should support the application.

The following are necessary:

(i) Two copies of the formal application (Form C.P.9).

(ii) Certificate of the fund in court (if any).

Delete "(iii) Consents of beneficiaries (where necessary) as to dispensing with final account.".

Where (as is usually the case) only directions are required the following are necessary:

(i) A statement as explained above (see paras 6B–42 and 6B–43).

(ii) The grant of representation.

Delete "(iii) Consents (where necessary) as to dispensing with final account.".

Where the receiver is the sole personal representative but is not the sole beneficiary, the consents in writing of the principal beneficiaries to dispensing with the final account of the receiver, if so desired, must be filed and, preferably, on the issue of the formal application or the filing of the statement as the case may be.

Where it is desired that funds should be transferred not to the personal representatives but to their solicitors or nominees, an authority and request to that effect signed by the personal representatives should be filed with the application (see *Woodhead v. Bates* [1963] 1 W.L.R. 926; [1963] 2 All E.R. 877).

A Transaction fee of £1,015 is payable where the Public Trustee has been appointed Receiver or £125 otherwise. See paras 6B–42, 6B–316 and 6B–337.

Costs

Normally the final order will pick up any outstanding costs, but where at the death of a patient there is pending an application for a settlement or a gift or a statutory will under s.96(1)(d) or (e) of the principal Act, or under s.1(3) of the Variation of Trusts Act 1958, the final order to wind up the court of Protection proceedings would not normally deal with the costs of such a pending application; but if directions are required, the application in question should be restored to the list to enable the question of the costs thereof to be dealt with separately. The personal representatives (if constituted) should be the persons to be notified, but if they have not been constituted, the court would consider whether or not **6B–46** those entitled to the estate were sufficiently represented to enable the matter to be dealt with in the absence of the personal representatives, neither would the costs of a pending application relating to the appointment of new trustees be dealt with by the final order, and the application should similarly be restored to the list if an order as to costs is required.

Order, settlement, entry and sealing
6B–47   Usually directions are given by way of a letter, but where an order is made it proceeds in much the same way as on a first application. See paras 6B–22 to 6B–25.

Transfer out of fund in Court
6B–48   As on an order determining proceedings on recovery, see para. 6B–38. As to realisation of Common Investment Fund units, see para. 6B–86.

Vacation of security
6B–49   As on an order determining proceedings on recovery (see para. 6B–39) except that the receipt for the balance found due on the passing of the final account will be that of the personal representatives, unless the receiver is the sole personal representative.

Passing final account
6B–50   See "Accounts", paras 6B–149 *et seq.*

(e) Application to Raise Money out of the Fund in Court for Duty on Death of Patient

Note
6B–51   "Duty" means Capital Transfer Tax, Inheritance tax or, where relevant, Estate, Succession or Legacy Duty.

Sometimes prior to grant of representation it is desired that part of the fund should be transferred to the Capital Taxes Office to meet duty. Should it be desired to tender any National Savings or Stocks on the National Savings Register not in court, the practice here indicated should be followed so far as applicable.

The application is made by way of formal application, unless the court otherwise directs.

Documents and evidence
For "r. 21" substitute: r. 19

6B–52   The application is made by the executors named in the will of the patient or (where the patient dies intestate) the persons entitled to apply for a grant of administration to his estate. The receiver, if acting by the same solicitors, should be joined as an applicant, but if not he should be notified and a copy of the application served on him at least two clear days before the return day (r.19). If the receiver is also dead, a certificate of death or the grant of administration (or sealed office copy) to his estate should be produced; but his personal representatives should not be notified unless so directed. The application should ask that:
   (1) Sufficient of the stock in court be sold to meet the tax (and interest) now payable, and that the balance of such fund in court be transferred to the personal representatives of the patient when constituted.
   (2) The deeds, securities, or other documents (if any) deposited with the Bank (or elsewhere) be delivered to such personal representatives when constituted. The application should also ask for the release from restriction of any other assets, *e.g.* furniture and effects, building society or bank accounts (*N.B.* not receivership bank account) held subject to the directions of the court. If the aforementioned items are held *only during the lifetime of the patient* subject to the directions of the court, no directions in the order will be required.
   (3) Direction as to costs as in application for final order, paras 6B–44 and 6B–45.

The affidavit in support should state:
   (1) The date of the death of the patient and whether the patient left a will and if so the date thereof and the executors (if any) appointed thereby and, if they are dead or if the patient dies intestate, that the applicants are the persons entitled to apply for administration.
   (2) That representation has not yet been obtained but the necessary papers to lead to a grant have been completed and are ready to be lodged in the Probate Registry.

(3) The approximate amount of the tax.
  (4) The stock which it is suggested should be sold to meet the tax.
  (5) That the facts therein deposed to are within the deponent's own knowledge and are true and that, where necessary, the deponent is authorised by his co-executor or co-applicant to make the affidavit.

The following are necessary:
  (i) Two copies of the formal application (Form C.P. 9).
  (ii) Affidavit in support.
  (iii) Certificate of Death.
  (iv) Certificate of the fund in court.

Order, settlement, entry and sealing

6B–53 As on a first application except that no "receiver's copy" of the order is issued, see paras 6B–22 to 6B–25.

Certificate of duty

6B–54 When the order has been completed, an office copy should be produced to the Capital Taxes Office who will send a requisition for the amount of tax payable to the Court Funds Office.

Final directions as to account and security

6B–55 When the personal representatives have been constituted, directions as to passing or dispensing with a final account and vacation of security (if any) should be applied for by lodging a statement (formal application not necessary); the grant should be produced.

Delete "The same consents are required to dispense with the account as on a final order, see paras 6B–44 and 6B–45.".

Transfer out of balance of fund

6B–56 The balance will be transferred out to the personal representatives when constituted upon the production of the grant to the Court Funds Office and, if the fund exceeds £5,000 in value, an affidavit of representation will also be required. See also paras 6B–38 and 6B–85.

Vacation of security

6B–57 As on final order (para. 6B–47).

Passing final account

6B–58 See "Accounts", paras 6B–149 *et seq.*

APPOINTMENT OF NEW TRUSTEES AND VESTING ORDERS

(a) Generally as to Jurisdiction

Statutory jurisdiction

6B–59 The removal from his office of a trustee under mental disability and the appointment, where necessary, of a new trustee in his place and the vesting of trust property are matters which may be effected out of court or may require relief either in the Court of Protection or the Chancery Division or county court, according to the circumstances.

The following enactments have special application:
  (1) s.96(1)(k) of the Mental Health Act 1983—exercise of a patient's power of appointing new trustee or retiring from a trust with (if necessary) a vesting order under subs.(2).
  (2) s.54(2) of the Trustee Act 1925—appointment by the Court of Protection of a new trustee in place of a patient with (if necessary) a vesting order.
  (3) s.36(9) of the Trustee Act 1925—giving of leave to a continuing (or refusing or retiring) trustee to exercise his *statutory* power of appointment.

Which method to adopt

6B–60 With a view to assisting the practitioner to decide what is the appropriate course and procedure to be followed in any particular case, the following working rules are given:

(a) Where the Patient is not a Trustee

6B–61 (1) Where the patient has no beneficial interest, and the assistance of the court is required, relief should be asked for in the Chancery Division (or county court, where appropriate; see Trustee Act 1925, s.67) but see note (4) below.

(2) s.54(2) of the Trustee Act 1925, does not apply.

(3) The only jurisdiction in the Court of Protection is under s.96(1)(k) of the Mental Health Act 1983, exercising a power of appointment (if any) vested in the patient, with, if necessary, a consequential vesting order under subs. (2).

(4) Where the patient is the person nominated by the trust instrument to exercise the power of appointing new trustees, such power should be exercised in the Court of Protection if the patient is beneficially interested and a receiver has been appointed (see *Re Blake* [1887] W.N. 173); otherwise new trustees may be appointed out of court by any of the persons so empowered by s.36 of the Trustee Act 1925. Where, however, the patient was the settlor it is appropriate for the power to be exercised in the Court of Protection under note (3) above, whether or not the patient has a beneficial interest.

(5) If the power vested in the patient is purely statutory, and there is no other person with a power capable of exercising the same, application may be made to the Court of Protection to exercise the power.

(b) Where the Patient is a Trustee

6B–62 (1) Where the patient has no beneficial interest and the assistance of the court is required, relief should be asked for in the Chancery Division (or other court, where appropriate; see Trustee Act 1925, s.67) but see note (5) below.

(2) If a vesting order is required and the matter is one coming within the scope of s.54(2) of the Trustee Act 1925, proceed under that section for an order appointing and vesting. This course is advocated even where the patient or some other person (who would require to be an applicant) is the person nominated by the trust instrument to appoint new trustees, see note (5).

(4) If a vesting order is not required, new trustees should be appointed out of court by any of the persons so empowered by s.36 of the Trustee Act 1925, but where the patient has some beneficial interest *in possession*, and the appointment is being made by the continuing (or refusing or retiring) trustee, by virtue of subs.(1)(b) of that section, the prior leave of the Court of Protection is necessary under subs.(9).

(5) If the patient is the person nominated by the trust instrument to exercise the power of appointing new trustees and he is beneficially interested and there is a receiver, the appointment should be made in the Court of Protection (see *Re Blake* [1887] W.N. 173) under s.96(1)(k) of the Mental Health Act 1983, by exercising the power, and where the patient was the settlor, this course should be followed, even if he has no beneficial interest. If a vesting order is required it is preferable, where possible, to proceed under s.54(2) of the Trustee Act 1925 for an order appointing and vesting (see notes (2) and (3)).

(6) Where there is with the patient a capable trustee who wishes to retire, the matter does not fall within s.54(2) of the Trustee Act 1925, though there would be jurisdiction under s.96(1)(k) of the Mental Health Act 1983.

(7) Where it is desired that the patient shall retire from the trust under s.39 of the Trustee Act 1925, without a new trustee being appointed in his place, application can be made under s.96(1)(k) of the Mental Health Act 1983, for an order authorising the receiver to exercise the power with (if necessary) a vesting order under subs.(2) of that section.

Generally, see Heywood and Massey, *Court of Protection Practice*, (12th ed., 1991) Chap. 15.

Vesting order, where necessary

6B–63 Usually no vesting provisions are required, unless the patient is a trustee. Where there stand in the name of the patient, either solely or jointly, mortgages or stocks or shares, etc. (see the Trustee Act 1925, s.40(4)) a vesting order is necessary, for, if the appointment of new trustees were made by deed either under s.96(1)(k) of the Mental Health Act 1983, or by the continuing trustee or other person empowered under s.36 of the Trustee Act 1925, such classes of property would not "follow the deed" under any express or implied vesting provisions under s.40 of the Trustee Act 1925.

Where, however, proceedings for appointment of new trustees are being taken under s.54 of the Trustee Act 1925 all property will be vested in the new trustees by or in pursuance of the order; there will be no deed of appointment.

Where new trustees are being appointed for the purposes of the Settled Land Act 1925, the order will not deal with the freehold and leasehold property (since—if vested in him—the legal estate remains in the tenant for life). Where land is vested in a patient as statutory owner (see the Settled Land Act 1925, s.23(1)(b)) the order will authorise the receiver to convey or join in conveying the land to the new statutory owners (see *ibid.*, s.7(4)).

(b) Application to Exercise Patient's Power of Appointment under Mental Health Act 1983, s.96(1)(k)

Mental Health Act 1983, s.96(1)(k)

6B–64 Under this enactment an order may be made in the Court of Protection for the exercise of any power vested in the patient, whether beneficially, or as guardian or trustee, or otherwise, and a consequential order can be made under *ibid.*, subs.(2). See *Re Fuller* [1900] 2 Ch.551; and *Re Shortridge* [1895] 1 Ch. 278. It is not the practice under this provision to authorise the exercise of functions of the patient in the administration of a trust, the proper course being to remove the patient from the trust.

Mode of application and applicants

For "r. 8) in Form B" substitute: r. 7) in Form A

6B–65 The application is made by way of formal application (r.7) in Form A the Schedule to the Rules. A transaction fee of £110 will be payable, see paras 6B–316 and 6B–337, and if the application is the first in the matter of the patient, a commencement fee of £230 will be payable.

For "r. 19" substitute: r.17

By virtue of r.17, applicants are the same as for an application under s.54(2) of the Trustee Act 1925, and, accordingly, governed by

For "r. 17" substitute: r.15

r.15. Normally, however, the receiver is the sole applicant, but a joint donee of a power should be joined as applicant.

Documents and evidence

6B–66 The formal application should ask that the receiver be authorised in the name and on behalf of the patient to exercise (or concur with A.B. in exercising) the power of appointment vested in the patient (and A.B.) by appointing C.D. (*full name, address and description*) to be a new trustee of the trusts of the will dated   of   (*as the case may be*) and, if necessary, for the purposes of the Settled Land Act 1925; if a vesting order is required it should be asked that any necessary consequential vesting order be made; and costs be provided for.

The following are the main documents and evidence required:
   (i) Two copies of the formal application prepared on Form C.P. 9.
   (ii) Affidavit in support as for an application under s.54(2) of the Trustee Act 1925 (see para. 6B–76).
   (iii) Affidavit of fitness, except where the proposed new trustee is a trust corporation or is the receiver.
   (iv) Special Undertaking by trustees (Form C.P. 14) except where proposed new trustee is a trust corporation; a copy should be attached to the deed of appointment when executed.
   (v) Where the patient is not a trustee and no vesting directions are required, an undertaking by the present trustees to transfer the investments comprised in the trust funds into the names of the new trustees when appointed.

The order

6B–67 The order, if made, will authorise the receiver in the name and on behalf of the patient to exercise the power, and to execute the necessary deed but it is not necessary for the deed to be settled by the court, the court relying on the solicitors as to the accuracy and sufficiency of its contents. Any vesting provision will be dependent and consequent upon the execution of the deed. The order is drafted and settled as on a first application. See paras 6B–22 and 6B–25.

Deed of appointment

6B–68 A fair copy of the Deed of Appointment, and the Supplemental Deed if any required by s.35 of the Settled Land Act 1925, or the further deed (if any) required by s.35 of the Trustee Act 1925, to be executed by the receiver in pursuance of the order should be lodged for record purposes. For the form of the recitals as required by the court, see paras 6B–173 and 6B–179.

Certificate of due execution

6B–69 Where a vesting provision is incorporated the order will read, "That upon the Certificate of the Court of the due execution of the said deed" (*i.e.* the deed appointing the new trustees) etc. (then follow the vesting provisions).

In order to procure this certificate an affidavit by the attesting witness of due execution of the deed by the appointor (exhibiting the deed) must be filed. See Form No. 87, Heywood and Massey, *Court of Protection Practice* (12th ed., 1991), p. 461. Not until the issue of this certificate do the vesting provisions under the order actually take effect.

(c) Application to Exercise Patient's Power of Retirement under Mental Health Act 1983, s.96(1)(k)

Mental Health Act 1983, s.96(1)(k)

6B–70 Under this enactment an order may be made for the exercise of the power conferred upon a patient who is a trustee, by s.39 of the Trustee Act 1925, of retirement from a trust without any appointment of a new trustee in his place, with (if necessary) a consequential vesting order under s.96(2), thus eliminating the patient.

Generally, however, the court prefers that a new trustee should be appointed in place of the patient if he has a beneficial interest. Accordingly, unless the remaining trustee or trustees is or includes a trust corporation, or the trust is practically at an end, or the number of trustees exceeds four, the application is unlikely to be successful. See also *Re Harrison* [1965] 1 W.L.R. 1492.

Mode of application and applicants

6B–71 Generally, as for an application to exercise power of appointment of new trustees (see para. 6B–64); in particular, the co-trustees and such other person, if any, as is empowered to appoint trustees (see the Trustee Act 1925, s.39) must be applicants or otherwise notified of the application. A transaction fee of £110 will be payable (paras and 6B–337) and if the application is the first in the matter of the patient, a commencement fee of £230 will be payable.

Documents and evidence

6B–72 As for an application to exercise a power of appointment of new trustees (see para. 6B–66) save that no affidavit of fitness and consent to act will be required and, the special undertaking (where required) will be given by the remaining trustees.

The order, deed of retirement, certificate of due execution

6B–73 As for an application to exercise a power of appointment of new trustees (see para. 6B–66) save that instead of references to a "deed of appointment", there will be references to a "deed of retirement" and the affidavit of due execution will require to prove the execution by all necessary parties other than execution by corporations within s.74(1) of the Law of Property Act 1925.

(d) Application to Appoint New Trustee under Trustee Act 1925, s.54(2)

Trustee Act 1925, s.54

6B–74 This section, as amended by the Mental Health Act 1983, Sched. 4, para. 4, provides as follows:

"**54.**—(1) Subject to the provisions of this section, the authority having jurisdiction under Part VII of the Mental Health Act 1983, shall not have power to make any order, or give any direction or authority, in relation to a patient who is a trustee if the High Court has power under this Act to make an order to the like effect.

(2) Where a patient is a trustee and a receiver appointed by the said authority is acting for him or an application for the appointment of a receiver has been made but not determined, then, except as respects a trust which is subject to an order for

administration made by the High Court, the said authority shall have concurrent jurisdiction with the High Court in relation to—
    (a) mortgaged property of which the patient has become a trustee merely by reason of the mortgage having been paid off;
    (b) matters consequent on the making of provision by the said authority for the exercise of a power of appointing trustees or retiring from a trust;
    (c) matters consequent on the making of provision by the said authority for the carrying out of any contract entered into by the patient;
    (d) property to some interest in which the patient is beneficially entitled but which, or some interest in which, is held by the patient under an express, implied or constructive trust.
    The Lord Chancellor may make rules with respect to the exercise of the jurisdiction referred to in this subsection.
    (3) In this section "patient" means a patient as defined by section 94(2) of the Mental Health Act 1983, or a person as to whom powers are exercisable and have been exercised under section 98 of that Act."

Part IV of the Trustee Act 1925, confers upon the High Court (or other court, see *ibid.*, s.67) extensive powers in regard to the appointment of new trustees and vesting orders and by virtue of s.54(2) and subject to the provisions thereof, these powers are exercisable in the Court of Protection where a patient is a trustee. As to the meaning of the words "the authority having jurisdiction under Part VII of the Mental Health Act 1983", see *ibid.*, s.111.

Settled Land Act trustees cannot be appointed under this section unless the patient is such a trustee but, where he is such a trustee, a new trustee appointed in his place thereunder is a trustee appointed by the court for the purposes of s.35(2) of the Settled Land Act 1925 (*Re E. F. Jackson*, January 28, 1932, unrep., CA transcript 32/401, *per* Romer L.J.).

Mode of application and applicants

For "Form B (r.8)" substitute: Form A (r.7)

The application is made by way of formal application in Form A (r.7) in the Schedule to the Rules.   **6B–75**

For "r. 17" substitute: r.15

Applicants are governed by r.15 and it should be noted that no person who is a patient should be notified unless and until the court so directs. As regards persons to be notified the practice is that all the trustees, if not applicants, should be notified, as should also the principal beneficiaries in England and Wales, leaving it to the court to direct who else should be notified. On an application for a vesting order only it is not necessary to notify beneficiaries unless in any particular case the court so directs (*Practice Note* [1908] W.N. 75). A donee of the power (other than the patient) should preferably be an applicant.

Documents and evidence

The following are the main documents and evidence required: **6B–76**
    (i) Two copies of the formal application prepared on Form C.P. 9.
    (ii) Affidavit in support (see below).
    (iii) Affidavit of fitness, except where the proposed new trustee is a trust corporation or is the receiver.
    (iv) Special Undertaking by trustee (Form C.P. 14) except where the proposed new trustee is a trust corporation. A copy should be attached to the working copy of the order when completed.

The master directed on October 1, 1959, that paragraphs 1, 2, 3 and 7 of the Practice Direction relating to title to proceedings in the Chancery Division and dated June 18, 1959, shall, so far as applicable, be followed in the Court of Protection (see *Practice Notes* [1959] 2 All E.R. 629 and *Practice Note* [1959] 3 All E.R. 320).

The affidavit in support should:
    (1) State the name, address and description of the applicant and the capacity in which he applies.
    (2) Describe the instrument (if any) creating the trust and set out the main trusts and the investment clause and in the case of land showing whether it is settled or is held upon trust for sale. The original trust instrument should be exhibited and if the original instrument cannot be produced a certified copy should be exhibited and an explanation why the original is not produced (see *Hansell v. Spink* [1943] Ch. 396 as to lost settlement). There is no need to exhibit an original grant of representation.
    (3) Show the devolution of the trust and, in the case of land, the legal estate, and if the

land is settled land whether or not there is a vesting instrument, and, if so, identify it. In the case of a trust arising under a will or intestacy, where the office has changed to that of trustee, show that administration has been completed and that the property in respect of which a vesting order is required is vested in the capacity of trustee and no longer as personal representative (see *Re King* [1964] Ch. 542, and *Re Ponder* [1921] 2 Ch. 59; *Re Yerburgh* [1928] W.N. 208; *Re Pitt* (1928) 44 T.L.R. 371; *Re Cockburn* [1957] Ch. 438).

(4) Define the patient's beneficial interest.

(5) Give the names and addresses of the other beneficiaries, whether in possession or in reversion; if any are minors or patients it should be stated. If a beneficiary has settled or charged his interest particulars should be given and names of the trustees or encumbrancers stated. In showing the devolution of beneficial interests deaths need not be strictly proved.

(6) Set out, with full details, the trust property, showing in whose names the various securities stand, and whether fully paid, and whether registered or in bearer form.

(7) In the case of joint ownership of land being held on December 31, 1925, in undivided shares—whether or not there were at that date any encumbrances effecting undivided shares (see paragraph 1(2) Pt IV, First Schedule to the Law of Property Act 1925).

(8) State the present trustees.

(9) Show all previous changes in the trusteeship, exhibiting all previous deeds of appointment or retirement, which if produced from proper custody are sufficient evidence of their authenticity; the execution need not be proved strictly unless for any reason it is desirable that this should be done. The dates of death of any deceased trustees should be given; a certificate of death must be exhibited in proof unless the death was 20 years prior to the application.

(10) State the names, addresses, ages and descriptions of proposed new trustees.

(11) State the name of the person in whom, and the circumstances in which, the power of appointment of new trustees is vested by the instrument or statute.

(12) State that the trust is not subject to an order for administration in the Chancery Division.

On an application for a vesting order alone consequent upon an appointment of a new trustee out of court, due execution of the deed upon which the application is founded must be proved strictly (see *Re Rice* (1886) 32 Ch.D. 35; and the Evidence Act 1938, s.3) unless it is 20 years old (*ibid.*, s.4) but only if the appointor is not a party to the application or, if a party, does not admit due execution (see also *Practice Note* [1934] W.N. 334).

The order

6B–77 Where an order is made under s.54(2) of the Trustee Act 1925, appointing new trustees and vesting the property, no deed of appointment is necessary; when the order is finally completed any necessary transfers in respect of stocks or shares, etc., should be executed by the new trustees. The order is drafted and settled in the usual way.

A transaction fee of £110 will be payable—see para. 6B–337.

(e) Application for Leave to Appoint New Trustee under Trustee Act 1925, s.36(9)

Trustee Act 1925, s.36(9)

6B–78 This enactment, as amended by the Mental Health Act 1983, Sched. 4, para. 4, provides that where a trustee is incapable by reason of mental disorder within the meaning of the Mental Health Act 1983, of exercising his functions as trustee and is also entitled *in possession* to some beneficial interest in the trust property, no appointment of a new trustee in his place shall be made by virtue of paragraph (b) of subs.(1) of that section unless leave to make the appointment has been given by the authority having jurisdiction under Pt VII of the Mental Health Act 1983. As to the meaning of "the authority," etc., see *ibid.*, s.111.

Mode of application and applicants

For "r. 8" substitute: r.7

6B–79 Where the matter is free from complication the court is usually prepared to grant the certificate of leave under r.7 without the issue of a formal application unless the application is the first in the matter of the patient, where it is by way of formal application in

For "Form B" substitute: Form A
Form A in the Schedule to the Rules.

For "r. 18" substitute: r.16
As to applicants, see r.16. Subject to r.16 and the following notes the procedure is the same as for an application under s.54(2) of the Trustee Act 1925, para. 6B–74.

For "rr. 21(5)(a) and 25" substitute: rr.19(5)(a) and 23
When the application is the first application in the matter the patient is served (Direction of the master, May 9, 1962) *i.e.* with a copy of the application—see rr.19(5)(a) and 23 (para. 6B–258).

Documents and evidence

6B–80 Unless the court concerned otherwise directs, all evidence in support of the application will be by unsworn statements or certificates and relevant documents should be produced without being exhibited (Practice Direction (Court of Protection) February 29, 1968; (1968) 112 S.J. 200).

Otherwise the same documents and evidence are required as for an application under s.54(2) of the Trustee Act 1925 (see para. 6B–76). Where no receiver has been appointed (or applied for) the evidence should give such particulars and information as are known of the patient's property and circumstances and medical evidence as to the patient's incapacity to exercise his function as trustee is required.

Certificate of leave

6B–81 The leave of the ourt is manifested by a certificate, a draft of which, if necessary, is sent to the solicitor. A transaction fee of £110 is payable and, if the application is the first in the matter of the patient, a commencement fee of £230.

Deed of appointment

6B–82 The deed will no longer require to be settled by the court, the court relying on the Solicitors for the accuracy and sufficiency of the contents (see para. 6B–173). For recitals, see para. 6B–179.

MANAGEMENT AND ADMINISTRATION

Maintenance

For "PTO" substitute: PGO

6B–83 The maintenance of the patient is the first consideration and will have priority over the creditors (*Re Plenderleith* [1893] 3 Ch. 332; and *Re Winkle* [1894] 2 Ch. 519); but the maintenance of his wife will not (*Re Winkle*). If the income is insufficient resort may be made to capital. The principle to be followed is that laid down in *Tye's Case* [1900] 1 Ch. 249, that the first object of the court and the PGO is to use the patient's property for his support. See also s.95 of the Mental Health Act 1983 (para. 6B–189) and r.66 (para.). The extent to which this is done out of capital in addition to income will depend on the age of the patient, the cost of maintenance, and the amount of his property. When there is every probability that he can be maintained out of interest and capital for his whole life, this should be done instead of creating a charge on his property enforceable at his death.

The coming into force of the National Health Service Act 1946, on July 5, 1948, brought to an end chargeability to local authorities in respect of the maintenance of patients maintained in mental hospitals, and consequently the question will only require to be considered in regard to liability arising prior to that date and in regards to patients in residential accommodation provided under Pt III of the National Assistance Act 1948, and, possibly, under s.21 of the National Health Service Act 1977. In the case of a rate-aided patient, the authority to whom he was chargeable could claim six years' past maintenance (*Re Newbegin* (1887) 36 Ch.D. 477; *Re Watson, Stamford Union v. Bartlett* [1899] 1 Ch. 72; see also *Re T.R.M.* [1939] Ch. 260) and in such cases the court was usually prepared to direct payment of such arrears or give a charge therefor, as the case might require.

Directions in regard to the maintenance of the patient are given in the first order. Any capital required to supplement income is usually raised annually.

Voluntary allowances

For "PTO" substitute: PGO

6B–84 Voluntary allowances are made out of the patient's estate in a proper case, especially if they have previously been made by the patient himself (see s.95(1)(c) of the Mental Health Act 1983). When applying for such an allowance a full disclosure should be made to the PGO of the applicant's means and circumstances.

As to bringing voluntary allowances into hotchpot see *Re Gist* [1906] 2 Ch. 280; and *Re Merrall* [1924] 1 Ch. 45.

Investments

For "PTO" substitute: PGO

6B–85 The provisions of the Trustee Investment Act 1961 do not apply to the investments of patients under the jurisdiction of the court. Nevertheless the court and the PGO bear in mind that they are dealing with the moneys of persons incapable of expressing their own wishes and consider a reasonably conservative policy should be adopted. The investments chosen by the patient prior to his incapacity are not disturbed without sufficient reason.

Advice on policy is given by an independent Honorary Investment Advisory Committee appointed by the Lord Chancellor, which meets at regular intervals. The court also has the services of a panel of stockbrokers. Normally, the periodic review of a patient's investments is referred to the brokers unless the receiver prefers to consult his own brokers.

Each estate is considered on its merits; and an investment policy laid down taking into account the age of the patient, his income requirements, whether resort to capital will be necessary, and so on. The first duty is to the patient himself, but subject to this the objective is to preserve the real value of the estate for the benefit of all concerned. Where a patient's income is likely to exceed by a reasonable margin the foreseeable total annual expenditure, future investment or a portfolio review may well be on the basis of what will be most beneficial for those who will take on the patient's death.

The Committee has recommended that unless the particular circumstances of an estate otherwise require, the investments of a patient should consist partly of fixed interest securities and partly of equities. What is the proper proportion of one to the other will chiefly depend on the period during which the court can expect to exercise jurisdiction. If the period is likely to be a long one, say 10 years or more, it would be reasonable to have up to about two-thirds in equities and one-third in fixed interest securities. The shorter the period the smaller should be the proportion of equities. Generally where the funds are not sufficiently large to warrant an individual investment portfolio the court favours investment in the Common Investment Funds (para. 6B–86), unit trusts and investment trust, thus securing "spread" of investment and investment management.

The balance of a portfolio should not be changed merely because by lapse of time the expected duration of the court's jurisdiction has become short.

Common investment funds

6B–86 Funds lodged in court may, but not necessarily, be invested in accordance with the Common Investment Funds Scheme under Pt VI of the Administration of Justice Act 1982: there are now two types of trust units, *i.e.* Capital and High Yield. The scheme now has a private sector manager. The unit prices are published in *The Financial Times* in the "F.T. Unit Trust Information Service".

The Capital Fund is substantially an equity fund. The High Yield Fund is a mixed fund of fixed interest stock and equities. It follows that an investment in the Capital Fund (as at present constituted) is to be regarded as an investment in equities.

These funds have certain advantages over other unit trusts. In particular, no initial charge is made on new purchases and the annual charge compares very favourably with the charges made by most commercial trusts. No brokerage or commission is payable.

In these circumstances the Committee had advised that where capital growth is required and income is not of primary importance, the whole of any cash requiring to be invested in equities can properly be invested in the Capital Fund. In a particular estate it may be possible to make out a case for investment in individual undertakings but in the normal course the court will expect the Capital Fund to be used.

When income is of importance an alternative to investing in the High Yield Fund is to invest part in the Capital Fund and to make up the required income by investing the balance in suitably chosen fixed-interest stock.

The only person who can hold such Common Investment Fund units is the Accountant General and they are not transferable. They must therefore either remain in court in the name of the Accountant General or be realised and the proceeds paid to the person entitled. Accordingly, upon determination of the proceedings on death or recovery, any units forming part of the fund in court must be realised.

Sale and purchase of property

For "PTO" substitute: PGO

6B–87 The court or the PGO may direct the sale and purchase of any property on the patients' behalf (s.96(1)(b) and (c) of the Mental Health Act 1983).

A specific direction in the order appointing the receiver, or in a subsequent order or a separate direction under seal, is normally necessary in regard to a sale of any sort, and where the property to be sold is land (either freehold or leasehold) an order is invariably necessary. Before directing the sale of any property, the court desires to know whether the property has been specifically bequeathed or devised by the will of the patient. Section 101(1) and (3) of the Mental Health Act 1983, automatically prevents ademption on a sale under an order of the court, and where it is desirable to identify the proceeds, the proceeds may be lodged to a special credit or otherwise earmarked (see para. 6B–111).

Under s.96(1)(k) of the Act, an order may be made for the receiver to exercise on behalf of a patient mortgagee a power of sale under the mortgage (see para. 6B–108) or his power to sell as tenant for life under the Settled Land Act 1925 (see para. 6B–100).

Practice as to sale of land and house property

6B–88 Unless the receiver has already been authorised to sell the property in the First General Order, or an Interim Order for Sale has been issued, it will be necessary to apply by letter for an Order authorising the sale. The letter should be accompanied by a statement showing the reasons for the proposed sale and confirming that the title is in order (*i.e.* that the patient has a good and marketable title to the property, the same being vested in him as (beneficial owner) (tenant for life within the meaning of the Settled Land Act 1925) in which capacity he offers it for sale). This course is suitable either for a sale by private treaty or by auction. Where the solicitors are unfamiliar with the patient's affairs and the land to be dealt with is not registered land, a search in the Land Charges Register is advisable before confirming the position as to title.

Note

6B–89 It should be borne in mind, when asking for office copies of the order or direction authorising sale, that one will have to be handed to the purchaser on completion.

Once an order or direction for sale has been made the following points should be noted:

1. For a sale by private treaty

For "PTO" substitute: PGO

6B–90 The court does not require to approve the terms of the contract itself (other than the purchase price), it being the responsibility of the solicitors acting in the sale to ensure that the contract is adequate in all respects. Usually a certificate of value (see para. 6B–175) by the selling agent should be lodged as soon as it is decided to sell the property in question and the approval of the PGO of the proposed asking price sought unless there are exceptional circumstances (see *below*). It would be as well if the certificate were to state the lowest acceptable price that could reasonably be expected for the property because if that price is approved, then it follows that any higher offer may be accepted without further reference to the PGO. If the highest offer obtained is less than the figure given in the certificate the approval of the PGO must be sought for the sale to proceed at the lower figure. If the property has been put on the market prior to any application and approval is sought merely to a price already negotiated, then the certificate will state merely that the price is, in the agent's judgment and opinion, the full and fair value of the property, and fully as much as would probably be obtained therefore at a sale by public auction and recommending confirmation. The certificate is to be given by a *qualified valuer* whose qualifications must be stated or by *someone with at least five years' experience* with his present firm or another firm practising in the locality. The following professional qualifications of valuers are acceptable to the court: FRICS, ARICS, FSVA and ASVA.

After "exceptional by the Court" delete: or PTO.

In exceptional circumstances, *e.g.* the sale or purchase of business property, or where a receiver is buying from a patient or there is some similar inter-family transaction or other circumstances deemed to be exceptional by the court , *a sworn affidavit of value by a qualified valuer* will be required before approval to the price can be given.

After "an order of the Court of Protection" delete: or a direction of the Public Trustee dated the ..... 19...

A contract (which should not contain any reference to mental disorder) should be entered into by the vendor acting by the receiver (or other named person) pursuant to an order of the Court of Protection. Subject to any necessary adaptation, the following special conditions should be included:—

(1) The amount of the deposit shall be £10 per cent of the purchase money and shall be paid to Messrs. ...... [*the solicitors in the matter*] as stakeholders.

(2) The vendor as (beneficial owner) (tenant for life) is selling by his receiver pursuant to an order of the Court of Protection

After "an order of the Court of Protection" delete: or a direction of the Public Trustee dated the ..... 19....

and an office-copy of the said order or of the relevant portion thereof will be handed over on completion and shall be deemed to be conclusive evidence of such authority to sell and the purchaser(s) shall not require the production of or make any requisition or objection in relation to any evidence matter or thing referred to in the said order or otherwise relating thereto.

(3) The purchase money shall be paid as directed or authorised by the relevant order or other direction of the court

After "other direction of the Court" delete: or the Public Trustee.

Notes

(i) The court will rely entirely upon the solicitors for the accuracy and sufficiency of the contents of the contract and the draft particulars and conditions will not be settled or approved by the court.

(ii) The address of the vendor (if inserted) should be his home address or that of the receiver, never that of an institution.

(iii) As to preparation of the conveyance or transfer, see paras 6B–174 and 6B–183.

(iv) Restrictive or other covenants. If the property is subject to any such covenants, the conditions should provide that the property will be sold "and will be conveyed" subject thereto and (unless it is clear that the vendor will not remain liable after parting with the property) that the purchaser shall in the conveyance enter into a covenant for indemnity in respect thereof.

At end of renumbered paragraph 6B-90 delete link line: [THE NEXT PARAGRAPH IS 6B-92].

2. Special condition on sale of leasehold property

6B–91 In an assignment on sale of leasehold property by an assignor who is expressed to convey "as beneficial owner" there is implied a covenant (*inter alia*) that all the covenants of the lease have been observed up to the time of the assignment; see the Law of Property Act 1925, Sched. II, Pt II; the Land Registration Act 1925, s.24(1)(a). It is, of course, notorious that covenants for repair and decoration are seldom completely performed at any given moment, and the purchaser is probably well aware of the actual condition of the property; but liability under the implied convenants depends not on knowledge of the grantee but on what is actually expressed in the conveyance. It is therefore important that the implied covenants should be restricted when it is known or suspected that there has been a breach of covenant.

In ordinary cases, therefore, every contract for the sale of leasehold property on behalf of a patient should contain a clause to the following effect:

"The purchaser shall in the assurance of the property covenant to indemnify the vendor and the vendor's estate and effects from and against all subsisting and future liabilities arising out of the state of repair and condition of the property and the assurance shall contain a declaration negativing any implied covenant by the vendor that the covenants contained in the said lease (underlease) and relating to the repair decoration painting or condition of the property have been performed."

3. For a sale by public auction

After "order of the Court of Protection" delete: or direction of the Public Trustee.

6B–92 The sale may be advertised as being made "by order of the Court of Protection ." The particulars and conditions of sale must not contain any reference to mental disorder or the name of the patient. Subject to any necessary adaptation the special conditions are set out in 1. above.

For "PTO" substitute: PGO

Not less than seven days before the date of the auction there should be lodged with the PGO for the purpose of fixing the reserves a certificate by an agent or deponent as to value and recommending reserves (and lotting, if necessary). The reserve biddings, as fixed by the PGO, will be forwarded to the auctioneer in a sealed envelope to be opened at the time of the sale and not before.

The result of the auction should be reported to the PGO as soon as possible by letter enclosing a certificate by the auctioneer showing the date of the sale, the purchaser's name and the purchase price.

Settlement and approval of the assurance

It is no longer necessary for draft deeds to be settled and approved by the court, the court relying on the solicitors for the accuracy and sufficiency of the contents. **6B–93**

Entry to property prior to completion

Upon exchange of contracts, no objection will be raised by the court to the purchaser being allowed: **6B–94**

  (i) to enter into occupation of the property prior to completion, provided that the contract contains a relevant condition similar to that in the National Conditions of Sale or the Law Society's General Conditions, and the solicitors for the patient take all necessary steps to safeguard patient's interest.

  (ii) access to the property to effect repairs or decorations prior to completion, provided the contract contains a provision or there is a subsequent agreement by the purchasers to the effect that if for any reason whether due to the default of the vendor or not the contract is not completed, the purchaser shall not have any claim against the vendor in respect of work done and the purchaser shall make good at his own expense any damage to the property.

Proceeds of sale

For "PTO" substitute: PGO

On completion, a statement should be forwarded to the PGO showing the approximate amount of the purchase money available for investment, after allowing for the payment off of any encumbrances and a reserve to cover costs and estate agents' charges. Solicitors will normally be asked to give an undertaking to receive the purchase money and deal with it as directed by the PGO. Pending the issue of directions by the PGO the proceeds of sale *must* be placed on deposit in the solicitor's name at the highest rate of interest available to him for deposits subject to the minimum period of notice for withdrawal. **6B–95**

Fees

A Transaction Fee of £145 is payable when dealing with the sale of property on behalf of a patient. See paras 6B–316 and 6B–337. **6B–96**

Purchase of property for the patient

For "PTO" substitute: PGO

As in paras 6B–88 and 6B–89, unless authority has already been obtained for purchase of property it will be necessary to apply to the PGO by letter for a direction authorising the purchase. The letter should be accompanied by a statement showing the reasons for the purchase and the approximate amount of the intended expenditure. If approval is given, an order or direction will issue authorising the receiver to purchase such freehold or leasehold property as the PGO shall approve. **6B–97**

Once an order or direction for purchase has been made, negotiations may proceed up to the exchange of contracts. However the PGO will need to approve the purchase price, and a certificate of value together with a surveyor's report should be lodged (see paras 6B–90 and 6B–91). The evidence of value should be to the effect that the price represents the fair market value of the property (see para. 6B–175).

Thereafter the procedure follows along similar lines as for a sale of property. If the patient is not an executing party, no reference should be made in the assurance to the fact that the purchaser is a patient, or that the purchase is proceeding pursuant to an order of the Court of Protection or direction of the Public Trustee or that the purchaser is acting by a receiver.

Estate agent's charges

1. The charges of estate agents and auctioneers selling freehold or leasehold property **6B–98**

pursuant to orders of the Chancery Division, Family Division, the Court of Protection, or divorce county courts will normally be considered reasonable by the court if they do not exceed the rate of commission which that agent would normally charge on a sole agency basis, and if they do not exceed $2^{1}/_{2}$ per cent of the sale price, exclusive of value added tax.

For "PTO" substitute: PGO

2. These charges are to include all commission, valuations, expenses and other disbursements, including making affidavits, the cost of advertising, and all other work except surveys. The allowance for a survey will be at the discretion of the PGO.

3. If:
   (a) an agent's charges do not fall within the limits set out in para. 1; or
   (b) there is a sale of any investment property, business property, or farm property; or
   (c) a property is sold in lots or by valuation,
an application must be made to the PGO to authorise the fee to be charged.

4. The limits set out in paras 1 and 2 above do not apply to sales of property for patients of the Court of Protection where an agreement has been concluded with the estate agent before the jurisdiction of the court has been invoked.

5. In matrimonial cases, either where the party who has been condemned in these costs has not agreed to the increased rate, or where the costs fall to be paid out of the legal aid fund, the higher charges will be subject to the discretion of the taxing officer.

6. This Practice Direction applies to all instructions for sale which are placed with estate agents and auctioneers after January 1, 1983.

Practice Direction (Estate Agents' and Auctioneers' Fees) (No.2) [1972] 1 W.L.R. 1431 and Practice Direction (Family Division: Sale of Land) [1972] 1 W.L.R. 1471 are hereby revoked.

By direction of the Vice-Chancellor and the President of the Family Division and with the concurrence of the Lord Chancellor.

(Practice Direction, December 22, 1982 [1983] 1 W.L.R. 86; (1983) 127 S.J. 40.)

Joint tenant and tenant in common

6B–99 When a patient holds land with other co-owners upon trust for sale, a new trustee must be appointed in his place or he must be otherwise discharged from the trust before the legal estate is dealt with under the trust for sale or under the powers vested in the trustees for sale (s.22(2) of the Law of Property Act 1925). By s.36(9) of the Trustee Act 1925, the leave of the court is required before any such appointment is made in a case by virtue of s.36(1)(b) where the patient has a beneficial interest in possession. For procedure, see para. 6B–18.

In view of the undertaking required to be filed on the making of the application for leave to appoint a new trustee not to sell without first obtaining approval as to price and to deal with the patient's share of the proceeds as may be directed, directions must be obtained before any sale by the new trustees. The same evidence as to value will be required as on a sale of the patient's absolute property (see paras 6B–90 and 6B–91).

A sale of the patient's beneficial interest in property (either as joint tenant or tenant in common) to a third party can, of course, be ordered at any time, but a new trustee in place of the patient will sometimes be required if the legal estate is not to remain outstanding. If, however, the purchaser is the co-owner it may also be possible to assure the patient's interest in the legal estate, inasmuch as it would not appear that such a transaction would be invalidated by s.22(2) of the Law of Property Act 1925. Generally see Heywood and Massey, *Court of Protection Practice* (12th ed., 1991) pp. 163–164.

Tenant for life

6B–100 The jurisdiction to authorise the exercise of a patient's powers as tenant for life derives from s.96(1)(k) of the Mental Health Act 1983.

In view of s.13 of the Settled Land Act 1925, the principal powers of the tenant for life cannot be exercised until the requisite vesting instrument has been executed. An authority under seal to procure the execution of the necessary vesting instrument will be issued. If execution of such instrument on behalf of the patient is unnecessary no reference to incapacity is to be made. Where the land is leasehold or freehold subject to a rent or covenants, and if execution on behalf of the patient is required, the authority will authorise the receiver in the name and on behalf of the patient to execute. In either case the draft vesting instrument must be submitted to the court for approval.

The prior leave of the court is required before any notices under s.101 of the Settled

Land Act 1925, can be given (*Re Ray's Settled Estates* (1884) 25 Ch.D. 464) where a sale of settled property is contemplated. The procedure to be followed is similar to that of a sale of the patient's absolute property under a general order (see paras 6B–88 and 6B–89). That order will authorise the receiver to give all necessary notices required by s.101 of the Settled Land Act 1925. The proceeds will be received by the trustees as capital moneys who will also be responsible for the payment of the taxed costs of the application and order and of the sale.

Generally, see Heywood and Massey, *Court of Protection Practice* (12th ed., 1991), pp. 151 (Leases) and 160 (Sales).

Business

6B–101 Under s.96(1)(f) of the Mental Health Act 1983, the court may direct the carrying on by a suitable person of any profession trade or business of the patient, and in such a case the following detailed directions to the receiver are usually incorporated in the order and should be strictly adhered to:

(a) To procure forthwith a valuation of the (stock in trade) (and fixtures and fittings) (and live and dead stock) as on the date hereof or as near thereto as may be possible (such valuation to be made by a competent valuer at a fee to be agreed and sanctioned by the court beforehand) and to file the same with the court at the earliest possible moment and to report to the court at the expiration of three months from the date thereof as to the position and prospects of the business.

(b) To open a new banking account earmarked for the business and to use such account exclusively for transactions relating to such business.

(c) To open a second new banking account earmarked for the receivership generally and to use such account for all receipts and payments not relating to the said business.

(d) No overdraft is to be incurred nor any existing overdraft increased in respect of either of the said banking accounts except under an authority bearing the seal of the court.

(e) The business account is not to be drawn upon except for purposes wholly relating to the business (except when profits are sufficient to permit drawings therefrom to be made for the credit of the receivership account) and the receivership account is not to be drawn upon for purposes of the business.

(f) In the event of drawings being made from the business on account of profits a cheque is to be drawn upon the business account in favour of the receivership account.

(g) To keep proper books of account of the said business.

(h) In the event of the court authorising the carrying on of the business after the expiration of the said period of three months to cause a balance sheet and profit and loss account to be prepared annually (generally by accountants) and such balance sheet and profit and loss account together with a report upon the said business are to be submitted to the court (within one month after the close of the account)(with the annual receivership account).

A receiver carrying on the business of the patient, under an order of the court, cannot be made personally liable for trade debts unless it can be shown that he held himself out as principal (*Plumpton v. Burkinshaw* [1908] 2 K.B. 572).

Dissolution of partnership

6B–102 The Court of Protection may order the dissolution of a partnership of which the patient is a member (s.96(1)(g) of the Mental Health Act 1983) but will only do so where there is a receiver and there are no partnership disputes; otherwise it may be necessary to apply in the Chancery Division. In any event the receiver may be authorised to give notice to dissolve, etc.

Limited companies

6B–103 It is not the practice, save in exceptional circumstances, to authorise the exercise by a receiver of a patient's voting rights in respect of his shareholding in a public company, but where he is a substantial shareholder in a private company other considerations will apply, *e.g.* whether he holds a controlling interest, or his holding is sufficiently substantial to influence the running of the company.

If the patient is a director of the company it may be that his mental incapacity disqualifies him from continuing to act as a director in which case the court will consider whether he should be replaced as a director by his receiver or some other person nominated by the court. In any case, it is important that his directorship be relinquished if only to avoid the possibility of his incurring any personal liability for misfeasance or breach of trust committed by his fellow directors during his incapacity.

Following his removal from directorship the possibility of his being granted a pension by the company should be explored.

Where it is desired to replace the patient as a director by the receiver or some other person, *e.g.* his accountant or solicitor, to enable the court to exercise control on the more important aspects of the company's affairs, the receiver will be authorised to exercise the patient's voting rights to procure such election. When necessary the receiver will be authorised to transfer to himself sufficient shares to enable him to qualify as a director, upon his undertaking to credit the patient's account with the dividends thereon and to retransfer the shares to the patient and to resign from the directorship if and when directed by the court to do so. Any remuneration received by the receiver in respect of the directorship will belong to him in his own right.

The Court's Order will also provide for the exercise by the receiver of the patient's voting rights in respect of the remainder of the patient's shares in the company but, as to certain matters, only subject to the prior approval of the court. Such matters are (a) borrowing (b) increase or reduction of capital (c) alterations or amendments of or additions to the Memorandum and Articles of Association of the company (d) fixing director's fees (e) appointment or removal of directors (f) winding up (g) sale of assets or goodwill (h) entering into partnership with any person or company.

The above specific limitations as to voting will normally be included in any order where, the patient being a large shareholder in a private company, the receiver is authorised to exercise the patient's voting rights.

The basic information required to be supplied to enable the court to consider the patient's position is:

(a) The total issued capital of the company.
(b) The number of shares held by the patient.
(c) The number of shares held by the other major shareholders.
(d) The number of shares (if any) required to be held by a director.
(e) The auditors' report and accounts of the company covering the three years previous to the application.
(f) A copy of the Memorandum and Articles of Association.
(g) A list of the present directors of the company.

Leases and surrenders

6B–104   The jurisdiction to authorise the granting of leases and accept surrenders derives from s.96(1)(b) and (c) of the Mental Health Act 1983.

A receiver by the order appointing him may sometimes be authorised to let property for periods not exceeding three years, but if there is a probability that sale may become desirable such authority will not be included. For longer periods an order may be required.

For "PTO" substitute: PGO

To obtain an order to grant a lease application should be made by letter setting out the facts. The order or direction will be an open order authorising the receiver, subject to the approval of the court or PGO, in the name and on behalf of the patient to grant a lease of the property in question and for that purpose to execute such documents as shall be necessary. When the proposed lease has been agreed the draft should be submitted to the court together with evidence of the sufficiency of the rent and the desirability of the terms by certificate of the estate agent. The draft should be exhibited to the evidence.

Performance of a contract

6B–105   The court may direct the carrying out of any contract entered into by the patient, either prior to incapacity or during incapacity (s.96(1)(h) of the Mental Health Act 1983). The adoption of a voidable contract for the purchase (and *semble,* sale) of freehold property entered into prior to the proceedings works conversion as from the date of the contract (*Baldwyn v. Smith* [1900] Ch. 588).

See also s.54(2)(c) of the Trustee Act 1925.

Exercise of power (including power to consent)

6B–106   Any such power may be exercised under s.96(1)(k) of the Mental Health Act 1983. It should be noted that powers of a patient as patron of a benefice are exercisable by the Lord Chancellor only and all inquiries in regard thereto should be made to The Lord Chancellor's Ecclesiastical Secretary, 10 Downing Street, London, SW1A 2AA.

Among the powers exercisable under this provision are the powers of a patient as tenant for life; the powers of a patient as mortgagee; power to bar an entail (see *Re Pares* (1879) 12 Ch.D. 333; *Re E. D. S.* [1914] 1 Ch. 618, and *Re R. H. C.* [1963] 1 W.L.R. 1095); power to appoint in favour of children (*Re A.* [1904] 2 Ch. 328); powers of guardianship of an infant child (*Re L. H. B.* [1935] 1 Ch. 643); the exercise of a power to appoint trustee (*Re Fuller* [1900] 2 Ch. 551).

The question whether the Court of Protection could authorise a receiver, on behalf of a patient, to give his consent under s.2(1)(d) of the Divorce Reform Act 1969 (now s.1(2)(d) of the Matrimonial Causes Act 1973) was raised in *Mason v. Mason* [1972] Fam. 302; [1972] 3 All E.R. 315. The President declined to say whether the Court of Protection could give such authority.

A transaction fee of £110 will be payable in most cases. See paras and 6B–337.

Grant of administration

If a patient is entitled to apply for a grant of representation to the estate of a deceased **6B–107** person, authority may be given by the Court of Protection for the receiver to apply for a grant for the use and benefit of the patient during his incapacity. Generally, see Heywood and Massey, *Court of Protection Practice* (12th ed., 1991) pp. 237 *et seq.* and the Non-Contentious Probate Rules 1987, r.35.

Where a patient is entitled to a grant but, either because no receiver has been appointed or for some other reason, no person has been authorised by the Court of Protection to apply for a grant or there is no lawful attorney acting under a registered enduring power of attorney and an application is being made for a grant under r.35(2)(c) of the Non-Contentious Probate Rules 1987, notice of the intended application is required to be given to the Court of Protection under r.35(5). The notice should include the name and address of the proposed administrator, his relationship to the deceased and the patient and short particulars of the deceased's estate and the extent of the patient's interest therein, and any proposals for dealing therewith for the benefit of the patient. The formal sealed acknowledgment issued by the court should be produced to the Probate Registry.

Patient mortgagee

Delete "or PTO".

Powers of a patient as mortgagee are exercisable under ss.95(1) and 96(1)(k) of the **6B–108** Mental Health Act 1983. An order or direction for the execution of a statutory receipt or reconveyance where the patient is beneficially entitled as mortgagee is applied for by letter (unless the court otherwise directs). The following undertaking should be included in the letter of application: "We undertake to produce on the hearing of the application the mortgage referred to in the within written application and any transfer of the said mortgage." The application must be supported by an affidavit by a solicitor dealing with (i) the patient's title to the mortgage and who is entitled to give a receipt; (ii) the title to the immediate equity of redemption and in whom vested; (iii) who is entitled to receive the deeds bearing in mind any subsequent incumbrances; and (iv) the amount due under the mortgage (capital and arrears of interest) bearing in mind any further advances, etc., or any moneys applied to protect the security.

The mortgagor should not be served, and if served is not entitled to his costs out of the patient's estate (*Re Phillips* (1869) L.R. 4 Ch.App. 629; and *Re Wheeler* (1852) 1 De G.M. & G. 434). The order or direction directs the receiver in the name and on behalf of the patient to execute the statutory receipt or to reconvey or transfer.

If the patient is one of several co-mortgagees and all of such mortgagees are living and each mortgagee is entitled to a definite amount of the mortgage money application can be made in the Court of Protection for the patient by his receiver to concur in the statutory receipt or transfer as the case may be, otherwise the appropriate proceedings must be taken for the appointment of a new trustee in place of the patient.

For form of statutory receipt see para. 6B–177.

In a proper case an order will be made for the advance of the patient's money on mortgage. The application would have to be supported by evidence as to value and the proposed advance should not normally exceed two-thirds of such valuation.

An application for sale by the patient as mortgagee would proceed substantially in the same manner as an application for sale of property belonging to a patient absolutely (paras 6B–87 *et seq.*); it must be shown that the power of sale has arisen.

Patient mortgagor

Delete "or the PTO".

6B–109 When a patient is the mortgagor of any of his property the mortgagee should communicate with the receiver or his solicitor if the question arises of enforcing the mortgage or any of the covenants arising thereunder. Under s.96(1)(b) of the Mental Health Act 1983, the court can authorise the charging or other disposition of or dealing with any property of the patient. Application is made by letter (unless otherwise directed).

Improvements

6B–110 When the patient is tenant for life and it is desired to expend money on improvements upon the settled property application should be made for leave for the receiver in the name and on behalf of the patient tenant for life to execute the required improvement, to give a direction to the Settled Land Act trustees for payment pursuant to s.75 of the Settled Land Act 1925, and, if there are no capital moneys available in the hands of the Settled Land Act trustees, to raise the money required on the security of the settled land or of any part thereof by a legal mortgage (Settled Land Act 1925, s.71(1)); or the application could be made for the money required to be advanced out of the patient's capital and a mortgage given by the trustees to the patient to secure the amount advanced (Settled Land Act 1925, s.68).

Preservation of interests in patient's property

6B–111 This is now governed by s.101 of the Mental Health Act 1983, to which reference should be made (para. 6B–198). Section 123(1) of the Lunacy Act 1890 which was replaced in the main by the Mental Health Act 1959, s.107, only applied to transactions wherein the element of conversion into money was present and did not apply, *e.g.* to the investment of money (*Re Walker* [1921] 2 Ch. 63) purchase of property (*Re Searle* [1912] 2 Ch. 365) and lodgment in court of funds *in specie* (*Re Palmer* [1945] Ch. 8). The definition of "disposal" in subs. (3) nullifies the effect of these decisions. See Sched. 5, para. 45 as to retrospective effect of s.101(1).

The paramount consideration is the interest of the patient, and the court pays no regard to those who come after, but in matters outside the ordinary course of management it is the duty of the court, so far as possible, not to alter the character of the patient's property or to interfere with any rights of succession (*Att.-Gen. v. Ailesbury* (1887) 12 App. Cas. 672).

As to proceeds of sale of real estate descending as realty, see *Re Matson* [1897] 2 Ch. 509; *Re Tugwell* (1885) 27 Ch.D. 309; *Re Alston* [1917] 2 Ch. 226.

When it is desired to relieve a legatee from the incidence of duty upon freehold property which has been purchased out of personal property bequeathed to the legatee (his interest being automatically preserved under s.101(1)) the court can give a direction under subs. (2) *ibid.*, that the property purchased shall, as long as it remains the property of the patient or forms part of his estate, be treated as personal property. The converse case of sale of real property and the acquisition in its place of personal property requires no direction of the court, and under subs. (1)(b) the property purchased would automatically be treated as real property.

As to devolution to the heir of a pre-1926 patient's interest in realty on his death intestate, without having recovered his testamentary capacity, see Administration of Estates Act 1925, s.51(2).

Creditors

6B–112 See ss.95(2) and 96(1)(i) of the Mental Health Act 1983. During the receivership proceedings the creditors are without remedy. They cannot obtain any payment unless the court in the exercise of its discretion, makes an order in their favour (*Re Seager Hunt* [1906] 2 Ch. 299). The patient's interest comes first, and if necessary the creditors will be ignored (*Re Plenderleith* [1893] 3 Ch. 332) or they can obtain a charging order under s.96(1)(b) and (j) of Mental Health Act 1983. After the patient's death the High Court, in administering his estate, will not be bound by any order of the Court of Protection directing payment of a dividend to creditors (*Re Seager Hunt* [1906] 2 Ch. 295); see also *Re Wheater* [1928] 1 Ch. 223. A creditor who is entitled to interest is to have it at 4 per cent together with the costs of proving his claim (*Re Hunt* [1902] 2 Ch. 318).

Where the property of a patient has become subject to the control of the Court of Protection by the appointment of a receiver, it cannot be seized under a writ of *fi. fa.* by an execution creditor of the patient; and the court will make an order dealing with his property, and for the payment thereout of costs and of an allowance for the maintenance of the patient—though not of his wife—in priority to any claim of the execution creditor; but subject to such allowance and to the costs incurred in relation to the patient's property, the order will be made without prejudice to any charge or priority which the creditor may have acquired by lodging his writ of *fi. fa.* with the sheriff (*Re Winkle* [1894] 2 Ch. 519, CA). An interim order has been made for the express purpose of protecting the patient's property from execution (*Re Pountain* (1888) 37 Ch.D. 609). Nevertheless, the jurisdiction of the Court of Protection does not interfere with the common law or statutory rights of a judgment creditor over funds which have not been brought within the control of the Court of Protection (*Re Brown* [1900] 1 Ch. 489) or with the rights of creditors to seize and sell by legal process property of the patient which at the time of seizure is not in the custody of such court, and the issuing of an application in the Court of Protection does not withdraw the property of the patient from such legal process by a creditor until an order is made showing that the court has actually taken the property under its protection (*Re Charles Clarke* [1898] 1 Ch. 336, CA, distinguishing *Re Winkle*). Further, an order authorising a person therein specified, in the name and on behalf of the patient to receive and give a discharge for all sums of money due to him, does not affect rights against the patient's property at law or in equity (such as a vendor's lien for unpaid purchase money) previously acquired by third persons (*Davies v. Thomas* [1900] 2 Ch. 462, explaining and distinguishing *Re Winkle*).

The Court of Protection will not normally pay statute barred debts (*Re Kenrick* [1907] 1 Ir. Ch. 480) but will recognise an honourable obligation on the part of the patient, and will order payment by way of bounty (*Re Whitaker* (1889) 42 Ch.D. 119). As to the admission of claims for the maintenance of what were formerly rate-aided patients, see "Maintenance," para. 6B–83.

For "PTO" substitute: PGO

Debts properly incurred by a receiver under the direction of the court or PGO will be paid; such debts are the liability of the patient and not of the receiver, unless he expressly pledges his credit (*Plumpton v. Burkinshaw* [1908] 2 K.B. 572; *Re E. G.* [1914] 1 Ch. 927).

Charging order

6B–113 A charging order of the High Court under O.50 may be obtained against property of a patient in respect of a judgment for debts incurred before incapacity, and may be enforced against the estate of the patient after his death; for the effect of a charging order does not depend upon the capacity of the judgment debtor to give a valid charge but upon the validity of the judgment (*Re Leavesley* [1891] 2 Ch. 1, CA). The High Court is not precluded from giving effect to a charging order made by it upon the interest of a patient in a fund in the High Court during his life without regard to his needs where that fund has not been brought within the control of the Court of Protection, and the balance only of the funds after satisfying the charge, will be transferred to Court of Protection administration (*Re Brown* [1900] 1 Ch. 489; see also *Horne v. Pountain* (1889) 23 Q.B.D. 264). On the other hand, where the fund in court is under the control of the Court of Protection that court will order a proper allowance for the maintenance of the patient to be made out of the capital and income of the fund, though the effect may be to make the capital insufficient for the payment of the creditors who have obtained charging orders on the fund, and such creditors are not entitled to have impounded an amount of capital sufficient to meet their demands (*Re Plenderleith* [1893] 3 Ch. 332). Whether the obtaining of a charging order is, under such circumstances, of any value, *quaere.* See remarks of Lindley L.J., in *Re Plenderleith* [1893] 3 Ch. 332; *cf. Re Winkle* [1894] 2 Ch. 519; *Re Seager Hunt* [1900] 2 Ch. 54; and *C. L. v. C. F. W.* [1928] P. 223 at 225.

O.50, does not apply to Court of Protection charging orders made under s.96(1)(b) and (j) of the Mental Health Act 1983 (*Re Cathcart* [1893] 1 Ch. 466, CA).

It is now the normal practice, though discretionary, for charging orders of the Court of Protection to carry simple interest at the judgment rate (see current Judgment Debts (Rate of Interest) Order).

Bankruptcy

6B–114 The county court may, *ex parte,* and without notice appoint any person to act for a patient. A person under mental disability, whether a receiver has been appointed or not, may be adjudicated bankrupt without the concurrence of the Court of Protection, but such adjudication and the appointment of a trustee in bankruptcy does not affect the direction and control of the debtor's property which may have already been assumed by the Court of Protection (*Re a Debtor (No.1 of 1941)* [1941] Ch. 487).

Where it is for the patient's benefit the Court of Protection will authorise the necessary steps to be taken with a view to the patient's adjudication as a bankrupt (*Re Lee* (1883) 23 Ch.D. 216; and *Re Farnham* [1895] 2 Ch. 799) but the receiver, as such, should take no further steps than the Court of Protection may have authorised (*Re R.S.A.* [1901] 2 K.B. 32).

A person under the jurisdiction of the Court of Protection, discharged from the mental hospital as recovered, who does not apply to determine the proceedings, cannot set up the Court of Protection order as a defence against bankruptcy (*Re Belton* [1913] W.N. 63).

Litigation by or against a patient

6B–115   Under s.96(1)(i) of the Mental Health Act 1983, the Court of Protection may make orders and give directions and authorities for the conduct of legal proceedings in the name of the patient or on his behalf. Proceedings in the High Court by or against a patient are regulated and governed by O.80, and the Matrimonial Causes Rules 1977, rr.112–114. See also "Matrimonial causes," para. 6B–134. County court proceedings are regulated and governed by the County Court Rules 1981. As to seeking directions of the Court of Protection in regard to contemplated legal proceedings, including divorce, involving a patient, see *Re W. (E. E. M.)* [1971] Ch. 123 at 143 as explained in *Re S. (F. G.)* [1973] 1 W.L.R. 178.

The general effect of all the above Rules of Court is that a receiver (or other person) duly authorised by the Court of Protection to conduct the proceedings in question on behalf of a patient is entitled to be next friend or guardian *ad litem*, as the case may be, save that in the county court the actual appointment of the guardian *ad litem* is made by the district judge.

The receiver should before bringing or defending an action have the sanction of the Court of Protection, otherwise he will act at his own risk as to costs (*Re Nottley* (1839) 3 Jur. (o.s.) 719). To obtain such authority a statement of facts should be filed with, where the patient is defendant or respondent, a copy of the writ or originating summons as the case may be. The facts should be set out sufficiently to enable the master to form an opinion of the merits of the action.

Unless it is plainly manifest that the receiver has no interest adverse to the patient, a certificate of no adverse interest should be filed. If the receiver has an adverse interest, either a new receiver should be appointed or, alternatively, the name and address, etc., of some other person should be submitted and the solicitor should file a certificate of no adverse interest and that the person proposed is a fit and proper person to act as next friend or guardian *ad litem* for the patient in the proceedings. In such a case the master may prefer that the Official Solicitor should conduct the proceedings and become next friend or guardian *ad litem*.

Legal aid does not apply to proceedings in the Court of Protection *per se*. Where, however, a patient as defined in reg. 3(3) of the Legal Aid (General) Regulations 1980 is to commence or to defend proceedings in a court to which the legal aid regulations apply, application should be made in accordance with reg. 15. Where the Court of Protection is already seised of the matter it will, where appropriate, issue any necessary authority for such application to be made on behalf of the patient.

Damages recovered on behalf of patient

Delete "or PTO".

6B–116   Damages recovered on behalf of a patient should be administered by the Court of Protection (*Leather v. Kirby* (HL) [1965] 1 W.L.R. 1489; and *M. v. Lester* (*Practice Note*) [1966] 1 W.L.R. 134). When applying to the Court of Protection for directions to deal with damages recovered under a High Court order, the Part I order must be produced. The Part II order should be lodged with the Court Funds Office as soon as possible (see below).

Where a plaintiff who is a patient within the meaning of the Mental Health Act 1983 has been awarded damages in an action in the Queen's Bench Division, the transfer of the damages will be facilitated if the judgment includes a provision to the following effect:

> "... that the defendant do within [   ] days pay the said sum of £[   ] into court to be placed to and accumulated in a Special Account pending an application by the next friend to the Court of Protection for the appointment of a receiver for the plaintiff and that upon such appointment being made the said sum of £[   ] together with any interest thereon [subject to a first charge under the Legal Aid Act 1988] be transferred to the Court of Protection to the credit of the plaintiff to be dealt with as the Court of Protection in its discretion shall think fit."

Similar provisions should be included in an order approving a compromise on behalf of a patient.

Once an award has been made or approved, the next friend and the plaintiff's carers will naturally be anxious to have access to it to meet the plaintiff's needs. Three steps can be taken by solicitors in such a case to expedite matters:

For "Public Trust Office" substitute: Public Guardianship Office

(1) Application may be made for the appointment of a receiver in anticipation of an award. Forms for this purpose are available from the Public Guardianship Office, Stewart House, 24 Kingsway, London WC2B 6JX. The next friend is usually the person to make the application and may also be the most suitable person to act as receiver.

(2) If the plaintiff was legally aided in the action, the award will effectively be frozen, because of the statutory charge, unless and until a reserve for costs can be agreed with the Legal Aid Board. The plaintiff's solicitors should therefore take urgent steps to obtain and complete the appropriate form of undertaking, which is available from the area office, by inserting a figure which is sufficient to cover the full extent of their claim upon the legal aid fund. This sum should take into account costs and disbursements already incurred or to be incurred, less any legal aid contribution which has been paid by the plaintiff and any *inter partes* costs which have been recovered from the defendant. The plaintiff's solicitor should then return the signed undertaking to the legal aid area office (who will inform the Court Funds Office by letter of the amount to be retained to cover the statutory charge) and should obtain an order from the court making the award directing the Court Funds Office to release to the area office the amount from the award to cover the statutory charge. The balance will then be released to the Court of Protection, once the Part II Order has been lodged.

(3) The solicitors in the matter should then follow the procedure known as "Lodging the Part II Order." A payment schedule (Form 200) should at once be prepared. This can be purchased from law stationers or copied from the precedent at para. 1209 in this volume. In the column headed "Details of payments, transfers or other operations required," they should insert "Transfer to Court of Protection credit," in the second column they should give the full name and address of the patient and in the third column they should insert the figure which represents the award, less the figure to be reserved for costs. In the space below, they should insert in the first column "Reserve for costs" and in the third column they should give details of that figure, as shown in the undertaking to the legal aid area office mentioned in paragraph (2) above. The solicitors should then forward the Form 200 for authentication to the District Registry which made the award. If the award was made in London and the patient is not also a minor, the form should be lodged in the Action Department of the Central Office at the Royal Courts of Justice. If the patient is also a minor, it should go to the Masters' Secretary's Office at the Royal Courts of Justice.

The court which made the award should be requested to forward the payment schedule (Form 200) to the Court Funds Office, Queen's Bench Division, 22 Kingsway, London WC2B 6LE. As soon as it is received there, arrangements will be made to carry the bulk of the award over to the Court of Protection, leaving the amount reserved for costs in the Special Account at the Court Funds Office to gain interest until the area office confirms that it can be released to the Court of Protection or to itself, as the case may be.

Practice Note (Transfer of Damages to Court of Protection) September 7, 1990 by the Senior Master of the Queen's Bench Division and the Master of the Court of Protection.

It is necessary to lodge a schedule of damages in accordance with Practice Direction (Damages: Personal Injuries) [1984] 1 W.L.R. 1127; [1984] 3 All E.R. 165.

Structured settlements involving patients

6B–117 Where damages are awarded in respect of injuries of a kind such as to make the appointment of a receiver by the court appropriate, the award should include an element for receivership management costs and Court of Protection fees (*Futej v. Lewandowski* (1980) 124 S.J. 777; and *Duller v. South East Lines Engineers* [1981] C.L.Y. 585). There have been a number of cases in which "structured settlements" involving plaintiffs who are patients have been approved. Under this arrangement, part of the plaintiff's award is provided in the form of an annuity under which payments are made which represent slices of the antecedent debt and which are treated as tax-free capital payments. The payments are index-linked, or increased at a fixed percentage each year and are guaranteed during the plaintiff's lifetime or for a minimum period of years, whichever is the longer (*Kelly v. Dawes*, Times, September 27, 1990 is the first reported case of a structured settlement).

Settlement on behalf of patient

6B–118 There is no power in the High Court to order a settlement on behalf of a patient and/or his family and dependants of damages awarded to him as a result of litigation there: this power is reserved to the Court of Protection under s.96(1)(d) of the Mental Health Act 1983, para. 6B–190. It follows that where such a settlement is contemplated, application should first be made to the Master of the Court of Protection.

Orders for Settlement of Personal Injury Awards to Patients

6B–119   Practice Note (Procedure for the Settlement of Personal Injury: Awards to Patients) November 15, 1996, made by the Master of the Court of Protection sets out as follows (this note supersedes the former Practice Note dated May 6, 1994):

1. Disregard of personal injury awards in assessing entitlement to benefits

6B–120   1.1 In certain circumstances, funds derived from personal injury awards may be disregarded for the purposes of assessment of entitlement to income support under the Income Support (General) Regulations or local authority funding under the National Assistance (Assessment of Resources) Regulations 1992. Similar exemptions apply for the purposes of Housing Benefit and Council Tax. Until recently, the establishment of a trust was believed to be the only way to take advantage of these exemptions, but it has recently become clear that, in the case of funds held subject to the jurisdiction of the Court of Protection, the creation of a formal trust may not always be necessary.

Minors' funds

6B–121   1.2 An additional disregard was introduced from October 1994 under paragraph 44 to Schedule 10 of the Income Support (General) Regulations 1987 (as amended by the Income-related Benefits Schemes (Miscellaneous Amendments) (No. 5) Regulations 1994). Accordingly, any sum of capital administered in the Court of Protection on behalf of a person under the age of 18 which is derived either (i) from an award of damages for personal injury to that child; or (ii) an award of compensation for the death of a parent will be disregarded for the purpose of the assessment of capital. Similar disregards were introduced in respect of eligibility for other benefits.

Adult patients' funds

Add after "the Public Trust Office": (now the Public Guardianship Office)

6B–122   1.3 On August 31, 1995, Social Security Commissioner Heald gave a decision (CIS/368/94) in which he held that a patient's funds derived from an award of compensation for personal injuries held subject to the control of the Public Trust Office (now the Public Guardianship Office) and the Court of Protection should be treated for capital assessment purposes under the income support legislation as if they were held on trust and should accordingly be disregarded. This is now reported at [1996] 3 J.S.S.L. D136. Enquiries made of the DSS indicate that no appeal is contemplated and representations have been made seeking clarification, possibly by way of amendments to the regulations. It is understood that a review of the general policy in this area is likely. Whilst this decision is not binding upon local authorities, indications are that it will be strongly persuasive (see para. 10.003 of the Charging for Residential Accommodation Guide which expressly contemplates an exemption for funds in the Court of Protection) and that for funding as well as benefits purposes, any capital derived from a personal injury award which is under the control of the Court of Protection can be disregarded without the necessity of placing it in a formal trust.

2. Orders for settlement of personal injury awards

6B–123   2.1 In cases where a formal trust (often known as a "special needs" trust) for a patient is required, there are two different methods by which it may be created.

An Application to the Court of Protection under section 96(1)(d) of the Mental Health Act 1983

6B–124   2.2 Under section 96(1)(d) the Court of Protection has power to order the creation of a settlement (that is to say, a trust) for a patient.

2.3 Where the amount of the award exceeds £30,000, the jurisdiction of the Court of Protection should be invoked by an application for the appointment of a receiver (where there is no existing receivership) and a formal application should also be made under section 96(1)(d) for the creation of a trust. The Official Solicitor will be asked to represent the patient for the purposes of the application and, depending upon the complexity of the case, an attended hearing may be required. The procedure set out in Procedure Note PN9 (obtainable from the Registrar) should be followed.

2.4 Where the amount of the award is below £30,000, a simplified procedure is available. In suitable cases, the Court of Protection may be prepared to deal with the application without asking the Official Solicitor to represent the patient and without requiring an attended hearing.

Settlement as part of the terms of compromise of litigation

2.5 The High Court has no power to order the settlement of an award of damages which is the absolute property of a patient (see RSC, O.80/12/5), this can only be done by the Court of Protection. However, there are procedures whereby an award of damages can be settled, by consent, in trust for the patient as part of the terms of compromise of the action between the plaintiff and the defendant, with the approval of the High Court, in circumstances where the award never becomes the absolute property of the patient. If the award is proposed to be settled as a term of the compromise of the litigation and not to become the plaintiff's absolute property, and the plaintiff is a patient (by reason of being incapable, through mental disorder, of managing his property and affairs), the Court of Protection should be asked to approve the terms of compromise, the form of the draft trust deed and the draft consent order before the final application for the approval of the High Court takes place. The Court of Protection will also need to consider what directions should be given as to other assets which may need administration, which may involve the appointment of a receiver.

6B–125

3. When are "special needs" trusts appropriate?

Possible disadvantages

3.1 In approving a compromise or a settlement under section 96(1)(d), the Court of Protection will have to consider not only the possible financial advantages to the patient in terms of preserved eligibility for public funding, but also the various possible disadvantages. These disadvantages may include a loss of supervision by the court, inflexibility, the imposition of a second layer of administration of the patient's affairs (which may be expensive), the difficulty of finding suitable trustees and, in the case of discretionary trusts, restricted access to the funds, the difficulty of finding alternative beneficiaries and possible tax disadvantages. Bare trusts are generally more straightforward. There may be no financial advantage in terms of preserved eligibility for public funding in setting up a trust if the income or capital are intended and used for an item of food, ordinary clothing or footwear, household fuel, rent in respect of which housing benefit is payable, council tax or water rate, even if paid to a third party as the regulations exclude such payments from the disregard (Income Support (General) Regulations 1987, Sched. 9, para. 15).

6B–126

Suitable cases

3.2 Normally, the Court of Protection will only approve the creation of a trust if this will result in some immediate and substantial benefit to the patient which will not accrue if the funds simply remain under a receivership. Accordingly, it is not considered that all cases where a person is entitled to public funding prior to the receipt of an award of damages should give rise to an application for a trust; in some cases it may be more appropriate to continue to manage the funds under a receivership. Also, if monies have been specifically received by the patient which will pay for all future care, these monies should generally remain available for that purpose.

3.3 The most suitable cases for settlement will therefore be those where such benefit to the patient can be demonstrated, and which also include one of the following features (i) the award is only small or (ii) in the case of a larger award, difficulties on liability or contributory negligence have resulted in substantially reduced damages, or (iii) the award does not include the cost of future care as an element of damages.

6B–127

Timing

3.4 It is not to be assumed that time is of the essence, so far as creating a trust is concerned. It is now clear that it is not necessary to set up a trust as soon as the award is received. Provided the funds attributable to the personal injury compensation have been

6B–128

kept separate from other assets and remain identifiable, a trust can be set up at any time that the advantages to the patient of doing so become apparent. In some cases, it may be appropriate for the award to be held under normal receivership arrangements for a period of time to enable arrangements for the care of the patient to be developed and settle down into a pattern.

3.5 Solicitors advising the next friend are often concerned to ensure that any trust is created as early as possible. This is usually because they are concerned that the patient will otherwise be treated as possessing capital of which he has deprived himself for the purpose of securing entitlement to income support, overlooking the exception provided in regulation 51(1) of the Income Support (General) Regulations 1987 (as amended by the Income Support (General) (Amendment No. 3) Regulations 1990). Also, requests for the Court of Protection to approve trusts informally prior to hearings in the High Court are often presented as urgent because a hearing date in the High Court is approaching. Whilst approval to the settlement of small awards can often be given very quickly where necessary, experience has shown that it is rarely satisfactory to rush the preparation of trusts involving substantial sums of money. These require careful consideration, even at the expense of some addition to the costs or an adjournment of the High Court application. Accordingly, even where an award is to be settled as a term of the compromise of the personal injury claim rather than by an application under section 96(1)(d), the Court of Protection may still direct the application to be dealt with by an attended hearing, and request the Official Solicitor to represent the patient for the purposes of the hearing of that application before the master.

4. Which method of setting up a trust should be chosen?

6B–129 4.1 The separate methods of creating a trust have certain different consequences, which may sometimes influence the choice.

The accumulation period

6B–130 4.2 Trusts set up following an order of the High Court can only be done in the form of a declaration of trusts by the trustees, whereas trusts set up by an order of the Court of Protection will take the form of a settlement, with the patient being the settlor. In the former case, the period over which income can be accumulated by the trustees is restricted to 21 years, whereas, in the case of trusts set up by an order of the Court of Protection, provision can be made for income to be accumulated, if appropriate, for the lifetime of the patient as section 164(1)(a) of the Law of Property Act 1925 applies.

Revocation

6B–131 4.3 Because of uncertainties about possible future changes in the benefits legislation, it is generally preferable for trusts to be revocable, to retain the flexibility to restore the capital to the patient absolutely, should this become desirable. There are, however, problems about including a power of revocation in trusts set up as part of the compromise of a personal injury claim, as the award has never been the absolute property of the patient and it is accordingly arguable that exercising a power of revocation would restore the funds to the defendants.

Inheritance tax

6B–132 4.4 All applications are expected to address the inheritance tax implications of the proposed settlement, where the relevant funds exceed the levels at which inheritance tax is charged. The method chosen to establish the trust may have an effect upon this. Also, the tax implications of the form of trust should be considered. For example, there may in some cases be advantages in setting up a trust under the trusts for disabled persons regime, by virtue of which the trust will be treated for inheritance tax purposes as an income in possession trust and the patient as an income beneficiary even though there may be a power to accumulate income (Inheritance Tax Act 1984, section 89). Fully discretionary trusts will be liable to the ten-year charge and to the proportionate (or exit) charge on assets leaving the settlement at other times. When discretionary trusts are applied for, it will generally be necessary to demonstrate that, notwithstanding any tax disadvantages, such a trust is in the patient's best interests.

The terms of the trust

6B–133 5.1 A number of precedent clauses are issued by the Court of Protection with Procedure

Note PN9. These are not prescriptive and are for guidance only. However, a number of general points arise.

5.2 Placing funds in trust may entail the Court of Protection giving up control, or partial control of the assets of a patient in derogation of the powers entrusted to it by the Mental Health Act 1983. Consequently, it is not to be assumed that the Court of Protection will automatically authorise a trust which gives complete discretion to the trustees as to the distribution of income and capital. In some cases, it may prefer to retain control of certain critical powers exercised by the trustees and of the trustees themselves, particularly in relation to the distribution of capital and the appointment of new trustees. It should be appreciated that if the involvement of the Court of Protection in a case is continuing on this account, then it is possible that a receivership will be necessary even if there are no assets apart from the assets in the trust to administer. In some cases, this may be regarded as an acceptable price to pay for the benefits obtained by placing the funds in trust. Sometimes a receiver may be needed to deal with income applied for the benefit of the patient or with assets in the patient's free estate and to deal with tax returns.

5.3 Further, it is not to be assumed that the Court of Protection will necessarily authorise discretionary trusts including beneficiaries other than the patient. It will be expected that the trust will be revocable, and that if the patient recovers his capacity, he will have the right to bring the trust to an end and call for the trust fund to be paid to him. In most cases, the trust should provide that on the death of the patient, the fund should be payable to his personal representatives for the benefit of his estate. Whilst it is possible for the Court of Protection to approve a trust which makes testamentary provision for the devolution of the fund after the patient's death for a patient who lacks testamentary capacity, it is nearly always more satisfactory to deal with this by way of a separate statutory will application which will also make provision for the devolution of any assets falling into the patient's free estate. If, exceptionally, the trust is to make testamentary provisions, it may also provide for a general or special power of appointment by will. The court will not, however, normally authorise the execution of a settlement which includes incidental testamentary provisions where the patient is still a minor.

5.4 As the principal beneficiary of the trust will be a patient, it is normally expected that the trust will include some method of regulating professional trustees' costs.

Matrimonial causes

Generally, see r.112 of the Matrimonial Causes Rules 1977 and Heywood and Massey, **6B–134** *Court of Protection Practice* (12th ed., 1991) pp. 243 *et seq*.

Under s.96(1)(i) of the Mental Health Act 1983, the master may authorise the receiver (or other person) to present a petition in the name or on behalf of a patient for matrimonial relief (see para. 10B-7 and *Baker v. Baker* (1860) 5 P.D. 152; affirmed (1860) 6 P.D. 12, and *Re W. (E. E. M.)* [1971] Ch. 123) nullity (see *Portsmouth v. Portsmouth* (1828) 1 Hagg. E.R. 355) presumption of death and dissolution of marriage, or judicial separation (see *Woodgate v. Taylor* (1861) L.J.P. 197).

The jurisdiction to authorise the bringing of a divorce suit on behalf of a patient was fully considered by Ungoed-Thomas J. in *Re W. (E. E. M.)* [1971] Ch.123.

Where a receiver (or other person) is authorised in the Court of Protection to bring a suit or defend a suit on behalf of a patient, he is entitled to be next friend or guardian *ad litem* without an order of the Divorce Court (Matrimonial Causes Rules 1977, r.112(4)).

Where a patient is a respondent in a suit and it is desired that the receiver should be authorised to conduct the proceedings on behalf of the patient, a statement of facts should be filed in the Court of Protection, accompanied by a copy of the petition and any other relevant documents. It may well be that the master may prefer that the Official Solicitor should act as guardian. The sealed authority of the master would be required before the receiver or the Official Solicitor could conduct the proceedings, and so become guardian under *ibid*. r.112(4) (*Re W. (E. E. M.)* as explained in *Re S. (F. G.)* [1973] 1 W.L.R. 178).

For "the Public Trustee" substitute: an officer of the court

In cases where the petitioning spouse is the receiver and the Official Solicitor is to act as guardian, the Official Solicitor will, normally, in accordance with the usual practice, bring the matter to the attention of the court so that it may consider the appointment of an officer of the court or some other person as new receiver in place of such spouse.

As to the importance of the duties and functions of the guardian *ad litem*, see *Timins v. Timins* [1938] 4 All E.R. 180; *Randall v. Randall* [1939] P.131; *Bailey v. Bailey* [1942] 2 All E.R. 89.

As to consent by a patient to a decree being granted, see *Mason v. Mason* [1972] Fam. 302; [1972] 3 All E.R. 315.

Settlement or gift of patient's property

6B–135 Under s.96(1)(d) of the Mental Health Act 1983, the court may direct a settlement or gift to be made of any property of the patient with any consequential directions under subs. (2). There is power to vary a settlement so made on the grounds of non-disclosure of material facts or substantial change in circumstances but this power is only exercisable by the Lord Chancellor or a nominated judge (s.96(3)).

For "r. 20" substitute: r.18

Application is by way of formal application supported by affidavit evidence. Applicants are governed by r.18 (para.). Generally as to practice, see Heywood and Massey, *Court of Protection Practice* (12th ed., 1991) pp. 196 *et seq*. See also paras 6B–136 to 6B–142. A transaction fee will be payable. See paras and 6B–337.

For reported cases, see *Re Freeman* [1927] 1 Ch. 479; *Re Greene* [1928] Ch. 528; *Re C. W. M.* [1951] 2 K.B. 714 and *Re C.* [1960] 1 W.L.R. 92. *Re C. E. F. D.* [1963] 1 W.L.R. 329 (costs); *Re R. H. C.* [1963] 1 W.L.R. 1095 (disentailing and resettlement). *Re D. M. L.* [1965] Ch. 1133 (meaning of "family" and "persons for whom patient might be expected to provide"); *Re L. (W. J. G.)* [1966] Ch. 135 (disentailing and meaning of "family," etc.); *Re T. B.* [1967] Ch. 247; [1966] 3 All E.R. 599 (settlement in favour of the illegitimate son of the patient).

Statutory wills

6B–136 Under s.96(1)(e) of the Mental Health Act 1983 the court has jurisdiction to provide for the making of a will, or a codicil, for a patient who does not possess testamentary capacity.

The court in drafting a will for a patient assumes that the patient is having a brief lucid interval at the time when the will is made. During that lucid interval, the patient is assumed to have a full knowledge of the past, and a full realisation that as soon as the will is executed he will relapse into the mental state that previously existed. The court considers not a hypothetical patient but the actual patient, with all the antipathies and affections he had while of full capacity, and seeks to make the will which he, acting reasonably, would have made. The patient is to be envisaged during the hypothetical lucid interval as being advised by a competent solicitor and, in normal cases, the patient is to be envisaged as taking a broad brush to the claims on his bounty rather than an accountant's pen (*Re D. (J.)* [1982] Ch. 237; [1982] 2 All E.R. 37).

A transaction fee of £475 will be payable. See paras and 6B–337.

Procedure on application for settlement, gift or statutory will

6B–137 Generally as to settlements (or gifts) of patients' property, see Heywood and Massey, *Court of Protection Practice* (12th ed., 1991), pp. 196 *et seq.*; and as to statutory wills, see *ibid.*, at pp. 191 *et seq*. See also para. as to applications by attorneys under registered enduring powers of attorney for orders to execute statutory wills and codicils.

In view of the affinity between applications for settlements and capital gifts and those for the execution of a will for the patient, the Master of the Court of Protection has issued the following Practice Note (1983) 133 L.J. 6124.

All applications

6B–138 This note refers to applications for the execution of wills and codicils under s.96(1)(e) of the Mental Health Act 1983 and for gifts and settlements under s.96(1)(d). The note is intended for the general guidance of solicitors as to the practice of the court.

For "r. 42 of the Court of Protection Rules 1994" substitute: r.40 of the Court of Protection Rules 2001

These applications usually require the attendance of the solicitor having the conduct of the proceedings. Country solicitors may attend or instruct London agents if they so wish. Counsel may be instructed in appropriate cases. It is frequently helpful if the applicant attends as well. Applications will normally be heard by the master in chambers, subject to r.39 of the Court of Protection Rules 1984 (succeeded by r.40 of the Court of Protection Rules 2001).

Parties

For "Rule 20 COPR 1004" substitute: Rule 18 COPR 2001

6B–139 Applications may be made by one or more of the persons specified in r.17 of the Court of Protection Rules 1984 (Rule 18 COPR 2001). The receiver, if not the applicant or one of the applicants, should be given notice of the hearing of the application. Otherwise, no person should be given notice until the court has so directed.

If the receiver is personally interested in the relief sought, or if there is any other reason for having the interests of the patient separately represented, it is likely that the court will direct that the patient be represented by the Official Solicitor, who must then be given notice by the applicant's solicitors.

The principles which guide the court in deciding who should be given notice of the hearing of an application are that, in general, all persons whose interests will be materially affected by the proposals should be notified, but the discretion is a wide one and will be exercised according to the particular facts of each case (see *Re B* [1987] 1 W.L.R. 552).

Service

For "r. 23 COPR 1994" substitute: r.21 COPR 2001

6B–140 Notice is drawn to r.20 of the Court of Protection Rules 1984 (r.21 COPR 2001) with regard to acceptance of service by solicitors (including the Official Solicitor).

Evidence

6B–141 Evidence must be by way of affidavit or affirmation, with relevant exhibits. The facts directly relating to the application should be set out in full and the following further information should be included:
  (1) Details of the patient's family, by way of a family tree showing the relationship between the patient and the other members of his family on both sides, naming the members of the family and giving their dates of birth or current ages.
  (2) Particulars of the patient's current assets, with updated valuations. (If there is a fund in court, an up-to-date transcript may be obtained from the

For "PTO" substitute: PGO

PGO by the receiver or the receiver's solicitors. The court will give any further help it can from the receivership papers, for example by confirming the correctness of information supplied by the receiver.)
  (3) A statement of the patient's needs (at present and expected in future) and general circumstances.
  (4) Full information as to the patient's general health at present and in the future.
  (5) Where a patient is living in National Health Service accommodation, information as to the likelihood of discharge to Part III local authority accommodation, to other fee-paying accommodation or to the patient's own home.
  (6) Full particulars of the resources of any proposed beneficiary, with details of the likely changes if the application succeeds.
  (7) A clear explanation of the incidence of capital and income tax liabilities as a result of the proposals.
  (8) An illustration of the effect of the proposals on the patient's resources, preferably in the form of a "before" and "after" schedule of assets and income.

Affidavits must conform with the requirements of the Practice Directions issued by the Lord Chief Justice on July 21, 1983 as amended on March 23, 1995 [1983] 1 W.L.R. 922; [1983] 3 All E.R. 33, and the master on August 15, 1984 *Practice Direction* [1984] 1 W.L.R. 1171; [1984] 3 All E.R. 128.

The execution of statutory wills and codicils

6B–142 As well as the matters common to all applications and mentioned above, attention is drawn to the following points:
  (a) Section 96(4)(b) of the Mental Health Act 1983 requires that the master must have reason to believe that the patient is incapable of making a valid will for himself. It can be assumed that in most cases the court will require recent evidence as to lack of testamentary capacity in the form of a letter or certificate (which should be the original document, not a photocopy) from a doctor. If recent evidence is not available, the court may adjourn the application and possibly call for a report from one of the Lord Chancellor's Medical Visitors on this question.
  (b) Section 97(1) of the Act directs how a statutory will is to be executed and attested. A suitable form is set out at the foot of this note (see para. 6B–181). Section 97(2) provides that section 9 of the Wills Act 1837, which relates to the execution and attestation of wills, shall not apply.
  (c) Having regard to section 97(4) of the Act, the evidence on the application should state the patient's domicile, whether any immovable property will be affected by the proposed will and, if so, the situation of that property if already belonging to the patient.

(d) Where a will for the patient already exists, the evidence in support of the application must substantiate the need for the execution of a further will or codicil. The consents to act of the executors named in the proposed will should be filed with the supporting evidence.
(e) The Court of Protection has no jurisdiction to adjudicate upon the validity of an existing will; it can only authorise the execution of a further will in the light of evidence submitted.
(f) Every application should be accompanied by a draft of the proposed statutory will, with a spare copy in case amendment is required.
(g) Statutory wills will not be sealed by the court until they have been executed and attested in accordance with the provisions of section 97(1) of the Act.
(h) In cases of extreme urgency, the court will make every effort to assist; a telephone call to the Registrar (020 7664 7352) or the Registrar's Assistant (020 7664 7208) is advisable. It may be sensible, for example, to provide for the will to be executed by someone more readily available in an emergency than the applicant; for example, the Official Solicitor.
(i) Full supporting information is needed even if the application seeks a codicil or new will addressed to a change of executors or other simple point because the court will need to review all the provisions of the existing will.

Gifts

Smaller gifts

For "PTO" substitute: PGO

6B–143 Gifts not exceeding £15,000 in any year that are insignificant in the context of a patient's assets, and gifts in consideration of marriage are usually considered on application to the PGO by letter only; no attendance, nor the issue of a formal application, is required.

Larger gifts

6B–144 If the proposed gifts do not fall within the above limits, a formal application must be issued. The notes on parties and evidence set out above will need to be followed.

Settlements, deeds of variation, deeds of family arrangement or the exercise of powers and similar dealings

6B–145 If a settlement, a deed of variation, a deed of family arrangement or the exercise of a power under section 96(1)(k) or any similar dealing is proposed, a draft of the deed that is proposed to be executed should be exhibited, with a spare copy in case amendment is required. Relevant settlements include those under insurance "Inheritance Trust" and similar schemes. The notes on parties and evidence set out above will need to be followed.

As to a proposed gift to the persons in charge of a private mental hospital, see *Re C. M. G.* [1970] Ch. 574.

A statutory will ordered by the master should be executed forthwith without delay notwithstanding the pendency of an appeal to the nominated judge (*Re D. (J.)* [1982] Ch. 237; [1982] 2 All E.R. 37).

Named charities may be "interested" persons (within the meaning of r.21(4) in proceedings for a new will where they have expectations under a previous will, as well as the Attorney-General, representing the interests of the public as beneficiaries of all charities. The court has a discretion whether to direct the joinder of the charities or the Attorney-General or both (*Re H. M. F.* [1976] Ch. 33; [1975] 2 All E.R. 795).

The giving of notice of an application to a husband or relatives is within the discretion of the court (*Re Davey (decd.)* [1981] 1 W.L.R. 164; [1980] 3 All E.R. 342). In that case, the court had dispensed with notice and ordered the execution of a statutory will and such had been properly executed. The patient died shortly afterwards and her husband appealed against the order. The will was held to be valid and, since the patient had died, irrevocable.

Testimony (perpetuation of)

6B–146 See O.39, r.15; and *Re Stoer* (1884) 9 P.D. 120.

The practice of the action to perpetuate testimony would appear to have fallen entirely into disuse. However, the jurisdiction remains and the law on this subject can be found as mentioned above. Section 96(1)(d) or (e) of the Mental Health Act 1983 enables any injustice in the vast majority of cases to be remedied.

Variation of Trusts Act 1958

For the guidance of those who have reason to apply to the court under s.1(3) of the Act, **6B–147** the master directed, on December 9, 1959, that:

(1) As soon as an originating summons under the Act to which a patient is a respondent has been issued in the Chancery Division, the Court of Protection should be notified and an authority sought for leave to conduct the proceedings on behalf of the patient.

(2) No application should be issued in the Court of Protection for relief under s.1(3) of the Act until the originating summons has been issued in the Chancery Division and evidence filed in support thereof, but the master will in suitable cases authorise counsel to be instructed on behalf of the patient to look after the patient's interest during negotiations for an arrangement.

(3) The application should only be entitled in the matter of the patient. The master will direct whether the patient is to be served or service dispensed with, and where the master considers that the patient should be separately represented he may request the Official Solicitor to act as a solicitor for the patient on the application.

(4) A copy of the originating summons (or an office copy if the arrangement is to be found in the summons itself) and office copies of the evidence in support thereof, together with the exhibits, should be lodged with the application and an affidavit filed stating how the patient will be affected by the arrangement and whether it is considered to be for or against his benefit.

(5) The master's order will make provision for subsequent approval of amendments which may be made to the arrangement after the date of the order. See *Re Sanderson's Settlement Trusts* [1961] 1 W.L.R. 36; [1961] 1 All E.R. 25n.

If the only consent to the proposed variation requiring judicial approval is that of a patient for whom a receiver is acting (or about to be applied for) there is no need to proceed under the Variation of Trusts Act 1958, since consent and authority to join in any necessary deed of variation on behalf of the patient may be given by the Court of Protection alone under Pt VII of the Mental Health Act 1983, either under one or other of the particular provisions of s.96 or the general provisions of s.95.

Where, however, the court in Chancery is being asked to approve an arrangement under the Act and a patient for whom a receiver is acting has an interest, it would not be proper for the Court of Protection to authorise the receiver to consent to the scheme on his behalf; in such a case it is for the Chancery Court, if it thinks fit, to approve the scheme, subject to the Court of Protection having determined that the variation would be for the patient's benefit under s.1(3) as set out above (*Re C. L.* [1969] 1 Ch. 587; [1968] 1 All E.R. 1104).

The term "benefit" in this context is not confined to some element of financial advantage: it is for a patient's benefit to do what he would have done if of full capacity (*Re C. L.*).

A transaction fee will be payable. See para. 6B–337.

Wills

For "Rule 72" substitute: Rule 70

Rule 70 empowers the court to call for production of testamentary dispositions executed **6B–148** by a patient. Normally the court directs that the patient's will is to be deposited at the receivership bank for safe custody. Since banks now charge for this service it is now the practice to allow the will to remain with the solicitors who prepared it to be held subject (during the lifetime of the patient) to the directions of the court, and the usual undertaking (Form C.P. 12) must be filed (see Practice Note [1935] W.N. 202).

When a patient whose affairs are under the jurisdiction of the court desires to make a will, the directions of the Cocurt should be obtained first, otherwise costs may be disallowed (see Practice Note [1935] W.N. 54). Medical evidence must be furnished to the effect that the patient is of testamentary capacity, *i.e.* capacity to understand the nature of the document proposed to be executed, the extent of the property to be disposed of, and the claims of those it is proposed to benefit or exclude (see *Banks v. Goodfellow* (1870) 5 Q.B. 549; and *Roe v. Nix* [1893] P.55). Evidence given by a hospital doctor should be given by one of consultant status. In some cases the court will request one of the Lord Chancellor's Medical Visitors to visit the patient and report as to testamentary capacity. The will should be witnessed by a solicitor and the hospital doctor, or the patient's medical attendant, as the case may require.

Where a patient does not possess testamentary capacity consideration should, where appropriate, be given to the execution of a statutory will on behalf of the patient. See paras 6B–136 to 6B–142.

Accounts

Duty to account

For "PTO" substitute: PGO

6B–149   Normally a receiver has to account annually to the anniversary of his appointment, although where special reasons exist the court or the PGO may direct that his accounts be taken to some other date (*e.g.* the close of a business year). In suitable cases accounts by the receiver are sometimes dispensed with. (Generally, see s.107 of the Mental Health Act 1983, and

For "r. 63" substitute: r.61

r.61.) Where the property of the patient is extensive and complicated the court or the PGO may direct the account to be certified by a chartered accountant or solicitor (see Heywood and Massey, *Court of Protection Practice* (12th ed., 1991), pp. 421–422).

For "r. 67" substitute: r.65

A final account of a receiver, where required to be passed, on the death of the patient (see *Re Walker* [1907] 2 Ch. 120) or receiver, will be made up to the date of death, but where the receiver has retired from office or for any other reason has been discharged, including the recovery of the patient, the account will require to be made up to the date of the order discharging the receiver. See r.65.

An account is required to be lodged within one month of the closing date thereof.

Form of account

For "PTO" substitute: PGO

6B–150   The receiver's account should be prepared on Form C.P. 28. This is sent by the PGO free of charge with the notice calling for the account. Endorsed on the form are full instructions as to how the account should be prepared, and as to what documents to accompany. It should be particularly noted that the account is essentially an account of actual receipts and payments within the accounting period. If any rents are collected, or outgoings on property paid, by the receiver (as distinct from agents) details should be shown in Form C.P. 28A, and the totals brought into the account.

The court is empowered to direct a receiver to render an account in a specific form and made up to a date of the court's choosing (*Re C. M. R.* (1982) 79 L.S.Gaz. 407).

In connection with the vouching of the account where the allowance for maintenance of the patient or any other person is for "so much as may be necessary not exceeding £. ... a year (or the net income)" the expenditure is required, so far as reasonably practicable, to be accounted for and vouched in detail but where the allowance is of a specified sum or net surplus income (unqualified) the allowance need not normally be accounted for in detail and only the amount charged pursuant to the allowance entered in the account; where, however, the court has reason to believe that such allowance has been misapplied the court can direct a proper account to be taken (see *Re French* (1868) 3 Ch. App. 317 at 318, *per* Lord Cairns L.J., and *Strangwayes v. Read* [1898] 2 Ch. 419).

Where the patient is living at home with his family, detailed accounts of expenditure on household expenses are not usually expected, provided the court is satisfied that the patient is enjoying proper care and attention. If the patient is the owner of the house, evidence of payment for rates, taxes, insurance premiums, repairs and any mortgage repayments may be required. In cases where a large establishment is maintained, more detailed information on household expenditure may be required, for example, books of account showing the wages and salaries paid to staff and the payments made in settlement of tradesmen's accounts. Vouchers for the entries in the account books should only be produced if requested.

Where there is a business the instructions for keeping accounts in connection with the business will be found in the directions given in the order. See para. 6B–101.

Lodging account

6B–151   The account should be lodged promptly. Such of the following documents as are applicable to the case should be lodged with the account:

> (a) Counterfoils of dividend warrants and any other vouchers for sums received, *if specifically requested.*
>
> (b) Form C.P. 28A (see above) where any rents are collected by or outgoings on property paid by receiver.

(c) Rent accounts (and, *if specifically requested*, vouchers in support of payments included therein) where any rents are collected by an agent.
(d) A copy of the trustee's income account where income is collected and distributed by the trustees.
(e) A copy of the audited accounts and balance sheet of any business or partnership in which the patient has an interest.
(f) Receipts for amounts paid, *if specifically requested*.
(g) The receivership bank account pass book (sheets) covering the period of the account.

As regards the receivership bank account, the receiver should keep a separate receivership account opened in his own name "as Receiver for (*Patient*)" into which, as far as possible, all sums received should be paid and from which all payments should be made.

Passing account

6B–152

The account will be examined and vouched by an officer of the Protection Division and, if necessary, a questionnaire will be sent. The matter as a whole will be reviewed and consideration will be given to the application or investment of the surplus balance of the account.

For "PTO" substitute: PGO

The PGO may disallow any excess of authorised allowances or other unauthorised payments. The circumstances will be considered and if disallowance is directed the offending items will be struck out of the account.

Upon the passing of the account directions will be given in respect of the costs thereof and any, if necessary, costs of general management. See para. 6B–171.

Annual administration fee

For "rr. 78, 79 and 86" substitute: rr.76, 78 and 83

6B–153

An annual fee is payable from the date of the issue of the first application until the termination of the proceedings. Generally as to the administration fee, see rr.76, 78 and 83 and the Appendix thereto.

The administration fee is payable on the first and on every subsequent anniversary of the date of the appointment of a receiver until the termination of the proceedings and is collected by a demand sent to the solicitor by post or by deduction from the fund in court.

At end of renumbered paragraph 6B-153 delete link line [THE NEXT PARAGRAPH IS 6B-158].

Method of payment of the annual administration fee

The fee is levied:

6B–154

(1) By a "demand" issued on the passing of the account (or on the settlement of a final order or order determining proceedings when the account is dispensed with). The demand form (certificate) gives full instructions as to payment which may be made either in cash accompanied by the certificate at the Protection Division, 24, Kingsway, London, WC2B 6JX, or by returning the certificate with a cheque (including a giro cheque) or postal order made payable to the Public Trust Office and crossed.

For "PTO" substitute: PGO

(2) By being carried over by the Accountant General of the Supreme Court from the fund in court to a special account entitled "Court of Protection Administration Fee Account". This is done on a "carry over" certificate issued by the PGO to the Accountant General.

Costs

General note

For "r. 87(1)" substitute: r.84(1)

6B–155

See the Court of Protection Rules, rr.87–92. Costs are in the discretion of the court (see *Re Cathcart* [1893] 1 Ch. 466 at 472, *per* Halsbury L.C.) and the court may order them to be paid by the patient or charged on or paid out of his estate or paid by any other party or any person attending the proceedings (r.84(1)). The order is enforceable in the same manner as an order as to costs made by the High Court (subs. (2)) but is appealable without leave and is not a charging order within the meaning of O.50, r.2 (*Re Cathcart* [1893] 1 Ch. 466).

Subject to the Court of Protection Rules and Civil Procedure Rules 1998, O.62 applies and the costs are assessed where required accordingly. They are awarded either on the indemnity basis (which is usually the case in receivership proceedings) or on the standard basis, but the court will not in either case allow costs which have been unreasonably incurred or are unreasonable in amount.

On assessment on the indemnity basis the court will resolve any doubts which it may have as to whether costs were unreasonably incurred or were unreasonable in amount in favour of the receiving party.

On assessment of costs on the standard basis the court will (a) only allow costs which are proportionate to the matters in issue, and (b) resolve any doubts which it may have as to whether costs were reasonably incurred or reasonable and proportionate in amount in favour of the paying party.

The rules against champerty (now obsolete) did not apply. A solicitor who fairly and properly conducts an objection to an application for the appointment of a receiver on a retainer from the patient ought to be allowed his costs in any event (see *Wentworth v. Tubb* (1842) 7 Jur.(o.s.) 738). A solicitor will not be deprived of his costs merely because he represents the patient and other parties as well, but where there is a conflict of interest, and the solicitor acts on behalf of the other parties rather than the patient, the costs may be disallowed (*Re Weston* (1903) 116 L.T.J. 34).

The receiver acts as agent for the patient, and solicitors instructed by the receiver are entitled to look to the patient's estate for payment; the relationship of "solicitor and client" does not exist between the solicitor and the receiver (*Re E. G.* [1914] 1 Ch. 927).

The costs of the notes of the judgment of the Lords Justices (in Lunacy) were allowed (*Re Cathcart*).

A surety is liable for costs directed to be paid by the receiver and which remain unsatisfied (*Re Graham* [1895] 1 Ch. 66).

6B–156 Practice Note (Taxation of Court of Protection Costs), August 11, 1995 made by the Master of the Court of Protection and the Chief Master, Supreme Court Costs Office, sets out as follows:

For "Public Trust Office" substitute: Public Guardianship Office

This Practice Note is issued in order to clear up any misunderstandings that may have arisen as to taxation procedures for Court of Protection costs. Solicitors are reminded that the court's jurisdiction extends to the management and administration of a patient's financial affairs only and it cannot be concerned with aspects of a patient's affairs which are not financial; and the costs of work beyond these limits will not be the subject of an order by the court or a direction by the Public Guardianship Office. Consequently no such costs will be allowed by the Supreme Court Taxing Office on assessment.

For "r. 89 of the Court of Protection Rules" substitute: r.86 of the Court of Protection Rules 2001

If solicitors believe that an item in their bill is properly chargeable as work relating to financial affairs, but that contention is not accepted by the Supreme Court Costs Office, they should bring in objections and, if that is unsuccessful, take the question to appeal. The Court of Protection itself cannot assist by reinstating any costs disallowed by the Supreme Court Costs Office, since the function of deciding the quantum of costs belongs to them, by reason of r.86 of the Court of Protection Rules 2001 and the Civil Procedure Rules 1998.

For "r. 90 of the Court of Protection Rules 1994" substitute: r.87 of the Court of Protection Rules 2001

In cases where the receiver is not a professional person, he or she is nonetheless expected to be able to carry out the whole range of a receiver's duties, as outlined in the Receiver's Handbook issued by the Public Trust Office. The court may, however, in suitable cases authorise a receiver (under r.87 of the Court of Protection Rules 2001) to employ at the patient's expense a solicitor or other professional person to do any work not usually requiring professional assistance. This authority should always be sought in appropriate cases. However, the rule does not extend the limits of a receiver's authority beyond financial affairs. Out-of-pocket expenses are allowed to non-professional receivers.

For "r. 90" substitute r.87

If the receiver is a solicitor, costs are allowed for the whole range of receivership duties, subject to detailed assessment, and there is no need for him or her to seek authority under r.87. Accountant-receivers are allowed remuneration fixed by the court and their fees are not liable to detailed assessment. As regards visits by solicitor-receivers to patients, or attendances by solicitor-receivers at case conferences, it has become apparent that, with more patients living in the community, patients may need a visit or require the receiver's help in connection with case conferences or similar attendances, which may be necessary in order to safeguard the financial interests of the patient. In such cases the Supreme Court Costs Office will accept well-founded arguments that the costs should be allowed on detailed assessment.

Practice Note (Authority to Solicitors to act for patients or donors), August 9, 1995 made by the Master of the Court of Protection sets out as follows: **6B–157**

In Court of Protection matters, problems may arise for solicitors in knowing for whom they act.

In the case of *Re EG* [1914] 1 Ch. 927, it is established that where a receiver has been appointed, the solicitor acting in the matter is acting for the patient and not for the receiver. The decision leaves undecided the question of who is the patient's solicitor in cases where more than one solicitor has been instructed to make an application for receivership or where a patient himself wishes to instruct another solicitor for a particular area of his affairs, for example, where he remains of testamentary capacity and wishes to instruct a different solicitor to draw up a will for him. Where more than one solicitor has been instructed, perhaps each by a different member of the patient's family, this places the solicitors in a position of uncertainty as to who is acting for the patient on the principle of *Re EG*.

A further difficulty may arise as a result of the case of *Yonge v. Toynbee* [1910] 1 K.B. 215, which decided that the retainer of a solicitor came to an end when the patient lost capacity (as an extension of the general rule that, except in the case of an enduring power of attorney, the mental incapacity of the principal revokes any agency). Nevertheless, incapacitated people may need solicitors to act for them and them alone.

For "Public Trust Office" substitute: Public Guardianship Office

Assuming that a patient or donor is within the jurisdiction of the Court of Protection, the solicitor's authority to act for him can be expressly confirmed by the Court of Protection. Solicitors are also entitled to look upon themselves as acting for a patient or donor and not for the person who has given them instructions (if that is not the patient or donor) from the time that an application which is in order is received by the Court of Protection or the Public Guardianship Office. This may, for example, be an application for the appointment of a receiver, for an order determining proceedings, for the appointment of a new receiver, for confirmation of the revocation of an enduring power of attorney or for some other relief or authorisation. Where two or more solicitors have been instructed (expressly or by implication) to act for the same patient or donor, preliminary directions should be sought from the court as to who will be deemed to be the solicitor in the matter.

A solicitor instructed by an applicant for receivership (or by an attorney) will be treated by the court as the patient's (or donor's) solicitor until an objection to the application, or a competing application, is received by the court. As soon as this happens, the solicitor instructed by the first applicant must elect whether to continue representing the patient or to represent the first applicant. If the solicitor elects to represent the first applicant, then it is for the court to decide whether the patient needs separate representation and if so, to instruct a different private solicitor or the Official Solicitor (if he agrees) to act for him. If the solicitor elects to remain as the patient's solicitor, then the first applicant will have to instruct another firm.

Solicitors will no doubt wish to make clear to the person from whom they take initial instructions relating to patients or donors that their client will be the patient or donor and that the solicitors will have a duty of confidentiality to the patient or donor, even if the instructions come from somebody else.

The court would like applicants and solicitors to be aware that if a reference which is received by the court in respect of an applicant is not satisfactory, no further enquiry will be made as to the applicant's suitability but the applicant will not be appointed as receiver. This may be considered unfair to the applicant but in the court's view, the best interests of the patient must come first.

Legal aid

The Legal Aid Act 1988 does not apply to proceedings in the Court of Protection, but as to its application to patients involved in proceedings in other courts, see paras 6B–115 *et seq.* **6B–158**

Lodgment of order to assess, etc.

The solicitors having the carriage of an order which directs detailed assessment of costs should send to or leave at the Supreme Court Costs Office, Court of Protection Branch, **6B–159**

Room 1–18, Cliffords Inn, Fetter Lane, London EC4A 1DQ, a copy of the order a request for detailed assessment suitably amended and a statement showing the names and addresses of the parties (if any) appearing in person and of the solicitor of the parties (if any).

A statement of parties however is not required unless the costs clause directs the taxation of costs of a party separately represented or unless the costs are payable other than out of the estate of a patient.

The copy order may be typed or photographed and should be properly endorsed with the title of the matter, the date of entry, and the name and address of the solicitor. The following is the form of certificate which should be signed in the name of the firm:

"I/We hereby certify this to be a true copy of the Order dated
as passed and entered."

(Signed)

The Bill will be assessed and returned by post. If desired an appointment for detailed assessment will be given.

Form of bill

6B–160 Every bill of costs should be headed with the full title of the matter, also the name of the party and date of the order directing the assessment as under:—

IN THE COURT OF PROTECTION   No ....
 In the matter of ...
 The costs of the ... to be
  assessed pursuant to Order dated ...

Bills of costs should be prepared on A4 paper bookwise, in accordance with Civil Procedure Rules 1998, Practice Direction supplementing Part 43.

As the names of solicitors have to appear in all certificates of costs, it is essential that the full forenames of a single practitioner or the correct title of a firm should be endorsed on the bill. In agency matters, copies of orders and bills should show the name of the country solicitor.

Small bills of costs, for any type of business, are now accepted in summary form provided that the narrative is adequate for the work done and a summary of the number of personal attendances, telephone attendances and letters is provided. Care should be taken that in such bills all disbursements are included and summarised.

Documents to accompany bill

6B–161 To facilitate the checking of the bills, before provisional assessment, all drafts of affidavits, deeds, orders, cases to counsel (if authorised) correspondence file, notes of attendances and vouchers should be lodged. In the case of sales of land the original contracts for sale, requisitions and draft transfers or conveyances should be lodged.

As to payment of estate agents' fees, see para. 6B–166.

At end of renumbered paragraph 6B-161 delete link line "[THE NEXT PARAGRAPH IS 6B-167]".

Prior costs

6B–162 (a) If such costs are due to the Solicitor acting in the proceedings, they may be included in his bill without special mention in the Order.

For "PTO" substitute: PGO

(b) Should the prior costs be due to another Solicitor, particulars thereof should be forwarded to the court. In either case a request must be obtained from the PGO referring such costs to a Costs Judge of the Supreme Court so that the amount due may be ascertained by him or under his direction (

For "r. 92 of the Court of Protection Rules 1994" substitute: r.89 of the Court of Protection Rules 2001

r.89 of the Court of Protection Rules 2001).

Receivership general management costs

6B–163 General management costs may be brought in for assessment at least every second year.

The bill and papers should be lodged with the Costs Office and the following request endorsed upon the front of the bill:

"I/We request that the within bill of costs of general management may be assessed

whereupon we will apply to the court with a recommendation as to how payment should be effected."
(Signed)
(Dated)

Costs of passing accounts are dealt with on the passing of the receivership account. Costs for income tax returns, recovering overpaid tax and the lodgment in court of any part of the balance on the account must be included in a bill of costs of general management. See also para. .

Unnecessary employment of solicitor

For "r.90" substitute: r.87

Special attention is drawn to r.87, which provides that no receiver, other "than the Official Solicitor, shall, unless authorised by the court, be entitled at the expense of the patient's estate to employ a solicitor or other professional person to do work not usually requiring professional assistance."

6B–164

Costs of preparing wills

Costs in respect of drawing wills for patients during the course of the proceedings will normally only be allowed against the patient's estate where the leave of the court has previously been obtained for the preparation of such will.

6B–165

Estate agents' fees

For "PTO" substitute: PGO

These should not be included in bills of costs as a disbursement. The limit on estate agents' commission is advised to solicitors in the note which accompanies the order for sale (PN4). If the commission (and other expenses) proposed exceeds that limit solicitors are required to obtain prior approval from the PGO before committing the estate to such expenditure. When prior approval has been obtained, or if it is not necessary, solicitors will continue with the sale in the normal way and pay the estate agents' fees. Estate agents' fees will appear neither in the bill of costs nor, normally, in the receiver's account, but in the completion statement which is produced to the PGO when directions are being sought for investment of the net proceeds of sale.

The court will normally consider estate agents' charges reasonable if they do not exceed $2^{1}/_{2}$ per cent of the sale price, to include all commission, expenses, etc. For full details of estate agents' charges solicitors should read the Practice Direction published jointly by the Chief Chancery Master, the Master of the Court of Protection, and the Senior Registrar of the Family Division, dated December 22, 1982 [1983] 1 All E.R. 160. See para. 6B–98.

6B–166

Assessed bills of costs

A receipt will be issued when the assessed bill is lodged, stamped and completed in the Costs Office, and this receipt must be produced on any future enquiry: Direction dated November 1968 of Chief Taxing Master (Practice Direction (1968) 118 New L.J. 1097).

6B–167

Certificate of costs

If the costs are payable out of the fund in court the office copy certificate of costs will be sent by the Costs Office direct to the Accountant General of the Supreme Court. London Solicitors must lodge with the Accountant General, Court Funds Office, 22 Kingsway, London, WC2B 6LE a form of postal request, but in country cases the Accountant General will forward this form direct to the solicitors.

Where the costs are not payable out of the fund in court the office copy certificate will be sent by post to the solicitors concerned.

6B–168

Fees on assessment

As from October 1, 1999, there shall be payable on the filing of a request for a detailed assessment of costs a fee of £160.

On an appeal against a decision made in a detailed assessment of costs or on an application to set aside a default costs certificate there shall be payable a fee of £50.

6B–169

Costs not assessed

Where an Order is referred for assessment and for any reason it is desired subsequently not to assess the costs, notification must be given to the Supreme Court Costs Office that an assessment will not take place.

6B–170

Second Cumulative Supplement

For precedents and Costs generally, see Heywood and Massey, *Court of Protection Practice* (12th ed., 1991), Chap. 20.

Fixed costs

6B–171   Some items of costs may be dealt with in accordance with a Practice Note issued by the master on September 1, 1983 (see Practice Note (1983) 133 New L.J. 6121) whereby fixed costs were introduced by agreement with the Law Society in respect of certain Court of Protection work.

It has been agreed with the Law Society that the amounts to be allowed will be increased as follows:

Category I	Work up to and including the date upon which the First General Order is entered. (The commencement fee of £50 and fees for medical evidence and evidence of notification of the patient may be added. Please produce receipts for fees paid)	£620 (plus VAT)
Category II	(a) Preparation and lodgment of a receivership account...	£160 (plus VAT)
	(b) Preparation and lodgment of a receivership account which has been certified by a solicitor under the provisions of the Practice Notes dated September 13, 1984 and March 5, 1985	£175 (plus VAT)
Category III	General management work in the second and subsequent years...	
	(a) where there are lay receivers...	£490 (plus VAT)
	(b) where there are solicitor-receivers...	£545 (plus VAT)

(Note: Categories II and III may be claimed together)

Category IV	Applications under s.36(9) of the Trustee Act 1925 for the appointment of a new trustee in the place of the patient, for the purpose of making title to land...	£300 (plus VAT)
Category V	In respect of Conveyancing, two elements will be allowable as follows: (a) a sum of £115 in every case to cover correspondence with the Court of Protection, the preparation of the Certificate or affidavit of value, having the documents sealed by the Court and all other work solely attributable to the Court of Protection, together with (b) a value element of $1/2$ per cent of the consideration up to £400,000 and $1/4$ per cent thereafter, with a minimum sum for this element of £315. As well as a fee for both above elements, VAT and disbursements will be allowed.	

In Category I, to all First General Orders sent out on or after January 1, 2001.
In Category II to all receivership accounts lodged on or after January 1, 2001.
In Category III to all general management costs in respect of years ended on or after January 1, 2001.
In Category IV to all certificates sent out on or after January 1, 2001.

In all categories, solicitors will continue to have the option of detailed assessment rather than accepting fixed costs, if they wish. If solicitors seek an order for detailed assessment of the costs under Category II as well as Category III, the relevant items for both categories should be included in the same bill.

Agreed costs

For "PTO" substitute: PGO

6B–172   If a solicitor's bill for costs incurred in the Court of Protection does not exceed £2,500 (excluding VAT and disbursements) solicitors may submit the bill to the PGO and suggest a figure which they would accept by way of costs. If the bill appears reasonable, the amount sought will be agreed by the PGO. However, if the PGO is unwilling to agree the amount because the bill does not appear reasonable, it may at its discretion direct the costs to be assessed.

To seek agreement of costs, solicitors should lodge a narrative bill with a summary of the work done, the hours spent and the level of fee-earner concerned, together with counsel's fee-notes and vouchers for any disbursements.

Where costs are sought to be agreed for types of work where there is provision for fixed costs, solicitors should note that only in exceptional cases will the court agree a bill higher than the fixed costs amount. The normal alternative to fixed costs will continue to be detailed assessment.

These arrangements apply to bills submitted to the court on or after January 1, 2001, whenever the work comprised in the bill was done, but does not apply in cases where a detailed assessment is already pending on January 1, 2001.

Deeds, Forms, Recitals, etc.

6B–173 Following the coming into effect of the Court of Protection Rules 1994 draft deeds are not, as a general rule settled and approved by the court, the court relying on the solicitors for the accuracy and sufficiency of the contents.

Only the relevant part of the particular order or direction should be recited. The order appointing the receiver need only be recited where the deed is being executed under a sealed direction, as distinct from an order.

In deeds generally, such as conveyances, leases, etc., the patient is the "party" and is cited as "A. B. (*the patient, no address*) acting by C.D. (*the Receiver*) of etc., pursuant to the hereinafter recited Order (hereinafter called 'the Receiver') ...". The fact of mental disability should not appear in the description of the patient.

The actual wording of the direction contained in the order should wherever possible be strictly adhered to in the recital thereof, except that the recital is in the past tense.

[Paras 6B–174 to 6B–181 inclusive constitute unchanged graphics.]

6B–182 The court no longer requires such an affidavit to be filed as a matter of general practice.

Part I

Application of Act

Application of Act: "mental disorder"

6B–185 **1.**—(1) The provisions of this Act shall have effect with respect to the reception, care and treatment of mentally disordered patients, the management of their property and other related matters.

(2) In this Act—

and other expressions shall have the meanings assigned to them in section 145 below.

(3) Nothing in subsection (2) above shall be construed as implying that a person may be dealt with under this Act as suffering from mental disorder, or from any form of mental disorder described in this section, by reason only of promiscuity or other immoral conduct, sexual deviancy or dependence on alcohol or drugs.

Part VII

Management of Property and Affairs of Patients

Judicial authorities and Court of Protection

6B–186 **93.**—(1) The Lord Chancellor shall from time to time nominate one or more judges of the Supreme Court (in this Act referred to as "nominated judges") to act for the purposes of this Part of this Act.

(2) There shall continue to be an office of the Supreme Court, called the Court of Protection, for the protection and management, as provided by this Part of this Act, of the property and affairs of persons under disability; and there shall continue to be a Master of the Court of Protection appointed by the Lord Chancellor under section 89 of the Supreme Court Act 1981.

(3) The Master of the Court of Protection shall take the oath of allegiance and judicial oath in the presence of the Lord Chancellor; and the Promissory Oaths Act 1868 shall have effect as if the officers named in the Second Part of the Schedule to that Act included the Master of the Court of Protection.

(4) The Lord Chancellor may nominate other officers of the Court of Protection (in this Part of this Act referred to as "nominated officers") to act for the purposes of this Part of this Act.

Exercise of the judge's functions: "the patient"

6B–187   94.—(1) Subject to subsection (1A) below, the functions expressed to be conferred by this Part of this Act on the judge shall be exercisable by the Lord Chancellor or by any nominated judge, and shall also be exercisable by the Master of the Court of Protection, by the Public Trustee or by any nominated officer, but—

    (a) in the case of the Master, the Public Trustee or any nominated officer, subject to any express provision to the contrary in this Part of this Act or any rules made under this Part of this Act,

    (aa) in the case of the Public Trustee, subject to any directions of the Master and so far only as may be provided by any rules made under this Part of this Act or (subject to any such rules) by directions of the Master,

    (b) in the case of any nominated officer, subject to any directions of the Master and so far only as may be provided by the instrument by which he is nominated;

and references in this Part of this Act to the judge shall be construed accordingly.

(1A) In such cases or circumstances as may be prescribed by any rules under this part of this Act or (subject to any such rules) by directions of the Master, the functions of the judge under this part of this Act shall be exercised by the Public Trustee (but subject to any directions of the Master as to their exercise).

(2) The functions of the judge under this Part of this Act shall be exercisable where, after considering medical evidence, he is satisfied that a person is incapable, by reason of mental disorder, of managing and administering his property and affairs; and a person as to whom the judge is so satisfied is referred to in this part of this Act as a patient.

Public Trustee's functions

6B–188   Section 94 was amended by the Public Trustee and Administration of Funds Act 1986 which came into operation on January 2, 1987.

This amended section enables the Public Trustee to carry out for the Court of Protection functions given to the court under enactments other than the Mental Health Act 1983. It is intended, for example, that the registration work given to the court under the Enduring Powers of Attorney Act 1985 should normally be undertaken within the Public Trust Office.

General functions of the judge with respect to property and affairs of patient

6B-189 **95.**—(1) The judge may, with respect to the property and affairs of a patient, do or secure the doing of all such things as appear necessary or expedient—
- (a) for the maintenance or other benefit of the patient,
- (b) for the maintenance or other benefit of members of the patient's family,
- (c) for making provision for other persons or purposes for whom or which the patient might be expected to provide if he were not mentally disordered, or
- (d) otherwise for administering the patient's affairs.

(2) In the exercise of the powers conferred by this section regard shall be had first of all to the requirements of the patient, and the rules of law which restricted the enforcement by a creditor of rights against property under the control of the judge in lunacy shall apply to property under the control of the judge; but, subject to the foregoing provisions of this subsection, the judge shall, in administering a patient's affairs, have regard to the interests of creditors and also to the desirability of making provision for obligations of the patient notwithstanding that they may not be legally enforceable.

Powers of the judge as to patient's property and affairs

6B-190 **96.**—(1) Without prejudice to the generality of section 95 above, the judge shall have the power to make such orders and give such directions and authorities as he thinks fit for the purposes of that section and in particular may for those purposes make orders or give directions or authorities for—
- (a) the control (with or without the transfer or vesting of property or the payment into or lodgment in the Supreme Court of money or securities) and management of any property of the patient;
- (b) the sale, exchange, charging or other disposition of or dealing with any property of the patient;
- (c) the acquisition of any property in the name or on behalf of the patient;
- (d) the settlement of any property of the patient, or the gift of any property of the patient to any such persons or for any such purposes as are mentioned in paragraphs (b) and (c) of section 95(1) above;
- (e) the execution for the patient of a will making any provision (whether by way of disposing of property or exercising a power or otherwise) which could be made by a will executed by the patient if he were not mentally disordered;
- (f) the carrying on by a suitable person of any profession, trade or business of the patient;
- (g) the dissolution of a partnership of which the patient is a member;
- (h) the carrying out of any contract entered into by the patient;
- (i) the conduct of legal proceedings in the name of the patient or on his behalf;
- (j) the reimbursement out of the property of the patient, with or

without interest, of money applied by any person either in payment of the patient's debts (whether legally enforceable or not) or for the maintenance or other benefit of the patient or members of his family or in making provision for other persons or purposes for whom or which he might be expected to provide if he were not mentally disordered;

(k) the exercise of any power (including a power to consent) vested in the patient, whether beneficially, or as guardian or trustee, or otherwise.

(2) If under subsection (1) above provision is made for the settlement of any property of a patient, or the exercise of a power vested in a patient of appointing trustees or retiring from a trust, the judge may also make as respects the property settled or trust property such consequential vesting or other orders as the case may require, including (in the case of the exercise of such a power) any order which could have been made in such a case under Part IV of the Trustee Act 1925.

(3) Where under this section a settlement has been made of any property of a patient, and the Lord Chancellor or a nominated judge is satisfied, at any time before the death of the patient, that any material fact was not disclosed when the settlement was made, or that there has been any substantial change in circumstances, he may by order vary the settlement in such manner as he thinks fit, and give any consequential directions.

(4) The power of the judge to make or give an order, direction or authority for the execution of a will for a patient—
(a) shall not be exercisable at any time when the patient is a minor, and
(b) shall not be exercised unless the judge has reason to believe that the patient is incapable of making a valid will for himself.

(5) The powers of a patient as patron of a benefice shall be exercisable by the Lord Chancellor only.

Settlement of property

6B–191 Notwithstanding subs.(3) of this section, if the court has directed a settlement of a patient's property for the benefit of, for example, his family, it is permissible to distribute any capital of the settled property during the lifetime of the patient. *Re C. W. H. T.* [1978] Ch. 67; [1978] 1 All E.R. 210.

Supplementary provisions as to wills executed under s.96

6B–192 97.—(1) Where under section 96(1) above the judge makes or gives an order, direction or authority requiring or authorising a person (in this section referred to as "the authorised person") to execute a will for a patient, any will executed in pursuance of that order, direction or authority shall be expressed to be signed by the patient acting by the authorised person, and shall be—
(a) signed by the authorised person with the name of the patient, and with his own name, in the presence of two or more witnesses present at the same time, and
(b) attested and subscribed by those witnesses in the presence of the authorised person, and
(c) sealed with the official seal of the Court of Protection.

(2) The Wills Act 1837 shall have effect in relation to any such will as if it were signed by the patient by his own hand, except that in relation to any such will—

(a) section 9 of that Act (which makes provision as to the signing and attestation of wills) shall not apply, and
(b) in the subsequent provisions of that Act any reference to execution in the manner required by the previous provisions of that Act shall be construed as a reference to execution in the manner required by subsection (1) above.

(3) Subject to the following provisions of this section, any such will executed in accordance with subsection (1) above shall have the same effect for all purposes as if the patient were capable of making a valid will and the will had been executed by him in the manner required by the Wills Act 1837.

(4) So much of subsection (3) above as provides for such a will to have effect as if the patient were capable of making a valid will—
(a) shall not have effect in relation to such a will in so far as it disposes of any immovable property, other than immovable property in England or Wales, and
(b) where at the time when such a will is executed the patient is domiciled in Scotland or Northern Ireland or in a country or territory outside the United Kingdom, shall not have effect in relation to that will in so far as it relates to any other property or matter, except any property or matter in respect of which, under the law of his domicile, any question of his testamentary capacity would fall to be determined in accordance with the law of England and Wales.

Note

As from January 1, 1983, the Wills Act 1837 must be read as amended by the Administration of Justice Act 1982.

Judge's powers in cases of emergency

98. Where it is represented to the judge, and he has reason to believe, that a person may be incapable, by reason of mental disorder, of managing and administering his property and affairs, and the judge is of the opinion that it is necessary to make immediate provision for any of the matters referred to in section 95 above, then pending the determination of the question whether that person is so incapable the judge may exercise in relation to the property and affairs of that person any of the powers conferred on him in relation to the property and affairs of a patient by this Part of this Act so far as is requisite for enabling that provision to be made.

Power to appoint receiver

99.—(1) The judge may by order appoint as receiver for a patient a person specified in the order or the holder for the time being of an office so specified.

(2) A person appointed as receiver for a patient shall do all such things in relation to the property and affairs of the patient as the judge, in the exercise of the powers conferred on him by sections 95 and 96 above, orders or directs him to do and may do any such thing in relation to the property and affairs of the patient as the judge, in the exercise of those powers, authorises him to do.

(3) A receiver appointed for any person shall be discharged by order of the judge on the judge being satisfied that person has become capable

of managing and administering his property and affairs, and may be discharged by order of the judge at any time if the judge considers it expedient to do so; and a receiver shall be discharged (without any order) on the death of the patient.

Note

6B–196 See *Re W. L. W.* [1972] Ch. 456; [1972] 1 All E.R. 433 and para. 6B–202.
"Expedient" in subs.(3) means, "expedient for the patient". (*Re N. (decd.)* [1977] 1 W.L.R. 676; [1977] 2 All E.R. 687, CA).

Vesting of stock in curator appointed outside England and Wales

6B–197 100.—(1) Where the judge is satisfied—
 (a) that under the law prevailing in a place outside England and Wales a person has been appointed to exercise powers with respect to the property or affairs of any other person on the ground (however formulated) that that other person is incapable, by reason of mental disorder, of managing and administering his property and affairs, and
 (b) that having regard to the nature of the appointment and to the circumstances of the case it is expedient that the judge should exercise his powers under this section,
 the judge may direct any stock standing in the name of the said other person or the right to receive the dividends from the stock to be transferred into the name of the person so appointed or otherwise dealt with as requested by that person, and may give such directions as the judge thinks fit for dealing with accrued dividends from the stock.
 (2) In this section "stock" includes shares and also any fund, annuity or security transferable in the books kept by any body corporate or unincorporated company or society, or by an instrument of transfer either alone or accompanied by other formalities, and "dividends"shall be construed accordingly.

Preservation of interests in patient's property

6B–198 101.—(1) Where any property of a person has been disposed of under this Part of this Act, and under his will or his intestacy, or by any gift perfected or nomination taking effect on his death, any other person would have taken an interest in the property but for the disposal—
 (a) he shall take the same interest, if and so far as circumstances allow, in any property belonging to the estate of the deceased which represents the property disposed of; and
 (b) if the property disposed of was real property any property representing it shall so long as it remains part of his estate be treated as if it were real property.
 (2) The judge, in ordering, directing or authorising under this Part of this Act any disposal of property which apart from this section would result in the conversion of personal property into real property, may direct that the property representing the property disposed of shall, so long as it remains the property of the patient or forms part of his estate, be treated as if it were personal property.
 (3) References in subsections (1) and (2) above to the disposal of property are references to—

(a) the sale, exchange, charging or other dealing (otherwise than by will) with property other than money,
(b) the removal of property from one place to another,
(c) the application of money in acquiring property, or
(d) the transfer of money from one account to another;
and references to property representing property disposed of shall be construed accordingly and as including the result of successive disposals.

(4) The judge may give such directions as appear to him necessary or expedient for the purpose of facilitating the operation of subsection (1) above, including the carrying of money to a separate account and the transfer of property other than money.

(5) Where the judge has ordered, directed or authorised the expenditure of money for the carrying out of permanent improvements on, or otherwise for the permanent benefit of, any property of the patient, he may order that the whole or any part of the money expended or to be expended shall be a charge upon the property, whether without interest or with interest at a specified rate; and an order under this subsection may provide for excluding or restricting the operation of subsection (1) above.

(6) A charge under subsection (5) above may be made in favour of such person as may be just, and in particular, where the money charged is paid out of the patient's general estate, may be made in favour of a person as trustee for the patient; but no charge under that subsection shall confer any right of sale or foreclosure during the lifetime of the patient.

Lord Chancellor's Visitors

102.—(1) There shall continue to be the following panels of Lord Chancellor's Visitors of patients constituted in accordance with this section, namely— **6B–199**
(a) a panel of Medical Visitors;
(b) a panel of Legal Visitors; and
(c) a panel of General Visitors (being Visitors who are not required by this section to possess either a medical or legal qualification for appointment).

(2) Each panel shall consist of persons appointed to it by the Lord Chancellor, the appointment of each person being for such term and subject to such conditions as the Lord Chancellor may determine.

(3) A person shall not be qualified to be appointed—
(a) to the panel of Medical Visitors unless he is a registered medical practitioner who appears to the Lord Chancellor to have special knowledge and experience of cases of mental disorder;
(b) to the panel of Legal Visitors unless he has a 10 year general qualification, within the meaning of section 71 of the Courts and Legal Services Act 1990.

(4) If the Lord Chancellor so determines in the case of any Visitor appointed under this section, he shall be paid out of money provided by Parliament such remuneration and allowances as the Lord Chancellor may, with the concurrence of the Treasury, determine.

SECOND CUMULATIVE SUPPLEMENT

Note
6B–200 Amended by the Courts and Legal Services Act 1990, Sched. 10, para. 51.

Function of Visitors
6B–201 **103.**—(1) Patients shall be visited by Lord Chancellor's Visitors in such circumstances, and in such manner, as may be prescribed by directions of a standing nature given by the Master of the Court of Protection with the concurrence of the Lord Chancellor.

(2) Where it appears to the judge in the case of any patient that a visit by a Lord Chancellor's Visitor is necessary for the purpose of investigating any particular matter or matters relating to the capacity of the patient to manage and administer his property and affairs, or otherwise relating to the exercise in relation to him of the functions of the judge under this Part of this Act, the judge may order that the patient shall be visited for that purpose.

(3) Every visit falling to be made under subsection (1) or (2) above shall be made by a General Visitor unless, in a case where it appears to the judge that it is in the circumstances essential for the visit to be made by a Visitor with medical or legal qualifications, the judge directs that the visit shall be made by a Medical or a Legal Visitor.

(4) A Visitor making a visit under this section shall make such report on the visit as the judge may direct.

(5) A Visitor making a visit under this section may interview the patient in private.

(6) A Medical Visitor making a visit under this section may carry out in private a medical examination of the patient and may require the production of and inspect any medical records relating to the patient.

(7) The Master of the Court of Protection may visit any patient for the purpose mentioned in subsection (2) above and may interview the patient in private.

(8) A report made by a Visitor under this section, and information contained in such a report, shall not be disclosed except to the judge and any person authorised by the judge to receive the disclosure.

(9) If any person discloses any report or information in contravention of subsection (8) above, he shall be guilty of an offence and liable on summary conviction to imprisonment for a term not exceeding three months or to a fine not exceeding level 3 on the standard scale or both.

(10) In this section references to patients include references to persons alleged to be incapable, by reason of mental disorder, of managing and administering their property and affairs.

Reports, disclosure and liability of Medical Visitors
6B–202 The nature of reports of the Lord Chancellor's Medical Visitors under this section, the questions of their disclosure and the liability of a visitor to be summoned to be examined and cross-examined thereon were considered in *Re W. L. W.* [1972] Ch. 456; [1972] 2 All E.R. 433. Section 103(8) enables the court to withhold disclosure of a report of a visitor and in this connection a distinction is drawn between the court's paternalistic jurisdiction, concerned for the care of an undoubted patient and the management of his property and affairs, on the one hand, and the question of whether a person should become or remain subject to such jurisdiction, on the other. Such latter question was held to be outside the court's paternalistic jurisdiction under the Act and that the principles of natural justice apply and, accordingly, an alleged patient should be allowed to test any disclosed report of a visitor: in such a case although the court has power under s.103(8), to keep the report to itself it then has to resolve any conflict of fact or medical opinion as best it can and should only in exceptional cases, when it would be injurious to the (alleged) patient, refuse to allow the report to be disclosed and questions put to the visitor (see below).

Further, on the question of disclosure, Goff J. expressed the view, as *obiter*, that when the question is the initial one of whether a person is a "patient" within s.94(2) of the Act or whether proceedings should be determined, the court should lean towards allowing disclosure, at least to the patient's legal and medical advisers, and should refuse it only where the court feels that the interest of the particular alleged patient would be served thereby. In other cases, the court should only direct disclosure if it sees a positive advantage.

Where a visitor's report, or information contained in such a report has been disclosed to any person in pursuance of s.103(8), the court may, on the application of any person who appears to the court to be interested, give leave for written questions relevant to the issues before the court to be put to the visitor by whom the report was made (Court of Protection Rules 1984 (r.27(1)).

It should be noted that, with the leave of the court, a witness summons may issue against a Lord Chancellor's Medical Visitor under the Court of Protection Rules 1984, r.47.

General powers of the judge with respect to proceedings

104.—(1) For the purposes of any proceedings before him with respect to persons suffering or alleged to be suffering from mental disorder, the judge shall have the same powers as are vested in the High Court in respect of securing the attendance of witnesses and the production of documents.

(2) Subject to the provisions of this section, any act or omission in the course of such proceedings which, if occurring in the course of proceedings in the High Court would have been a contempt of the court, shall be punishable by the judge in any manner in which it could have been punished by the High Court.

(3) Subsection (2) above shall not authorise the Master, or any other officer of the Court of Protection to exercise any power of attachment or committal, but the Master or officer may certify any such act or omission to the Lord Chancellor or a nominated judge, and the Lord Chancellor or judge may upon such certification inquire into the alleged act or omission and take any such action in relation to it as he could have taken if the proceedings had been before him.

(4) Subsections (1) to (4) of section 36 of the Supreme Court Act 1981 (which provides a special procedure for the issue of writs of subpoena ad testificandum and duces tecum so as to be enforceable throughout the United Kingdom) shall apply in relation to proceedings under this Part of this Act with the substitution for references to the High Court of references to the judge and for references to such writs of references to such document as may be prescribed by rules under this Part of this Act for issue by the judge for securing the attendance of witnesses or the production of documents.

Appeals

105.—(1) Subject to and in accordance with rules under this Part of this Act, an appeal shall lie to a nominated judge from any decision of the Master of the Court of Protection or any nominated officer.

(2) The Court of Appeal shall continue to have the same jurisdiction as to appeals from any decision of the Lord Chancellor or from any decision of a nominated judge, whether given in the exercise of his original jurisdiction or on the hearing of an appeal under subsection (1) above, as they had immediately before the coming into operation of Part VIII of the Mental Health Act 1959 as to appeals from orders in lunacy made by the Lord Chancellor or any other person having jurisdiction in lunacy.

Note

6B-205   An appeal to the Court of Appeal under subs.(2) lies without leave. See para. 6B-9.

Rules of procedure

6B-206   **106.**—(1) Proceedings before the judge with respect to persons suffering or alleged to be suffering from mental disorder (in this section referred to as "proceedings") shall be conducted in accordance with the provisions of rules made under this Part of this Act.

(2) Rules under this Part of this Act may make provision as to—
- (a) the carrying out of preliminary or incidental inquiries;
- (b) the persons by whom and manner in which proceedings may be instituted and carried on;
- (c) the persons who are to be entitled to be notified of, to attend, or to take part in proceedings;
- (d) the evidence which may be authorised or required to be given in proceedings and the manner (whether on oath or otherwise and whether orally or in writing) in which it is to be given;
- (e) the administration of oaths and taking of affidavits for the purposes of proceedings; and
- (f) the enforcement of orders made and directions given in proceedings.

(3) Without prejudice to the provisions of section 104(1) above, rules under this Part of this Act may make provision for authorising or requiring the attendance and examination of persons suffering or alleged to be suffering from mental disorder, the furnishing of information and the production of documents.

(4) Rules under this Part of this Act may make provision as to the termination of proceedings, whether on the death or recovery of the person to whom the proceedings relate or otherwise, and for the exercise, pending the termination of the proceedings, of powers exercisable under this Part of this Act in relation to the property or affairs of a patient.

(5) Rules under this Part of this Act made with the consent of the Treasury may—
- (a) make provision as to the scale of costs, fees and percentages payable in relation to proceedings, and as to the manner in which and funds out of which such costs, fees and percentages are to be paid;
- (b) contain provision for charging any percentage upon the estate of the person to whom the proceedings relate and for the payment of costs, fees and percentages within such time after the death of the person to whom the proceedings relate or the termination of the proceedings as may be provided by the rules; and
- (c) provide for the remission of fees and percentages.

(6) A charge upon the estate of a person created by virtue of subsection (5) above shall not cause any interest of that person in any property to fail or determine or to be prevented from recommencing.

(7) Rules under this Part of this Act may authorise the making of orders for the payment of costs to or by persons attending, as well as persons taking part in, proceedings.

Security and accounts

6B-207   **107.**—(1) Rules under this Part of this Act may make provision as to the giving of security by a receiver and as to the enforcement and discharge of the security.

(2) It shall be the duty of a receiver to render accounts in accordance with the requirements of rules under this Part of this Act, as well after his discharge as during his receivership; and rules under this Part of this Act may make provision for the rendering of accounts by persons other than receivers who are ordered, directed or authorised under this Part of this Act to carry out any transaction.

General provisions as to rules under Part VII

108.—(1) Any power to make rules conferred by this Part of this Act shall be exercisable by the Lord Chancellor. **6B–208**

(2) Rules under this Part of this Act may contain such incidental and supplemental provisions as appear requisite for the purposes of the rules.

Effect and proof of orders, etc.

109.—(1) Section 204 of the Law of Property Act 1925 (by which orders of the High Court are made conclusive in favour of purchasers) shall apply in relation to orders made and directions and authorities given by the judge as it applies in relation to orders of the High Court. **6B–209**

(2) Office copies of orders made, directions or authorities given or other instruments issued by the judge and sealed with the official seal of the Court of Protection shall be admissible in all legal proceedings as evidence of the originals without any further proof.

Reciprocal arrangements in relation to Scotland and Northern Ireland as to exercise of powers

110.—(1) This Part of this Act shall apply in relation to the property and affairs in Scotland or Northern Ireland of a patient in relation to whom powers have been exercised under this Part of this Act, or a person as to whom powers are exercisable and have been exercised under section 98 above as it applies in relation to his property and affairs in England and Wales unless a curator bonis, tutor, judicial factor, committee, receiver or guardian has been appointed for him in Scotland or, as the case may be, Northern Ireland. **6B–210**

(2) Where under the law in force in Scotland or Northern Ireland with respect to the property and affairs of persons suffering from mental disorder a curator bonis, tutor, judicial factor, committee, receiver or guardian has been appointed for any person, the provisions of that law shall apply in relation to the person's property and affairs in England and Wales unless he is a patient in relation to whom powers have been exercised under this Part of this Act, or a person as to whom powers are exercisable and have been exercised under section 98 above.

(3) Nothing in this section shall affect any power to execute a will under section 96(1)(e) above or the effect of any will executed in the exercise of such a power.

(4) In this section references to property do not include references to land or interests in land but this subsection shall not prevent the receipt of rent or other income arising from land or interests in land.

Construction of references in other Acts to judge or authority having jurisdiction under Part VII

111.—(1) The functions expressed to be conferred by any enactment **6B–211**

not contained in this Part of this Act on the judge having jurisdiction under this Part of this Act shall be exercisable by the Lord Chancellor or by a nominated judge.

(2) Subject to subsections (3) and (3A) below, the functions expressed to be conferred by any such enactment on the authority having jurisdiction under this Part of this Act shall, subject to any express provision to the contrary, be exercisable by the Lord Chancellor, a nominated judge, the Master of the Court of Protection by the Public Trustee or a nominated officer.

(2A) The exercise of the functions referred to in subsection (2) above by the Public Trustee shall be subject to any directions of the Master and they shall be exercisable so far only as may be provided by any rules made under this Part of this Act or (subject to any such rules) by directions of the Master.

(3) The exercise of the functions referred to in subsection (2) above by a nominated officer shall be subject to any directions of the Master and they shall be exercisable so far only as may be provided by the instrument by which the officer is nominated.

(3A) In such cases or circumstances as may be prescribed by any rules under this Part of this Act or (subject to any such rules) by directions of the Master, the functions referred to in subsection (2) above shall be exercisable by the Public Trustee (but subject to any directions of the Master as to their exercise).

(4) Subject to the foregoing provisions of this section—
- (a) references in any enactment not contained in this Part of this Act to the judge having jurisdiction under this Part of this Act shall be construed as references to the Lord Chancellor or a nominated judge, and
- (b) references in any such enactment to the authority having jurisdiction under this Part of this Act shall be construed as references to the Lord Chancellor, a nominated judge, the Master of the Court of Protection or a nominated officer.

Public Trustee's functions

6B–212   Section 111 was amended by the Public Trustee and Administration of Funds Act 1986 which came into operation on January 2, 1987.

This amended section allows the Public Trustee to carry out work on behalf of the Court of Protection (which is a separately constituted entity outside the Public Trust Office structure). The Public Trustee undertakes the administrative tasks whereas matters requiring judicial decision are dealt with by the court. Whilst it enables the Public Trustee to carry out the functions given to the court under Pt VII of the Mental Health Act 1983 such authority is subject to the directions of the Master or so far as provided by rules. The Master is able to direct not only what functions under Pt VII of the Mental Health Act 1983 should be carried out by the Public Trustee but how this function should be exercised.

Interpretation of Part VII

6B–213   112. In this Part of this Act, unless the context otherwise requires—

Disapplication of certain enactments in relation to persons within the jurisdiction of the judge

6B–214   113. The provisions of the Acts described in Schedule 3 to this Act which are specified in the third column of that Schedule, so far as they make special provision for persons suffering from mental disorder, shall not have effect in relation to patients and to persons as to whom powers are exercisable and have been exercised under section 98 above.

Part IX

Offences

Forgery, false statements, etc.

126.—(1) Any person who without lawful authority or excuse has in his custody or under his control any document to which this subsection applies, which is, and which he knows or believes to be, false within the meaning of Part I of the Forgery and Counterfeiting Act 1981, shall be guilty of an offence.

(2) Any person who without lawful authority or excuse makes or has in his custody or under his control, any document so closely resembling a document to which subsection (1) above applies as to be calculated to deceive shall be guilty of an offence.

(3) The documents to which subsection (1) above applies are any documents purporting to be—
- (a) an application under Part II of this Act;
- (b) a medical or other recommendation or report under this Act; and
- (c) any other document required or authorised to be made for any of the purposes of this Act.

(4) Any person who—
- (a) wilfully makes a false entry or statement in any application, recommendation, report, record or other document required or authorised to be made for any of the purposes of this Act; or
- (b) with intent to deceive, makes use of any such entry or statement which he knows to be false,

shall be guilty of an offence.

(5) Any person guilty of an offence under this section shall be liable—
- (a) on summary conviction, to imprisonment for a term not exceeding six months or to a fine not exceeding the statutory maximum, or to both;
- (b) on conviction on indictment, to imprisonment for a term not exceeding two years or to a fine of any amount, or to both.

Note

Amended by the Mental Health (Patients in the Community) Act 1995, Sched. 1, para. 17.

Obstruction

129.—(1) Any person who without reasonable cause—
- (a) refuses to allow the inspection of any premises; or
- (b) refuses to allow the visiting, interviewing or examination of any person by a person authorised in that behalf by or under this Act; or
- (c) refuses to produce for the inspection of any person so authorised any document or record the production of which is duly required by him; or
- (d) otherwise obstructs any such person in the exercise of his functions,

shall be guilty of an offence.

(2) Without prejudice to the generality of subsection (1) above, any person who insists on being present when required to withdraw by a person authorised by or under this Act to interview or examine a person in private shall be guilty of an offence.

(3) Any person guilty of an offence under this section shall be liable on summary conviction to imprisonment for a term not exceeding three months or to a fine not exceeding level 4 on the standard scale or to both.

MISCELLANEOUS PROVISIONS

Part X

Miscellaneous and Supplementary

Correspondence of patients

6B–218   134.—(1) A postal packet addressed to any person by a patient detained in a hospital under this Act and delivered by the patient for dispatch may be withheld from the Post Office—
- (a) if that person has requested that communications addressed to him by the patient should be withheld; or
- (b) subject to subsection (3) below, if the hospital is a special hospital and the managers of the hospital consider that the postal packet is likely—
  - (i) to cause distress to the person to whom it is addressed or to any other person (not being a person on the staff of the hospital); or
  - (ii) to cause danger to any person;

and any request for the purposes of paragraph (a) above shall be made by a notice in writing given to the managers of the hospital, the registered medical practitioner in charge of the treatment of the patient or the Secretary of State.

(2) Subject to subsection (3) below, a postal packet addressed to a patient detained in a special hospital under this Act may be withheld from the patient if, in the opinion of the managers of the hospital, it is necessary to do so in the interests of the safety of the patient or for the protection of other persons.

(3) Subsections (1)(b) and (2) above do not apply to any postal packet addressed by a patient to, or sent to a patient by or on behalf of—
- (a) any Minister of the Crown or Member of either House of Parliament;
- (b) the Master or any other officer of the Court of Protection or any of the Lord Chancellor's Visitors;
- (c) the Parliamentary Commissioner for Administration, the Welsh Administration Ombudsman the Health Service Commissioner for England, the Health Service Commissioner for Wales or a Local Commissioner within the meaning of Part III of the Local Government Act 1974;
- (d) a Mental Health Review Tribunal;
- (e) a Health Authority or Special Health Authority, a local social services authority, a Community Health Council or a proba-

tion committee (within the meaning of the Probation Service Act 1993);
(f) the managers of the hospital in which the patient is detained;
(g) any legally qualified person instructed by the patient to act as his legal adviser; or
(h) the European Commission of Human Rights or the European Court of Human Rights.

(4) The managers of a hospital may inspect and open any postal packet for the purposes of determining—
(a) whether it is one to which subsection (1) or (2) applies, and
(b) in the case of a postal packet to which subsection (1) or (2) above applies, whether or not it should be withheld under that subsection;
and the power to withhold a postal packet under either of those subsections includes power to withhold anything contained in it.

(5) Where a postal packet or anything contained in it is withheld under subsection (1) or (2) above the managers of the hospital shall record that fact in writing.

(6) Where a postal packet or anything contained in it is withheld under subsection (1)(b) or (2) above the managers of the hospital shall within seven days give notice of that fact to the patient and, in the case of a packet withheld under subsection (2) above, to the person (if known) by whom the postal packet was sent; and any such notice shall be given in writing and shall contain a statement of the effect of section 121(7) and (8) above.

(7) The functions of the managers of a hospital under this section shall be discharged on their behalf by a person on the staff of the hospital appointed by them for that purpose and different persons may be appointed to discharge different functions.

(8) The Secretary of State may make regulations with respect to the exercise of the powers conferred by this section.

(9) In this section "hospital" has the same meaning as in Part II of this Act, "postal packet" has the same meaning as in the Post Office Act 1953 and the provisions of this section shall have effect notwithstanding anything in section 56 of that Act.

Note

Amended by the Probation Service Act 1993, Sched. 3, para. 7; and the Health Authorities Act 1995, Sched. 1, para. 107(10). Subs. (3)(c) amended by the Government of Wales Act 1998 (c.38), s.125, Sched. 12, para. 22.

6B–219

Protection for acts done in pursuance of this Act

139.—(1) No person shall be liable, whether on the ground of want of jurisdiction or on any other ground, to any civil or criminal proceedings to which he would have been liable apart from this section in respect of any act purporting to be done in pursuance of this Act or any regulations or rules made under this Act, or in, or in pursuance of anything done in, the discharge of functions conferred by any other enactment on the authority having jurisdiction under Part VII of this Act, unless the act was done in bad faith or without reasonable care.

6B–220

(2) No civil proceedings shall be brought against any person in any court in respect of any such act without the leave of the High Court; and

no criminal proceedings shall be brought against any person in any court in respect of any such act except by or with the consent of the Director of Public Prosecutions.

(3) This section does not apply to proceedings for an offence under this Act, being proceedings which, under any other provision of this Act, can be instituted only by or with the consent of the Director of Public Prosecutions.

(4) This section does not apply to proceedings against the Secretary of State or against a Health Authority or Special Health Authority or against a National Health Service trust established under the National Health Service and Community Care Act 1990.

(5) In relation to Northern Ireland the reference in this section to the Director of Public Prosecutions shall be construed as a reference to the Director of Public Prosecutions for Northern Ireland.

Note

6B–221   Amended by the National Health Service and Community Care Act 1990, Sched. 9, para. 24(7); and the Health Authorities Act 1995, Sched. 1, para. 107(11).

Application for leave under this section to bring proceedings against any person must be made to a judge in Chambers. See O.32, r.9 (1)(b).

An application under subs.(2) is an interlocutory matter coming within the Supreme Court Act 1981, s.18 and a decision thereon is accordingly not appealable without leave (*Moore v. Commissioner of Metropolitan Police* [1968] 1 Q.B. 26; [1967] 2 All E.R. 827 (decision under T.A. 1925)).

The nature of the acts covered by the section and the protection afforded to members of the nursing staff of hospitals in consequence were considered in *R. v. Bracknell Justices, ex p. Griffiths* [1975] 2 W.L.R. 291; [1975] 1 All E.R. 900. See also report of the appeal to the House of Lords [1975] 3 W.L.R. 140; [1975] 2 All E.R. 881.

The section does not apply to proceedings brought by informal patients (*R. v. Runighian* [1977] Crim.L.R. 361).

See articles in (1979) 129 New L.J. 213 and [1979] J.S.W.L. 337.

Supplemental

General provisions as to regulations, orders and rules

6B–222   **143.**—(1) Any power of the Secretary of State or the Lord Chancellor to make regulations, orders or rules under this Act shall be exercisable by statutory instrument.

(2) Any Order in Council under this Act and any statutory instrument containing regulations or rules made under this Act or any order made under section 54A or 65 above shall be subject to annulment in pursuance of a resolution of either House of Parliament.

(3) No order shall be made under section 45A(10), 68(4) or 71(3) above unless a draft of it has been approved by a resolution of each House of Parliament.

Note

6B–223   Amended by the Criminal Justice Act 1991, s.27; the Crime (Sentences) Act 1997, Sched. 4, para. 12; and the Health Authorities Act 1995, Sched. 1, para. 107(13).

Application to Scotland

6B–224   **146.** Sections 42(6), 80, 88 (and so far as applied by that section sections 18, 22 and 138), 104(4), 110 (and so much of Part VII of this Act as is applied in relation to Scotland by that section), 116, 122, 128 (except so far as it relates to patients subject to guardianship), 137, 139(1), 141, 142, 143 (so far as applicable to any Order in Council extending to Scotland) and 144 above shall extend to Scotland together with any amendment or repeal by this Act of or any provision of Schedule 5 to this Act relating to any enactment which so extends; but, except as aforesaid and except so far as it relates to the interpretation or commencement of the said provisions, this Act shall not extend to Scotland.

Application to Northern Ireland

147. Sections 81, 82, 86, 87, 88 (and so far as applied by that section sections 18, 22 and 138), 104(4), 110 (and so much of Part VII as is applied in relation to Northern Ireland by that section), section 128 (except so far as it relates to patients subject to guardianship), 137, 139, 141, 142, 143 (so far as applicable to any Order in Council extending to Northern Ireland) and 144 above shall extend to Northern Ireland together with any amendment or repeal by this Act of or any provision of Schedule 5 to this Act relating to any enactment which so extends; but except as aforesaid and except so far as it relates to the interpretation or commencement of the said provisions, this Act shall not extend to Northern Ireland.

6B–225

At end of renumbered paragraph 6B-226 delete link line [THE NEXT PARAGRAPH IS 6B-232].

Court of Protection Rules 2001

6B–226

(S.I. 2001 No. 824)

6B–227

ARRANGEMENT OF RULES

PART I

PRELIMINARY

RULE
1. Title and Commencement 6B–227.1
2.— Interpretation 6B–228
3. Exercise of the court's functions 6B–229
4.— Computation of time 6B–230
5. Power to vary time 6B–231

PART II

EXERCISE OF JURISDICTION

6. Exercise of jurisdiction 6B–232

PART III

APPLICATIONS

7.— Forms of application 6B–233
8.— Procedure for short order or direction without appointment of a receiver 6B–234
9.— Date for hearing 6B–235
10. Consolidation of Proceedings 6B–236
11. Power to direct applications by officer of the court or Official Solicitor 6B–237
12.— Representation of patient by receiver 6B–238
13. Representation of patient by the Official Solicitor 6B–239
14.— Persons under a disability 6B–240
15. Application under section 54 of the Trustee Act 1925 . . . . .6B–241
16. Application under section 36(9) of the Trustee Act 1925 . . . . .6B–242
17. Application under section 96(1)(k) of the Act 6B–243
18. Application for settlement or gift of patient's property or for execution
    of will of patient 6B–244

PART IV
SERVICE

19.—	Notice of hearing	.6B–245
20.	Mode of service	.6B–246
21.	Service on solicitor	.6B–247
22.	Substituted service	.6B–248
23.—	Service on person under a disability	.6B–249
24.—	Notification of application for appointment of receiver, etc.	.6B–250
25.—	Notification to next of kin etc. of intention to make application for appointment of receiver	.6B–251
26.—	Certificate of service or notification	.6B–252

PART V
EVIDENCE

27.—	Affidavit evidence	.6B–253
28.—	Unsworn evidence	.6B–254
29.—	Written questions to Visitors	.6B–255
30.	Cross-examination of deponent	.6B–256
31.	Administration of oaths	.6B–257
32.—	Filing of written evidence	.6B–258
33.—	Use of evidence in subsequent proceedings	.6B–259
34.—	Evidence to be filed on a first application for receiver, etc	.6B–260
35.—	Evidence of patient's recovery or death and inquiry by court as to whether patient has recovered	.6B–261
36.	Proof of amount due to public authority	.6B–262

PART VI
HEARING OF PROCEEDINGS

37.—	Privacy of applications	.6B–263
38.	Persons attending the hearing	.6B–264
39.	Representation at hearing	.6B–265
40.	Reference of proceedings to judge	.6B–266
41.	Reference of proceedings to Master	.6B–267

PART VII
RECEIVERS

42.—	Interim provision	.6B–268
43.—	Remuneration of receiver	.6B–269
44.	Appointment of receivers with survivorship	.6B–270

PART VIII
ENTRY AND ENFORCEMENT OF ORDERS

45.	Sealing and filing of orders	.6B–271
46.—	Entry of order after notification to a patient	.6B–272
47.	Enforcement of orders	.6B–273

PART IX
SUMMONSES AND ORDERS FOR ATTENDANCE OF WITNESSES AND OTHER PERSONS

48.—	Summoning of witnesses	.6B–274
49.—	Powers of court where undue delay, etc.	.6B–275
50.	Order for examination of patient	.6B–276

PART X
AMENDMENT

51.—	Amendment of application	.6B–277
52.	Clerical mistakes and slips	.6B–278
53.	Endorsement of amendment	.6B–279

PART XI
REVIEWS AND APPEALS

54.—	Review of decision not made on an attended hearing	6B–280
55.—	Appeal from a decision made on an attended hearing	6B–281

PART XII
SECURITY

56.—	Receiver to give security	6B–282
57.	Manner of giving security	6B–283
58.	Lodgement of security	6B–284
59.	Discharge of security where new security given	6B–285
60.	Maintenance of security by bond	6B–286

PART XIII
ACCOUNTS

61.—	Passing of accounts	6B–287
62.	Application of balance due from receiver	6B–288
63.	Default by receiver	6B–289
64.	Payment of maintenance and costs	6B–290
65.—	Final accounts	6B–291
66.	Accounting by other persons	6B–292

PART XIV
INQUIRIES

67.—	Inquiries as to desirability of appointment of receiver, etc	6B–293
68.	Inspection of a patient's property	6B–294
69.	Inquiries as to prior dealing with the patient's property	6B–295
70.	Inquiries as to testamentary documents executed by patient	6B–296
71.	Power to direct other inquiries	6B–297

PART XV
CUSTODY AND DISPOSAL OF FUNDS AND OTHER PROPERTY

72.	Statement of property retained or deposited	6B–298
73.—	Stock in name of patient or receiver	6B–299
74.	Disposal of property on patient's recovery or death	6B–300
75.—	Copies of documents in court	6B–301

PART XVII
FEES

76.—	Appendix of fees	6B–302
77.	Commencement fee	6B–303
78.—	Administration fee	6B–304
79.	Transaction fee	6B–305
80.	Fee on detailed assessment of costs	6B–306
81.—	Receivership fees	6B–307
82.	Winding up fee	6B–308
83.—	Remission and postponement	6B–309

PART XVIII
COSTS

84.—	Costs generally	6B–310
85.	Applications under sections 36(9) and 54 of the Trustee Act 1925	6B–311
86.—	Civil Procedure rules to apply	6B–312
87.—	Costs of unnecessary employment of solicitor, etc not to be allowed	6B–313
88.	Costs of Official Solicitor	6B–314
89.	Ascertainment of costs not relating to the proceedings	6B–315

PART XIX
APPROVAL OF DEEDS

90.	Approval of deeds	6B–316

SECOND CUMULATIVE SUPPLEMENT

PART XX
TRANSITIONAL PROVISIONS

91.— Transitional provisions..6B–317

PART XXI
REVOCATION

92. Revocation of previous rules 6B–318

PART I

PRELIMINARY

Title and Commencement

6B–227.1   1. These Rules may be cited as the Court of Protection Rules 2001[1] and shall come into force on 1st April 2001.

Interpretation

6B–228   2.——(1) In these Rules, unless the context otherwise requires— expressions used in the Supreme Court Act 1981 shall have the same meanings as they have for the purposes of that Act;

"the Act" means the Mental Health Act 1983;

"attended hearing" means a hearing where one or more of the parties to the proceedings have been invited to attend the court for the determination of the application;

"court" means the Court of Protection;

"direction" means a direction or authority given under the seal of the court;

"entered" means entered in the books of the court;

"filed" mean filed in the court office;

"function" means any power, discretion or function conferred by the Act;

"hearing" means an attended or unattended hearing;

"judge" means the Lord Chancellor or a nominated judge;

"Master" means the Master of the Court of Protection;

"medical certificate" means a certificate by a registered medical practitioner that a patient is incapable, by reason of mental disorder, of managing and administering his property and affairs;

"order" includes a certificate, direction or authority of the court under seal;

"patient" includes a person who is alleged to be or who the court has reason to believe may be incapable by reason of mental disorder of managing and administering his property and affairs;

"receiver" means a receiver appointed under section 99(1) of the Act;

"seal" means an official seal of the Court and "sealed" shall be construed accordingly;

---

[1] 1981, c. 5.

"stock" includes shares in any fund, annuity or security transferable in the books kept by any body corporate or unincorporated company or society, or by an instrument of transfer either alone or accompanied by other formalities and includes any dividends paid in respect of them;

"Visitor" means one of the Lord Chancellor's Visitors.

(2) In these Rules—
   (a) any reference to a numbered rule is a reference to the rule of these Rules so numbered in these Rules;
   (b) any reference in a rule to a numbered paragraph is a reference to the paragraph so numbered in the rule in which the reference occurs;
   (c) a form referred to by letter alone means the form so designated in the Schedule to these Rules or a form to the same effect with such variations as the circumstances may require or the court may approve and in all cases shall include a Welsh translation of the form.

Exercise of the court's functions

3. Where any function (in whatever words) is expressed by these Rules to be exercisable by the court then, subject to the provisions of the Act, that functions may be exercised— 6B–229
   (a) by a judge;
   (b) by the Master;
   (c) to the extent to which he is authorised to exercise it under section 94 of the Act, by any nominated officer.

Computation of time

4.——(1) Where a period of time fixed by these Rules or by any order or direction of the court for doing an act expires on a day on which the court office for doing that act is closed and for that reason the act cannot be done on that day, the act shall be done in time if done on the next day on which that office is open. 6B–230

(2) Where the act is required to be done within a specified period after or from a specified date, the period begins immediately after that date.

(3) Where any period of time as mentioned in paragraph (1) is less than six days, any day on which the court office is closed shall not be included in that computation.

Power to vary time

5. The court may extend or abridge the time limited by these Rules or any order or direction of the court for doing any act or taking any proceedings upon such terms as the court thinks fit and notwithstanding, in the case of an extension, that the time so limited has expired. 6B–231

PART II

EXERCISE OF JURISDICTION

Exercise of jurisdiction

6. Except where these Rules otherwise provide, any function may be exercised— 6B–232

(a) without fixing an appointment for a hearing;
(b) by the court of its own motion or at the instance or on the application of any person interested;
(c) whether or not any proceedings have been commenced in the court with respect to the patient.

PART III

APPLICATIONS

Forms of application

6B–233 7.——(1) Subject to paragraph (3), a first application to the court for the appointment of a receiver shall state the name and address of the applicant and the proposed receiver and their relationship (if any) to the patient in such manner as the court shall direct and an application to the court respecting the exercise of any of its other jurisdiction in relation to a patient, may be made by letter unless the court otherwise directs that it should be formal, in which case it shall be made in Form A.

(2) An application for the appointment of a receiver shall be treated as an application for the appointment as receiver of the person named in the application or some other suitable person.

(3) On grounds of urgency the court may dispense with the need for an application in writing.

(4) An application relating to the committal of a person for contempt of court shall be made to a judge but all other applications to the court shall be made in the first instance to the Master.

Procedure for short order or direction without appointment of a receiver

6B–234 8.——(1) Without prejudice to the generality of Rule 6, if it appears to the court that—
(a) the property of the patient does not exceed £10,000 in value; or
(b) it is otherwise appropriate to proceed under this rule,
and that it is not necessary to appoint a receiver for a patient, the court may make a short order or direction under this rule whether or not the application was made for the appointment of a receiver for the patient.

(3) A short order or direction under this rule is an order or direction directing an officer of the court or some other suitable person named in the order or direction to deal with the patient's property (or any part of it), or with his affairs, in any manner authorised by the Act and specified in the order or direction.

Date for hearing

6B–235 9.——(1) Upon receiving an application under rule 7 the court shall fix a date for the hearing of the application unless it considers that the application can properly be dealt with without a hearing, and on this ground the court may cancel any hearing fixed under this paragraph.

(2) Where a hearing is fixed under paragraph (1) an officer shall notify the applicant, by letter, of the date and time of the hearing.

Consolidation of Proceedings
10. The court may allow one application to be made in respect of two or more patients or may consolidate an application relating to two or more patients, if in its opinion the proceedings relating to them can be more conveniently dealt with together. **6B–236**

Power to direct applications by officer of the court or Official Solicitor
11. Where, in the opinion of the court, an application ought to be made for the appointment or discharge of a receiver or for a direction with regard to the exercise of any other function with respect to the property and affairs of a patient, and there appears to be no other suitable person able and willing to make the application, or the court for any other reason thinks fit, the court may direct that the application be made by an officer of the court or, if he consents, the Official Solicitor. **6B–237**

Representation of patient by receiver
12.——(1) Except as mentioned in rule 18(c), (d) and (e), an application on behalf of a patient for whom a receiver has been appointed shall, unless the court otherwise directs, be made by a receiver in his own name. **6B–238**

(2) Subject to any directions given by the court, a patient for whom a receiver has been appointed may be represented by the receiver at any hearing relating to the patient or of which the patient has been given notice.

Representation of patient by the Official Solicitor
13. Where, in any proceedings, the court considers that the interests of the patient are not adequately represented, the court may, with the consent of the Official Solicitor, direct that the Official Solicitor shall act as a solicitor for the patient either generally in the proceedings or for any particular purpose connected with the proceedings, except that it shall not be necessary to appoint the Official Solicitor to be receiver or guardian ad litem for the patient. **6B–239**

Persons under a disability
14.——(1) In this rule, "person under a disability" means a minor or a patient for whom no receiver has been appointed. **6B–240**

(2) A person under a disability shall not make an application in proceedings relating to another person except by his next friend and shall not resist an application in any such proceedings except by his guardian ad litem.

(3) Where a person is to be appointed next friend or guardian ad litem of a person under a disability in substitution for the person previously acting as next friend or guardian ad litem, the appointment shall

be made by the court but, except for this, an order of the court appointing a next friend or guardian ad litem of a person under a disability shall not be necessary.

(4) Before the name of any person is used in any proceedings as next friend or guardian ad litem of a person under a disability there shall be filed—
 (a) a written consent of the first-mentioned person to act as next friend or (as the case may be) guardian ad litem of the person under a disability in the proceedings, and
 (b) a certificate by the solicitor acting for the person under a disability certifying—
  (i) that he knows or believes that the person to whom the certificate relates is a minor or patient giving (in the case of a patient) the grounds of his knowledge or belief, and
  (ii) except where the person named in the certificate is the Official Solicitor, that the person so named has no interest in the proceedings adverse to that of the person under a disability.

Application under section 54 of the Trustee Act 1925

6B–241 15. An application to the court with respect to the jurisdiction referred to in section 54(2) of the Trustee Act 1925 may be made only by—
 (a) the receiver for the patient, or
 (b) any person who has made an application for the appointment of a receiver which has not yet been fully determined, or
 (c) a continuing trustee, or
 (d) any other person who, according to the practice of the Chancery Division, would have been entitled to make the application if it had been made in the High Court.

Application under section 36(9) of the Trustee Act 1925

6B–242 16. No person other than a co-trustee, or other person with power to appoint a new trustee, may make an application to the court under section 36(9) of the Trustee Act 1925 for leave to appoint a new trustee in place of a patient.

Application under section 96(1)(k) of the Act

6B–243 17. The provisions of rule 15 shall apply with such modifications as may be necessary to an application under section 96(1)(k) of the Act for an order for the exercise of any power vested in a patient of appointing trustees or retiring from a trust.

Application for settlement or gift of patient's property or for execution of will of patient

6B–244 18. An application under section 96(1)(d) of the Act for an order for the settlement or gift of any property of a patient, or an application under section 96(1)(e) of the Act for an order of execution for a patient of a will, may be made only by—

(a) the receiver for the patient, or
(b) any person who has made an application for the appointment of a receiver which has not yet been determined, or
(c) any person who, under any known will of the patient or under his intestacy, may become entitled to any property of the patient or any interest in it, or
(d) any person for whom the patient might be expected to provide if he were not mentally disordered, or
(e) any attorney acting under a registered enduring power of attorney, or
(f) any other person whom the court may authorise to make it.

PART IV

SERVICE

Notice of hearing

19.——(1) Except where these rules provide otherwise or the court directs otherwise, the applicant shall give notice of the hearing of an application in accordance with the following provisions of this rule.   6B–245

(2) Where a receiver has been appointed for a patient he shall, unless he is the applicant, be given notice of the hearing of any application relating to the patient.

(3) Where the application is one to which rules 15 or 17 relate, notice of the hearing of the application shall also be given to every person who would have been required to be served with the application notice if the application had been made to the High Court.

(4) Notice of the hearing of the application shall also be given to such other persons who appear to the court to be interested as the court may specify.

(5) Notice of a hearing shall be given—
  (a) in the case of a first application for the appointment of a receiver, or an application under rule 16, not less than ten clear days and
  (b) in the case of any other application, not less than two clear days before the date fixed for the hearing.

(6) For the purposes of this rule notice of a hearing shall be given to the person concerned in such manner as the court may direct.

Mode of service

20. Except where these rules otherwise provide, any document required by these Rules to be served on any person shall be served by—   6B–246
  (a) delivering it to him personally;
  (b) sending it to him by first class post or through a document exchange at his last known address; or
  (c) by transmitting it to him at his last known address by fax or other electronic means.

Service on solicitor

21. Where a solicitor acting for the person to be served with any document endorses on the document or a copy of it a statement that he   6B–247 accepts service on behalf of that person, the document shall be deemed to have been duly served on that person and to have been served on the date on which the endorsement was made.

Substituted service

6B–248   22. Where it appears to the court that it is impracticable for any reason to serve a document in accordance with rule 20, the court may make an order for substituted service of the document by taking such steps as the court may direct to bring it to the notice of the person to be served.

Service on person under a disability

6B–249   23.——(1) Unless the court otherwise directs, any document required by these Rules to be served on a person who is a minor or patient (in this rule referred to as a person under a disability) shall be served—
    (a) in the case of a minor who is not also a patient, on his parent or guardian or, if he has no parent or guardian, on the person with parental responsibility as defined in section 3 of the Children Act 1989[1];
    (b) in the case of a patient—
      (i) on his receiver or, if he has no receiver,
      (ii) on the person acting in pursuance of an order or direction under rule 8, or, if there is no such person,
      (iii) on an attorney acting under a registered power of attorney, or, if there is no such attorney,
      (iv) on the person with whom he resides or in whose care he is;
and must be served in a manner required by these Rules.

(2) Notwithstanding anything in paragraph (1), the court may order that any document which has been served on the person under a disability or on a person other than a person mentioned in that paragraph shall be deemed to be duly served on the person under a disability.

(3) Nothing in this rule shall apply to an order required by rule 42 to be served on a patient.

Notification of application for appointment of receiver, etc.

6B–250   24.——(1) Where—
    (a) a first application is made for the appointment of a receiver for a patient or for an order authorising a person to do any act or carry out any transaction on behalf of a patient without appointing him receiver, or
    (b) the court proposes to make a short order or direction;
the patient shall be notified in such manner as the court may direct.

(2) Where the patient is a minor, notification under paragraph (1) shall be given to his parent or guardian or, if he has no parent or guardian, to the person with parental responsibility within the meaning of the Children Act 1989.

---

[1] 1989, c. 41.

Notification to next of kin etc. of intention to make application for appointment of receiver

25.——(1) Where an applicant proposes to make an application for the appointment of a receiver or a new receiver, the applicant shall give notice of his intention to—
    (a) all relatives of the patient who have the same or a nearer degree of relationship to the patient than the applicant or proposed receiver; and
    (b) such other persons who appear to the court to be interested as the court may specify;
    unless the court directs that such notification shall be dispensed with.

(2) For the purposes of this rule, notice of the intention to make an application is given if the person concerned is notified, in such manner as the court may direct, of the identities of the patient, the applicant and the proposed receiver and supplied with such additional information as the court may direct.

6B–251

Certificate of service or notification

26.——(1) If the court so directs, a certificate of service showing where, when, how and by whom service was effected shall be filed as soon as practicable after service of a document has been effected in accordance with these Rules.

(2) The provisions of paragraph (1) shall apply to the giving of notification under rules 24 and 25 as they apply to the service of documents and references in that paragraph to service shall accordingly be construed as including references to notification and the giving of notification respectively.

6B–252

PART V

EVIDENCE

Affidavit evidence

27.——(1) Except where these Rules provide otherwise, evidence in proceedings governed by these Rules shall be given by affidavit.

(2) An affidavit for use in proceedings under these Rules may be sworn—
    (a) in England or Wales, before any person authorised to take affidavits under the Commissioners for Oaths Acts 1889 and 1891[1], under the Solicitors Act 1974[2], or under the Courts and Legal Services Act 1990[3] or before any officer of the court of, or above, the rank of higher executive officer;
    (b) outside England and Wales, before any person before whom an affidavit may be sworn for use in the Supreme Court.

6B–253

Unsworn evidence

28.——(1) Notwithstanding rule 27(1), the court may accept and act upon a statement of facts or other such evidence, whether oral or writ-

6B–254

---

[1] 1889 c. 10; 1891 c. 50.
[2] 1974, c. 47.
[3] 1990, c. 41.

ten, as the court considers sufficient, although not given on oath and whether or not it would be admissible in a court of law apart from this rule.

(2) The court may give directions as to the manner in which a statement of facts or other written evidence under paragraph (1) is to be given but subject to such directions any such statement or other evidence shall—
> (a) be drawn up in numbered paragraphs and dated; and
> (b) be signed by the person by whom it is given.

Written questions to Visitors

6B-255   29.——(1) Where a Visitor's report, or information contained in such a report, has been disclosed to any person in pursuance of section 103(8) of the Act, the court may, on the application of any person who appears to the court to be interested, give leave for written questions relevant to the issues before the court to be put to the Visitor by whom the report was made.

(2) The questions sought to be put to the Visitor shall be submitted to the court, which may put to the Visitor with such amendments (if any) as it thinks fit and the Visitor shall give his replies in writing to the questions so put.

(3) The court may disclose the replies given by the Visitor under this rule to any person who appears to the court to be interested, or to his legal or medical adviser, on such conditions (if any) as it thinks fit.

(4) No Visitor shall be required to give written evidence for the purpose of any proceedings to which these rules relate, other than in accordance with this rule.

(5) In this rule, "Visitor" means a Medical or Legal Visitor.

Cross-examination of deponent

6B-256   30. Any person who has made an affidavit or given a certificate or other written evidence for use in proceedings under these Rules may be ordered by the court to attend for cross-examination.

Administration of oaths

6B-257   31. The court may direct that an oath be administered to any witness or interpreter in any proceedings before the court.

Filing of written evidence

6B-258   32.——(1) Before an affidavit certificate or other evidence is used in any proceedings under these rules it shall be filed but the court may make an order on the basis of such evidence before it is filed if the person tendering it undertakes to file it before the order is drawn up.

(2) There shall be endorsed on every affidavit, certificate or other written evidence the name and address of the solicitor, if any, acting for the person on whose behalf it is filed.

Use of evidence in subsequent proceedings

6B-259   33.——(1) Except where the court otherwise directs, evidence which has been used in any proceedings relating to a patient may be used at any subsequent stage of those proceedings or in any other proceedings relating to the same patient or to another member of the patient's family.

(2) Without prejudice to paragraph (1), the Master may, upon application being made for that purpose, authorise the use of such evidence in any legal proceedings that he may specify.

Evidence to be filed on a first application for receiver, etc

34.——(1) Where a first application has been made for the appointment of a receiver for a patient or for a short order or direction under rule 8 authorising any person to do any act or carry out any transaction on behalf of a patient without appointing him receiver—   **6B–260**
- (a) the applicant shall, unless the court otherwise directs, file a medical certificate and evidence of family and property; and
- (b) the court may—
   - (i) require the applicant to produce to it such evidence as it shall direct of the suitability of the applicant to be appointed a receiver or to do any such act or carry out any such transaction without being appointed receiver; and
   - (ii) make such enquiries as it shall think fit with regard to the suitability of the applicant for such appointment.

(2) In this rule, "evidence of family and property" means a certificate or, if the court so directs, in a particular case, an affidavit giving particulars of the patient's relatives and such other persons as the court may direct, property and affairs and of the circumstances giving rise to the application.

(3) Rule 28 applies to unsworn evidence of family and property as it applies to unsworn evidence generally.

Evidence of patient's recovery or death and inquiry by court as to whether patient has recovered

35.——(1) Where at any stage of proceedings relating to a patient the court has reason to believe that the patient has recovered or has died, the court may require medical evidence of the recovery or evidence of the death (as the case may be) to be furnished to it by such person as it thinks appropriate.   **6B–261**

(2) The court shall, from time to time, review a patient's case where a medical certificate provided to the court expressed an opinion that there is a possibility of mental recovery and make such inquiries and carry out such investigations as it thinks fit to establish whether or not the patient has recovered.

Proof of amount due to public authority

36. The amount due to any public authority for the past maintenance of a patient may, unless the court otherwise directs, be proved by the filing of an account certified under the hand of the proper officer of the authority.   **6B–262**

PART VI

HEARING OF PROCEEDINGS

Privacy of applications

6B-263 **37.**——(1) Every application shall be heard in chambers unless, in the case of an application for a hearing by the judge, the judge otherwise directs.

(2) The court shall give such directions as it thinks fit concerning the privacy of applications made to it.

Persons attending the hearing

6B-264 **38.** Subject to rule 14 the court may determine what persons are to be entitled to attend at any stage of the proceedings relating to a patient.

Representation at hearing

6B-265 **39.** Where two or more persons appearing at a hearing are represented by the same legal representative, the court may, if it thinks fit, require any of them to be separately represented.

Reference of proceedings to judge

6B-266 **40.** Where a function of the court is not being exercised by a judge, the court, after giving such direction as it thinks fit, shall refer to the judge any proceedings or any question arising in any proceedings which ought, by virtue of any enactment or in its opinion, to be considered by the judge.

Reference of proceedings to Master

6B-267 **41.** The judge may refer any proceedings before him or any question arising in them to the Master for inquiry and report.

PART VII

RECEIVERS

Interim provision

6B-268 **42.**——(1) Where in the opinion of the court it is necessary to make immediate provision in relation to the property and affairs of a patient for any of the matters referred to in section 95(1) of the Act—

    (a) the court may by certificate or direction direct or authorise any named person to do any act or carry out any transaction specified in the certificate or direction; or

    (b) the court may by order appoint an interim receiver for the patient and, subject to any direction given by the court, such appointment shall continue until further order.

(2) An order appointing an interim receiver shall, unless the court otherwise directs, be served upon the patient within such time as the order may specify and the patient may, within such further time as the order may specify, apply under rule 54 for the review of the order by the court or, if the order was made by a judge, apply to have the order set aside.

Remuneration of receiver

43.——(1) Where a receiver is appointed for a patient, the court may, during the receivership, allow the receiver remuneration for his services at such amount or at such rate as it considers reasonable and proper and any remuneration so allowed shall constitute a debt due to the receiver from the patient and his estate. **6B–269**

(2) No request by a receiver to have the sum payable for this remuneration fixed after the death or recovery of the patient shall be entertained unless the court has during the receivership directed that remuneration be allowed and the request is made within six years from the date of the receiver's discharge.

Appointment of receivers with survivorship

44. Where in the opinion of the court two or more persons ought to be appointed receivers of the same patient and more than one of them ought to continue to act after the death or discharge of any of the others, the court when appointing them receivers direct that the receivership shall continue in favour of the surviving or continuing receiver or receivers. **6B–270**

PART VIII

ENTRY AND ENFORCEMENT OF ORDERS

Sealing and filing of orders

45. Every order, certificate, direction or authority of the court which is drawn up shall, when entered, be sealed and filed. **6B–271**

Entry of order after notification to a patient

46.——(1) Where— **6B–272**
    (a) an order is made on a first application appointing a receiver for a patient or directing or authorising any person to do any act or carry out any transaction on behalf of a patient without appointing him receiver; or
    (b) an order or direction with respect to a patient's property under rule 8, the order or direction shall not be entered until the expiration of ten clear days after the patient has been notified in accordance with rule 24(1) unless such notification is dispensed with.

(2) Nothing in paragraph (1) shall prevent the entry of an interim order, certificate or direction under rule 42 for the protection of a

patient's property or for the application of a patient's property for his benefit.

Enforcement of orders
6B–273 47. Every writ of execution or other process for the enforcement of an order of the court shall be issued out of the Central Office of the Supreme Court.

PART IX

SUMMONSES AND ORDERS FOR ATTENDANCE OF WITNESSES AND OTHER PERSONS

Summoning of witnesses
6B–274 48.——(1) In any proceedings under these Rules the court may allow or direct any person to take out a witness summons in Form B requiring the person named in it to attend before the court and give oral evidence or produce any document.

(2) An application by a person allowed to take out a witness summons shall be made by filing a statement giving—
    (a) the name and address of the person making the application and of his solicitor, if any;
    (b) the name, address and occupation of the proposed witness;
    (c) particulars of any document which the proposed witness is to be required to produce; and
    (d) the grounds on which the application is made.

(3) A witness summons shall be served on the witness personally a reasonable time before the day fixed for his attendance and he shall be entitled to the same conduct money and payment of expenses and loss of time as if he had been summoned to attend the trial of an action in the High Court.

Powers of court where undue delay, etc
6B–275 49.——(1) If the court is dissatisfied with the conduct of any proceedings or the carrying out of an order whether by reason of undue delay or otherwise, the court may require the person having the conduct of the proceedings, or any other person appearing to be responsible, to explain the delay or any other cause of dissatisfaction, and may then make such order for expediting the proceedings or otherwise as may be appropriate.

(2) For the purposes of paragraph (1), the court may direct any person to make any application and to conduct any proceedings and carry out any directions which the court may specify; and the court may, if it thinks fit and he consents, appoint the Official Solicitor to act as solicitor for the patient in the proceedings in the place of any solicitor previously acting for him.

Order for examination of patient
6B–276 50. In any proceedings relating to a patient, a judge or Master may make an order for the patient's attendance at such time and place as he

may direct for examination by the Master, a Visitor or any medical practitioner.

PART X

AMENDMENT

Amendment of application

51.——(1) The court may allow or direct an applicant, at any stage of the proceedings, to amend his application in such manner and on such terms as to costs or otherwise as may be just.   **6B–277**

(2) The amendment may be effected by making in writing the necessary alterations to the application, but if the amendments are so numerous or of such a nature or length that written alterations would make it difficult or inconvenient to read, a fresh application amended as authorised or directed may be issued.

Clerical mistakes and slips

52. The court may at any time correct any clerical mistakes in an order or direction or any error arising in an order or direction from any accidental slip or omission.   **6B–278**

Endorsement of amendment

53. Where an application, order or direction has been amended under rule 51 or 52, a note shall be placed on it showing the date on which it was amended and the alteration shall be sealed.   **6B–279**

PART XI

REVIEWS AND APPEALS

Review of decision not made on an attended hearing

54.——(1) Any person who is aggrieved by a decision of the court that was made without an attended hearing may apply to the court within fourteen days of the date on which the decision was given to have the decision reviewed by the court.   **6B–280**

(2) No review shall lie from any decision under rule 83 of these Rules.

(3) On considering an application for review the court may either confirm or revoke the previous decision or make any other order or decision which it thinks fit.

(4) Any person aggrieved by any order or decision of the court made on considering an application for review may apply to the court for an attended hearing.

Appeal from a decision made on an attended hearing

55.——(1) Any person aggrieved by a decision of the court made on an attended hearing may, within fourteen days from the date of entry of   **6B–281**

the order or (as the case may be) from the date of the decision, appeal to a nominated judge.

(2) The applicant shall within the fourteen days—
  (a) serve a notice of appeal in Form C on—
    (i) every person who appeared, or was represented before, the court when the order or decision was made or given, and
    (ii) any other person whom the court may direct; and
  (b) lodge a copy of the notice at the court office.

(3) The time and place at which the appeal is to be heard shall be fixed by the court and it shall cause notice of the time and place so fixed to be sent to the appellant who shall immediately send notice of it to every person who has been served with notice of the appeal.

(4) No evidence further to that given at the hearing shall be filed in support of or in opposition to the appeal without leave of the court.

PART XII

SECURITY

Receiver to give security

6B–282 56.——(1) Where an order is made appointing a person other than an officer of the court or the Official Solicitor as receiver for a patient—
  (a) the person appointed shall, unless the court otherwise directs, give such security for the due performance of his duties as the court may approve and shall give it before acting as receiver unless the court allows it to be given subsequently; and
  (b) the order shall not be entered until the person appointed has given to the satisfaction of the court any security required to be given by him before acting.

(2) The court may from time to time vary or dispense with any security required.

Manner of giving security

6B–283 57. Subject to any directions of the court, security may be given in any one of the following ways, or partly in one of those ways and partly in another—
  (a) by a bond approved by the court and given by the person giving security and also by—
    (i) an insurance company, a group of underwriters or a bank approved by the court; or
    (ii) with the approval of the court, two personal sureties; or
  (b) in such other manner as the court may approve.

Lodgement of security

6B–284 58. Any security given by lodgment of money or stock shall be dealt with in accordance with the terms of the direction filed when the lodgment was made.

Discharge of security where new security given
59. Where a receiver is authorised or directed to give new security, and—
    (a) the new security has been completed; and
    (b) he has paid or secured to the satisfaction of the court any balance due from him,
the former security shall, unless the court otherwise directs, be discharged.

6B–285

Maintenance of security by bond
60. Every person who has given security by a bond shall, whenever his accounts are passed, or the court so directs, satisfy the court—
    (a) that any premiums payable in respect of the bond have been duly paid;
    (b) if the bond was given by personal sureties, that each surety is living and within the jurisdiction and has neither been adjudicated bankrupt nor compounded with his creditors,
and, if the court is not so satisfied, it may require new security to be given or may give such other directions as it thinks fit.

6B–286

PART XIII

ACCOUNTS

Passing of accounts
61.——(1) Every receiver shall—
    (a) annually;
    (b) on the death or recovery of the patient for whom he has been appointed receiver; and
    (c) at any other time that the court may direct
        deliver his accounts to the court within such time and in such manner as the court shall direct.
(2) The receiver shall answer such requisitions on his accounts as the court shall raise and in such manner and in such time as the court shall direct.
(3) On the passing of any accounts the court shall make all proper allowances out of the patient's estate, including an allowance in respect of the reasonable and proper costs of the receiver in passing the accounts.
(4) The court may direct that a receiver need not account under this rule or may dispense with the passing of any accounts at any time at which they would otherwise require to be passed.

6B–287

Application of balance due from receiver
62. The balance found due from a receiver on the passing of his accounts or so much of it as the court may direct, shall—
    (a) be paid by the receiver into court to the credit of the proceedings and invested in such manner as the court may direct, or

6B–288

(b) be invested or otherwise dealt with by the receiver in such manner as the court may direct.

Default by receiver

6B–289 63. Where a receiver fails to comply with rule 61 or 62 or fails to pay into court or invest or otherwise deal with any money in accordance with any direction of the court, the court may disallow any remuneration which would otherwise be due to the receiver and, if he has made default in paying into court or investing or otherwise dealing with any money, may charge him with interest on it at such rate as the court may reasonably fix, for the period of his default.

Payment of maintenance and costs

6B–290 64. Unless otherwise directed, any money ordered to be paid by a receiver for maintenance shall be paid out of income and any costs ordered to be paid by a receiver may, when agreed, assessed by way of detailed assessment or fixed, be paid out of any moneys coming into his hands, after providing for any maintenance and fees payable under these Rules.

Final accounts

6B–291 65.——(1) Every receiver shall, on the death or recovery of the patient for whom he has been appointed receiver, deliver his final account to the court within such time and in such manner as the court shall direct.

(2) On the discharge or death of a receiver, the receiver, or in the case of his death, his personal representatives, shall deliver a final account to the court within such time as the court shall direct.

(3) The court shall pass the final account of a receiver from the date of the receiver's last account or, if no account of his has previously been passed, from the date of his appointment, unless in the opinion of the court the passing of such accounts may properly be dispensed with.

(4) If a balance is found due from a receiver or his estate, he or his personal representatives (as the case may be) shall pay it into court or otherwise deal with as the court may direct.

(5) If a balance is found due to the receiver or his estate, it shall be paid to him or his personal representatives (as the case may be) by the patient or out of the patient's estate.

(6) On payment of any balance found due from a receiver, or if no balance is found due from him or the passing of his accounts has been dispensed with under paragraph (1), the security of the receiver shall be discharged.

Accounting by other persons

6B–292 66. Rules 63 to 65 shall also apply, to the extent directed by the court, to any person who is—

    (a) directed to deal with the patient's property or affairs under rule 8;

(b) directed or otherwise authorised to act under rule 42(1)(a); or
   (c) appointed an interim receiver under rule 42(1)(b),
as they apply to a receiver.

PART XIV

INQUIRIES

Inquiries as to desirability of appointment of receiver, etc
67.——(1) Where the court has reason to believe that a receiver should be appointed for a patient or that any other function of the court should be exercised with respect to the property and affairs of a patient, the court may direct—
   (a) a Medical or Legal Visitor, or, if he consents, the Official Solicitor or any other appropriate person to visit the patient and report to the court whether it is desirable in the interests of the patient that an application should be made for that purpose, and, in the case of a report by a Medical or Legal Visitor, whether there is any other matter which the court should consider before exercising its functions in relation to a patient's property and affairs; or
   (b) a Medical Visitor to visit the patient and report to the court on the capacity of the patient to manage and administer his property and affairs.

(2) On receiving any report pursuant to paragraph (1), the court may—
   (a) direct an application to be made pursuant to rule 11; or
   (b) if the report is by a Medical Visitor and the court is satisfied that the patient is incapable, by reason of mental disorder, of managing and administering his property and affairs, make an order appointing a receiver or exercising any other function with respect to the patient's property and affairs.

(3) The court may direct a General Visitor or any other appropriate person to visit the patient and report whether it is desirable for any functions in relation to the patient's property and affairs to be exercised.

(4) On receiving any report pursuant to paragraph (3)—
   (a) the court may direct that an application be made pursuant to rule 11; or
   (b) the court may exercise any function conferred on it in relation to a patient's property and affairs.

6B–293

Inspection of a patient's property
68. For the purpose of any proceedings relating to the property of a patient—
   (a) the court may inspect the property or direct an officer of the court, the Official Solicitor (if he consents) or any other appropriate person to inspect the property, make any necessary enquiries and report to the court; and
   (b) the court may, if it thinks fit and of its own motion, make such an inspection and inquiries or direct some other appropriate person to do so and report to it.

6B–294

Inquiries as to prior dealing with the patient's property

6B–295 69. In any proceedings relating to a patient the court may make or cause to be made such inquiries as it thinks fit as to any dealing with the patient's property before the commencement of the proceedings and as to the patient's mental capacity at the time of such dealing.

Inquiries as to testamentary documents executed by patient

6B–296 70. The court may make or cause to be made inquiries whether any person has in his possession or under his control or has any knowledge of any testamentary document executed by a patient, and may direct that person to answer the inquiries on oath and to produce any such document which is in his possession or under his control and to deal with it in such manner as the court may direct.

Power to direct other inquiries

6B–297 71. The court may make or cause to be made any other inquiries which it or he may consider necessary or expedient for the proper discharge of its functions under the Act of these rules.

PART XV

CUSTODY AND DISPOSAL OF FUNDS AND OTHER PROPERTY

Statement of property retained or deposited

6B–298 72. Where under a direction of the court any furniture or effects of a patient are allowed to remain in the possession of, or deposited with, any person, that person shall, unless the court otherwise directs, sign and file an inventory of the furniture or effects and an undertaking not to part with them during the patient's lifetime except on a direction under seal.

Stock in name of patient or receiver

6B–299 73.——(1) Where any stock—
  (a) is standing in the name of a patient beneficially entitled to it; or
  (b) is standing in the name of a receiver in trust for a patient, or as part of his property, and the receiver dies intestate or himself becomes incapable by reason of mental disorder of acting as receiver, or is out of the court's jurisdiction, or it is uncertain whether he is still alive, or he neglects or refuses to transfer the stock or to receive and pay over the dividends as the court directs,
  the court may order some proper person to transfer the stock into the name of the receiver or, as the case may be, a new receiver for the patient or into court or otherwise deal with it as the court may direct and also to receive and pay over the dividends as the court directs.
  (2) Where an order made under paragraph (1) or under section 100

of the Act directing stock to be transferred into court, the person required to effect the transfer shall be—
    (a) in the case of stock standing in the stock register kept by the Bank of England or any other bank or by the Crown Agents for Overseas Governments and Administrations, some proper officer of the bank or Crown Agents;
    (b) in any other case, some proper officer of the company or other body whose stock is to be transferred,
and that person shall, if so ordered, receive any sum accrued due before the transfer by way of dividend, bonus or periodical payment in respect of the stock and pay it into court to the general account of the patient or to a separate account or otherwise deal with it as the court may direct.

Disposal of property on patient's recovery or death

74.——(1) On the recovery of a patient the court may order any money, securities or other property belonging to the patient, or forming part of his estate, or remaining under the control of, or held under the directions of the court, to be transferred to the person who appears to be entitled to it.   **6B–300**

(2) On the death of a patient the court may direct any money, securities or other property belonging to the patient or forming part of his estate, remaining under the control of, or held under the direction of the court, to be transferred to the person who appears to be entitled to it.

(3) If no grant of representation has been taken out to the estate of a deceased patient and it appears to the court that the assets of the estate, after deduction of debts and funeral expenses, do not exceed £5,000 in value, the court may, if it thinks fit, provide for payment of the funeral expenses out of any funds in court standing to the credit of the deceased and order that any such funds, or the balance of them, or any other property of the patient remaining under the control, or held under the directions, of the court be paid, transferred, delivered or released (as appropriate) to the personal representative of the deceased when constituted or to the person who appears to be entitled to apply for a grant of representation to his estate.

(4) The court may at any time, pending notification to him of the grant of representation to the estate of a patient, direct that any money or securities which belonged to the patient when he died and were not already in court shall be transferred to the court.

Copies of documents in court

75.——(1) Any person who has filed an affidavit or other document shall, unless the court otherwise directs, be entitled, on request, to be supplied with a copy of it.   **6B–301**

(2) The person having the conduct of any proceedings shall, unless the court otherwise directs, be entitled, on request, to be supplied by the court with a copy of any order, certificate, authority, direction or other document made, given or prepared by the court in the proceedings.

(3) Any other person may, on request, be supplied with a copy of any such document as is mentioned in paragraph (1) or (2), if the court is satisfied that he has good reason for requiring it and that it is not reasonably practicable for him to obtain it form the person entitled to bespeak a copy from the court.

(4) Any copy of any document supplied under paragraphs (1), (2) or (3) shall, if so required, be marked as an office copy.

PART XVII

FEES

Appendix of fees

6B-302 76.——(1) The Appendix to these Rules, in this Part of these Rules described as "the Appendix", shall apply so as to fix the fees payable pursuant to the following provisions of this Part of these Rules.

(2) Subject to paragraph (3), the fee specified in the Appendix shall be taken in respect of proceedings governed by these Rules.

(3) The fee prescribed by rule 78 and contained in the corresponding provisions of the Appendix shall not be payable where an officer of the court has been appointed and is acting as receiver for the patient.

(4) Subject to paragraph (5), the person by whom any fee (other than a fee payable under rule 82) is payable shall, unless the court otherwise directs make the payment out of the income of the patient or, if dead, out of his estate.

(5) Where the payment of a fee is made by the Accountant General then, unless the court directs that payment is to be made out of the income of the fund, the Accountant General shall meet the fee from any cash sums held in court to the account of the patient.

Commencement fee

6B-303 77. A commencement fee shall be payable on any first application for the appointment of a receiver in respect of any patient.

Administration fee

6B-304 78.——(1) An administration fee shall be payable—
  (a) on the first and every subsequent anniversary of the date of the appointment of a receiver, until the termination of the proceedings, and at such other times either during the proceedings or at their termination as the court may direct;
  (b) where the period for which the administration fee is payable is for less than one year, the fee payable shall be the proportion of the full fee as such period bears to one year.

(2) The court shall annually, or at such other intervals as may be convenient, issue a certificate in respect of each patient stating—
  (a) the amount of the administration fee payable in respect of the patient at the date of the certificate;
  (b) the period in respect of which the administration fee is payable; and

(c) the name of the person by whom the payment is made.

(3) Upon the issue of a certificate under this rule the amount of the fee shall be charged upon the patient's estate, and the payment shall be made within such time (not exceeding one month from the date of the certificate) as the court may allow.

(4) In any case in which it appears to the court that amount of the fee certified under this rule has been wrongly assessed, the court may direct that the fee is to be adjusted as it appears to it to be convenient.

(5) No administration fee shall be taken where the proceedings are terminated less than four weeks from the date of issue of the first application for the appointment of a receiver.

Transaction fee

79.——(1) A transaction fee shall be payable in respect of any order or direction or, as the case may be, any application for an order or direction to be made in exercise of the specific powers conferred by—

    (a) paragraphs (d), (e), (h) or (k) of section 96(1) of the Act;
    (b) section 100 of the Act;
    (c) sections 36(9) and 54 of the Trustee Act 1925; and
    (d) section 1(3) of the Variation of Trusts Act 1958.

(2) A transaction fee shall be payable in respect of an application for authorisation of a person under section 20 of the Trusts of Land and Appointment of Trustees Act 1996.

(3) In a special case, the standard fee payable in accordance with the Appendix shall be increased in accordance with the Appendix where there is readily ascertainable pecuniary consideration in the nature of capital arising to or provided by the patient (otherwise than by way of a loan to, or repayment of a loan by, the patient), no account being taken of the possible capitalisation of the value of rents or interests or other income payments.

(4) Where a transaction is to be approved under an order or direction mentioned in paragraph (1), or authorisation is to be given as mentioned in paragraph (2), the fee shall be taken—

    (a) in a special case, upon the approval of the transaction;
    (b) otherwise, upon the making of the application for the order, direction or authorisation
    and the court shall issue a certificate stating the amount payable.

(5) A transaction fee as specified in paragraph 3(4) of the Appendix shall be payable on application for the appointment of a new receiver.

(6) A transaction fee as specified in paragraph 3(5) of the Appendix shall be payable upon the making of the application for an order or direction to be made in exercise of the specific powers conferred by paragraph (b) of section 96(1) of the Act, offering or authorising the sale of any land as defined in the Law of Property Act 1925[1].

(7) Except where the court otherwise directs, no fee shall be payable under this rule upon the sale or purchase of personal chattels or any investment for the time being authorised by law for the investment of

---

[1] The definition of "land" in section 205(1)(x) was amended by Schedule 4 to the Trusts of Land and Appointment of Trustees Act 1996.

trust property or in securities quoted on any stock exchange in the United Kingdom.
    (8) In this rule—
- (a) "special case" means an order made by the court under paragraphs (d) or (h) of the Act or under section 1(3) of the Variation of Trusts Act 1958; and
- (b) references to an application for an order or direction include (without limitation) an application for an order or direction made at the same time as a first application for the appointment of a receiver or other originating process.

Fee on detailed assessment of costs

6B–306   **80.** A fee is payable in respect of the detailed assessment of costs and on an appeal against a decision made in a detailed assessment of costs.

Receivership fees

6B–307   **81.**——(1) An appointment fee shall be payable, as set out in paragraph 5 of the Appendix, upon the appointment of an officer of the court as receiver for a patient.

(2) In cases where an officer of the court is receiver a receivership administration fee shall be payable—
- (a) on the first and every subsequent anniversary of the date of his appointment as receiver, until the termination of the proceedings, and at such other times either during the proceedings or at their termination as the court may direct;
- (b) where the period for which the administration fee is payable is for less than one year, the fee payable shall be the proportion of the full fee as such period bears to one year.

(3) The court shall annually, or at such other intervals as may be convenient, issue a certificate in respect of each patient stating—
- (a) the amount of the administration fee payable in respect of the patient at the date of the certificate;
- (b) the period in respect of which the administration fee is payable; and
- (c) the name of the person by whom the payment is made.

(4) No administration fee shall be taken where the proceedings are terminated less than four weeks from the date of issue of the first application for the appointment of a receiver.

Winding up fee

6B–308   **82.** A winding up fee shall be payable on the death of a patient in cases where a receiver has been appointed.

Remission and postponement

6B–309   **83.**——(1) The court may remit or postpone the payment of the whole or part of any fee where in its opinion hardship might otherwise be caused to the patient or his dependants or the circumstances are otherwise exceptional.

(2) The court may remit a payment of the whole or any part of any fee where the cost of calculation and collection would be disproportionate to the amount involved.

PART XVIII

COSTS

Costs generally

84.——(1) All costs incurred in relation to proceedings under these Rules and not provided by way of remuneration under rule 43, shall be in the discretion of the court and it may order or direct them to be paid by the patient or charged on or paid out of his estate by any other person attending or taking part in the proceedings.

(2) Every order made or direction given under paragraph (1) shall be enforceable in the same manner as an order as to costs made by the High Court.

(3) An order or direction that costs incurred during the lifetime of a patient be paid out of or charged on his estate may be made within six years after his death.

6B–310

Applications under sections 36(9) and 54 of the Trustee Act 1925

85. The court may make any such order with respect of the costs of an application under section 36(9) or 54 of the Trustee Act 1925 as the High Court could make under section 60 of that Act in relation to any matter referred to in that section.

6B–311

Civil Procedure rules to apply

86.——(1) Subject to the provisions of these Rules, Parts 43, 44, 47 and 48 of the Civil Procedure Rules 1998[1] ("the 1998 Rules") shall apply, with the modification in paragraph (2) and such other modifications as may be necessary, to costs incurred in relation to proceedings under these Rules as they apply to costs incurred in relation to proceedings in the High Court.

(2) The modifications referred to in paragraph (1) are—
   (a) in rule 43.2(1)(c) of the 1998 Rules, costs officer shall include—
      (i) a judge;
      (ii) the Master;
   (b) in rule 43.2(1)(d) of the 1998 Rules, authorised court officer shall include an officer of the court;
   (c) rule 44.3(2) of the 1998 Rules (costs follow the event) does not apply;
   (d) rules 44.9 to 44.12 of the 1998 Rules (costs on small claims and fast tracks and on track allocation or reallocation) do not apply;

6B–312

---

[1] As amended by S.I.s 1999 No. 1008, 2000 No. 221, 2000 No. 940, 2000 No. 1317 and 2000 No. 2092.

(e) rules 48.1 to 48.3 (costs payable by or to particular persons) and 48.7 to 48.10 (costs relating to solicitors and other legal representatives) of the 1998 Rules do not apply.

Costs of unnecessary employment of solicitor, etc not to be allowed

6B–313 87.——(1) No receiver for a patient, other than the Official Solicitor, shall, unless authorised by the court, be entitled at the expense of the patient's estate to employ a solicitor or other professional person to do any work not usually requiring professional assistance. Where two or more persons having the same interest in relation to the matter to be determined attend any hearing by separate legal representatives, they shall not be allowed more than one set of costs of that hearing unless the court certifies that the circumstances justify separate representation.

Costs of Official Solicitor

6B–314 88. Any costs incurred by the Official Solicitor in relation to proceedings under these Rules or in carrying out any directions given by the court, and not provided for by remuneration under rule 43, shall be paid by such person on or out of such funds as the court may direct.

Ascertainment of costs not relating to the proceedings

6B–315 89. Where in any proceedings relating to a patient a claim is made against his estate in respect of any costs alleged to have been incurred by him or on his behalf or otherwise than in relation to proceedings, the court may refer the claim to a costs judge of the Supreme Court so that the amount due to the claimant may be ascertained by him or under his direction.

PART XIX

APPROVAL OF DEEDS

Approval of deeds

6B–316 90. The seal of the court on any deed or other document shall be evidence that its terms have been approved by the court.

PART XX

TRANSITIONAL PROVISIONS

Transitional provisions

6B–317 91.——(1) Where any matter is pending before the Public Trustee before the coming into force of these Rules, which, by virtue of these Rules relates to a function exercised by the court, the court shall decide the matter in accordance with these Rules.

(2) Where any review or appeal is pending before the court or the Public Trustee before the coming into force of these Rules, it shall be dealt with in accordance with the provisions of these Rules.

PART XXI

REVOCATION

Revocation of previous rules

92. The Court of Protection Rules 1994[1], the Court of Protection (Amendment) Rules 1999[2] and the Court of Protection (Amendment) Rules 2000[3] are hereby revoked.

6B–318

Powers of Attorney

The Enduring Powers of Attorney Act 1985

The Enduring Powers of Attorney Act 1985 came into operation pursuant to (Commencement) Order 1986 (S.I. 1986 No.125) on March 10, 1986, and enables powers of attorney to be created which will survive any subsequent mental incapacity of the donor and makes provision in connection with such powers.

6B–319

For "Court of Protection (Enduring Powers of Attorney) Rules 1994" substitute: Court of Protection (Enduring Powers of Attorney) Rules 2001

The Act is set out at paras 6B–340 *et seq.* The rules are the Court of Protection (Enduring Powers of Attorney) Rules 2001. These are made pursuant to s.10(1)(d) of the Enduring Powers of Attorney Act 1985, and ss.106, 107 and 108 of the Mental Health Act 1983 and are referred to in this Section as "EPA Rules" for the purpose of distinguishing them from the

For "Court of Protection Rules 1984" substitute: Court of Protection Rules 2001

Court of Protection Rules 2001, which apply equally to proceedings under the Enduring Powers of Attorney Act 1985 save that in case of inconsistency or ambiguity the EPA Rules prevail. There are also the Enduring Powers of Attorney (Prescribed Form) Regulations 1990 and these are made pursuant to s.2(2) of the Enduring Powers of Attorney Act 1985. They are set out at paras 6B–421 *et seq.*

Forms

For "r. 3(3)" substitute: r.3(2)

See EPA Rules r.3(2) and Sched. 1 to the EPA Rules. The following forms may be obtained (free of charge) from the Court of Protection:

6B–320

Notice of intention to register	EP 1
Application for registration	EP 2
General form of application	EP 3
Application for search	EP 4

The form of enduring power of attorney itself is not provided by the court but can be purchased from any law stationer. It may of course be prepared by the practitioner himself but in any event it must (subject to the transitional provisions set out in reg. 4) be in the prescribed form (see reg. 2 and the Schedule to the Regulations (paras 6B–423 and 6B–457)).

Fees

For "r. 27" substitute: r.26

See EPA Rules, r.26 and Sched. 2 to the EPA Rules (paras and 6B–453). Payment of fees may be made as follows:

6B–321

(i) In cash at Protection Division, 24 Kingsway, London WC2B 6JX; or
(ii) By cheque or postal order made payable to the

---

[1] S.I. 1994 No. 3046
[2] S.I. 1999 No. 2504
[3] S.I. 2000 No. 2025

For "Public Trust Office" substitute: Public Guardianship Office
Public Guardianship Office and crossed and sent by post.

Enduring Power of Attorney

Characteristics

6B–322   These are fully described in s.2 of the Act (see para. 6B–344) but basically such a power must (subject to the transitional provisions set out in reg. 5) be executed in the manner and form prescribed in reg. 3 of the Regulations and the schedule thereto (see paras 6B–424, 6B–456 and 6B–457). The donor at the time of execution must be mentally capable of understanding what the enduring power is and what it is intended to do (*Re K, Re F* [1988] Ch. 310) and have attained 18 years. An enduring power may confer a general authority, a specific authority or a general or specific authority subject to conditions and restrictions.

Action on incapacity of donor

For "rr. 7(1) and 16" substitute: rr.6(1)

6B–323   If the attorney has reason to believe that the donor is or is becoming mentally incapable he is obliged to make application to the court for the registration of the instrument creating the power. Before making such an application, the attorney is required pursuant to s.4(3) of the Act and the First Schedule thereto to give notice of the application in Form EP 1 in Sched. 1 to the EPA Rules (see paras 6B–351, 6B–404 and 6B–408) to those relatives entitled to receive notice and any co-attorney (by first-class post) and to the donor himself (personally). (See EPA Rules, 15 rr.6(1) and 15, paras and 6B–428.) An application to dispense with notice must be made before any application for registration is made. (See

For "r. 6(2)" substitute: r.6(2)

EPA Rules, r.6(2).)

Mode of application

For "Public Trust Office" substitute: Public Guardianship Office

6B–324   Application for registration in Form EP 2 in Sched. 1 to the EPA Rules must be lodged with the Public Guardianship Office not later than three days after the date on which notice was given or leave to dispense with notice was given. (See EPA Rules,

For "r. 8" substitue: r.7

r.7). The application must be accompanied by the original power of attorney and a remittance of £75 made payable to the

For "PTO" substitute: PGO

PGO in respect of the fee. (See EPA Rules,

For "r. 27" substitute: r.26

r.26).

Objections to registration

For "r. 10(1)" substitute: r.9(1)

6B–325   Any objection to registration under s.6(5) of the Act must, pursuant to EPA Rules r.9(1), set out:
  (a) The name and address of the objector
  (b) The name and address of the donor if he is not the donor
  (c) Any relationship of the objector to the donor
  (d) The name and address of the attorney and
  (e) The grounds for objecting to registration of the enduring power of attorney

For "r. 10(2)" substitute: r.9(2)

Any objection to registration received by the court on or after the date of registration shall be treated by the court as an application to cancel the registration. (See EPA Rules, r.9(2).)

On receipt of any objection the court will fix an appointment to hear the objection and will give such directions as are necessary and in particular whether any further information is required or whether any other persons are to be notified of the hearing.

Upon supervening incapacity and until the power is registered the attorney may not do anything under the authority of the power except:—
- (a) to maintain the donor or prevent loss to his estate; or
- (b) to maintain himself or other persons in so far as section 3(4) permits, or
- (c) as authorised or directed by the court.

Delete: a nominated officer of.

Any objection to registration will be considered by the court and will be subject on application by any aggrieved person within

For "eight days to review by the master" substitute: fourteen days to review by the court

fourteen days to review by the court. (See EPA Rules,

For "r. 24" substitute: r.23

r.23). An appeal from

For "the master lies to" substitute: a decision made by the court on an attended hearing lies to

a decision made by the court on an attended hearing lies to a nominated judge in the usual way. (See EPA Rules,

For "r. 25" substitute: r.24

r.24).

Registration

For "PTO" substitute: PGO

Where there is no objection to registration or any objection has been withdrawn or dismissed the enduring power of attorney will be registered. The PGO will, after retaining a copy, return the original instrument duly sealed and stamped with the date of registration to the applicant attorney. **6B–326**

After registration

The effect of registration is that: **6B–327**
- (a) no revocation of the power by the donor shall be valid except as provided in section 8(3) (para. 6B–364);
- (b) no disclaimer of the power shall be valid until the attorney gives notice of it to the PTO;
- (c) the donor may not alter the scope of the power.

The court may pursuant to s.8(1):
- (a) determine any question as to the meaning or effect of the power;
- (b) give directions with respect to the management or disposal by the attorney of the property and affairs of the patient, the rendering of accounts by the attorney and his remuneration or expenses;
- (c) require the attorney to furnish information or produce documents;
- (d) give any consent or authorisation to act which the attorney would have to obtain from a mentally capable donor;
- (e) authorise the attorney to benefit himself or other persons;
- (f) relieve the attorney from any liability which he may incur on account of a breach of duty.

Leave to bring an application

For "r. 22" substitute: r.21

Any person other than a person who has been served with a notice of intention to register an enduring power of attorney shall apply to the court for leave to make application for relief specified in the Act. (See EPA Rules, r.21). **6B–328**

Any other application (other than an application for registration)

The court is primarily concerned with applications for registration and consequently it is not intended to deal here, with the scope of an attorney's authority under and enduring power which is governed by s.3 of the EPA Act and of course any restrictions or conditions imposed by the instrument itself. In the ordinary course of events, following registration of an enduring power of attorney, the court does not expect to be further involved in any dealings with the donor's affairs. Apart from the registration process, the court's powers under the EPA Act are mainly directed to the proper supervision of the attorney and to **6B–329** giving necessary supplementary consents and authorisations which are not inconsistent with the restrictions imposed by the donor (Re R. [1990] 2 W.L.R. 1219, where the applicant was not the attorney).

For "r. 9(1)" substitute: r.8(1)

Any person other than a person who has been served with notice of intention to register an enduring power of attorney must apply to the court, as mentioned in para. 6B–328, for leave to make any application for relief specified in the EPA Act. Such application may, pursuant to EPA Rules, r.8(1), be made by letter unless the court directs that the application should be formal, in which case it should be made on Form EP 3.

It has been found in practice that situations arise which call for three particular applications.

Delete: or the PTO.

First, it may be necessary for the attorney in the course of his stewardship to realise an asset which is specifically bequeathed or devised by the donor's will. If the donor was testamentary capacity, he is able to make a new will to cater for the changed circumstances. Otherwise, the devise or bequest will be adeemed. However, s.101 of the Mental Health Act 1983 provides that where any property of a person has been disposed of under Pt VII of that Act, and under his will or his intestacy or by any gift perfected or nomination taking effect on his death any other person would have taken an interest in the property but for the disposal, that person shall take the same interest in any property belonging to the estate of the deceased which represents the property disposed of. It is therefore open to the attorney or any other person entitled to make an application for the appointment of a Receiver and for an order for the sale of the asset in question under the provisions of Pt VII of the Act mentioned above to preserve the devise. Such an application would have to be made in form CP. 1 supported with the evidence usually required in connection with a receivership application (that is to say, evidence of the donor's incapacity to manage and administer his property and affairs by reason of mental disorder (Form CP. 3) and a certificate of family and property (Form (CP. 5). It may be possible for the court to deal with the application by issuing a Short Procedure Order under

For "r. 9 of the Court of Protection Rules 1994" substitute: r.8 of the Court of Protection Rules 2001

r.8 of the Court of Protection Rules 2001 and thereafter to direct (pursuant to s.2(11) of the EPA Act 1985) that the EPA shall not be revoked by the exercise by the court of its powers under the Mental Health Act 1983.

Secondly, the attorney may wish to re-organise the donor's affairs with a view to mitigating the incidence of inheritance tax. If such a scheme involves an element of gift which goes beyond the gifts permitted by s.3(5) of the EPA Act and the instrument itself, an application to the court for the necessary relief will most probably be necessary.

Thirdly, it may be considered that for any one of a variety of reasons the will of a donor who lacks testamentary capacity is no longer appropriate to his circumstances and does not reflect his current wishes. The procedure for making an application for a statutory will is dealt with below.

Cancellation of registration

Delete: direct the Public Trustee to

6B–330   The court shall cancel the registration of any power:
(a) on confirming the revocation of the power or receiving notice of disclaimer;
(b) on giving a direction revoking the power or exercising any of its powers under the Mental Health Act 1983;
(c) on being satisfied that the donor is and is likely to remain mentally capable;
(d) on being satisfied that the power has expired or has otherwise been revoked;
(e) on being satisfied that the power was not valid when registration was effected;
(f) on being satisfied that fraud or undue pressure was used;
(g) on being satisfied the attorney is unsuitable.

On the death of a donor or attorney the original instrument, any office copies thereof and evidence of death should be forwarded to the court.

Searches of the register

For "r. 14" substitute: r.13

6B–331   Any person may upon payment of a fee of £25 request the court in Form EP. 4 to search the register and to say whether an enduring power has been registered. (See EPA Rules, r.13).

The Master of the Court of Protection issued the following Practice Direction on February 28, 1989.

Practice Direction: Enduring Powers of Attorney Act 1985

6B–332 The Enduring Powers of Attorney (Prescribed Form) Regulations 1987 (see paras 6B–421 et seq.)

Inclusion of Marginal Notes

The Enduring Powers of Attorney (Prescribed Form) Regulations 1987 came into force on November 1, 1987 and any enduring power of attorney executed on or after July 1, 1988 has to be in the form prescribed by those regulations in order to be a valid enduring power of attorney.

Regulation 2(1) of the regulations provides that a valid form must include the requisite explanatory information and all the relevant marginal notes. Regulation 2(2) refers to omissions or deletions of one of the various pairs of alternatives given in the form and allows omission or deletion of the corresponding marginal note.

Section 2(6) of the Enduring Powers of Attorney Act 1985 provides that an instrument differing in an immaterial respect in form or mode of expression from the prescribed form shall be treated as sufficient in point of form and expression.

Consequently, marginal notes may only be omitted if they are irrelevant (regulation 2(1)), correspond to the omitted or deleted one of a pair of alternatives (regulation 2(2)) or constitute an immaterial difference from the prescribed form (section 2(6)).

On several occasions recently, solicitors have submitted for registration enduring powers of attorney bearing no marginal notes at all, on the basis that the instrument had in each case been drawn up by the solicitors after the various choices had been explained to the donor and he had selected the options he wished to include and had decided the precise terms of the power.

There is no provision in the regulations for differences in form where donors prepare the form themselves and where solicitors prepare the form. Solicitors should therefore include in the forms to be completed by their client all marginal notes unless they come within one of the exceptions already mentioned.

Practice Direction (Court of Protection) (Power of Attorney: Form) [1989] 1 W.L.R. 311; [1989] 2 All E.R. 64.

Termination of enduring power of attorney

6B–333 An enduring power of attorney may be revoked by the donor; by the court; or automatically. The donor may revoke the power in the same way as he is able to do at common law provided an application for registration has not been made. Revocation by the donor after registration of the power is not valid unless and until it is confirmed by the court.

It is open to the court to revoke the power on exercising of any of its powers under Pt VII of the Mental Health Act 1983 (EPA Act 1985, s.2(11)) and in practice it usually so directs. The court also directs revocation of the power if it finds that fraud or undue pressure was used to induce the donor to create the power or concludes that the attorney is not suitable.

For "PTO" substitute: PGO

An enduring power of attorney is automatically revoked by the bankruptcy of the attorney whatever the circumstances of the bankruptcy. The power may also be terminated by the attorney exercising his right to disclaim the power. However, he is required to give notice of disclaimer to the donor or, if he has reason to believe that the donor is or is becoming mentally incapable or if the power has been registered, to the PGO.

An enduring power of attorney will be terminated by the death of the donor or the death, mental incapacity or, as already mentioned, the bankruptcy of the attorney.

Protection of attorney and third parties

Delete "and the PTO"

6B–334 The main function of the court is to receive and consider applications for registration and following registration does not expect to be further involved in relation to the attorney's dealings with the donor's affairs unless anything untoward is reported or an application such as mentioned above is made. It is not thought necessary to deal here with the protection of the attorney and third parties for which provision is made in s.9 of the

EPA Act. However, it is stressed that subss. (1) (2) (3) and (4) of s.9 which afford protection after the enduring power has been registered are wider than those given by the Powers of Attorney Act 1971. Further, subs. (5) enables the attorney and third parties to disregard any attempted revocation by the donor until it has been confirmed by the court.

Applications by attorneys under registered enduring powers of attorney for orders for execution of statutory wills and codicils

Generally

6B–335 Guidance as to the practice and procedure of the court in connection with applications for statutory wills and codicils is given at paras 6B–137 to 6B–146. The following notes give additional information for use in cases where the application is made by an attorney under a registered enduring power of attorney, and should be read in conjunction with the notes at paras 6B–137 to 6B–146.

Although applications may be accepted from attorneys if the enduring power is registered, it will be appreciated that the court will have little knowledge in those cases of the donor's family or property and will probably have received no medical evidence at all concerning the donor's mental condition.

Medical evidence

6B–336 The jurisdiction to order the execution of a statutory will or codicil is conferred by s.96(1)(e) of the Mental Health Act 1983 and is only exercisable in respect of someone who is a "patient" (defined in the Act as a person who is incapable, by reason of mental disorder, of managing and administering his property and affairs). The court will need to see medical evidence of such incapacity (s.94(2) of the Act) and the best way in which that evidence can be supplied is on form CP. 3, the usual form of medical evidence in receivership matters, which gives a great deal of helpful information as well as giving a categorical statement of incapacity to satisfy the requirements of the Act. An enduring power of attorney is able to be registered at a stage where the donor is becoming, but has not yet necessarily become, mentally incapable and consequently the fact that the enduring power of attorney has been registered is not in itself sufficient evidence of mental incapacity.

Furthermore, medical evidence is also always required specifically stating that the donor is not of testamentary capacity—see paragraph 1(a) at para. 6B–142.

Parties

6B–337 Applications for statutory wills are governed by the Mental Health Act 1983 and not by the Enduring Powers of Attorney Act 1985. There is guidance at para. 6B–142 as to those who may apply and those who should be joined.

Additionally, in cases arising out of enduring powers of attorney, if the power appoints joint attorneys to act jointly, both or all must concur in making the application. If joint attorneys have been appointed to act jointly and severally, and not all are making the application, those who are not applicants should be given notice of the hearing of the application, together with such other persons as the court may direct. The Official Solicitor may be directed to represent the donor.

Evidence

6B–338 It is stressed that the information mentioned in notes 1(a) to (h) at para. 6B–143 will be required, with full details, since the court will have no other particulars of the donor's family or property.

At end of renumbered paragraph 6B–338 delete link line [THE NEXT PARAGRAPH IS 6B–358].

Enduring Powers of Attorney Act 1985

(1985 c. 29)

ARRANGEMENT OF SECTIONS

Enduring powers of attorney

SECT.
1. Enduring power of attorney to survive mental incapacity of donor. 6B–340
2. Characteristics of an enduring power. 6B–344
3. Scope of authority, etc. of attorney under enduring power 6B–348
4. Duties of attorney in event of actual or impending incapacity of donor 6B–351
5. Functions of court prior to registration 6B–355
6. Functions of court on application for registration 6B–358
7. Effect and proof of registration, etc.. . . . . .6B–361
8. Functions of court with respect to registered power 6B–364
9. Protection of attorney and third persons where power invalid or revoked 6B–368

Supplementary

10. Application of Mental Health Act provisions relating to the court 6B–372
11. Application to joint and joint and several attorneys. 6B–375
12. Power of Lord Chancellor to modify pre-registration requirements in certain cases 6B–378
13. Interpretation 6B–380
14. Short title, commencement and extent. 6B–382

SCHEDULES:
Schedule 1—Notification Prior to Registration 6B–384
Part I   Duty to Give Notice to Relatives and Donor. 6B–384
Part II   Contents of Notices 6B–386
Part III Duty to Give Notice to Other Attorneys 6B–387
Part IV   Supplementary 6B–388
Schedule 2—Further Protection of Attorney and Third Persons .6B–389
Schedule 3—Joint and Joint and Several Attorneys 6B–390
Part I   Joint Attorneys 6B–390
Part II   Joint and Several Attorneys 6B–391

Enduring powers of attorney

Enduring power of attorney to survive mental incapacity of donor

1.—(1) Where an individual creates a power of attorney which is an enduring power within the meaning of this Act then—

(a) the power shall not be revoked by any subsequent mental incapacity of his; but

(b) upon such incapacity supervening the donee of the power may not do anything under the authority of the power except as provided by subsection (2) below or as directed or authorised by the court under section 5 unless or, as the case may be, until the instrument creating the power is registered by the court under section 6; and

(c) section 5 of the Powers of Attorney Act 1971 (protection of donee and third persons) so far as applicable shall apply if and so long as paragraph (b) above operates to suspend the donee's authority to act under the power as if the power had been revoked by the donor's mental incapacity.

(2) Notwithstanding subsection (1)(b) above, where the attorney has made an application for registration of the instrument then, until the application has been initially determined, the attorney may take action under the power—

(a) to maintain the donor or prevent loss to his estate; or
(b) to maintain himself or other persons in so far as section 3(4) permits him to do so.

(3) Where the attorney purports to act as provided by subsection (2) above, then, in favour of a person who deals with him without knowledge that the attorney is acting otherwise than in accordance with paragraph (a) or (b) of that subsection, the transaction between them shall be as valid as if the attorney were acting in accordance with paragraph (a) or (b).

Definitions

6B–341   "enduring power", "the court" (s.13(1)).

Subsection (1)

6B–342   This subsection provides that an enduring power is not revoked by the mental incapacity of the donor and in that event, and until the instrument is registered with the Court of Protection, makes it clear that the authority of the attorney is suspended except to the limited extent that the Act otherwise provides. Although suspension is removed on registration, it does not restore full authority retrospectively.

The effect of s.1(1)(c) is to confer upon attorneys and third parties the protection given by the Powers of Attorney Act 1971 when the donor of an enduring power has become mentally incapable.

Subsection (2)

6B–343   This subsection enables the attorney to act with limited authority pending registration, provided he has applied for registration. The attorney is able, pursuant to s.5, to apply to the court for any further powers he requires pending registration.

Characteristics of an enduring power

6B–344   **2.**—(1) Subject to subsections (7) to (9) below and section 11, a power of attorney is an enduring power within the meaning of this Act if the instrument which creates the power—
(a) is in the prescribed form; and
(b) was executed in the prescribed manner by the donor and the attorney; and
(c) incorporated at the time of execution by the donor the prescribed explanatory information.

(2) The Lord Chancellor shall make regulations as to the form and execution of instruments creating enduring powers and the regulations shall contain such provisions as appear to him to be appropriate for securing—
(a) that no document is used to create an enduring power which does not incorporate such information explaining the general effect of creating or accepting the power as may be prescribed; and
(b) that such instruments include statements to the following effect—
  (i) by the donor, that he intends the power to continue in spite of any supervening mental incapacity of his;
  (ii) by the donor, that he read or had read to him the information explaining the effect of creating the power;
  (iii) by the attorney, that he understands the duty of registration imposed by this Act.

(3) Regulations under subsection (2) above—
(a) may include different provision for cases where more than one

attorney is to be appointed by the instrument than for cases where only one attorney is to be appointed; and

(b) may, if they amend or revoke any regulations previously made under that subsection, include saving and transitional provisions.

(4) Regulations under subsection (2) above shall be made by statutory instrument which shall be subject to annulment in pursuance of a resolution of either House of Parliament.

(5) An instrument in the prescribed form purporting to have been executed in the prescribed manner shall be taken, in the absence of evidence to the contrary, to be a document which incorporated at the time of execution by the donor the prescribed explanatory information.

(6) Where an instrument differs in an immaterial respect in form or mode of expression from the prescribed form the instrument shall be treated as sufficient in point of form and expression.

(7) A power of attorney cannot be an enduring power unless, when he executes the instrument creating it, the attorney is—

(a) an individual who has attained eighteen years and is not bankrupt; or

(b) a trust corporation.

(8) A power of attorney under section 25 of the Trustee Act 1925 (power to delegate trusts etc. by power of attorney) cannot be an enduring power.

(9) A power of attorney which gives the attorney a right to appoint a substitute or successor cannot be an enduring power.

(10) An enduring power shall be revoked by the bankruptcy of the attorney whatever the circumstances of the bankruptcy.

(11) An enduring power shall be revoked on the exercise by the court of any of its powers under Part VII of the Mental Health Act 1983 if, but only if, the court so directs.

(12) No disclaimer of an enduring power, whether by deed or otherwise, shall be valid unless and until the attorney gives notice of it to the donor or, where section 4(6) or 7(1) applies, to the court.

(13) In this section "prescribed" means prescribed under subsection (2) above.

Definitions

"enduring power", "trust corporation", "the court", and "notice" (s.13(1)). "prescribed" (s.2(13)).

6B–345

General note

This section deals with the formal requirements and characteristics of an enduring power. A power which is not an enduring power within the meaning of the Act is at best an ordinary power of attorney which will be revoked by the mental incapacity of the donor. Joint attorneys must be appointed to act jointly or jointly and severally and there is no restriction on the appointment of a number of attorneys by separate instruments.

6B–346

Subsection (8)

A power of attorney under s.25 of the Trustee Act 1925 can only be for a period not exceeding 12 months whereas the mental incapacity of the donor might last for a much longer period.

6B–347

Scope of authority, etc. of attorney under enduring power

3.—(1) An enduring power may confer general authority (as defined in subsection (2) below) on the attorney to act on the donor's behalf in rela-

6B–348

tion to all or a specified part of the property and affairs of the donor or may confer on him authority to do specified things on the donor's behalf and the authority may, in either case, be conferred subject to conditions and restrictions.

(2) Where an instrument is expressed to confer general authority on the attorney it operates to confer, subject to the restriction imposed by subsection (5) below and to any conditions or restrictions contained in the instrument, authority to do on behalf of the donor anything which the donor can lawfully do by an attorney.

(3) Subject to any conditions or restrictions contained in the instrument, an attorney under an enduring power, whether general or limited, may (without obtaining any consent) execute or exercise all or any of the trusts, powers or discretions vested in the donor as trustee and may (without the concurrence of any other person) give a valid receipt for capital or other money paid.

(4) Subject to any conditions or restrictions contained in the instrument, an attorney under an enduring power, whether general or limited, may (without obtaining any consent) act under the power so as to benefit himself or other persons than the donor to the following extent but no further, that is to say—

> (a) he may so act in relation to himself or in relation to any other person if the donor might be expected to provide for his or that person's needs respectively; and
> (b) he may do whatever the donor might be expected to do to meet those needs.

(5) Without prejudice to subsection (4) above but subject to any conditions or restrictions contained in the instrument, an attorney under an enduring power, whether general or limited, may (without obtaining any consent) dispose of the property, of the donor by way of gift to the following extent but no further, that is to say—

> (a) he may make gifts of a seasonal nature or at a time, or on an anniversary, of a birth or marriage, to persons (including himself) who are related to or connected with the donor, and
> (b) he may make gifts to any charity to whom the donor made or might be expected to make gifts,
> provided that the value of each such gift is not unreasonable having regard to all the circumstances and in particular the size of the donor's estate.

Definition

6B–349 "enduring power" (s.13(1)).

Subsection (3)

6B–350 This subsection was introduced following the decision in *Walia v. Michael Naughton Ltd*, *The Times*, December 1, 1984, which decided that an attorney may only exercise the functions and powers of a trustee if such functions and powers are delegated to him by a power made under s.25 of the Trustee Act 1925. By virtue of s.2(8) of the Act, a power made under s.25 of the Trustee Act 1925 cannot be an enduring power.

ACTION ON ACTUAL OR IMPENDING INCAPACITY OF DONOR

Duties of attorney in event of actual or impending incapacity of donor

6B–351 **4.**—(1) If the attorney under an enduring power has reason to believe that the donor is or is becoming mentally incapable subsections (2) to (6) below shall apply.

(2) The attorney shall, as soon as practicable, make an application to the court for the registration of the instrument creating the power.

(3) Before making an application for registration the attorney shall comply with the provisions as to notice set out in Schedule 1.

(4) An application for registration shall be made in the prescribed form and shall contain such statements as may be prescribed.

(5) The attorney may, before making an application for the registration of the instrument, refer to the court for its determination any question as to the validity of the power and he shall comply with any direction given to him by the court on that determination.

(6) No disclaimer of the power shall be valid unless and until the attorney gives notice of it to the court.

(7) Any person who, in an application for registration, makes a statement which he knows to be false in a material particular shall be liable—
- (a) on conviction on indictment, to imprisonment for a term not exceeding two years or to a fine, or both; and
- (b) on summary conviction, to imprisonment for a term not exceeding six months or to a fine not exceeding the statutory maximum, or both.

(8) In this section and Schedule 1 "prescribed" means prescribed by rules of the court.

Definitions
"enduring power", "mentally incapable", "the court", "notice", "statutory maximum", "rules of the court" (s.13(1)). "prescribed" (s.4(8)).

6B–352

General note
Registration is the cornerstone of the Act and besides safeguarding against abuse of the power it protects attorneys and third parties as provided in s.9 in cases where an instrument did not create a valid power of attorney.

6B–353

Subsection (2)
An attorney must give notice of his application for registration to the donor, any co-attorney and certain relatives as provided in Sched. 1. See r.14 of the EPA Rules as to the mode of service. If the attorney does not make application for registration when he has reason to believe that the donor is or is becoming mentally incapable he is at risk that the donor has in fact so become and his authority has been suspended.

6B–354

Functions of court prior to registration

5. Where the court has reason to believe that the donor of an enduring power may be, or may be becoming, mentally incapable and the court is of the opinion that it is necessary, before the instrument creating the power is registered, to exercise any power with respect to the power of attorney or the attorney appointed to act under it which would become exercisable under section 8(2) on its registration, the court may exercise that power under this section and may do so whether the attorney has or has not made an application to the court for the registration of the instrument.

6B–355

Definitions
"the court", "enduring power", "mentally incapable" (s.13(1)).

6B–356

General note

6B–357 This section enables the court, prior to registration, to take any necessary steps to protect the interests of a donor who may be or who may be becoming mentally incapable.

Functions of court on application for registration

6B–358 6.—(1) In any case where—
   (a) an application for registration is made in accordance with section 4(3) and (4), and
   (b) neither subsection (2) nor subsection (4) below applies,
   the court shall register the instrument to which the application relates.

(2) Where it appears to the court that there is in force under Part VII of the Mental Health Act 1983 an order appointing a receiver for the donor but the power has not also been revoked then, unless it directs otherwise, the court shall not exercise or further exercise its functions under this section but shall refuse the application for registration.

(3) Where it appears from an application for registration that notice of it has not been given under Schedule 1 to some person entitled to receive it (other than a person in respect of whom the attorney has been dispensed or is otherwise exempt from the requirement to give notice) the court shall direct that the application be treated for the purposes of this Act as having been made in accordance with section 4(3), if the court is satisfied that, as regards each such person—
   (a) it was undesirable or impracticable for the attorney to give him notice; or
   (b) no useful purpose is likely to be served by giving him notice.

(4) If, in the case of an application for registration—
   (a) a valid notice of objection to the registration is received by the court before the expiry of the period of five weeks beginning with the date or, as the case may be, the latest date on which the attorney gave notice to any person under Schedule 1, or
   (b) it appears from the application that there is no one to whom notice has been given under paragraph 1 of that Schedule, or
   (c) the court has reason to believe that appropriate inquiries might bring to light evidence on which the court could be satisfied that one of the grounds of objection set out in subsection (5) below was established,
   the court shall neither register the instrument nor refuse the application until it has made or caused to be made such inquiries (if any) as it thinks appropriate in the circumstances of the case.

(5) For the purposes of this Act a notice of objection to the registration of an instrument is valid if the objection is made on one or more of the following grounds, namely—
   (a) that the power purported to have been created by the instrument was not valid as an enduring power of attorney;
   (b) that the power created by the instrument no longer subsists;
   (c) that the application is premature because the donor is not yet becoming mentally incapable;
   (d) that fraud or undue pressure was used to induce the donor to create the power;
   (e) that, having regard to all the circumstances and in particular the attorney's relationship to or connection with the donor, the attorney is unsuitable to be the donor's attorney.

(6) If, in a case where subsection (4) above applies, any of the grounds of objection in subsection (5) above is established to the satisfaction of the court, the court shall refuse the application but if, in such a case, it is not so satisfied, the court shall register the instrument to which the application relates.

(7) Where the court refuses an application for registration on ground (d) or (e) in subsection (5) above it shall by order revoke the power created by the instrument.

(8) Where the court refuses an application for registration on any ground other than that specified in subsection (5)(c) above the instrument shall be delivered up to be cancelled, unless the court otherwise directs.

Definitions
"the court", "notice", "enduring power", "mentally incapable" (s.13(1)).   **6B–359**

Subsection (3)
This subsection enables the court to proceed with an application where for the reasons mentioned an attorney has not given the required notices. The court may also dispense with the giving of notices as provided in Sched. 1, paras 3(2) and 4(2), the former subsection applying also to any co-attorney.   **6B–360**

LEGAL POSITION AFTER REGISTRATION

Effect and proof of registration, etc.

7.—(1) The effect of the registration of an instrument under section 6 is that—   **6B–361**

(a) no revocation of the power by the donor shall be valid unless and until the court confirms the revocation under section 8(3);
(b) no disclaimer of the power shall be valid unless and until the attorney gives notice of it to the court;
(c) the donor may not extend or restrict the scope of the authority conferred by the instrument and no instruction or consent given by him after registration shall, in the case of a consent, confer any right and, in the case of an instruction, impose or confer any obligation or right on or create any liability of the attorney or other persons having notice of the instruction or consent.

(2) Subsection (1) above applies for so long as the instrument is registered under section 6 whether or not the donor is for the time being mentally incapable.

(3) A document purporting to be an office copy of an instrument registered under this Act or under the Enduring Powers of Attorney (Northern Ireland) Order 1987 shall, in any part of the United Kingdom, be evidence of the contents of the instrument and of the fact that it has been so registered.

(4) Subsection (3) above is without prejudice to section 3 of the Powers of Attorney Act 1971 (proof by certified copies) and to any other method of proof authorised by law.

Note
Amended by the Enduring Powers of Attorney (Northern Ireland Consequential Amendment) Order 1987 (S.I. 1987 No. 1628).   **6B–362**

Definitions

6B-363 "the court", "notice", "mentally incapable" (s.13(1)).

Functions of court with respect to registered power

6B-364 8.—(1) Where an instrument has been registered under section 6, the court shall have the following functions with respect to the power and the donor of and the attorney appointed to act under the power.

(2) The court may—
- (a) determine any question as to the meaning or effect of the instrument;
- (b) give directions with respect to—
  - (i) the management or disposal by the attorney of the property and affairs of the donor;
  - (ii) the rendering of accounts by the attorney and the production of the records kept by him for the purpose;
  - (iii) the remuneration or expenses of the attorney, whether or not in default of or in accordance with any provision made by the instrument, including directions for the repayment of excessive or the payment of additional remuneration;
- (c) require the attorney to furnish information or produce documents or things in his possession as attorney;
- (d) give any consent or authorisation to act which the attorney would have to obtain from a mentally capable donor;
- (e) authorise the attorney to act so as to benefit himself or other persons than the donor otherwise than in accordance with section 3(4) and (5) (but subject to any conditions or restrictions contained in the instrument);
- (f) relieve the attorney wholly or partly from any liability which he has or may have incurred on account of a breach of his duties as attorney.

(3) On application made for the purpose by or on behalf of the donor, the court shall confirm the revocation of the power if satisfied that the donor has done whatever is necessary in law to effect an express revocation of the power and was mentally capable of revoking a power of attorney when he did so (whether or not he is so when the court considers the application).

(4) The court shall cancel the registration of an instrument registered under section 6 in any of the following circumstances, that is to say—
- (a) on confirming the revocation of the power under subsection (3) above or receiving notice of disclaimer under section 7(1)(b);
- (b) on giving a direction revoking the power on exercising any of its powers under Part VII of the Mental Health Act 1983;
- (c) on being satisfied that the donor is and is likely to remain mentally capable;
- (d) on being satisfied that the power has expired or has been revoked by the death or bankruptcy of the donor or the death, mental incapacity or bankruptcy of the attorney or, if the attorney is a body corporate, its winding up or dissolution;
- (e) on being satisfied that the power was not a valid and subsisting enduring power when registration was effected;
- (f) on being satisfied that fraud or undue pressure was used to induce the donor to create the power; or

(g) on being satisfied that, having regard to all the circumstances and in particular the attorney's relationship to or connection with the donor, the attorney is unsuitable to be the donor's attorney.

(5) Where the court cancels the registration of an instrument on being satisfied of the matters specified in paragraph (f) or (g) of subsection (4) above it shall by order revoke the power created by the instrument.

(6) On the cancellation of the registration of an instrument under subsection (4) above except paragraph (c) the instrument shall be delivered up to be cancelled, unless the court otherwise directs.

Definitions

"the court", "mentally capable", "notice", "mental incapacity", "enduring power" (s.13(1)). **6B–365**

General note

The court has the same powers under s.5 where prior to registration it has reason to believe that the donor may be or may be becoming mentally incapable. **6B–366**

Subsection (6)

If the court cancels registration because it is satisfied the donor is mentally capable and is likely to remain so, the enduring power will revert to being an unregistered enduring power. **6B–367**

PROTECTION OF ATTORNEY AND THIRD PARTIES

Protection of attorney and third persons where power invalid or revoked

9.—(1) Subsections (2) and (3) below apply where an instrument which did not create a valid power of attorney has been registered under section 6 (whether or not the registration has been cancelled at the time of the act or transaction in question). **6B–368**

(2) An attorney who acts in pursuance of the power shall not incur any liability (either to the donor or to any other person) by reason of the non-existence of the power unless at the time of acting he knows—
    (a) that the instrument did not create a valid enduring power; or
    (b) that an event has occurred which, if the instrument had created a valid enduring power, would have had the effect of revoking the power; or
    (c) that, if the instrument had created a valid enduring power, the power would have expired before that time.

(3) Any transaction between the attorney and another person shall, in favour of that person, be as valid as if the power had then been in existence, unless at the time of the transaction that person has knowledge of any of the matters mentioned in subsection (2) above.

(4) Where the interest of a purchaser depends on whether a transaction between the attorney and another person was valid by virtue of subsection (3) above, it shall be conclusively presumed in favour of the purchaser that the transaction was valid if—
    (a) the transaction between that person and the attorney was completed within twelve months of the date on which the instrument was registered; or
    (b) that person makes a statutory declaration, before or within three months after the completion of the purchase, that he

had no reason at the time of the transaction to doubt that the attorney had authority to dispose of the property which was the subject of the transaction.

(5) For the purposes of section 5 of the Powers of Attorney Act 1971 (protection of attorney and third persons where action is taken under the power of attorney in ignorance of its having been revoked) in its application to an enduring power the revocation of which by the donor is by virtue of section 7(1)(a) above invalid unless and until confirmed by the court under section 8(3) above, knowledge of the confirmation of the revocation is, but knowledge of the unconfirmed revocation is not, knowledge of the revocation of the power.

(6) Schedule 2 shall have effect to confer protection in cases where the instrument failed to create a valid enduring power and the power has been revoked by the donor's mental incapacity.

(7) In this section "purchaser" and "purchase" have the meanings specified in section 205(1) of the Law of Property Act 1925.

Definitions

6B–369 "enduring power" (s.13(1)). "purchaser", "purchase" (s.9(7)).

Subsections (1) (2) (3) and (4)

6B–370 The protection afforded by these subsections to the attorney and third parties, which are wider than those given by the Powers of Attorney Act 1971, apply after the enduring power has been registered.

Subsection (5)

6B–371 This subsection enables the attorney and third parties to disregard any attempted revocation by the donor until it has been confirmed by the court.

Supplementary

Application of Mental Health Act provisions relating to the court

6B–372 **10.**—(1) The provisions of Part VII of the Mental Health Act 1983(relating to the Court of Protection) specified below shall apply to persons within any proceedings under this Act in accordance with the following paragraphs of this subsection and subsection (2) below, that is to say—

    (a) section 103 (functions of Visitors) shall apply to persons within this Act as it applies to persons mentioned in that section;

    (b) section 104 (powers of judge) shall apply to proceedings under this Act with respect to persons within this Act as it applies to the proceedings mentioned in subsection (1) of that section;

    (c) section 105(1) (appeals to nominated judge) shall apply to any decision of the Master of the Court of Protection or any nominated officer in proceedings under this Act as it applies to any decision to which that subsection applies and an appeal shall lie to the Court of Appeal from any decision of a nominated judge whether given in the exercise of his original jurisdiction or on the hearing of an appeal under section 105(1) as extended by this paragraph;

    (d) section 106 except subsection (4) (rules of procedure) shall apply to proceedings under this Act and persons within this Act as it applies to the proceedings and persons mentioned in that section.

(2) Any functions conferred or imposed by the provisions of the said

Part VII applied by subsection (1) above shall be exercisable also for the purposes of this Act and the persons who are "within this Act" are the donors of and attorneys under enduring powers of attorney whether or not they would be patients for the purposes of the said Part VII.

(3) In this section "nominated judge" and "nominated officer" have the same meanings as in Part VII of the Mental Health Act 1983.

Definitions

"nominated judge", "nominated officer" (s.10(3)). "enduring power" (s.13(1)).   **6B–373**

General note

This section extends the powers given by the Mental Health Act 1983 to donors whether   **6B–374** or not they are patients within the meaning of that Act and whether or not the instrument creating the enduring power has been registered.

Application to joint and joint and several attorneys

11.—(1) An instrument which appoints more than one person to be an   **6B–375** attorney cannot create an enduring power unless the attorneys are appointed to act jointly or jointly and severally.

(2) This Act, in its application to joint attorneys, applies to them collectively as it applies to a single attorney but subject to the modifications specified in Part I of Schedule 3.

(3) This Act, in its application to joint and several attorneys, applies with the modifications specified in subsections (4) to (7) below and in Part II of Schedule 3.

(4) A failure, as respects any one attorney, to comply with the requirements for the creation of enduring powers, shall prevent the instrument from creating such a power in his case without however affecting its efficacy for that purpose as respects the other or others or its efficacy in his case for the purpose of creating a power of attorney which is not an enduring power.

(5) Where one or more but not both or all the attorneys makes or joins in making an application for registration of the instrument then—

    (a) an attorney who is not an applicant as well as one who is may act pending the initial determination of the application as provided in section 1(2) (or under section 5);

    (b) notice of the application shall also be given under Schedule 1 to the other attorney or attorneys; and

    (c) objection may validly be taken to the registration on a ground relating to an attorney or to the power of an attorney who is not an applicant as well as to one or the power of one who is an applicant.

(6) The court shall not refuse under section 6(6) to register an instrument because a ground of objection to an attorney or power is established if an enduring power subsists as respects some attorney who is not affected thereby but shall give effect to it by the prescribed qualification of the registration.

(7) The court shall not cancel the registration of an instrument under section 8(4) for any of the causes vitiating registration specified in that subsection if an enduring power subsists as respects some attorney who is not affected thereby but shall give effect to it by the prescribed qualification of the registration.

(8) In this section—

"prescribed" means prescribed by rules of the court; and
"the requirements for the creation of enduring powers" means the provisions of section 2 other than subsections (10) to (12) and of regulations under subsection (2) of that section.

Definitions

6B–376 "enduring powers", "notice", "the court", "rules of the court" (s.13(1)). "prescribed", "the requirements for the creation of enduring powers" (s.11(8)).

Subsection (1)

6B–377 This subsection invalidates an EPA which purports to appoint a succession of attorneys or substitutes and if it does it will at best be an ordinary power of attorney which will be revoked on the donor becoming mentally incapacitated.

Power of Lord Chancellor to modify pre-registration requirements in certain cases

6B–378 **12.**—(1) The Lord Chancellor may by order exempt attorneys of such descriptions as he thinks fit from the requirements of this Act to give notice to relatives prior to registration.

(2) Subject to subsection (3) below, where an order is made under this section with respect to attorneys of a specified description then, during the currency of the order, this Act shall have effect in relation to any attorney of that description with the omission of so much of section 4(3) and Schedule 1 as requires notice of an application for registration to be given to relatives.

(3) Notwithstanding that an attorney under a joint or joint and several power is of a description specified in a current order under this section, subsection (2) above shall not apply in relation to him if any of the other attorneys under the power is not of a description specified in that or another current order under this section.

(4) The power to make an order under this section shall be exercisable by statutory instrument which shall be subject to annulment in pursuance of a resolution of either House of Parliament.

General note

6B–379 No order under this section has yet been made (February 2000).

Interpretation

6B–380 **13.**—(1) In this Act—

(2) Any question arising under or for the purposes of this Act as to what the donor of the power might at any time be expected to do shall be determined by assuming that he had full mental capacity at the time but otherwise by reference to the circumstances existing at that time.

Note

6B–381 Section 13 repealed in part by the Statute Law (Repeals) Act 1993.

Short title, commencement and extent

6B–382 **14.**—(1) This Act may be cited as the Enduring Powers of Attorney Act 1985.

(2) This Act shall come into force on such day as the Lord Chancellor appoints by order made by statutory instrument.

(3) This Act extends to England and Wales only except that section

7(3) and section 10(1)(b) so far as it applies section 104(4) of the Mental Health Act 1983 extend also to Scotland and Northern Ireland.

Note

The Act came into force on March 10, 1986 (S.I. 1986 No.125).

SCHEDULES

SCHEDULE 1

Notification Prior to Registration

Part I

Duty to Give Notice to Relatives and Donor

Duty to give notice to relatives

1. Subject to paragraph 3 below, before making an application for registration the attorney shall give notice of his intention to do so to all those persons (if any) who are entitled to receive notice by virtue of paragraph 2 below.

2.—(1) Subject to the limitations contained in sub-paragraphs (2) to (4) below, persons of the following classes (referred to in this Act as "relatives") are entitled to receive notice under paragraph 1 above—

  (a) the donor's husband or wife;
  (b) the donor's children;
  (c) the donor's parents;
  (d) the donor's brothers and sisters, whether of the whole or half blood;
  (e) the widow or widower of a child of the donor;
  (f) the donor's grandchildren;
  (g) the children of the donor's brothers and sisters of the whole blood;
  (h) the children of the donor's brothers and sisters of the half blood;
  (i) the donor's uncles and aunts of the whole blood; and
  (j) the children of the donor's uncles and aunts of the whole blood.

(2) A person is not entitled to receive notice under paragraph 1 above if—

  (a) his name or address is not known to the attorney and cannot be reasonably ascertained by him; or
  (b) the attorney has reason to believe that he has not attained eighteen years or is mentally incapable.

(3) Except where sub-paragraph (4) below applies, no more than three persons are entitled to receive notice under paragraph 1 above and, in determining the persons who are so entitled, persons falling within class (a) of sub-paragraph (1) above are to be preferred to persons falling within class (b) of that sub-paragraph, persons falling within class (b) are to be preferred to persons falling within class (c) of that sub-paragraph; and so on.

(4) Notwithstanding the limit of three specified in sub-paragraph (3) above, where—

  (a) there is more than one person falling within any of classes (a) to (j) of sub-paragraph (1) above, and

(b) at least one of those persons would be entitled to receive notice under paragraph 1 above,

3.—(1) An attorney shall not be required to give notice under paragraph 1 above to himself or to any other attorney under the power who is joining in making the application, notwithstanding that he or, as the case may be, the other attorney is entitled to receive notice by virtue of paragraph 2 above.

(2) In the case of any person who is entitled to receive notice under paragraph 1 above, the attorney, before applying for registration, may make an application to the court to be dispensed from the requirement to give him notice; and the court shall grant the application if it is satisfied—

(a) that it would be undesirable or impracticable for the attorney to give him notice; or
(b) that no useful purpose is likely to be served by giving him notice.

Duty to give notice to donor

6B-385 4.—(1) Subject to sub-paragraph (2) below, before making an application for registration the attorney shall give notice of his intention to do so to the donor.

(2) Paragraph 3(2) above shall apply in relation to the donor as it applies in relation to a person who is entitled to receive notice under paragraph 1 above.

PART II

CONTENTS OF NOTICES

6B-386 5. A notice to relatives under this Schedule—
(a) shall be in the prescribed form;
(b) shall state that the attorney proposes to make an application to the Court of Protection for the registration of the instrument creating the enduring power in question;
(c) shall inform the person to whom it is given that he may object to the proposed registration by notice in writing to the Court of Protection before the expiry of the period of four weeks beginning with the day on which the notice under this Schedule was given to him;
(d) shall specify, as the grounds on which an objection to registration may be made, the grounds set out in .

6. A notice to the donor under this Schedule—
(a) shall be in the prescribed form;
(b) shall contain the statement mentioned in paragraph 5(b) above; and
(c) shall inform the donor that, whilst the instrument remains registered, any revocation of the power by him will be ineffective unless and until the revocation is confirmed by the Court of Protection.

PART III

DUTY TO GIVE NOTICE TO OTHER ATTORNEYS

6B-387 7.—(1) Subject to sub-paragraph (2) below, before making an application for registration an attorney under a joint and several power shall give notice of his intention to do so to any other attorney under the power who is not joining in making the application; and paragraphs 3(2) and 5 above shall apply in relation to attorneys entitled to receive notice by virtue of this paragraph as they apply in relation to persons entitled to receive notice by virtue of paragraph 2 above.

(2) An attorney is not entitled to receive notice by virtue of this paragraph if—
- (a) his address is not known to the applying attorney and cannot reasonably be ascertained by him; or
- (b) the applying attorney has reason to believe that he has not attained eighteen years or is mentally incapable.

Part IV

Supplementary

8.—(1) For the purposes of this Schedule an illegitimate child shall be treated as if he were the legitimate child of his mother and father. **6B–388**

(2) Notwithstanding anything in section 7 of the Interpretation Act 1978 (construction of references to service by post), for the purposes of this Schedule a notice given by post shall be regarded as given on the date on which it was posted.

SECTION 2(2)   **SCHEDULE 2**

Further Protection of Attorney and Third Persons

1. Where— **6B–389**
   - (a) an instrument framed in a form prescribed under creates a power which is not a valid enduring power; and
   - (b) the power is revoked by the mental incapacity of the donor, paragraphs 2 and 3 below shall apply, whether or not the instrument has been registered.

2. An attorney who acts in pursuance of the power shall not, by reason of the revocation, incur any liability (either to the donor or to any other person) unless at the time of acting he knows—
   - (a) that the instrument did not create a valid enduring power; and
   - (b) that the donor has become mentally incapable.

3. Any transaction between the attorney and another person shall, in favour of that person, be as valid as if the power had then been in existence, unless at the time of the transaction that person knows—
   - (a) that the instrument did not create a valid enduring power; and
   - (b) that the donor has become mentally incapable.

4. Section 9(4) shall apply for the purpose of determining whether a transaction was valid by virtue of paragraph 3 above as it applies for the purpose of determining whether a transaction was valid by virtue of section 9(3).

SECTION 2(7)   **SCHEDULE 3**

Joint and Joint and Several Attorneys

Part I

Joint Attorneys

1. In , the reference to the time when the attorney executes the instrument shall be read as a reference to the time when the second or last attorney executes the instrument. **6B–390**

2. In section 2(9) and (10), the reference to the attorney shall be read as a reference to any attorney under the power.

3. In section 5, reference to the attorney shall be read as including references to any attorney under the power.

4. Section 6 shall have effect as if the ground of objection to the registration of the instrument specified in subsection (5)(e) applied to any attorney under the power.

5. In section 8(2), references to the attorney shall be read as including references to any attorney under the power.

6. In section 8(4), references to the attorney shall be read as including references to any attorney under the power.

PART II

JOINT AND SEVERAL ATTORNEYS

6B–391 7. In section 2(10), the reference to the bankruptcy of the attorney shall be construed as a reference to the bankruptcy of the last remaining attorney under the power; and the bankruptcy of any other attorney under the power shall cause that person to cease to be attorney, whatever the circumstances of the bankruptcy.

8. The restriction upon disclaimer imposed by section 4(6) applies only to those attorneys who have reason to believe that the donor is or is becoming mentally incapable.

Court of Protection (Enduring Powers of Attorney) Rules 2001

6B–392 (S.I. 2001 No. 825)

ARRANGEMENT OF RULES

PART I

PRELIMINARY

RULE
1. Title and commencement 6B–392.1
2. Application. 6B–393
3.— Interpretation 6B–394
4. Exercise of court's functions 6B–395
5.— Computation of time 6B–396

PART II

APPLICATIONS

6.— Notice of intention to register. 6B–397
7. Time limits 6B–398
8.— Form of application 6B–399
9.— Objections to registration 6B–400
10.— Exercise of the court's powers and functions under the provisions of the 1985 Act. 6B–401
11. Consolidation of proceedings. 6B–402
12.— Registration of an enduring power of attorney. 6B–403
13.— Searches of the register and copies of registered enduring powers of attorney 6B–404

PART III

HEARINGS

14.— Notice of hearing 6B–405
15.— Mode of giving documents. 6B–406
16. Giving documents to a solicitor 6B–407
17. Alternative method of giving documents. 6B–408
18. Use of evidence in subsequent proceedings. 6B–409
19.— Copies of documents in court. 6B–410

20.	Summoning of witnesses	.6B–411
21.	Leave to bring an application	.6B–412
22.	Notification of decision	.6B–413

PART IV
Reviews and Appeals

23.—	Review of decision not made on an attended hearing	.6B–414
24.—	Appeal from decision made on an attended hearing	.6B–415

PART V
Cancellation of Registration

25.—	Cancellation of a registered power of attorney	.6B–416

PART VI
Fees

26.—	Schedule of fees	.6B–417

PART VII
Transitional Provisions

27.—		.6B–418

PART VIII
Revocation

28.	Revocation of previous Rules	.6B–419
	Schedules:	
	SCHEDULE 2—FEES	.6B–420

PART I

PRELIMINARY

Title and commencement

1. These Rules may be cited as the Court of Protection (Enduring Powers of Attorney) Rules 2001 and shall come into force on 1st April 2001.

6B–392.1

Application

2. Subject to the provisions of these Rules, the Court of Protection Rules 2001 shall apply to the proceedings under the Enduring Powers of Attorney Act 1985.

6B–393

Interpretation

3.——(1) In these Rules, unless the context otherwise requires—
expressions used in the Supreme Court Act 1981 shall have the same meanings as they have in that Act;
    "the Act" means the Enduring Powers of Attorney Act 1985;
    "the 1983 Act" means the Mental Health Act 1983;
    "the 2001 Rules" means the Court of Protection Rules 2001;
    "applicant" includes an objector;
    "application" includes an objection;
    "attended hearing" means a hearing where one or more of the par-

6B–394

ties to the proceedings have been invited to attend the court for the determination of the application;

"the court" means the Court of Protection;

"direction" means a direction or authority given under the seal of the court;

"enduring power of attorney" shall be construed in accordance with section 2 of the Act;

"entered" means entered in the register of enduring powers of attorney kept by the court;

"filed" means filed in the court office;

"hearing" means an attended or unattended hearing;

"judge" means the Lord Chancellor or a judge nominated under section 93(1) of the 1983 Act;

"Master" means the Master of the Court of Protection;

"nominated officer" means an officer of the court nominated under section 93(4) of the 1983 Act;

"order" means an order of the court under seal and includes a certificate, direction or authority of the court under seal;

"relative" means one of the persons referred to as relatives and entitled to receive notice under the provisions of paragraphs 1 and 2 of Schedule 1 to the Act;

"seal" means an official seal of the court and "sealed" shall be construed accordingly.

(2) In these Rules—
  (a) any reference to a numbered rule or to a numbered Schedule is a reference to the rule of, or the Schedule to, these Rules so numbered in these Rules;
  (b) any reference in a rule to a numbered paragraph is a reference to the paragraph so numbered in the rule in which the reference occurs; and
  (c) a form referred to by a letter alone means the form so designated in Schedule 1 or a form to the same effect with such variations as the circumstances may require and the court may approve and in both cases shall include a Welsh translation of the form.

Exercise of court's functions

6B–395   4. Where any discretion, power or function is (in whatever words) expressed by these Rules to be exercisable by the court then, subject to the provisions of the Act, that discretion, power or other function may be exercised—
  (a) by a judge;
  (b) by the Master;
  (c) to the extent to which he is authorised to exercise it under section 94 of the 1983 Act, by a nominated officer.

Computation of time

6B–396   5.——(1) Where a period of time fixed by the Act or by these Rules or by a judgment, order or direction for doing any act expires on a day on which the court office is closed and for that reason cannot be done on that day, the act shall be done in time if done on the next day on which the office is open.

(2) Where the act is required to be done within a specified period after or from a specified date, the period begins immediately after that date.

(3) Where any period of time, fixed as mentioned in paragraph (1), is three days or less, any day on which the court office is closed shall not be included in the computation of that period.

PART II

APPLICATIONS

Notice of intention to register

6.——(1) Notice of the attorney's intention to apply to register an enduring power of attorney shall be given in Form EP1 to the donor and to those relatives entitled to receive such notice and to any co-attorney, all such notices to be served within fourteen days of each other.

(2) An application to dispense with such notice shall be made in Form EP3 before any application for registration is made and shall be accompanied by the original power of attorney.

6B–397

Time limits

7. An application to register an enduring power of attorney shall be made in Form EP2 and shall be lodged with the court office not later than 10 days after the date on which—
    (a) notice has been given to the donor and every relative entitled to receive notice and every co-attorney; or
    (b) leave has been given to dispense with notice
whichever may be the later.

6B–398

Form of application

8.——(1) Subject to the provisions of rules 6 and 7 and to the following provisions of this rule, an application may be made by letter unless the court directs that it should be formal, in which case it shall be made in Form EP3.

(2) Any application made by letter to the court, other than an objection to registration, shall include the name and address of the applicant, the name of the donor if he is not the applicant, the form of relief or determination required and the grounds for the application.

6B–399

Objections to registration

9.——(1) Any objection to registration shall be made in writing and shall set out—
    (a) the name and address of the objector;
    (b) the name and address of the donor if he is not the objector;

6B–400

(c) any relationship of the objector to the donor;
(d) the name and address of the attorney; and
(e) the grounds for objecting to registration of the enduring power of attorney.

(2) Any objection to registration received by the court on or after the date of registration shall be treated by the court as an application to cancel the registration.

Exercise of the court's powers and functions under the provisions of the 1985 Act

6B–401   10.——(1) This rule shall apply to applications made to the court—
(a) for relief or for determination of any question under sections 1(1)(b), 4(5), 5, 6(3), 6(4), 8(2), 8(3), 8(4) or 11(5)(c) of the Act; or
(b) under paragraphs 2(1), 3(2), 4(2) or 7(1) of Schedule 1 to the Act,
which are not made simultaneously with an application for registration of an enduring power of attorney.

(2) On receipt of an application, the court may decide either that no hearing shall be held, in which case the application shall be dealt with by written representations, or it may fix an appointment for directions or for the application to be heard.

(3) The court may at any time, on application or of its own motion, give such direction as it thinks proper with regard to any matter arising in the course of an application.

(4) Notification of an appointment for directions or a hearing shall be given by the applicant to the attorney (if he is not the applicant), to any objector and to any other person directed by the court to be notified.

(5) The applicant, the attorney (if he is not the applicant) and any person given notice of the hearing may attend or be represented.

(6) If it appears to the court that any order for relief should be made or any question determined, the court may make such order or give such directions as it thinks fit, of its own motion.

(7) Where an attorney seeks to disclaim an enduring power of attorney pursuant to sections 4(6) or 7(1)(b) of the Act, the disclaimer shall not take effect earlier than the day on which the notice of disclaimer is received at the court.

Consolidation of proceedings

6B–402   11. The court may consolidate any application for registration or relief or any objection to registration if it considers that the proceedings may be dealt with more conveniently together.

Registration of an enduring power of attorney

6B–403   12.——(1) Where there is no objection to the registration of an enduring power of attorney or any objection has been withdrawn or dismissed, the enduring power of attorney shall be registered and sealed by the court.

(2) The court shall retain a copy of the registered enduring power of

attorney and shall return the original instrument to the applicant attorney.

(3) Any alterations which appear on the face of the instrument when an application for registration is made shall be sealed.

(4) Any qualification to registration imposed by reason of section 11(6) or (7) of the Act shall be noted on the register and on the instrument and sealed.

(5) The date of registration shall be the date stamped by the court on the instrument at the time of its registration.

Searches of the register and copies of registered enduring powers of attorney

13.——(1) On payment of the appropriate fee, any person shall be entitled to request the court in Form EP4 to search the register and to state whether an enduring power of attorney has been registered and the court shall so state in Form EP5.

6B–404

(2) The court may supply a person with an office copy of a registered enduring power of attorney if it is satisfied that he has a good reason for requesting a copy and that it is not reasonably practicable to obtain a copy from the attorney.

(3) For the purposes of this rule, an office copy is a photocopy or a facsimile copy of an enduring power of attorney, marked as an office copy and sealed.

(4) An office copy of an enduring power of attorney need not contain the explanatory information endorsed on the original power.

PART III

HEARINGS

Notice of hearing

14.——(1) Except where these rules otherwise provide or the court otherwise directs, the following minimum periods of notice of a hearing shall be given by the applicant—

6B–405

    (a) ten clear days in the case of—
        (i) an application to dispense with notice to the donor;
        (ii) an application to dispose of the donor's property prior to registration; and
        (iii) an objection to registration of an enduring power of attorney; and
    (b) seven clear days in the case of any other application.

(2) Unless the court otherwise directs, notice of a hearing shall be given to the attorney, the donor, every relative, any co-attorney and to such other persons who appear to the court to be interested as the court may specify.

(3) The court may extend or abridge the time limited by these Rules or any order or direction for doing any act upon such terms and notwithstanding in the case of an extension that the time so limited has expired.

(4) For the purpose of this rule, notice of a hearing is given if the ap-

plicant sends a copy of the application, endorsed by the court with the hearing date, to the person concerned.

Mode of giving documents

6B–406 15.——(1) Any document required by these Rules to be given to the donor shall be given to him personally.

(2) Except where these Rules otherwise provide, any document required by these Rules to be given to any person shall be given to him by—

    (a) sending it to him by first class post or through a document exchange; or

    (b) transmitting it to him by fax or other electronic means.

Giving documents to a solicitor

6B–407 16. Where a solicitor acting for the person to be given any document, other than the donor, endorses on that document, or on a copy of it, a statement that he accepts the document on behalf of that person, the document shall be deemed to have been duly given to that person and to have been received on the date that the endorsement was made.

Alternative method of giving documents

6B–408 17. Where it appears to the court that it is impracticable for any document to be given to a person in accordance with rule 15(2), the court may give such directions for the purpose of bringing the document to the notice of the person to whom it is addressed as it thinks fit.

Use of evidence in subsequent proceedings

6B–409 18. Except where the court otherwise directs, evidence which has been used in any proceedings relating to a donor may be used at any subsequent stage of those proceedings or in any other proceedings before the court.

Copies of documents in court

6B–410 19.——(1) Any person who has filed an affidavit or other document shall, unless the court otherwise directs, be entitled on request to be supplied with a copy of it.

(2) An attorney or his solicitor may have a search made for and may inspect and request a copy of any document filed in proceedings relating to the enduring power of attorney under which the attorney has been appointed.

(3) Subject to paragraphs (1) and (2), no documents filed in the court shall be open to inspection without the leave of the court and no copy of any such document or an extract from it shall be taken by or issued to any person without such leave.

Summoning of witnesses

6B–411 20. Any witness summons required to be issued in any proceedings under these Rules shall be in Form EP6.

Leave to bring an application

21. Any person other than a person who has been served with a notice of intention to register an enduring power of attorney shall apply to the court for leave to make an application for relief specified in the Act.

6B–412

Notification of decision

22. All persons to whom notice is to be given under rule 10(4) shall be notified by the applicant of the court's decision and shall also be sent by the applicant a copy of any order made or direction given.

6B–413

PART IV

REVIEWS AND APPEALS

Review of decision not made on an attended hearing

23.——(1) Any person who is aggrieved by a decision of the court that was made without an attended hearing may apply to the court within fourteen days of the date on which the decision was given to have the decision reviewed by the court.

6B–414

(2) On considering an application for review, the court may either confirm or revoke the previous decision or give any other order or decision which it thinks fit.

(3) Any person aggrieved by any order or decision of the court made on considering an application for review may apply to the court for an attended hearing.

Appeal from decision made on an attended hearing

24.——(1) Any person aggrieved by an order or decision of the court made on an attended hearing, may, within fourteen days from the date of entry of the order or as the case may be, from the date of the decision, appeal to a nominated judge.

6B–415

(2) The appellant shall within fourteen days—
   (a) serve notice of appeal in form EP7 on every person who is directly affected by the decision and on any other person whom the court may direct; and
   (b) lodge a copy of the notice at the court.

(3) The court shall fix a time and place at which the appeal is to be heard and shall cause notice of the time and place to be sent to the appellant, who shall immediately send notice of it to every person who has been served with notice of the appeal.

(4) No evidence further to that given at the hearing shall be filed in support of, or in opposition to, the appeal without leave of the court.

PART V

CANCELLATION OF REGISTRATION

Cancellation of a registered power of attorney

25.——(1) Where the court is satisfied that one of the circumstances listed in section 8(4) of the Act applies, it shall cancel the registration of

6B–416

the enduring power of attorney in question and send a notice to the attorney requiring him to deliver the original instrument to the court.

(2) Where the court—
- (a) receives a notice of disclaimer under section 7(1)(b) of the Act;
- (b) is satisfied that the enduring power of attorney has been revoked by the death or bankruptcy of the donor; or
- (c) is satisfied that the enduring power of attorney has been revoked by the death or bankruptcy of the attorney or, if the attorney is a body corporate, its winding up or dissolution;

it shall cancel the registration of the enduring power of attorney and send notice to the attorney, or, (where appropriate) to his personal representative or to the liquidator or receiver of a body corporate, requiring him or them to deliver the original instrument to the court.

(3) Where the instrument creating an enduring power of attorney has been lost or destroyed, the attorney shall give to the court written details of that date of such loss or destruction and of the circumstances in which the loss or destruction occurred.

(4) Where registration has been cancelled for any reason other than that set out in section 8(4)(c) of the Act, the court shall mark the power of attorney as cancelled.

(5) Any notices issued by the court under this rule may contain a warning that failure to comply with the notice may lead to punishment for contempt of court.

PART VI

FEES

Schedule of fees

6B–417 26.——(1) Fees shall be payable in accordance with the provisions of Schedule 2.

(2) The fees specified in column 2 of Schedule 2 shall apply in respect of the corresponding event referred to in column 1.

(3) The person liable to pay the fee for the registration of a power of attorney shall, unless the court otherwise directs, make the payment out of the assets of the donor.

PART VII

TRANSITIONAL PROVISIONS

6B–418 27.——(1) Where any matter is pending before the Public Trustee before the coming into force of these Rules which by virtue of these Rules relates to a function to be exercised by the court, the court shall deal with the matter in accordance with these Rules.

(2) Where any review or appeal is pending before the court or the Public Trustee before the coming into force of these Rules, it shall be dealt with in accordance with the provisions of these Rules.

PART VIII

REVOCATION

Revocation of previous Rules

28. The Court of Protection (Enduring Powers of Attorney) Rules 1994 and the Court of Protection (Enduring Powers of Attorney) (Amendment) Rules 1999 are hereby revoked.

6B–419

RULE 26 SCHEDULE 2

FEES

Column 1	Column 2
Item	Fee
Registration Fee	
1. On lodging an application for registration of an enduring power of attorney.	£75.00
Search Fee	
2. On application for a search of the register.	£25.00

6B–420

Enduring Powers of Attorney (Prescribed Form) Regulations 1990

(S.I. 1990 No.1376)

Introductory note

The Enduring Powers of Attorney (Prescribed Form) Regulations 1987 (S.I. 1987 No. 1612), which revoked the 1986 Regulations (S.I. 1986 No. 126), have themselves been revoked by the Enduring Powers of Attorney (Prescribed Form) Regulations 1990 (S.I. 1990 No.1376). An EPA made in the form which was prescribed at the time may be registered at any time thereafter; but if it is made on a form which was out-of-date when the EPA was made, it will be invalid. There are transitional periods allowed by the 1987 and the 1990 Regulations and consequently there are some overlaps between the relevant periods.

The 1986 prescribed form could be used for EPAs created between March 10, 1986 and June 30, 1988, the 1987 prescribed form for those created between November 1, 1987 and July 30, 1991 and the 1990 prescribed form for those from July 31, 1990 onwards. (See 1986 Regulations, regs 1 and 3; 1987 Regulations, regs 1, 2 and 4 and 1990 Regulations, regs 1, 2 and 5.)

The form prescribed by the 1990 Regulations was necessary because of the coming into force (also on July 31, 1990) of s.1 of the Law of Property (Miscellaneous Provisions) Act 1989. This is the section which abolishes the need for deeds to be sealed by people who execute them, although signing is still required. The facility for signing by direction is extended to enduring powers of attorney by the new regulations, so that a donor, if incapable of signing or making a mark on the document, is able to instruct someone else to sign the EPA on his behalf. If an EPA is being signed by direction, two witnesses to the signing will be needed.

6B–421

Citation and commencement

1. These Regulations may be cited as the Enduring Powers of Attorney (Prescribed Form) Regulations 1990 and shall come into force on 31st July 1990.

6B–422

Prescribed form

6B-423 2.—(1) Subject to paragraphs (2) and (3) of this regulation and to regulation 4, an enduring power of attorney must be in the form set out in the Schedule to these Regulations and must include all the explanatory information headed "About using this form" in Part A of the Schedule and all the relevant marginal notes to Parts B and C. It may also include such additions (including paragraph numbers) or restrictions as the donor may decide.

(2) In completing the form of enduring power of attorney—
- (a) there shall be excluded (either by omission or deletion)—
  - (i) where the donor appoints only one attorney, everything between the square brackets on the first page of Part B; and
  - (ii) one and only one of any pair of alternatives;
- (b) there may also be so excluded—
  - (i) the words on the second page of Part B "subject to the following restrictions and conditions", if those words do not apply;
  - (ii) the attestation details for a second witness in Parts B and C if a second witness is not required; and
  - (iii) any marginal notes which correspond with any words excluded under the provisions of this paragraph and the two notes numbered 1 and 2 which appear immediately under the heading to Part C.

(3) The form of execution by the donor or by an attorney may be adapted to provide—
- (a) for a case where the donor or an attorney signs by means of a mark; and
- (b) for the case (dealt with in regulation 3) where the enduring power of authority is executed at the direction of the donor or of an attorney; and the form of execution by an attorney may be adapted to provide for execution by a trust corporation.

(4) Subject to paragraphs (1) (2) and (3) of this regulation and to regulation 4, an enduring power of attorney which seeks to exclude any provision contained in these Regulations is not a valid enduring power of attorney.

Execution

6B-424 3.—(1) An enduring power of attorney in the form set out in the Schedule to these Regulations shall be executed by both the donor and the attorney, although not necessarily at the same time, in the presence of a witness, but not necessarily the same witness, who shall sign the form and give his full name and address.

(2) The donor and an attorney shall not witness the signature of each other nor one attorney the signature of another.

(3) Where an enduring power of attorney is executed at the direction of the donor—
- (a) it must be signed in the presence of two witnesses who shall each sign the form and give their full names and addresses; and
- (b) a statement that the enduring power of attorney has been executed at the direction of the donor must be inserted in Part B;

(c) it must not be signed by either an attorney or any of the witnesses to the signature of either the donor or an attorney.

(4) Where an enduring power of attorney is executed at the direction of an attorney—
 (a) paragraph 3(a) above applies; and
 (b) a statement that the enduring power of attorney has been executed at the direction of the attorney must be inserted in Part C;
 (c) it must not be signed by either the donor, an attorney or any of the witnesses to the signature of either the donor or an attorney.

4. Where more than one attorney is appointed and they are to act jointly and severally, then at least one of the attorneys so appointed must execute the instrument for it to take effect as an enduring power of attorney, and only those attorneys who have executed the instrument shall have the functions of an attorney under an enduring power of attorney in the event of the donor's mental incapacity or on the registration of the power, whichever first occurs. **6B–425**

Revocation

5. The Enduring Powers of Attorney (Prescribed Form) Regulations 1987 are hereby revoked, except that— **6B–426**
 (a) a power executed in the form prescribed by those Regulations and executed by the donor before 31st July 1991 shall be capable (whether or not seals are affixed to it) of being a valid enduring power of attorney;
 (b) regulation 3(3) shall apply to a power executed by the donor before 31st July 1991 under the provisions of those Regulations and the form of enduring power of attorney prescribed by those Regulations may be modified accordingly.

6D TRUSTEES

PUBLIC TRUSTEE RULES 1912

OFFICES

Add at end of paragraph 3(2):

3.—(2) The Office of the Public Trustee is at 81 Chancery Lane London WC2A 1DD; DX 0012 London Chancery Lane WC2. Telephone 020 7911 7100; Fax 020 7911 7105; e-mail enquiries@offsol.gsi.gov.uk **6D–88**

SECTION 7

LEGAL REPRESENTATIVES – COSTS AND LITIGATION FUNDING

Regulation 3(1)(b)

Add new paragraph after 7A–18:

7A–18.1 The Regulation requires that the CFA must specify how much of the percentage increase relates to the cost of the legal representative of the postponement of the payment of his fees and expenses. This element of the success fee is not recoverable from a paying party. This continues the principle laid down by the Court of Appeal in a decision under the earlier rules, *Hunt v. R M Douglas (Roofing) Ltd., The Times,* November 23, 1987, CA.

Recoverability of Success Fees and Insurance Premiums

Add new paragraph after 7A–33:

7A–33.1 The Court of Appeal has considered four main questions:
  (i) the time at which it is appropriate to enter into a CFA and take out an ATE policy;
  (ii) the reasonableness of the success fee when a claim is quickly resolved without the need for court proceedings;
  (iii) whether the claimants are entitled to recover an ATE premium where there has been no need to commence proceedings;
  (iv) the reasonableness of ATE premiums.

After a hearing at which representatives of interested bodies were also allowed to make representations the court found:
  (i) it is in principle permissible for a claimant to enter into a CFA with a success fee and to take out ATE insurance when he first consults his solicitor and before the solicitor writes a letter of claim and receives the prospective defendant's response;
  (ii) in relation to modest and straightforward claims for compensation resulting from road traffic accidents where a CFA is agreed at the outset, 20% is the maximum uplift that can reasonably be agreed in such a case;
  (iii) ATE premiums are in principle recoverable as part of a claimant's costs even though his claim is quickly resolved without the need for proceedings;
  (iv) The court requested a Costs Judge to investigate and report on the reasonableness of ATE premiums.

The court also considered that it is open to a solicitor and to a client to agree a two stage success fee at the outset of proceedings. It gave an example of an uplift agreed at 100% subject to a reduction to a maximum of 5% should the claim settle before the end of the period fixed by a pre-action protocol. Such an uplift would normally reflect the risks of the individual case. The court suggests that once the necessary data becomes available consideration will need to be given to the question whether the requirement to act reasonably mandates the agreement of a two stage success fee in a case where a CFA with a success fee is agreed at the outset: *Callery v. Gray* [2001] E.W.C.A. Civ. July 17.

The Court of Appeal subsequently held that the words "insurance against the risk of incurring a costs liability" in section 29 of the Access to Justice Act 1999 mean "insurance against the risk of incurring a costs liability that cannot be passed on to the opposite party". In the particular case the small element of cover for "own costs insurance" could be regarded as falling within the description of insurance against the risk of liability within section 29 and the premium of £350 was held to be reasonable.

The circumstances in which and the terms upon which "own costs" cover would be reasonable in relation to other policies so that the whole premium could be recovered as costs would have to be determined by the courts when dealing with individual cases. Other issues mentioned in the Costs Judge's Report would fall to be judicially determined as and when they arose in individual cases. A copy of the Report was annexed to the Court of Appeal judgment with the warning that the views expressed might be helpful but were not definitive: *Callery v. Gray (No.2)* [2001] E.W.C.A. Civ. July 31.

1. SUMMARY JURISDICTION OF THE COURT OVER SOLICITORS

Jurisdiction to enforce undertakings given by solicitors

Add after third paragraph:

Where a solicitor gives an undertaking, but not in the capacity as a solicitor, the court has no inherent jurisdiction to enforce the undertaking. In the particular case the solicitor had had no ostensible authority to bind the partnership and the undertaking could not therefore be enforced against a partner: *Ruparel v. Awan* [2001] Lloyds Rep. 258, David Donaldson QC.   **7C–213**

3. SOLICITORS' LIENS AND CHARGING ORDERS

General or retaining lien

Add after "Paragon Finance Plc v. Rosling King, May 26, 2000, per Hart J.":

The claimants terminated their solicitors' retainer and sought delivery up of documents. The solicitors retained the documents under their lien pending payment of outstanding fees. The court refused to make an order for delivery up of the documents on payment of the balance of the fees into court on the basis that the only possible prejudice to the claimant was the possibility of not being able to recover any overpayment it was found to have made. The court found there was no reason to suppose that the solicitors would not be able to repay the amount of any overpayment and the balance came down in favour of not making the order. In the absence of convincing evidence of the solicitors' inability to pay any overpayment, the claimant in fact suffered no prejudice if the court made no order: *Paragon Finance Plc v. Rosling King* [2001] E.W. Ch. June 12, Hart J.   **7C–227**

After "Ismail v. Richards Butler" for "The Times, February 2, 1996" substitute:
[1996] 3 W.L.R. 129

Add after "A. v. B., [1984] 1 All E.R. 265":
, Leggatt J.

SECTION 8

LIMITATION

Scope and operation of the Act

Add at end of fifth paragraph:

Further, the amended statutory provisions subsequent to the Limitation Act 1939 have been held not to deprive the defendant of accrued limitation defences where the cause of action, for physical abuse, accrued before June 4, 1954. The defendants were entitled to rely on the regime of the unamended 1939 Act: *McDonnell v. Congregation of Christian Brothers Trustee*, Daily Telegraph, March 20, 2001.   **8–3**

Note

Add at end:

For a case deciding that the 10 years time limit under s.11A(3) is a period of limitation for the purposes of CPR 19.5(3) (a case of mistake in naming the original defendant) see *H (a child) v. Merck & Co. Inc.* [2001] C.P. Rep. 80.   **8–19**

Actions for damages for personal injuries or death

Add at end:

The defendant may, in a case where the cause of action arose sufficiently long ago, be entitled to rely on accrued limitation defences under the new regime of the unamended Limitation Act 1939: see *McDonnell v. Congregation of Christian Brothers Trustees*, cited at 8.3 above.   **8–26**

Add after paragraph which begins "This view has been reinforced...":

This decision was followed in *Fennan v. Anthony Hodari & Co.* [2001] Lloyd's Rep. PN 183, CA (a case where the claimant did not know that the defendant's omission to tell her the nature and effect of a document amounted to a breach of duty of care).   **8–30**

Add after "The Times, May 2, 2000, CA":

See also *Steeds v. Peverel Management Services Ltd*, The Times, May 16, 2001, CA.   **8–74**

(3) Mistake in name of party

8–87 For "19.4(3)(a)" substitute:
19.5(3)(a)

Add at end:

He has been held, in a case where the Claimant's representatives were genuinely mistaken in their conclusion that the producer of a vaccine had been the original defendant, that there is no reason to place a restrictive interpretation on the word "mistake" for the purposes of s.35(6)(a) or of CPR 19.5(3): see *H (a child) v. Merck & Co. Inc.* [2001] C.P. Rep. 80.

SECTION 9

JURISDICTIONAL AND PROCEDURAL LEGISLATION

9A MAIN STATUTES

Introductory note

9A–2 *In the second sentence delete "has itself".*

Interpretation

9A–3 *After "Whereas the J.A. 1925 was a consolidating statute, the S.C.A. 1981 is not a mere consolidating statute but is" add a comma.*

The High Court

9A–16 *Delete the second paragraph.*

Liability to proceedings

9A–38 For "(Habeas Corpus Act 1679, 31 Car. 2, c.2)" substitute:
Habeas Corpus Act 1679, 31 Car. 2, c.2

"incapable of acting"

9A–44.1 For "*Locabail (U.K.) Ltd v. Bayfield Properties Ltd (Leave to Appeal)* [2000] 2 W.L.R. 870, *The Times*, November 19, 1999, CA" substitute:
Locabail (U.K.) Ltd v. Bayfield Properties Ltd [2000] Q.B. 451, CA

Add after "*Hoekstra v. H.M. Advocate*, *The Times*, April 14, 2000":

; *Medicaments and Related Classes of Goods (No.2), Re* [2001] 1 W.L.R. 700, CA; *Taylor v. Lawrence* [2001] EWCA Civ. 119, January 25, 2001, CA, (unreported)

Add at end after "(unreported)":

; *Save and Prosper Pensions Ltd v. Homebase Ltd*, March 2, 2000 (unreported) (Judge Rich QC)

Appeals in civil matters
(7)

9A–47 *Add at end of paragraph (7):*

Although s.55(1) of the Access to Justice Act 1999 s.55(1) (Second appeals) does not apply to these appeals, a robust attitude to the "prospect of success" criterion (CPR r.52.3(6)) should be adopted in these cases (*Cooke v. Secretary of State for Social Security* [2001] EWCA Civ 734, April 25, 2001, CA, unrep.).

"all purposes of or incidental to"

Add the following numbered paragraph:

9A–47.1 In judicial review proceedings, the High Court has an inherent jurisdiction to make ancillary orders temporarily releasing an applicant from detention, and by virtue of s.15(3), on appeal in those proceedings, the Court of Appeal could make like order (*R. (Sezek) v. Secretary of State for the Home Department, The Times*, June 20, 2001, CA).

Application of High Court enforcement provisions to Court of Appeal judgments

For "Times, January 6, 1998, CA" substitute: **9A–48**
9A–48[1998] 1 W.L.R. 1074, CA

In the heading, for ""leap-frog" appeals" substitute: "leap-frog" petitions

Appeals directly from the High Court to the House of Lords— "leap-frog" petitions

For text of exisitng paragraph, substitute: **9A–50**
See the A.J.A. 1969, s.13 (para. 9B–41 below) and Practice Directions and Standing Orders Applicable to Civil Appeals, Direction 6 and see paras 4A–25 and 4A–115 (above).

Jurisdiction to hear appeals from High Court

Add new paragraph before the last paragraph:
As to appeals from the Court of Appeal against an order of the High Court refusing **9A–50.1**
permission to appeal, see *Foenander v. Bond Lewis & Co* [2001] EWCA Civ 759; [2001] 2 All E.R. 1019, CA.

Restrictions on appeals

In the first sentence of the first paragraph, for "court of Appeal" substitute:
Court of Appeal   **9A–55**

Add after "[2000] 1 W.L.R. 586, HL":
; *Henry Boot Construction (U.K.) Ltd v. Malmaison Hotel (Manchester) Ltd* [2001] 1 All E.R. 193, CA; [2000] 2 Lloyd's Rep. 625, CA.

Add the following paragraph before the last paragraph:
The leading House of Lords Authority on the phrase "in any criminal cause or matter" is *Amand v. Home Secretary and Minister of Defence of Royal Netherlands Government* [1943] A.C. 147, HL, see *United States Government v. Montgomery* [2001] UKHL 3; [2001] 1 W.L.R. 196, HL, where the Amand case and other authorities are examined.

Jurisdiction exercisable by the High Court

In the final sentence of the first paragraph for ": in" substitute:
;   **9A–58**

In the final paragraph for "in this s.19" substitute:
in s.19

Inherent jurisdiction of the Court

Add after "[2000] 2 All E.R. 29)":
; *R. (Sezek) v. Secretary of State for the Home Department, The Times*, June 20, 2001, CA **9A–59**
(ancillary order in judicial review proceedings temporarily releasing an applicant from detention). Note also, *Harley v. McDonald* [2001] UKPC 18; [2001] 2 W.L.R. 1749, PC (jusisdiction to award costs personally against practitioner where serious dereliction of duty).

Jurisdiction to be exercised by single judge

For "In re Fletcher, Times, June 12, 1984" substitute:
In *Re Fletcher, The Times*, June 12, 1984   **9A–60**

Other cases as to jurisdiction

Bail

For "See, further, Archbold, Criminal Pleading, Evidence and Practice (1999) paras 3–186 to 3–194." substitute:
See, further, Archbold, Criminal Pleading, Evidence and Practice (2001) paras 3–186 to **9A–64**
3–194.

Jurisdiction where proceedings raising "academic" or "hypothetical" point of law

At the end of the second paragraph for "and R. v. Hackney London Borough Council, ex p. Jarram, June 14, 1999 (unrep.))." substitute:

9A–68 R. v. Hackney London Borough Council, Ex p. Jarram, June 14, 1999 (unrep.)), R. (Tshikangu) v. Newham LBC, The Times, April 27, 2001 (Stanley Burnton J).

At the end of the forth paragraph for "Note also R. v. Secretary of State for Health, ex p. Imperail Tobacco Ltd., The Times, December 20, 2000. H.L." substitute:

Note also R. v. Secretary of State for Health, Ex p. Imperial Tobacco Ltd [2001] 1 W.L.R. 127, HL.

9A–77 *For the heading "Note", substitute:*

rules of court

Matters relating to trial on indictment

For "(subsection (3))." substitute:

9A–81.1 (subsection (3)) (see also s.28(1))

For "R. v. Maidstone Crown Court, ex p. Harrow London Borough Council, The Times, May 14, 1999, D.C." substitute:

R. v. Maidstone Crown Court Ex p. Harrow LBC [1999] 3 All E.R. 542; The Times, May 14, 1999, DC

In the last line for "indictment." substitute:

indictment); see also R. v. Canterbury Crown Court, Ex p. Regentford Ltd, The Times, February 6, 2001, DC, and R. v. Leicester Crown Court, Ex p. Commissioners for Customs and Excise, The Times, February 23, 2001, DC.

Note

For "This section gives statutory force to the provisions of CPR Sched. 1, RSC O.53. For a full account see Vol. 1, paras sc53.14.1 et seq." substitute:

9A–85 For relevant rules of court, see CPR Pt 54 (Judicial Review); see Vol.1 paras 54.0.1 et seq.

Award of interest on debts and damages

In the second sentence of the first paragraph, after "the Act of 1934" add:

9A–105 (see para. 9B–442 below)

Application for injunctions

For "(O.T. Africa Line Ltd. v. Fayad Hijazy, The Times, November 28, 2000, Aikens J.)." substitute:

9A–112 (O.T. Africa Line Ltd v. Hijazy (The Kribi), [2001] 1 Lloyd's Rep. 76, Aikens J.). The 1998 Act requires that a marginally higher threshold test than that which applied previously should apply in all applications for interlocutory injunctions likely to affect freedom of expression (Imutran Ltd v. Uncaged Campaigns Ltd [2001] 2 All E.R. 385, Sir Andrew Morritt V.-C.).

Applications for order

For "For practice and procedure, see CPR Schedule 1, O.94, r. 15 and commentary thereon (Vol. 1, para. sc94.15 et seq.)." substitute:

9A–134 For practice and procedure, see CPR Schedule 1, O.94, r.15 and commentary thereon (Vol. 1, para. sc94.15 et seq.).

Applications for leave

9A–135 *In first sentence delete "in Chambers".*

Effect of this section

In the first sentence for "CPR Sched. 1, RSC O.53 (Applications for judicial review)" substitute:

9A–138 CPR Pt 54 (Judicial Review)

Note

For "Secondly, there are the power" substitute:
  Secondly, there are the powers **9A–152**

Effect of section

In the second list item numbered (b) delete "to 9A–177 below". **9A–155**

In the list item numbered (c) for "(see paras 9A–178 to 9A–191 below)" substitute:
(paras 9A–161 to 9A–178)

B. Section 49(2)

Final determination and avoidance of multiplicity of proceedings

Add at end of the fourth paragraph:
  The relationship between the rule in *Henderson v. Henderson* and the court's inherent jurisdiction to protect its processes from abuse was examined in *Johnson v. Gore Wood & Co* [2001] 2 W.L.R. 72, HL. **9A–160**

For "(1999) 149 New L.J. 1254" substitute:
  [2000] 1 W.L.R. 230

C. Section 49(3)

Stay of proceedings

Add at end:
  As there is a public interest in the finality of litigation, proceedings may be stayed on the grounds that they are an abuse of process to prevent a defendant from being vexed twice in the same matter (*Johnson v. Gore Wood & Co* [2001] 2 W.L.R. 72, HL); but whether an action should be stayed on this basis should be judged broadly on the merits, taking account of all public and private interests involved and all the facts of the case, the crucial question being whether the claimant was in all the circumstances misusing or abusing the process of the court (*ibid.*). See also, *Stevens v. School of Oriental and African Studies, The Times*, February 2, 2001 (Pumphrey J.) (a stay to prevent, what was in substance, a re-litigation of earlier proceedings, was, in the circumstances, a reasonable exercise of the court's inherent jurisdiction and did not infringe the Human Rights Act 1998 Sched.1, art.6). **9A–161**

Stay under particular statutes

Add new paragraph at end:
  The court has, in addition to the power granted under the Arbitration Act 1996, s.9 (see para. 2B–114 above), an inherent jurisdiction to stay proceedings, and this jurisdiction may be exercised if good sense and litigation management make it desirable for the matter to be referred to arbitration (*Al-Naimi v. Islamic Press Agency Inc.* [2000] 1 Lloyd's Rep. 522, CA). **9A–162**

Stay under the CPR

For paragraph which begins "Practice Direction (Transitional Arrangements)..." substitute:
  Existing proceedings that did not come before a judge between April 26, 1999, and April 25, 2000, were stayed by operation of CPR r.51.1 and Practice Direction (Transitional Arrangements) para. 19(i). Any party to those proceedings may apply for the stay to be lifted (para. 1 9(2) (see Vol. 1 paras 51.1.2 & 51PD–019). **9A–163**

Nature or effect of a stay of proceedings

After the second paragraph add the following new paragraph:
  For considerations relevant to the question whether a stay should take effect forthwith or at a later stage in the development of the proceedings (*e.g.* after the disclosure of documents and exchange of witness statements had been completed), see *Synstar Computer Service (U.K.) Ltd v. I.C.L. (Sorbus) Ltd, The Times*, May 1, 2001 (Lightman J.) **9A–165**

Concurrent civil proceedings

In the fifth paragraph, for "that question or issue shall be" substitute:
  that the question or issue should be **9A–168**

Delete text of penultimate paragraph and substitute:
  Recent authorities on the matters referred to above include: *Re B (Minors: Abduction), The Times,* November 6, 1992; *Chorion Plc. v. Lane, The Times,* April 7, 1999; *Steans Fashions Ltd. v. Legal and General Assurance Society Ltd, The Times,* December 31, 1994, CA. See further authorities referred to in para. 9A–161 above.

Concurrent civil and criminal proceedings

Add new paragraph at end:

9A–169 Where civil proceedings in the form of an application under the Directors Disqualification Act 1986 were stayed pending the outcome of a related criminal proceedings, and, after the completion of the criminal proceedings, the Secretary of State applied to restore the application, the civil proceedings were not barred by the doctrine of double recovery, and the continuation of the civil proceedings was not an abuse of process (*Re Cedarwood Productions Ltd, The Times,* July 12, 2001, CA).

Effect of this section

Add new paragraph at end:

9A–261 The jurisdiction of the court to refuse to grant an injunction sought to restrain continuing trespass and breach of covenant and to award damages in lieu under s.50 was authoritatively reviewed in *Jaggard v. Sawyer* [1995] 1 W.L.R. 269, CA. It has been held at first instance that, since the coming into effect of the Human Rights Act 1998 Sched. 1 Pt. 1, damages for future infringements of a claimant's rights may be awarded under s.50 in lieu of an injunction (*Marcic v. Thames Water Utilities Ltd.*, [2000] 3 All E.R. 698(Judge Richard Havery QC)).

"costs ... shall be in the discretion of the court"

At end, delete the last sentence and add new paragraphs:

9A–265 The breadth of the discretion was emphasised by the House of Lords in *Aiden Co Ltd v. Interbulk Ltd (The Vimeira) (No.2)* [1986] A.C. 965, HL, where it was held that it includes a power to award costs against a person who is not a party to the proceedings. In modern times, the jurisdiction to order that costs should be paid by a person who, though not actually a party to the proceedings, is sufficiently involved in them in support of a losing party for it to be appropriate for the court to order that they should bear at least some or a proportion of the winning party's costs (see further para. 9A–265A below), has been explained and developed in a number of cases. Significant authorities include the following: *Symphony Group Plc v. Hodgson* [1994] Q.B. 179, CA; *Tharros Shipping Co Ltd v. Bias Shipping Ltd (The Griparion) (No.3)* [1995] 1 Lloyd's Rep. 541; *Murphy v. Young & Co's Brewery Plc* [1997] 1 W.L.R. 1591, CA; *Faryab v. Smyth,* August 28, 1998, CA, unrep.; *Pendennis Shipyard Ltd v. Magrathea (Pendennis) Ltd* [1998] 1 Lloyd's Rep. 315; *TGA Chapman Ltd v. Christopher* [1998] 1 W.L.R. 12, CA; *Gloucestershire HA v. MA Torpy &Partners Ltd (t/a Torpy &Partners) (No.2),* [1999] Lloyd's Rep. I.R. 303; *Globe Equities Ltd v. Globe Legal Services Ltd, The Times,* April 14, 1999, CA, unrep.; *Fulton Motors Ltd v. Toyota (G.B.) Ltd,* July 23, 1999, CA, unrep.; *Stocznia Gdanska SA v. Latreefers Inc, The Times,* March 15, 2000, CA; *Cormack v. Washbourne, The Times,* March 30, 2000, CA; *Secretary of State for Trade and Industry v. Aurum Marketing Ltd, The Times,* August 10, 2000, CA; *Secretary of State for Trade and Industry v. Backhouse, The Times,* February 23, 2001, CA; *Hamilton v. Al Fayed (No.3), The Times,* July 25, 2001 (Morland J.).

  Normally, orders made by the court in the exercise of the discretion to award costs referred to in s.51(1) are made at the end of the proceedings to which they relate (whether interlocutory, final or appeal). However the discretion is wide enough to enable the court to make an order for costs in advance, based on assumptions as to the possible outcomes (and, therefore, the possible costs liabilities) of the proceedings. Depending on the circumstances, such orders may be aptly described as "prospective", "pre-emptive" or "protective" costs orders. The clearest example is where the court makes an order that a party involved in legal proceedings in the capacity of trustee should be entitled to his own costs out of the fund and should be indemnified by the fund against any award for costs which may be made against him (*Re Beddoe, Downes v. Cottam* [1893] 1 Ch. 547, CA) (see Vol. 1 para. 48.15.5). In certain circumstances the costs protection enjoyed by trustees may be extended to beneficiaries (*Re Buckton, Buckton v. Buckton* [1907] 2 Ch. 406; *D'Abo v. Paget (No.2), The Times,* August 10, 2000). The protection has also been extended to minority shareholders (*Wallersteiner v. Moir (No.2)* [1975] Q.B. 373), to beneficiaries under pension funds (*McDonald v. Horn* [1995] 1 All E.R. 961, CA; *Machin v. National Power Plc.*, July 31, 1998, unrep. (Carnwarth J.)), and to insurance policy-holders (*Re AXA Equity and Law Life Assurance Society Plc*, *The Times*, December 19, 2000 (Evans-Lombe J.)). In modern times, pre-emptive costs orders have been sought in circumstances quite different to the trust and trust-related circumstances noted above, in particular in judicial review applications where organisations acting in the public interest are involved. It has been held that, in exceptional circumstances, pre-emptive costs orders may be granted in such "public interest challenge" cases; see *R. v. Lord Chancellor, Ex p. Child Poverty Action Group*, [1999] 1 W.L.R. 347 (Dyson J.); *R. v. Hammersmith and Fulham LBC, Ex p. CPRE London Branch*, October 26, 1999, unrep. (Richards J.); *R. v. Secretary of State for the Environment, Ex p. O'Byrne*, *The Times*, November 12, 1999 (Hooper J.); cf. *Hodgson v. Imperial Tobacco Ltd* [1998] 1 W.L.R. 1056, CA.

Composition of the Court of Appeal

In the final sentence for "Court of Appeal (Civil Division) Order 1982" substitute:
    Court of Appeal (Civil Division) Order 1982 (S.I. 1982 No. 543)   **9A–274**

Subs. (1)

For "Practice Direction (Court Sitting)" substitute:
    Practice Direction (Court Sittings)   **9A–288**

Subs. (2)

For "As to sitting in vacations, see Practice Direction (Court of Appeal (Civil Division)), supplementing CPR Pt 52." substitute:
    Para. 10.8 of *Practice Direction (Court of Appeal (Civil Division))*, [1999] 1 W.L.R. 1027, CA   **9A–289**
(sub nom Practice Note (Court of Appeal : Procedure) [1999] 2 All E.R. 490, CA) states that the Court of Appeal will sit in vacation on such days as the Master of the Rolls may direct and may hear such appeals and applications as the Court may direct. Details of the number of courts sitting in August and September will be published each year, normally before Easter.

Jurisdiction of a single judge or any officer or member of court staff to hear incidental applications

In the second paragraph, for "RSC 0.59, r. 2B" substitute:
    RSC O.59, r.2B   **9A–292**

Re-distribution of business

For "The distribution of business among the Division" substitute:

Business conducted in camera   **9A–300**

For "Hallam-Eames v. Merrett Syndicates Ltd., Times, June 16, 1995" substitute:
    Hallam-Eames v. Merrett Syndicates Ltd, *The Times*, June 16, 1995   **9A–319**

"application ...not later than such time before trial as may be prescribed"

Add at end:
    Subject to the terms of s.69(l), either party to a defamation action has a right to trial by   **9A–326.1**
jury, and the power to make procedural rules under Civil Procedure Act 1997, s.4 does not permit the restriction of that fundamental right; consequently, although in terms CPR r.24.2 makes no exception for defamation cases, summary judgment should not be granted where one party was entitled to exercise his right to jury trial and wished to do so (*Safeway Stores Plc. v. Tate* [2001] 2 W.L.R. 1377, CA; see also *Elite Model Management Corporation v. British Broadcasting Corporation*, March 14, 2001, unrep., Eady J.).
    If there is a material issue of fact in a libel case, s.69(l) entities a party to have that issue determined by a jury; however it is for the judge to decide whether there really is such an issue (*Alexander v. Arts Council of Wales*, *The Times* April 27, 2001, CA). Where the judge comes to the conclusion that the evidence, taken at its highest, is such that a jury properly directed could not properly reach a necessary factual conclusion, it is his duty, upon a submission being made, to withdraw that issue from the jury; but where there is a risk that the judge's view on particular issue might be overturned on appeal it is desirable that it should be left to the jury (*ibid.*).

Effect of section

9A-337 In the last sentence for "ben" substitute:
been

For the heading "Sending by post" substitute:
"sending ... in the manner prescribed"

9A-433 For "Power to make provision for recorded delivery service is given by the Recorded Delivery Service Act 1962, Sched., para. 4." substitute:

    The principal purpose behind the granting to the Lord Chancellor of power to may make rules prescribing the manner in which court documents are to be produced to any court or tribunal is to facilitate production by post. The rule-making power as contained in J.A. 1925 s.220, the predecessor of s.136, insofar as it applied to production by post was confined to the making of rules permitting production by registered post. Rules to this effect were found in the Supreme Court Documents (Production) Rules 1926 (S.R. & 0) 1926 No. 461). After the coming into force of the Recorded Delivery Service Act 1962 those Rules, insofar as they permitted production by registered post, were to be read as also permitting production by recorded delivery service. The 1926 Rules were superseded by Practice Direction (Court Documents) para. 5.6 (see Vol. 1 para. 5PD–005). In terms, sub-para. (4) of para. 5.6 follows the 1926 Rules and permits production by the court by registered post. However, by virtue of the 1962 Act (referred to above) production by recorded delivery service is permitted. See further, Vol. 1 para. 5.1.4.

Jurisdiction of county courts

In the second paragraph, for "(Courts and Legal Services Act 1990, s.1(1)) and its jurisdiction to grant relief of the Anton Piller and Mareva injunction variety is restricted (see County Court Remedies Regulations 1991, reg. 2, see para. 9B–81)." substitute:

9A-485 (Courts and Legal Services Act 1990, s.1(10)) (see para. 9B–6 below), or to grant relief prescribed by the County Court Remedies Regulations 1991, reg. 2 (see para. 9B–81 below).

Add at end of second paragraph:
Note also s.17 (Abandonment of part of claim to give court jurisdiction).

Civil Courts Order

Add at end before ".":
9A-489 (see para. 11–7 below)

"any action founded on contract or tort"

Add at end:
9A-513 As to whether a particular claim is an action "founded on contract", see *Hutchings v. Islington LBC* [1998] 3 All E.R. 445, CA.

"any order which could be made by the High Court"

For "Anton Piller orders and Mareva injunctions" substitute:
9A-549 seizing orders and freezing injunctions

Add at end:
See also *C v. K (Ouster Order: Non-Parent)* [1996] 2 F.L.R. 506 (Wall J.) (molestation and ouster injunctions as injunctive relief).

"Transfer of the proceedings"

Add at end:
9A-553 For transfer of Chancery work from the High Court to a county court and patents county court, see Chancery Guide Chps. 13 and 23 (paras 1–108 and 1–140 above). For observations on time when transfer takes effect, see *Kings Quality Homes Ltd v. AJ Paints Ltd* [1998] 1 W.L.R. 124, CA (jurisdiction of county court judge to hear appeal from order made by district judge before proceedings transferred from High Court to a county court).

Subs. (3), Courts and Legal Services Act 1990, s.1

Add new paragraph at end:
9A-560 For transfer of proceedings from a county court to the High Court in insolvency proceedings, see *Bullard & Taplin Ltd, Re* [1996] B.C.C. 973 (Knox J.), *Licence Holder, Re* [1997]

B.C.C. 666 (Carnwath J.), *Re Debtors (No. 13-Misc-2000 and No. 14-Misc-2000), The Times,* April 10, 2000 (Neuberger J.).

Orders for provisional damages for personal injuries

In the last line, for "Wilson v. Ministry of Defence [1991] 1 All E.R. 638." substitute:
    Willson v. Ministry of Defence [1991] 1 All E.R. 638 and *Curi v. Colina, The Times,* October 14, 1998, CA.   **9A–581**

Rules of Court

Add at end:
    Note also CPR rr.25.5, 31.17 and 48.1.   **9A–589A**

Section 60 - Right of audience

Right of audience

In s.60(3), for the definition of "local authority" after "section 3 of the Police Act 1996" add:
    the Service Authority for the National Intelligence Service, the Service Authority for the National Crime Squad,   **9A–607**

Note

For "and the Environment Act 1995, s.78, Sched. 10." substitute:
    the Environment Act 1995, s.78, Sched. 10, the Police Act 1996, s.103 and Sched. 7, Pt I, para. 1, the Police Act 1997, s.134 and Sched. 9, para. 45.   **9A–608**

Power to award interest on debts and damages

After "CPR, r12.6." add:
    For interest on judgment under CPR r.14.4 (admission of whole of claim for specified amount of money) where interest claimed under s.69, see CPR r.14.14.   **9A–634**

Add at end:
In the exercise of its discretion, the court may reduce the rate at which interest on an award of damages is payable or reduce the period for which interest is payable. Since the coming into effect of the CPR, this power has been increasingly used by the courts as a sanction where parties fail to comply with procedural rules, practice directions and case management orders. The Court of Appeal has encouraged the use of this sanction as an alternative to more serious sanctions (*e.g.* striking out); see, *e.g. Biguzzi v. Rank Leisure Plc* [1999] 1 W.L.R. 1926, CA; *Baron v. Lovell, The Times,* September 14, 1999, CA; *Abbahall Ltd v. Smee,* January 24, 2000, CA, unrep.; *Walsh v. Misseldine,* February 29, 2000, CA, unrep.; *UYB Ltd v. British Railways Board, The Times,* November 15, 2000, CA; *Adcock v. Co-operative Insurance Society Ltd, The Times,* April 26, 2000, CA; note also Practice Direction (Protocols) para. 2.3 (see Civil Procedure 2000 Vol. 1, para. C1–002.

Finality of judgments and orders

In the third paragraph, for the sentence which begins "Authority for this is provided by in re Barrell Enterprises [1973] 1 W.L.R. 19, C.A." substitute
    Authority for this is provided by *Re Barrell Enterprises* [1973] 1 W.L.R. 19, CA   **9A–636**

Add after "Spice Girls Ltd. v. Aprillia World Service B.V. (No. 3), The Times September 12, 2000, Arden J.":
; *Mamidoil-Jetoil Greek Petroleum SA v. Okta Crude Oil Refinery AD (No.2)* [2001] 1 Lloyd's Rep. 591, Thomas J.; *Compagnie Noga d'Importation et d'Exportation SA v. Abacha (No.2),* (2001) 151 N.L.J. 693, Rix L.J.

At end of the penultinate paragraph for "effect." substitute:
effect; see also *Royal Brompton Hospital NHS Trust v. Hammond (No.7),* [2001] EWCA Civ 778.

Register of judgments and orders

Add at end:
    For an analysis of the question whether a claim may be brought for negligence or breach   **9A–643**

of statutory duty where the register is inaccurate, see *Du Bey v. Lord Chancellor's Department and Registry Trust*, June 9, 2000, unrep. (Gray J.).

Interest on judgment debts, etc.

9A-649

For "*amended by S.I. 1996 No. 2516*" substitute:
as amended

Add at end of first paragraph:
See further Vol. 1 para. 40.8.1, and note CPR rr.40.8, 44.12, 47.8 and 47.14.

Practice Directions

9A-652

Add after "April 27, 1997":
(see para. 9A-839 below)

GENERAL RULES OF PROCEDURE

County court rules

9A-653

In section 75 for "[Omitted]" substitute:
75. [*Omitted by Civil Procedure Act 1997 Sched. 2, para. 2.*]

Application of practice of High Court

9A-655

For "*Jephson Homes Housing Association Ltd v. Moisejevs*, November 1, 2000, C.A., unrep." substitute:
Jephson Homes Housing Association Ltd v. Moisejevs, [2001] 2 All E.R. 901, CA

PART IV

Appeals: general provisions

9A-656

In paragraph 77(1), for "and to any orders" substitute:
77.—(1) and to any order

Administrative and clerical expenses of garnishees

9A-719

For "*see S.I. 1996 No. 3098*" substitute:
see Attachment of Debts (Expenses) Order S.I. 1996 No. 3098

Power to commit for contempt

9A-742

Add at end of the first paragraph:
See *Manchester City Council v. McCann* [1999] 2 W.L.R. 590, CA.

Civil procedure Act 1997

Sched. 1

Add at end:

9A-832

In *Safeway Stores Plc v. Tate* [2001] 2 W.L.R. 1377, CA, it was said that the power to make procedural rules under s.4 does not permit the restriction of a party's right to trial by jury in a defamation claim (*cf. Alexander v. Arts Council of Wales, The Times*, April 27, 2001, CA).

Delete paragraph 9A-863.1

Delete paragraphs 9A-868 to 9A-877, then add new link line.

[THE NEXT PARAGRAPH IS 9A-878.]

9A-867 *Delete paragraphs 9A-879 to 9A-883, then add new link line.*

[THE NEXT PARAGRAPH IS 9A-884.]

Below "Access to Justice Act 1999 (Destination of Appeals) Order 2000" for "2000" substitute: **9A–878**

Access to Justice Act 1999 (Destination of Appeals) Order 2000

(S.I. 2000 1071

Below heading "Access to Justice Act 1999 (Destination of Appeals) Order 2000" for "1071" substitute:
No. 1071) (L. 10) **9A–884**

Introductory note

Add new paragraph after 9A–884:
See also CPR Pt 52. **9A–884.1**
This Order was made under the Access to Justice Act 1999, s.56, and came into effect on May 2, 2000. That section gives the Lord Chancellor power to provide by Order that appeals which would lie to (a) a county court, (b) the High Court, or (c) the Court of Appeal, shall lie instead to another of those courts, as specified in the Order.

In Article 1(2)(b) delete "[2]".
In Article 1(4)(b)(i) delete "[3]". **9A–885**
In Article 1(4)(b)(ii) delete ")" immediately preceding "any".
In Article 2(a) delete "[4]".
In Article 4(a) delete "[5]".

9B OTHER STATUTES AND REGULATIONS

For the title substitute:
Enforcement of traffic penalties
Delete text of paragraph 1(a) and substitute:
    8A.—(1) **9B–153.1**
        (a) increased penalty charges provided for in charge certificates issued under–
            (i) paragraph 6 of Schedule 6 to the 1991 Act[1]; and
            (ii) paragraph 8 of Schedule 1 to the London Local Authorities Act 1996.[2]

Add after paragraph (b):
; and

Add new paragraph after (b):
        (c) fixed penalties are payable under notices issued under regulation 5 of the Road Traffic (Vehicle Emissions) (Fixed Penalty) Regulations 1997 [3]

Add new paragraph after 9B–155:
Enforcement of possession orders against trespassers
    8B.—(1) A judgment or order of a county court for possession of land **9B–155.1** made in a possession claim against trespassers may be enforced in the High Court or a county court.
    (2) In this article "a possession claim against trespassers" has the same meaning as in Part 55 of the Civil Procedure Rules 1998.

---

[1] The Road Traffic Act 1991 c.40
[2] 1996 c.ix ; paragraph 8 of Schedule 1 was amended by paragraph 7 of Schedule 2 to the London Local Authorities Act 2000 (c. vii) and Schedule 1 is repealed by Schedule 31 to the Transport Act 2000 (c. 38) on such day as the Secretary of State may by order provide.
[3] S.I. 1997 No. 3058

SECTION 11

COURTS DIRECTORY

CIRCUIT ARRANGEMENTS

11–4

Circuit Administrator	Trial Centres	Group Manager
MIDLAND AND OXFORD CIRCUIT The Priory Courts, 33 Bull Street, Birmingham, B4 6DW In Midland and Oxford Circuit entry, for "Tel: 0121 681 3201" substitute: Tel: 0121 681 3226 *In Midland and Oxford Circuit entry, for "Fax: 0121 681 3202" substitute:* Fax 0121 681 3060 DX 701981 Birmingham 7		
	Newcastle	3rd Floor, Merchant House, *In North Eastern Circuit, Newcastle entry, for "The Cloth Market," substitute:* 30 Cloth Market, Newcastle upon Tyne, NE1 1EE Tel: 0191 232 7102 Fax: 0191 232 6784
	Sheffield	Sovereign House, Queen's Street, *In North Eastern Circuit, Sheffield entry, for "Sheffield, S1 2DW", substitute:* Sheffield, S1 2ES Tel: 0114 275 5866 Fax: 0114 275 5284
	Luton	7 George Street, Luton, LU1 2AA *In South-Eastern Circuit, Luton entry, for "Tel: 01582 522 080" substitute:* Tel: 01582 522 086 Fax: 01582 522 081 DX: 120504 LUTON 6

Circuit Administrator	Trial Centres	Group Manager	11–4
	Cardiff	2nd Floor, Churchill House, Churchill Way, *In Wales and Chester, Cardiff entry, for "Cardiff, CF1 2HH" substitute:* Cardiff, CF10 4HH *For "Tel: 02920 344 381 /344 239" substitute:* Tel: 02920 415520 *For "Fax: 029 2041 5529" substitute:* Fax: 02920 415511 DX: 121723 CARDIFF 9	
	Mold	*In Wales and Chester, Mold entry, delete the address details and replace with:* The Law Courts Civil Centre, Mold, Flintshire, CH7 1AE Tel: 01352 754410 Fax: 01352 759804 DX: 702521 Mold *In Western Circuit, Exeter entry, delete the address details and replace with:* Ground Floor Pembroke House Southernhay Gardens Exeter, EX1 1UN Tel: 01392 455900 Fax: 01392 455909 *In Western Circuit, Winchester entry, delete the address details and replace with:* Swindon Combined Courts The Law Courts Islington Street Wiltshire, SN1 2HG Tel: 01793 690570 Fax: 01793 690575 DX: 98430 Swindon 5	

11-7 COUNTY COURT DIRECTORY

BARNET BT	St Mary's Court Regents Park Road Finchley London N3 1BQ	Tel: (020) 8346 4272 *For "Fax: (020) 8343 1324" substitute:* Fax: (020) 8346 1324 DX: 122570 Finchley-2 (Church End)
BRENTFORD BF	Alexandra Road High Street Brentford Middx TW8 0JJ	*In Brentford BF entry, for "Tel: (020) 8560 3424" substitute:* Tel: (020) 8580 7300 Fax: (020) 8568 2401 DX: 97840 Brentford-2
CLERKENWELL CK	33 Duncan Terrace Islington London N1 8AN	*In Clerkenwell CK entry, for "Tel: (020) 7359 7347" substitute:* Tel: (020) 7359 8458 Fax: (020) 7354 1166 DX: 58284 Islington
PENZANCE PZ	Trevear Alverton Penzance Cornwall *In Penzance PZ entry, for "TR18 4JH" substitute:* TR18 4GH	Tel: 01736 362987 Fax: 01736 330595 DX: 136900 PENZANCE 2
ROMFORD RM	2a Oaklands Avenue Romford Essex RM1 4DP	Tel: 01708 750677 *In Romford RM entry, for "Fax: 01708 756654" substitute:* Fax: 01708 756653 DX: 975530 Romford-2
SHREWSBURY SY	*In Shrewsbury SY entry, delete address details and replace with:* Cambrian Business Centre Chester Street Shrewsbury Shropshire SY1 1NA	

INDEX

References to paragraph numbers in square brackets are to Volume 2

Accountant General, Office of
rules, [6A-18]-[6A-23]

Accounts
Court of Protection Rules
 balance due, [6B-288]
 costs, [6B-290]
 default, [6B-289]
 final, [6B-291]
 maintenance payments, [6B-290]
 passing, [6B-287]
 third parties, by, [6B-291]
persons under mental disorder
 fee, [6B-153], [6B-154]
 format, [6B-150]
 generally, [6B-149]
 lodgment, [6B-151]
 passing, [6B-152]
receivers
 mental health, [6B-34], [6B-40], [6B-50], [6B-58]
receivers (mental health)
 death of patient, discharge on, [6B-50]
 new appointment, [6B-34]
 recovery of patient, discharge on, [6B-40]
 tax, payment of, [6B-58]

Acknowledgment of service
landlord and tenant claims
 new tenancy claims, 56PD-007

Administration of Justice Act 1970
general provisions
 housing, [3A-31]-[3A-32]
 mortgage actions, [3A-31]-[3A-32]

Administration of Justice Act 1973
mortgage actions, [3A-48]

Administration of Justice Act 1985
appeals
 s.50, sc93.20

Admiralty claims
goods and materials supplied, [2A-162]
Practice Direction
 introduction, [2A-8]

Admiralty proceedings
claims
 introduction, [2A-8]
 generally, [2A-5]

Practice Direction
 generally, [2A-5]
 undertakings, [2A-123]-[2A-124]

Affidavit evidence
Court of Protection
 death, proof of, [6B-182]
 generally, [6B-253]

Agent of overseas principal, service on
generally, 6.16

Allocation of claims
alteration, [9A-300]
assessment of damages
 county court, 2BPD-011
county court
 assessment of damages, 2BPD-011
 road traffic debts, [9B-153.1]
High Court
 alteration, [9A-300]
 road traffic debts, [9B-153.1]

Allocation of jurisdiction
UK, within
 generally, [5-3]

Amendments
Court of Protection Rules
 clerical errors, [6B-278]
 endorsement, [6B-279]
 generally, [6B-277]

Anti-social behaviour
injunctions
 applications, cc49.6B
 generally, [3A-949]

Appeals
arbitration proceedings
 Court of Appeal, to, [2B-256]
county court, from
 generally, [9A-656]-[9A-657.1]
Court of Appeal, to
 arbitration, [2B-256]
Court of Protection
 introduction, [6B-9]
 Rules, [6B-281]
 statutory basis, [6B-204]-[6B-205]
Crown Court, from
 statutory basis, [9A-77]
Crown Court, to
 jurisdiction, [9A-152]

197

enduring powers of attorney, [6B-415]
House of Lords (civil cases), to
  practice directions, [4A-5]-[4A-75]
House of Lords (criminal cases), to
  practice directions, [4B-1]-[4B-65]
small claims
  Practice Direction, 52PD-015A

Appeals by way of case stated
Crown Court, by
  jurisdiction, [9A-77]
statutory basis
  Crown Court, [9A-77]

Appeals from county court
Court of Appeal, to
  generally, [9A-657.1]
  introduction, [9A-47]-[9A-47.1]
generally, [9A-656]-[9A-657.1]
"leapfrog"
  generally, [9A-657.1]
  introduction, [9A-47]-[9A-47.1]

Appeals from High Court
Court of Appeal, to, [9A-47]-[9A-47.1]

Appeals procedure
county court, and
  specific provisions, 52PD-038
High Court, and
  specific provisions, 52PD-038
Practice Directions
  evidence, 8PD-005
  section A claims, 8BPD-005-8BPD-006
  section B claims, 8BPD-007-8BPD-012
small claims
  Practice Direction, 52PD-015A

Appeals to Court of Appeal
High Court, from, [9A-47]-[9A-47.1]

Appeals to Crown Court
jurisdiction, [9A-152]

Appeals to High Court
Administration of Justice Act 1985, under
  s.50 proceedings, sc93.20
Leasehold Reform Act 1967, under,
  sc93.15

Appendix
House of Lords criminal appeal
  form, [4B-62]

Applications
arbitration proceedings
  meaning, [2B-17]
Companies Act 1985, under
  generally, [2F-1]
Court of Protection Rules

amendment, [6B-277]-[6B-279]
contents, [6B-233]
direction to make, [6B-237]
Official Solicitor, by, [6B-239]
person under disability, by, [6B-240]
receiver, by, [6B-238]
s.36(9) TA 1925, [6B-242]
s.54(2) TA 1925, [6B-241]
s.96(1)(d) TA 1925, [6B-244]
s.96(1)(k) TA 1925, [6B-243]
short order, [6B-234]
enduring powers of attorney
  generally, [6B-324]-[6B-328]
  rules, [6B-397]-[6B-404]
  statutory basis, [6B-351]-[6B-360]
Insurance Companies Act 1982, under
  generally, [2F-1]
judicial review, [9A-85]

Applications to county court
Family Law Reform Act 1969, under,
  cc47.5
Housing Act 1996, under, cc49.6B
Post Office Act 1969, under, cc49.15

Applications to High Court
Landlord and Tenant Acts, under,
  sc97.1-sc97.19

Arbitration
enforcement of award
  And see Arbitration award
  Arbitration Act 1950, [2B-84]
  Practice Direction, [2B-67]

Arbitration Act 1950
schedules, [2B-84]

Arbitration appeals
Court of Appeal, to, [2B-256]

Arbitration award
enforcement (from 25th March 2002),
  70.5
enforcement of foreign award
  Convention text, [2B-84]
  Practice Direction, [2B-67]

Arbitration (International Investment Disputes) Act 1966
registration of awards, [2B-67]

Arbitration proceedings
appeals
  statutory basis, [2B-256]
applications
  meaning, [2B-17]
enforcement of award
  And see Arbitration award
  Convention text, [2B-84]
  Practice Direction, [2B-67]

INDEX

Practice Direction
  applications, [2B-17]
  enforcement, [2B-67]

Assessment of damages
allocation of claims
  county court, 2BPD-011

Assignment
secure tenancy
  exchange, by, [3A-381]

Assignment of business
county court
  road traffic debts, [9B-153.1]
High Court
  alteration, [9A-300]

Assured shorthold tenancy
meaning
  pre-Housing Act 1996, [3A-738]
possession proceedings
  statutory basis, [3A-748]-[3A-748.1]

Assured tenancy
forms of order, [3A-649.1]
grounds for possession
  generally, [3A-642]-[3A-649.2]
  Ground 2, [3A-842]
  Ground 3, [3A-843]
  Ground 4, [3A-845]
  Ground 5, [3A-846]
  Ground 7, [3A-848]
meaning
  generally, [3A-607]
periodic tenancy
  succession, [3A-719]
possession
  court's discretion, [3A-672]
  grounds, [3A-642]-[3A-649B]
reasonableness
  appeals, [3A-649.2]
  ECHR, and, [3A-649.3]
  generally, [3A-642]-[3A-649]
security of tenure
  generally, [3A-633]
  possession, [3A-649]
  succession, [3A-719]

Asylum-seekers
introduction, [3A-28.10]
support for
  generally, [3A-1184.1]
  introduction, [3A-1176]

Anti-social behaviour, injunctions against
Practice Direction
  bail, ccpd49-002
  medical examination and report, ccpd49-003
  warrant of arrest, ccpd49-001

Attorney, powers of
And see Enduring powers of attorney
fees, [6B-321]
forms, [6B-320]
generally, [6B-319], [6B-322]-[6B-338]
prescribed forms, [6B-421]-[6B-426]
rules, [6B-392]-[6B-449]
statutory text, [6B-339]-[6B-391]

Audience, rights of
county court
  generally, [9A-607]-[9A-608]
  Lord Chancellor, by direction of, [9A-612]

Bail
jurisdiction, [9A-64]

Bankruptcy
persons under mental disorder, [6B-114]

Barristers
wasted costs, order for
  generally, 48.7

Beneficiaries
representation, sc15.14

Bodily tests, application for
county court, in
  editorial introduction, cc47.0.2
  generally, cc47.5

Brussels Convention 1968
implementation, [5-3]

Camera, **in**
conduct of business, [9A-319]

Case stated, appeals by
Crown Court
  statutory basis, [9A-77]
statutory basis
  Crown Court, from [9A-77]

Case statement
House of Lords civil appeal
  exchange, [4A-52]
  generally, [4A-49]
  lodgment, [4A-52]
House of Lords criminal appeal
  exchange, [4B-44]
  generally, [4B-41]
  lodgment, [4B-44]

Certificates of judgment
generally, cc22.8

Certiorari
jurisdiction, [9A-81.1]

Chambers, proceedings in
conduct of business, [9A-319]

Chancel Repairs Act 1932
claims from 15th October 2001
Practice Direction, 56PD-029

Charging orders
n.b. from 25th March 2002
application, 73.3
consideration of application, 73.8
contents of Part, 73.0.1
discharge, 73.9
editorial introduction, 73.0.2
enforcement, 73.10
generally, 73.2
interim order, 73.4-73.7
scope of Part, 73.1
variation, 73.9

Charging orders
n.b. prior to 25th March 2002
bill of costs, [7C-133]-[7C-134]
chargeable property, [9B-219]
county court
  And see Charging orders (CCR)
  generally, cc31.1-cc31.4
fixed costs, 45.5.6
High Court
  And see Charging orders (RSC)
  generally, sc50.1-sc50.9A.1
persons under mental disorder, [6B-114]
procedural guide, D1-029
Queen's Bench Guide, [1A-76]
solicitors, by
  enforcement, [7C-242]
  generally, [7C-232]
  priority, [7C-239]
  procedure, [7C-240]-[7C-241]
  relevant property, [7C-236]-[7C-238]
  statutory basis, [7C-133]-[7C-134], [7C-233]-[7C-235]
  generally, [7C-233]-[7C-235]
  Solicitors Act 1974, [7C-133]-[7C-134]
starting proceedings, 8BPD-002
statutory basis
  chargeable property, [9B-219]
  generally, [9B-217]-[9B-218]
  supplementary provision, [9B-220]
stop notice, [9B-222]-[9B-223]
time limits, E1-012

Charging orders (CCR)
contents of Order, cc31.0.1
editorial introduction, cc31.0.2
effect, cc31.3
enforcement, cc31.4
forms, cc31.0.4
order absolute, cc31.2
order nisi, cc31.1
related sources, cc31.0.3
sale, order for, cc31.4

Charging orders (RSC)
bankrupt, against
  effect, sc50.1.26
  generally, sc50.1.6
beneficial interests, against
  generally, sc50.1.7, sc50.1.29
  legal estate, sc50.1.31
  trustees interest, sc50.1.9, sc50.1.30, sc50.4-sc50.4.1
  trusts, sc50.1.8
chargeable property
  beneficial interests, sc50.1.29
  funds in court, sc50.1.32
  generally, sc50.1.5
  land, sc50.1.27-sc50.1.28
  legal estate, sc50.1.31
  list, sc50.1.25
  trustees interest, sc50.1.30
confiscation orders, and
  claim form, sc115.3-sc115.3.10
  discharge, sc115.5-sc115.5.1
  generally, sc115.4-sc115.4.4
  receiver, appointment of, sc115.8-sc115.8.3
  variation, sc115.6-sc115.6.2
contents of Order, sc50.0.1
costs, sc50.1.39-sc50.1.40
court's powers
  discretion, sc50.1.4, sc50.1.24
  generally, sc50.1.2
  jurisdiction, sc50.1.3, sc50.1.22
criteria
  debts payable by instalment, sc50.1.20
  generally, sc50.1.19
  miscellaneous, sc50.1.21
discharge
  generally, sc50.1.14, sc50.1.41
  procedure, sc50.7-sc50.7.1
disposal, validity of, sc50.5-sc50.5.2
editorial introduction, sc50.0.2
effect
  generally, sc50.1.17
  insolvent debtors, sc50.1.26
enforcement by sale
  generally, sc50.1.18
  procedure, sc50.9A-sc50.9A.1
estate of deceased person, sc50.1.37
forms, sc50.0.4
funds in court, against
  generally, sc50.1.11, sc50.1.32
  procedure, sc50.6-sc50.6.1
  stop orders, sc50.10-sc50.10.12
  generally, sc50.1, sc50.1.16
injunction in aid
  generally, sc50.1.13, sc50.1.35
  procedure, sc50.9-sc50.9.1
insolvent company, against
  effect, sc50.1.26
  generally, sc50.1.6
interest, sc50.1.39
jurisdiction, sc50.1.3, sc50.1.22
legal estate, against, sc50.1.31
limitation periods, sc50.1.15
money in court, sc50.6-sc50.6.1

nature, sc50.1.17
order absolute
  death of debtor, sc50.1.37
  generally, sc50.1.36, sc50.3-sc50.3.1
order nisi, sc50.1.35
order to show cause, sc50.2-sc50.2.1
procedure
  criteria, sc50.1.19-sc50.1.21
  evidence, sc50.1.34
  generally, sc50.1.12, sc50.1.33
  related sources, sc50.0.3
securities, against
  generally, sc50.1.10
  procedure, sc50.5-sc50.5.2
  prohibition of transfer, sc50.15-sc50.15.1
  stop notices, sc50.11-sc50.14.6
stop notices
  amendment, sc50.13-sc50.13.1
  effect, sc50.12-sc50.12.1
  generally, sc50.11-sc50.11.1
  withdrawal, sc50.14-sc50.14.1
stop orders, sc50.10-sc50.10.12
transfer to county court, sc50.1.23
trustee's interest, against
  generally, sc50.1.9, sc50.1.30
  procedure, sc50.4-sc50.4.1
trusts, against, sc50.1.8

Circuit administration
list of addresses, [11-4]

Civil Procedure Act 1997
Civil Procedure Rules
  generally, [9A-832]

Civil Procedure Rules
generally, [9A-828]-[9A-832]]

Claim forms
service
  agent of overseas principal, on, 6.16
  summary possession, proceedings for (CCR)
    evidence, cc24.2
    generally, cc24.1
    service, cc24.3

Claims in admiralty proceedings
goods and materials supplied, [2A-162]
Practice Direction
  introduction, [2A-8]

Claims *in rem*
introduction, [2A-8]

CLCC Business List Guide
Appendices, [2C-399]

Commercial Court Guide
service out of the jurisdiction

generally, [2C-46]
procedure, [2C-265]
starting proceedings
  service out of the jurisdiction, [2C-46]

Committal (CCR)
statutory provisions
  generally, [9A-742]

Companies
insolvency of
  Practice Directions, B1-001

Companies Act 1985, applications under
applications
  generally, [2F-1]

Compensation for improvements claims
certification of improvement, 56PD-013
defendant, 56PD-011

Composition of court
Court of Appeal (civil division)
  generally, [9A-274]

Conditional fee agreements
contents
  success fees, [7A-18.1]
insurance premiums, recovery of
  introduction, [7A-32.1]-[7A-33.1]
success fees
  introduction, [7A-32.1]-[7A-33.1]
  prescribed requirements, [7A-18.1]

Consolidation
Court of Protection, [6B-236]
enduring powers of attorney, [6B-402]

Constitution of courts
High Court, [9A-16]

Consumer credit
credit
  definition, [3B-21]
enforcement orders
  generally, [3B-231]
exempt agreement, [3B-37]
extortionate credit bargains
  reopening, [3B-261]
total charge for credit
  calculation, [3B-331]
unfair terms
  enforcement, [3B-455]

Consumer Credit (Total Charge for Credit) Regulations 1980
calculation, [3B-331]

Contempt of court
matters exempt from disclosure in court, [3C-27]

Contempt of Court Act 1981
general provisions
strict liability, [3C-27]

Contentious probate proceedings
counterclaim
non-probate proceedings, in, [2G-17]
editorial introduction, [2G-1]
Practice Direction
counterclaim, [2G-17]
editorial introduction, [2G-1]

Contract, actions in
generally, [9A-513]
persons under mental disorder, [6B-105]

Conveyance
persons under mental disorder, [6B-174]

Costs
Court of Protection, in
agreed, [6B-172]
application of CPR, [6B-312]
estate agency fees, [6B-98], [6B-166]
fixed, [6B-171]
generally, [6B-155]-[6B-157], [6B-310]
legal aid, [6B-158]-[6B-170]
Official Solicitor, of, [6B-314]
receivership management fees, [6B-163]
ss.36(9) & 54 TA 1925 applications, of, [6B-311]
unnecessary legal services, of, [6B-313]
unrelated proceedings, of, [6B-314]
House of Lords civil appeal
petition for leave, [4A-24]
petition of appeal, [4A-57]
House of Lords criminal appeal
petition for leave, [4B-20]
petition of appeal, [4B-49]
legal representatives, relating to
wasted costs order, 48.7
statutory basis
generally, [9A-265]
wasted costs order
generally, 48.7

Counterclaim
contentious probate proceedings
non-probate proceedings, in, [2G-17]

County court
appeals from
generally, [9A-656]-[9A-657.1]
committal
generally, [9A-742]
Directory list, [11-7]

districts, [9A-489]
enforcement
execution, warrant of, [9A-695]
garnishee order, [9A-719]
execution, warrant of
sale of goods, [9A-695]
garnishee proceedings, [9A-719]
jurisdiction
introduction, [9A-485]
practice directions, [9A-652]
provisional damages, [9A-581]
RSC, application of, [9A-655]
sale of goods
third party claims, [9A-695]
seized goods
sale of, [9A-695]
transfer
county court, to, [9A-553]
High Court, to, [9A-560]
transfer to county court
generally, [9A-553]
transfer to High Court
order of county court, by, [9A-560]

County court, appeals from
Court of Appeal, to
generally, [9A-657.1]
generally, [9A-656]-[9A-657.1]
"leapfrog"
generally, [9A-657.1]

County court jurisdiction
contract, actions in
generally, [9A-513]
exercise of
remedies, [9A-549]
remedies, [9A-549]
statutory basis
introductory note, [9A-485]
tort, actions in
generally, [9A-513]

County court procedure
audience, rights of
generally, [9A-607]-[9A-608]
Lord Chancellor, by direction of, [9A-612]
discovery
personal injury actions, [9A-589A]
interest
generally, [9A-634]
judgment debt, [9A-649]
judgment
finality, [9A-636]
interest, [9A-649]
register, [9A-643]
jury trial
generally, [9A-627]
order
finality, [9A-636]
interest, [9A-649]
register, [9A-643]
personal injury actions, discovery in

generally, [9A-589A]
practice directions, [9A-652]
rules
  application of RSC, [9A-655]
  generally, [9A-653]
transfer
  county court, to, [9A-553]
  High Court, to, [9A-560]
transfer to county court
  generally, [9A-553]
transfer to High Court
  order of county court, by, [9A-560]

County Courts Act 1984
appeals, [9A-656]-[9A-657.1]
constitution, [9A-489]
jurisdiction
  introduction, [9A-485]
transfer of proceedings, [9A-553]-[9A-560]

Court documents
production
  statutory provisions, [9A-443]

Court Funds Office
rules, [6A-18]-[6A-23]

Court Funds Rules 1987
arrangement of rules, [6A-18]
definitions, [6A-22]-[6A-23]

Court of Appeal
appeals to
  arbitration, [2B-256]
composition (civil division)
  generally, [9A-274]
enforcement, [9A-48]
jurisdiction
  civil courts, appeals from, [9A-47]-[9-47A]
  generally, [9A-48]
  High Court, appeals from, [9A-50]-[9A-50.1]
  restrictions on, [9A-55]
sittings
  statutory basis, [9A-288]-[9A-289]

Court of Protection
address, [6B-2]
appeals
  introduction, [6B-9]
  Rules, [6B-281]
  statutory basis, [6B-204]-[6B-205]
attorney, powers of
  And see Enduring powers of attorney
  fees, [6B-321]
  forms, [6B-320]
  generally, [6B-319], [6B-322]-[6B-338]
  prescribed forms, [6B-421]-[6B-426]
  rules, [6B-392]-[6B-449]
  statutory basis, [6B-339]-[6B-391]

Chancery Division, [6B-7]
detailed assessment of costs payable by
  generally, 47.17A-47.17A.1
  Practice Direction, 47PD-017
extra-jurisdictional property, [6B-6]
fees
  administration, [6B-304]
  commencement, [6B-303]
  detailed assessment, [6B-306]
  generally, [6B-302]
  introduction, [6B-11]
  postponement, [6B-309]
  receivership, [6B-307]
  remission, [6B-309]
  transactions, [6B-305]
  winding up, [6B-308]
forms
  And see Court of Protection forms
  deeds and recitals, [6B-173]-[6B-182]
  introduction, [6B-10]
introduction, [6B-2]
judges, [6B-3]
London agents, use of, [6B-5]
Masters, [6B-4]
minors under disability, [6B-8]
persons under mental disorder
  And see Persons under mental disorder
  accounts, [6B-149]-[6B-154]
  administration of affairs, [6B-83]-[6B-148]
  costs, [6B-155]-[6B-172]
  management of affairs, [6B-83]-[6B-148]
  receivers' accounts, [6B-149]-[6B-154]
  receivers', appointment of, [6B-12]-[6B-34]
  receivers', discharge of, [6B-35]-[6B-50]
  taxation, [6B-51]-[6B-58]
  vesting orders, [6B-59]-[6B-82]
raising taxes on death of patient, [6B-51]-[6B-58]
receiver
  And see Receiver
  accounts, [6B-149]-[6B-154]
  appointment, [6B-12]-[6B-34]
  discharge, [6B-35]-[6B-50]
  powers and duties, [6B-83]-[6B-148]
receiver, appointment of
  first, [6B-12]-[6B-27]
  new, [6B-28]-[6B-34]
  vesting orders, [6B-59]-[6B-82]
receiver, discharge of
  death, on, [6B-41]-[6B-50]
  recovery, on, [6B-35]-[6B-40]
  vesting orders, [6B-59]-[6B-82]
rules
  And see Court of Protection Rules
  accounts, [6B-287]-[6B-292]
  amendment, [6B-277]-[6B-279]
  appeal, [6B-280]-[6B-281]
  applications, [6B-233]-[6B-244]
  arrangement of, [6B-227]
  copies, [6B-301]

costs, [6B-310]-[6B-315]
deeds, [6B-316]
enforcement, [6B-271]-[6B-273]
evidence, [6B-253]-[6B-262]
exercise of jurisdiction, [6B-232]
fees, [6B-302]-[6B-309]
hearings, [6B-263]-[6B-267]
inquiries, [6B-293]-[6B-297]
preliminary, [6B-227.1]-[6B-231]
property dealing, [6B-298]-[6B-300]
receivers, [6B-268]-[6B-270]
security, [6B-282]-[6B-286]
service, [6B-245]-[6B-252]
summonses, [6B-274]-[6B-276]
transitional provisions, [6B-317]-[6B-318]
statutory basis
And see Mental Health Act 1983
application, [6B-185]
introduction, [6B-1]
management of affairs, [6B-186]-[6B-214]
offences, [6B-215]-[6B-217]
supplementary provisions, [6B-218]-[6B-225]
vesting orders
And see Vesting orders
appointment of receiver, [6B-64]-[6B-69]
appointment of trustee, [6B-74]-[6B-82]
generally, [6B-59]-[6B-63]
retirement of receiver, [6B-70]-[6B-73]

Court of Protection forms
affidavit proving death, [6B-182]
appointment of new trustees, leave for, [6B-179]
certificate of examination of deed, [6B-180]
certificate of recovery, [6B-182]
certificate of value, [6B-175]
conveyance, [6B-174]
order for purchase, [6B-176]
order for sale, [6B-173]
statutory receipt, [6B-177]
statutory will, [6B-181]
transfer, [6B-178]

Court of Protection Rules
accounts
balance due, [6B-288]
costs, [6B-290]
default, [6B-289]
final, [6B-291]
maintenance payments, [6B-290]
passing, [6B-287]
third parties, by, [6B-291]
amendment
clerical errors, [6B-278]
endorsement, [6B-279]
generally, [6B-277]
appeal, [6B-281]
applications
amendment, [6B-277]-[6B-279]
contents, [6B-233]
direction to make, [6B-237]
Official Solicitor, by, [6B-239]
person under disability, by, [6B-240]
receiver, by, [6B-238]
s.36(9) TA 1925, [6B-242]
s.54(2) TA 1925, [6B-241]
s.96(1)(d) TA 1925, [6B-244]
s.96(1)(k) TA 1925, [6B-243]
short order, [6B-234]
arrangement of sections, [6B-227]
citation, [6B-227.1]
copies, [6B-301]
consolidation, [6B-236]
costs
CPR Costs Rules, [6B-312]
generally, [6B-310]
Official Solicitor, [6B-314]
TA 1925 applications, [6B-311]
unrelated actions, [6B-314]
unnecessary legal services, [6B-313]
deeds, [6B-316]
definitions, [6B-228]
enforcement, [6B-271]-[6B-273]
evidence
administration of oaths, [6B-257]
affidavit, [6B-253]
cross-examination, [6B-256]
death of patient, of, [6B-261]
filing, [6B-258]
first appointment of receiver, on, [6B-260]
public authority, amount due to, [6B-262]
recovery of patient, of, [6B-261]
subsequent use, [6B-259]
unsworn, [6B-254]
Visitors, questions to, [6B-255]
examination of patient, [6B-276]
fees
administration, [6B-304]
commencement, [6B-303]
detailed assessment, [6B-306]
generally, [6B-302]
postponement, [6B-309]
receivership, [6B-307]
remission, [6B-309]
transactions, [6B-305]
winding up, [6B-308]
forms
And see Court of Protection forms
generally, [6B-173]-[6B-182]
functions
court, [6B-229]
jurisdiction, [6B-232]
hearings
date, [6B-235]
persons attending, [6B-264]
privacy, [6B-263]
representation, [6B-265]
inquiries
appointment of receiver, [6B-293]

execution of documents, [6B-296]
further inquiries, [6B-297]
inspection of property, [6B-294]
prior dealing of property, [6B-295]
orders
  enforcement, [6B-273]
  entry, [6B-272]
  filing, [6B-271]
  sealing, [6B-271]
property
  disposal, [6B-300]
  statement, [6B-298]
  stock, [6B-299]
receivers
  interim appointment, [6B-268]
  remuneration, [6B-269]
  security, [6B-282]-[6B-286]
  survivorship appointment, [6B-270]
references
  judge, to, [6B-266]
  Master, to, [6B-267]
reviews, [6B-280]
security
  bond, [6B-286]
  discharge, [6B-285]
  generally, [6B-282]
  lodgment, [6B-284]
  manner, [6B-283]
service
  certificate of, [6B-252]
  generally, [6B-245]
  method, [6B-246]
  next of kin, on, [6B-251]
  patient, on, [6B-250]
  person under disability, on, [6B-249]
  solicitor, on, [6B-247]
  substituted, [6B-248]
time
  generally, [6B-230]
  variation, [6B-231]
transitional provisions, [6B-317]-[6B-318]
witness summonses, [6B-274]-[6B-276]

Court, powers of the
statement of case
  dispensing with statements, 16.8

Courts Directory
Circuit Arrangements [11-2]
county courts, [11-7]
District Registries, [11-5]

Credit
definition, [3B-21]

Crown Court
appeals by way of case stated
  statutory provisions, [9A-77]
appeals to
  jurisdiction, [9A-151]-[9A-152]
jurisdiction
  appeals from, [9A-77]
  appeals to, [9A-152]

Crown proceedings (RSC)
enforcement
  attachment of debts, sc77.16

Damages
injunctions, [9A-261]
interest
  county court, [9A-634]
  High Court, [9A-105]
patients, for
  benefit disregards, [6B-120]-[6B-122]
  generally, [6B-116]
  settlements, [6B-118]
  special needs trusts, [6B-123]-[6B-133]
  structured settlements, [6B-117]
persons under mental disorder
  benefit disregards, [6B-120]-[6B-122]
  generally, [6B-116]
  settlements, [6B-118]-[6B-119]
  special needs trusts, [6B-123]-[6B-133]
  structured settlements, [6B-117]
special needs trusts
  generally, [6B-123]-[6B-125]
  method, [6B-129]-[6B-132]
  relevant cases, [6B-126]-[6B-128]
  terms, [6B-133]
specific performance, and
  generally, [9A-261]

Date of knowledge
generally, [8-26], [8-31]

Death
proof of
  persons under mental disorder, [6B-182]

Debt actions, interest in
county court, [9A-634]
High Court, [9A-105]

Debts, interest on
county court, [9A-634]
High Court, [9A-105]

Declaration
jurisdiction, [9A-81.1]

Default judgment
evidence, 12PD-004
Practice Direction
  evidence, 12PD-004

Defective Premises Act 1972
landlord's duty, [3A-44]

Defective products
time limits, [8-19]

Derivative claims
generally, 19.9

Disability, persons under
management of property and affairs
And see Person under mental disorder
Court of Protection Rules, [6B-227]-[6B-318]
generally, [6B-1]-[6B-182]
Mental Health Act 1983, [6B-184]-[6B-225]
powers of attorney, [6B-319]-[6B-426]

Disclosure
county court
personal injury actions, [9A-589A]

Discovery
county court
personal injury actions, [9A-589A]

Distribution of business
alteration, [9A-300]
assessment of damages
county court, 2BPD-011
county court
assessment of damages, 2BPD-011
road traffic debts, [9B-153.1]
High Court
alteration, [9A-300]
road traffic debts, [9B-153.1]

District Registries
list of, [11-5]

Divorce proceedings
persons under mental disorder, [6B-134]

DNA tests, application for
county court, in
editorial introduction, cc47.0.2
generally, cc47.5

Documents
House of Lords criminal appeal form, [4B-62]

EC Council Regulations
service of judicial documents
extrajudicial documents, 6.48
final provisions, 6.49-6.57
general provisions, 6.33-6.35
judicial documents, 6.36-6.47

Enduring powers of attorney
appeal, [6B-415]
applications
attorney's duties, [6B-351]-[6B-354]
contents, [6B-399]
court's powers, [6B-355]-[6B-360]
generally, [6B-324]-[6B-328], [6B-397]
objections, [6B-400]
rules, [6B-397]-[6B-404]
statutory basis, [6B-351]-[6B-360]
time limits, [6B-398]
attorney
applications by, [6B-340]-[6B-338]
authority of, [6B-348]-[6B-350]
duties of, [6B-351]-[6B-354], [6B-353]-[6B-388]
liability of, [6B-334], [6B-368]-[6B-371], [6B-389]
authority of attorney, [6B-348]-[6B-350]
cancellation
generally, [6B-330]
rules, [6B-416]
characteristics, [6B-344]-[6B-367]
court powers
exercise, [6B-401]
on application, [6B-358]-[6B-360]
post-registration, [6B-364]-[6B-367]
pre-registration, [6B-355]-[6B-356]
duties of attorney
generally, [6B-351]-[6B-354]
modification of, [6B-378] -[6B-379]
notification, [6B-384]-[6B-388]
effect
generally, [6B-327], [6B-340]-[6B-343]
statutory basis, [6B-361]-[6B-367]
execution, [6B-424]-[6B-425]
fees
generally, [6B-321]
rules, [6B-417], [6B-420]
forms
And see Enduring power of attorney forms
generally, [6B-320]
prescribed, [6B-332], [6B-421]-[6B-426]
generally, [6B-319], [6B-322]-[6B-323]
hearings
decision, [6B-413]
evidence, [6B-406]-[6B-410]
generally, [6B-405]
joint and several attorneys
generally, [6B-375]-[6B-377]
miscellaneous provisions, [6B-390]-[6B-391]
liability of attorney
generally, [6B-334]
statutory basis, [6B-368] -[6B-371], [6B-389]
notice procedure
content, [6B-386]
donors, to, [6B-385]
other attorneys, [6B-387]
relatives, to, [6B-384]
supplementary provisions [6B-388]
objections
generally, [6B-325]
rules, [6B-400]
prescribed forms
And see Enduring power of attorney forms

206

INDEX

Court of Protection direction, [6B-332]
regulations, [6B-421]-[6B-426]
registration
    application, [6B-324]
    cancellation, [6B-330], [6B-416]
    court powers, [6B-355]-[6B-360]
    duties of attorney, [6B-351]-[6B-354]
    effect, [6B-327], [6B-361]-[6B-367]
    leave, [6B-328]
    objections, [6B-325]
    procedure, [6B-326]
    proof, [6B-361]-[6B-367]
    searches for, [6B-331]
review, [6B-414]
revocation, [6B-404]
rules
    And see Enduring Powers of Attorney Rules 2001
    appeal, [6B-415]
    applications, [6B-397]-[6B-404]
    cancellation of registration, [6B-416]
    fees, [6B-417], [6B-420]
    generally, [6B-395]-[6B-396]
    hearings, [6B-405]-[6B-413]
    review, [6B-414]
searches
    generally, [6B-331]
    rules, [6B-404]
statutory basis
    And see Enduring Powers of Attorney Act 1985
    authority of attorney, [6B-348]-[6B-350]
    court powers, [6B-358]-[6B-367]
    generally, [6B-340]-[6B-367]
    liability of attorney, [6B-368] -[6B-371]
    procedure, [6B-351]-[6B-356]
    termination, [6B-333]
witness summons, [6B-411]

Enduring Powers of Attorney Act 1985
And see Enduring powers of attorney
arrangement of sections, [6B-339]
authority of attorney, [6B-348]-[6B-350]
characteristics, [6B-344]-[6B-367]
citation, [6B-382]-[6B-383]
commencement, [6B-382]-[6B-383]
court powers, [6B-355]-[6B-360], [6B-364]-[6B-367]
definitions, [6B-380]-[6B-381]
duties of attorney, [6B-351]-[6B-354], [6B-384]-[6B-388]
effect of registration, [6B-361]-[6B-363]
forms, [6B-320], [6B-332], [6B-421]-[6B-426]
generally, [6B-340]-[6B-343]
joint and several attorneys, [6B-375]-[6B-377]
liability of attorney, [6B-368]-[6B-371], [6B-389]
protection of interest, [6B-355]-[6B-356]
rules, [6B-392]-[6B-449]
schedules, [6B-384]-[6B-391]
supplementary provisions, [6B-372]-[6B-379], [6B-390]-[6B-391]

Enduring powers of attorney forms
generally, [6B-320]

Enduring Powers of Attorney (Prescribed Form) Regulations 1990
citation [6B-422]
contents [6B-423]
execution, [6B-424]-[6B-425]
introductory note, [6B-421]
revocation, [6B-404]

Enduring Powers of Attorney Rules 2001
appeal, [6B-415]
applications
    contents, [6B-399]
    generally, [6B-397]
    objections, [6B-400]
    time limits, [6B-398]
arrangement of rules, [6B-392]
cancellation of registration, [6B-416]
consolidation, [6B-402]
court's powers, [6B-401]
definitions, [6B-394]
fees, [6B-417], [6B-420]
forms
    And see Enduring powers of attorney forms
    generally, [6B-320]
general provisions, [6B-392.1]-[6B-396]
hearings
    decision, [6B-413]
    evidence, [6B-406]-[6B-410]
hearings
    generally, [6B-405]
    witness summons, [6B-411]
registration
    cancellation, [6B-416]
    generally, [6B-403]
reviews, [6B-414]
revocations, [6B-419]
schedule, [6B-420]
searches, [6B-404]
time computation, [6B-416]
transitional provisions, [6B-418]
witness summons, [6B-411]

Enforcement
n.b. from 25th March 2002
arbitration awards, of, 70.5
charging orders
    and see Charging orders
    application, 73.3
    consideration of application, 73.8
    contents of Part, 73.0.1
    discharge, 73.9
    editorial introduction, 73.0.2
    enforcement, 73.10
    generally, 73.2
    interim order, 73.4-73.7
    scope of Part, 73.1

variation, 73.9
contents of Part, 70.0.1
definitions, 70.1
editorial introduction, 70.0.2
foreign judgments, of, 70.5
garnishee proceedings
  and see Garnishee proceedings
  application, 72.3
  consideration of application, 72.8
  contents of Part, 72.0.1
  costs, 72.11
  debtors in hardship, 72.7
  editorial introduction, 72.0.2
  effect of order, 72.9
  interim orders, 72.4-72.6
  money in court, 72.10
  scope of Part, 72.1
  types of order, 72.2
information from judgment debtors
  and see Oral examination
  application, 71.2
  contents of Part, 71.0.1
  creditor's affidavit, 71.5
  editorial introduction, 71.0.2
  failure to comply, 71.8
  hearing, 71.6-71.7
  scope of Part, 71.1
  service of order, 71.3
  travelling expenses, 71.4
methods, 70.2
non-party, by or against, 70.4
oral examination
  and see Oral examination
  application, 71.2
  contents of Part, 71.0.1
  creditor's affidavit, 71.5
  editorial introduction, 71.0.2
  failure to comply, 71.8
  hearing, 71.6-71.7
  scope of Part, 71.1
  service of order, 71.3
  travelling expenses, 71.4
scope of Part, 70.1
setting aside judgment, and, 70.6
stop notices
  and see Stop notices
  amendment, 73.19
  contents of Part, 73.0.1
  definition, 73.16
  discharge, 73.21
  editorial introduction, 73.0.2
  effect, 73.18
  request, 73.17
  scope of Part, 73.1
  variation, 73.21
  withdrawal, 73.20
stop orders
  and see Stop orders
  application, 73.12
  contents of Part, 73.0.1
  definition, 73.11
  discharge, 73.15
  editorial introduction, 73.0.2
  funds in court, for, 73.13
  scope of Part, 73.1
  securities, for, 73.14
  variation, 73.15
third party debt orders
  and see Garnishee proceedings
  application, 72.3
  consideration of application, 72.8
  contents of Part, 72.0.1
  costs, 72.11
  debtors in hardship, 72.7
  editorial introduction, 72.0.2
  effect of order, 72.9
  interim orders, 72.4-72.6
  money in court, 72.10
  scope of Part, 72.1
  types of order, 72.2
transfer of proceedings, 70.3
tribunal awards, of, 70.5

Enforcement
n.b. prior to 25th March 2002
execution, warrant of
  sale of goods, [9A-695]
garnishee proceedings
  county court, [9A-719]

Enforcement (CCR)
n.b. prior to 25th March 2002
garnishee proceedings
  expenses, [9A-719]

Enforcement (RSC)
n.b. prior to 25th March 2002
crown proceedings
  attachment of debts, sc77.16
equitable execution, receiver appointed by way of
  application of Order, sc51.A1
  generally, sc51.1-sc51.3
possession of land judgment, of
  generally, sc45.3

Enforcement orders
generally, [3B-231]

Equitable jurisdiction
generally, [9A-155]
multiplicity of actions, [9A-160]
stay of proceedings
  change of law, pending, [9A-167]
  concurrent proceedings, [9A-168]-[9A-169]
  costs payment, pending, [9A-166]
  court of its own motion, by, [9A-164]
  CPR, under, [9A-163]
  EC Convention actions, [9A-171]-[9A-176]
  EC investigation, [9A-177]
  effect, [9A-165]
  examples, [9A-178]
  forum non conveniens, [9A-170]
  generally, [9A-161]

lis alibi pendens, [9A-170]
nature, [9A-165]
statute, under, [9A-162]

Equitable execution, receivers appointed by way of
accounts, sc51.3.9
criteria, sc51.1
relevant Master, sc51.2

Equity, rules of
generally, [9A-155]
multiplicity of actions, avoidance of, [9A-160]
stay of proceedings
generally, [9A-161]-[9A-169]

European Convention on Human Rights
House of Lords civil appeal, [4A-75]

European jurisdiction
Brussels Convention
implementation, [5-3]

Evidence
Court of Protection
administration of oaths, [6B-257]
affidavit, [6B-253]
cross-examination, [6B-256]
death of patient, of, [6B-261]
filing, [6B-258]
first appointment of receiver, on, [6B-260]
public authority, amount due to, [6B-262]
recovery of patient, of, [6B-261]
subsequent use, [6B-259]
unsworn, [6B-254]
Visitors, questions to, [6B-255]
default judgment, and, 12PD-004
summary possession, proceedings for, cc24.2

Execution, warrant of
sale of goods
third party claims, [9A-695]
seized goods
sale of, [9A-695]

Exempt agreement
consumer credit, and, [3B-37]

Expert evidence
Practice Direction
questions to experts, 35PD-004
written questions
Practice Direction, 35PD-004

Extension of time for service
House of Lords criminal appeal, [4B-6]

Extortionate credit bargains
reopening
restrictions, [3B-261]

Fees
Court of Protection
administration, [6B-304]
commencement, [6B-303]
detailed assessment, [6B-306]
generally, [6B-302]
introduction, [6B-11]
postponement, [6B-309]
receivership, [6B-307]
remission, [6B-309]
transactions, [6B-305]
winding up, [6B-308]
enduring powers of attorney
generally, [6B-321]
rules, [6B-417], [6B-420]
powers of attorney
generally, [6B-321]
rules, [6B-417], [6B-420]

Fixed costs
person under mental disorder, [6B-171]

Foreign judgment, enforcement of
generally, [5-3]

Forfeiture for non-payment of rent
county court
generally, [3A-290]-[3A-291]

Forms
Court of Protection
And see Court of Protection forms
deeds and recitals, [6B-173]-[6B-182]
introduction, [6B-10]
enduring powers of attorney
generally, [6B-320]
prescribed, [6B-421]-[6B-426]
powers of attorney
generally, [6B-320]
prescribed, [6B-421]-[6B-426]
prescribed
And see Prescribed forms
enduring powers of attorney, [6B-421]-[6B-426]

Funding arrangements
commentary
insurance premiums, [7A-32.1]-[7A-33.1]
success fees, [7A-32.1]-[7A-33.1]
insurance premiums, recovery of
introduction, [7A-32.1]-[7A-33.1]
success fee, recovery of
introduction, [7A-32.1]-[7A-33.1]

Funds in court
rules

contents table, [6A-18]
preliminary, [6A-22]-[6A-23]

Garnishee proceedings
n.b. from 25th March 2002
application, 72.3
consideration of application, 72.8
contents of Part, 72.0.1
costs, 72.11
debtors in hardship, 72.7
editorial introduction, 72.0.2
effect of order, 72.9
interim orders, 72.4-72.6
money in court, 72.10
scope of Part, 72.1
types of order, 72.2

Garnishee proceedings
n.b. prior to 25th March 2002
county court
And see Garnishee proceedings (CCR)
generally, cc30.1-cc30.15
fixed costs, 45.5.6
forms
CCR, cc30.0.4
RSC, sc49.0.4
High Court
And see Garnishee proceedings (RSC)
generally, sc49.1-sc49.10.2
Queen's Bench Guide, [1A-75]
procedural guide, D1-028
statutory basis
generally, [9A-124]-[9A-128]
National Savings Bank deposits, [9A-454]
time limits, E1-011, E1-021

Garnishee proceedings (CCR)
n.b. prior to 25th March 2002
application, cc30.2
cognate RSC, cc30.0.5
contents of Order, cc30.0.1
costs, cc30.13
crown proceedings, cc42.14-cc42.14.1
directions, cc30.8
discharge, cc30.11
district judge's powers, cc30.15
editorial introduction, cc30.0.2
expenses, [9A-717]-[9A-719]
firm, debt of, cc30.14
forms, cc30.0.4
generally, cc30.1
hearing, cc30.9
money in court, cc30.12
notice of non-indebtedness, cc30.5
order absolute, cc30.7
order to show case, cc30.3-cc30.3.1
procedural guide, D1-028
related sources, cc30.0.3
transfer, cc30.10

Garnishee proceedings (RSC)
n.b. prior to 25th March 2002

appeals, sc49.4.7
applications
bank accounts, sc49.2.3
evidence, sc49.2.2
generally, sc49.2-sc49.2.1
order nisi, sc49.2.4
attachable debts
deposit accounts, sc49.1.14-sc49.1.16
exemptions, sc49.1.40-sc49.1.74
generally, sc49.1.17-sc49.1.39
contents of Order, sc49.0.1
costs
bank's expenses, sc49.10.2
generally, sc49.10-sc49.10.1
court's powers, sc49.1.7
crown, against, sc49.1.3, sc77.16-sc77.16.3
discharge, sc49.8-sc49.8.1
dispute of liability, sc49.5-sc49.5.3
editorial introduction, sc49.0.2
exempt garnishees, sc49.1.16
estate of deceased person, against, sc49.1.5
forms, sc49.0.4
generally, sc49.1-sc49.1.1
limitation periods, sc49.1.2
money in court, sc49.9-sc49.9.1
no dispute of liability, sc49.4-sc49.4.7
order absolute, sc49.4-sc49.4.7
order to show cause
effect, sc49.3.2-sc49.3.3
garnishee's position, sc49.3.15-sc49.3.20
garnishor's position, sc49.3.4-sc49.3.14
generally, sc49.3-sc49.3.1
parties
creditors, sc49.1.8
debtors, sc49.1.12
exempt persons, sc49.1.16
partnership, against, sc49.1.4
procedural guide, D1-028
purpose, sc49.1.6
Queen's Bench Guide, [1A-75]
reciprocal enforcement, sc49.1.9
related sources, sc49.0.3
setting aside, sc49.4.5
third party claims, sc49.6-sc49.6.1

Geneva Convention, enforcement pursuant to
Convention text, [2B-84]
Practice Direction, [2B-67]

Grant of administration
persons under mental disorder, [6B-107]

Grounds for possession
assured tenancy
generally, [3A-642]-[3A-649.2]
reasonableness, [3A-649]-[3A-649.2]
protected tenancy
reasonableness, [3A-184]-[3A-184.2]
secure tenancy

reasonableness, [3A-342]-[3A-342.2]

Grounds for possession (assured tenancy)
generally, [3A-642]-[3A-649.2]
Ground 1, [3A-841]
Ground 2, [3A-842]
Ground 3, [3A-843]
Ground 4, [3A-845]
Ground 5, [3A-846]
Ground 7, [3A-848]
mandatory
  commentary, [3A-841]-[3A-848]
reasonableness
  appeals, [3A-649.1]
  ECHR, and, [3A-649.2]
  generally, [3A-642]-[3A-649]

Grounds for possession (protected tenancy)
Case 1
  commentary, [3A-264]
  effect, [3A-178]
reasonableness
  appeals, [3A-184.1]
  ECHR, and, [3A-184.2]
  generally, [3A-184]

Grounds for possession (secure tenancy)
reasonableness
  appeals, [3A-342.1]
  ECHR, and, [3A-342.2]
  generally, [3A-342]

Hearings
Court of Protection
  date, [6B-235]
  persons attending, [6B-264]
  privacy, [6B-263]
  representation, [6B-265]
enduring powers of attorney
  decision, [6B-413]
  evidence, [6B-406]-[6B-410]
  generally, [6B-405]
  witness summons, [6B-411]
summary possession, proceedings for
  generally, cc24.5

High Court
appeals from
  statutory basis, [9A-47]-[9-47A]
conduct of business
  camera, in, [9A-319]
  jury, [9A-326.1]
constitution, [9A-16]
Crown court appeals, [9A-75]-[9A-77]
distribution of business
  alteration, [9A-300]
interest, [9A-105]
jurisdiction
  equitable, [9A-155]-[9A-169]
  generally, [9A-56]-[9A-85]
jury trial
  generally, [9A-326.1]
practice
  privilege against incrimination, [9A-337]

High Court jurisdiction
bail, [9A-64]
certiorari, [9A-81.1]
equitable
  generally, [9A-155]-[169]
exercise of, [9A-60]
generally, [9A-58]
hypothetical cases, [9A-68]
inherent, [9A-59]
judicial review, [9A-85]
mandamus, [9A-81.1]
prohibition, [9A-81.1]

High Court powers
injunctions
  procedure, [9A-112]
interest, [9A-105]
pre-action discovery
  generally, [9A-95]
variation of sentence, [9A-138]
vexatious litigation
  procedure, [9A-134]-[9A-135]

Homelessness
asylum-seekers
  eligibility for assistance, [3A-1016.1]
eligibility for assistance
  asylum-seekers, [3A-1016.1]
  persons from abroad, [3A-1015]
generally
  introductory note, [3A-973]
  meaning, [3A-975.1]
intentionally homeless
  generally, [3A-1061.1]
interim duty to accommodate
  generally, [3A-1036]
  priority need, [3A-1038.1]-[3A-1039]
local authority duties
  priority need and not intentionally homeless, [3A-1082]-[3A-1083]
local authority functions
  guidance, [3A-995]
meaning
  generally, [3A-975.1]
priority need and not intentionally homeless
  generally, [3A-1082]-[3A-1083]
referral
  generally, [3A-1106]
review of decisions
  appeal from, [3A-1135.2]
  generally, [3A-1125]
Secretary of State's functions
  guidance, [3A-995]

House of Lords appeal
High Court, from

introduction, [9A-50]
"leapfrog" appeals
introduction, [9A-50]

House of Lords civil appeals
case statement
  exchange, [4A-52]
  generally, [4A-49]
  lodgment, [4A-52]
costs
  petition for leave, [4A-24]
  petition of appeal, [4A-57]
human rights, and, [4A-75]
petition for leave to appeal
  admissibility, [4A-5]
  consideration on papers, [4A-19]
  costs, [4A-24]
  respondent's objections, [4A-20]
  title, [4A-13]
petition of appeal
  anonymity, [4A-31.1]
  case statement, [4A-49]-[4A-52]
  costs, [4A-57]
  reporting restrictions, [4A-31.1]
  statement of case, [4A-49]-[4A-52]
  statement of facts and issues, [4A-38]
  title, [4A-30]
respondent's objections, [4A-20]
statement of case
  exchange, [4A-52]
  generally, [4A-49]
  lodgment, [4A-52]
statement of facts and issues
  generally, [4A-38]
title
  petition for leave, [4A-13]
  petition of appeal, [4A-30]

House of Lords criminal appeals
appendix
  form, [4B-62]
case statement
  exchange, [4B-44]
  generally, [4B-41]
  lodgment, [4B-44]
consideration on papers, [4B-15]
costs
  petition for leave, [4B-20]
  petition of appeal, [4B-49]
documents
  form, [4B-62]
extension of time
  petition for leave, [4B-6]
human rights, and, [4B-65]
leave to appeal
  England & Wales, in, [4B-1]
  Northern Ireland, in, [4B-1]
petition for leave to appeal
  costs, [4B-20]
  extension of time, [4B-6]
  form, [4B-9]
  leave to appeal, [4B-1]
  preliminary procedure, [4B-15]-[4B-16]
  respondent's objections, [4B-16]
  time limits, [4B-6]
  title of appeal, [4B-9]
petition of appeal
  anonymity, [4B-26.1]
  appendix, [4B-33]-[4B-38]
  case statement, [4B-41]-[4B-44]
  costs, [4B-49]
  reporting restrictions, [4B-26.1]
  statement of case, [4B-41]-[4B-44]
  statement of facts and issues, [4B-32]
  title of appeal, [4B-25]
reporting restrictions, [4B-26]-[4B-26.1]
respondent's objections, [4B-16]
statements of case
  exchange, [4B-44]
  generally, [4B-41]
  lodgment, [4B-44]
statement of facts and issues
  generally, [4B-32]
time limits
  petition for leave, [4B-6]
title of appeal
  petition for leave, [4B-9]
  petition of appeal, [4B-25]

Housing
agricultural occupancy, [3A-776]
anti-social behaviour
  injunctions, [3A-949]
assured shorthold tenancy
  generally, [3A-738]
  possession, [3A-748]-[3A-748.1]
assured tenancy
  generally, [3A-607]
  notice of possession, [3A-841]-[3A-848]
  security of tenure, [3A-633]-[3A-672]
  succession, [3A-719]
homelessness
  assistance, [3A-1015]-[3A-1016.1]
  generally, [3A-973]-[3A-975.1]
  interim duty, [3A-1036]-[3A-1039]
  local authority duties, [3A-1061.1]-[3A-1083]
  local authority functions, [3A-995]
  referral, [3A-1106]
  review of decisions, [3A-1125]
protected tenancy
  generally, [3A-89]
secure tenancy
  assignment, [3A-381]
  generally, [3A-322]-[3A-331]
  possession, [3A-342]-[3A-348]
  succession, [3A-357]
statutory basis
  Administration of Justice Act 1970, [3A-31]-[3A-32]
  Administration of Justice Act 1973, [3A-48]
  County Courts Act 1984, [3A-290]-[3A-291]
  Housing Act 1985, [3A-302]-[3A-381]
  Housing Act 1988, [3A-607]-[3A-848]

Housing Act 1996, [3A-949]-[3A-1135.2]
Immigration and Asylum Act 1999, [3A-1176]-[3A-1216]
Landlord and Tenant Act 1985, [3A-487]
National Assistance Act 1948, [3A-28.1]-[3A-28.10]
Rent Act 1977, [3A-89]-[3A-264]
statutory tenancy
change of tenant, [3A-232]

Housing Act 1985
general provisions
housing associations, [3A-302]
secure tenancy, [3A-322]

Housing Act 1988
general provisions
agricultural occupancy, [3A-776]
assured shorthold tenancy, [3A-738], [3A-748]-[3A-748.1]
assured tenancy, [3A-607], [3A-633]-[3A-672], [3A-719], [3A-841]-[3A-848]
protected tenancy, [3A-776]
restricted contract, [3A-783.1]

Housing Act 1996
applications
generally, cc49.6B
general provisions
homelessness, [3A-973]-[3A-1135.2]
injunctions against anti-social behaviour, [3A-949]

Housing association
meaning
HA 1985, [3A-302]
HA 1988, [3A-607]

Human rights
House of Lords
civil appeal, [4A-75]
criminal appeal, [4B-65]

Hypothetical cases
appeals to Court of Appeal, [9A-68]
statutory basis
procedure, [9A-112]

Immigration and Asylum Act 1999
introduction, [3A-1176]

Incidental decisions in Court of Appeal
jurisdiction, [9A-292]

Information from judgment debtors
n.b. from 25th March 2002
and see Oral examination
application, 71.2

contents of Part, 71.0.1
creditor's affidavit, 71.5
editorial introduction, 71.0.2
failure to comply, 71.8
hearing, 71.6-71.7
scope of Part, 71.1
service of order, 71.3
travelling expenses, 71.4

Injunctions
anti-social behaviour
Practice Direction, ccpd49-001-ccpd49-003
damages, [9A-261]

Inquiries
Court of Protection
appointment of receiver, [6B-293]
execution of documents, [6B-296]
further inquiries, [6B-297]
inspection of property, [6B-294]
prior dealing of property, [6B-295]

Insolvency proceedings
Practice Directions
generally, B1-001

Insurance Companies Act 1982, applications under
applications
generally, [2F-1]

Insurance premiums, recovery of
introduction, [7A-32.1]-[7A-33.1]

Interest
county court
debt and damages, [9A-634]
judgment debt, on, [9A-649]
damages, on
county court, [9A-634]
High Court, [9A-105]
debts, on
county court, [9A-634]
High Court, [9A-105]
High Court, [9A-105]
liquidated demand, on
county court, [9A-634]
High Court, [9A-105]
statutory basis, [9A-105]

Interest on judgment debt
county court, in
statutory basis, [9A-649]

Joinder
summary possession proceedings
CCR, cc24.4

Judges
liability, [9A-38]

rates and tax cases, [9A-44.1]
tenure, [9A-38]

Judgment
county court, in
finality, [9A-636]
interest, [9A-649]
register, [9A-643]

Judgment in default
evidence, 12PD-004
Practice Direction
evidence, 12PD-004

Judgments
CCR
certificate of judgment, cc22.8

Judicial review
application, [9A-85]
jurisdiction, [9A-85]

Jurisdiction
Crown Court
appeals from, [9A-77]
appeals to, [9A-152]
equitable
generally, [9A-155]-[9A-169]
High Court
generally, [9A-55]-[9A-85]
solicitors
undertakings, enforcement of, [7C-213]

Jury, trial by
county court, in
generally, [9A-627]
High Court
generally, [9A-326.1]

Knowledge, date of
generally, [8-26], [8-31]

Land, recovery of
statutory basis
statutory tenancy, [3A-232]

Landlord and Tenant Act 1927 claims
claims from 15th October 2001
Practice Direction, 56PD-011-56PD-013
claims prior to 15th October 2001 (CCR)
generally, cc43.3
issue of proceedings, cc43.4
claims prior to 15th October 2001 (RSC)
allocation of claims, sc97.2-sc97.2.2
applications, sc97.4-sc97.4.1
assignment of proceedings, sc97.2-sc97.2.2
issue of proceedings, sc97.3-sc97.3.1, sc97.5-sc97.5.2
transfer of proceedings, sc97.11

Landlord and Tenant Act 1954 claims
claims from 15th October 2001
Practice Direction, 56PD-007-56PD-008
claims prior to 15th October 2001 (CCR)
authorisation of s.38(4) agreement, cc43.9
new tenancy, cc43.6-cc43.8
procedure, cc43.5
rateable value, cc43.11
service, cc43.10
claims prior to 15th October 2001 (RSC)
assignment of proceedings, sc97.2-sc97.2.2
authorisation of s.38(4) agreement, sc97.6A-sc97.6A.2
certificate under s.37(4), sc97.10-sc97.10.1
interim rent, sc97.9A-sc97.9A.2
issue of proceedings, sc97.3-sc97.3.1
new tenancy, sc97.6-sc97.9.1
parties, sc97.8-sc97.8.1
procedure, sc97.3-sc97.3.1
relief under s.16, sc97.12
transfer of proceedings, sc97.11

Landlord and Tenant Act 1985 claims
claims prior to 15th October 2001, cc43.1

Landlord and Tenant Act 1987 claims
claims prior to 15th October 2001 (CCR)
s.19, under, cc43.17
s.24, under, cc43.18
s.29, under, cc43.19
s.38, under, cc43.20-cc43.20.1
s.40, under, cc43.20-cc43.20.1
service of notice of proceedings, cc43.21
tenants' associations, cc43.22
claims prior to 15th October 2001 (RSC)
assignment of proceedings, sc97.2-sc97.2.2
generally, sc97.2-sc97.3.1, sc97.8-sc97.8.1, sc97.14-sc97.19
issue of proceedings, sc97.3-sc97.3.1
parties, sc97.8-sc97.8.1
s.19, under, sc97.14-sc97.14.1
s.24, under, sc97.15-sc97.15.1
s.29, under, sc97.16-sc97.16.1
s.38, under, sc97.17
s.40, under, sc97.17
service of notice of proceedings, sc97.18
tenants' associations, sc97.19

Landlord and tenant claims
n.b. from 15th October 2001
Chancel Repairs Act 1932, under
Practice Direction, 56PD-029
compensation for improvements claims
certification of improvement, 56PD-013
defendant, 56PD-011
Landlord and Tenant Act 1927, under
Practice Direction, 56PD-0011-56PD-

013
Landlord and Tenant Act 1954, under
  Practice Direction, 56PD-007-56PD-008
new tenancy claims
  Practice Direction, 56PD-007
Practice Direction
  Chancel Repairs Act 1932, 56PD-029
  definitions, 56PD-001
  LTA 1927 claims, 56PD-011-56PD-013
  LTA 1954 claims, 56PD-007-56PD-008

Landlord and tenant claims
and see below under individual Acts
n.b. prior to 15th October 2001
applications under LTA 1927
  CCR, cc43.3-cc43.4
  RSC, sc97.2-sc97.5.2
applications under LTA 1954
  CCR, cc43.5-cc43.11
  RSC, sc97.6-sc97.12
applications under LTA 1985
  CCR, cc43.16
applications under LTA 1987
  CCR, cc43.17-cc43.22
  RSC, sc97.14-sc97.19

"Leapfrog" appeals
county court, from
  generally, [9A-656]-[9A-657.1]
Court of Appeal, to
  generally, [9A-656]-[9A-657.1]
House of Lords, to
  introduction, [9A-50]

Leasehold Reform Act 1967
appeals, sc93.15

Leave to appeal
House of Lords civil case
  petitions for, [4A-5]-[4A-24]
House of Lords criminal appeal
  England & Wales, in, [4B-1]
  Northern Ireland, in, [4B-1]
  petition for, [4B-6]-[4B-20]

Leave to appoint new trustees
generally, [6B-176]

Leave to register enduring power of attorney
generally, [6B-328]

Legal representative
costs against
  wasted costs order, 48.7

Liens
types, [7C-227]

Limitation period
date of knowledge
  generally, [8-26], [8-31]
defective products, [8-19]
generally, [8-3]
mistake in name of party, [8-87]
pending actions
  mistake in name of party, [8-87]
personal injury
  defective products, [8-19]
personal injury (discretionary exclusion)
  exercise of, [8-74]

Liquidated demand, interest on
county court, [9A-634]
High Court, [9A-105]

Local housing authorities
duty of
  introduction, [3A-28.3]-[3A-28.8.1]

Lord Chancellor's Visitors
functions, [6B-201]-[6B-202]
generally, [6B-199]-[6B-200]

Mandamus
jurisdiction, [9A-81.1]

Matrimonial proceedings
persons under mental disorder, [6B-134]

Mental disorder, person under
accounts
  fee, [6B-153], [6B-154]
  format, [6B-150]
  generally, [6B-149]
  lodgment, [6B-151]
  passing, [6B-152]
allowances, [6B-149]-[6B-154]
bankruptcy, [6B-114]
business
  company, [6B-103]
  generally, [6B-101]
  partnership, [6B-102]
charging orders, [6B-113]
contracts, [6B-105]
costs
  agreed, [6B-172]
  estate agency, [6B-98], [6B-166]
  fixed, [6B-171]
  generally, [6B-155]-[6B-157]
  legal aid, [6B-158]-[6B-170]
  receivership management, [6B-163]
creditors, [6B-112]
damages
  benefit disregards, [6B-120]-[6B-122]
  generally, [6B-116]
  settlements, [2C-214], [6B-118]-[6B-119]
  special needs trusts, [6B-123]-[6B-133]
  structured settlements, [2C-214], [6B-117]
divorce, [6B-134]

exercise of power, [6B-106]
fees
  administration, [6B-304]
  commencement, [6B-303]
  detailed assessment, [6B-306]
  generally, [6B-302]
  introduction, [6B-11]
  postponement, [6B-309]
  receivership, [6B-307]
  remission, [6B-309]
  transactions, [6B-305]
  winding up, [6B-308]
forms
  And see Court of Protection forms
  deeds and recitals, [6B-173]-[6B-182]
  introduction, [6B-10]
grant of administration, [6B-107]
investment, [6B-85]-[6B-86]
management, [6B-83]
matrimonial causes, [6B-134]
mortgagee, [6B-108]
mortgagor, [6B-109]
property
  charging order, [6B-113]
  estate agent's charges, [6B-98]
  generally, [6B-87]
  gift, [6B-135], [6B-137]-[6B-141], [6B-143]-[6B-144]
  improvements, [6B-110]
  jointly owned property, [6B-99]
  leases, [6B-104]
  preservation of interest, [6B-111]
  purchase, [6B-97]
  sale, [6B-88]-[6B-96]
  settlement, [6B-135], [6B-137]-[6B-141], [6B-145]
  tenancy for life, [6B-100]
receiver
  And see Receiver
  accounts, [6B-149]-[6B-154]
  appointment, [6B-12]-[6B-34]
  discharge, [6B-35]-[6B-50]
  powers and duties, [6B-83]-[6B-148]
receiver, appointment of
  first, [6B-12]-[6B-27]
  new, [6B-28]-[6B-34]
  vesting orders, [6B-59]-[6B-82]
receiver, discharge of
  death, on, [6B-41]-[6B-50]
  recovery, on, [6B-35]-[6B-40]
  vesting orders, [6B-59]-[6B-82]
special needs trusts
  generally, [6B-123]-[6B-125]
  method, [6B-129]-[6B-132]
  relevant cases, [6B-126]-[6B-128]
  terms, [6B-133]
statutory wills, [6B-136]-[6B-142]
structured settlements, [6B-117]
taxation, [6B-51]-[6B-58]
testimony. perpetuation of, [6B-146]
trusts, variation of, [6B-147]
vesting orders
  And see Vesting orders
  receiver, [6B-64]-[6B-73]

trustee, [6B-74]-[6B-82]
generally, [6B-59]-[6B-63]
wills
  generally, [6B-148]
  statutory, [6B-136]-[6B-142]

Mental Health Act 1983
And see Person under mental disorder
application of
  generally, [6B-185]
  Northern Ireland, [6B-210], [6B-225]
  Scotland, [6B-210], [6B-224]
arrangement of sections, [6B-184]
correspondence of patients, [6B-218]-[6B-335]
definitions, [6B-185], [6B-213]
general provisions, [6B-208]-[6B-214]
generally, [6B-1]
nominated judge
  appeal from, [6B-204]-[6B-205]
  definition, [6B-213]
  functions, [6B-187]-[6B-189]
  generally, [6B-186]
  powers, [6B-190]-[6B-203]
nominated officer
  definition, [6B-213]
offences
  forgery, [6B-215]-[6B-216]
  obstruction, [6B-217]
powers of judge
  conduct of proceedings, [6B-203]
  curator, appointment of, [6B-197]
  emergencies, [6B-194]
  generally, [6B-190]-[6B-191]
  preservation of property, [6B-198]
  receiver, appointment of, [6B-195]-[6B-196]
  Visitors, appointment of, [6B-199]-[6B-202]
  wills, [6B-192]-[6B-193]
procedural rules, [6B-206]
Public Trustee's functions, [6B-211]-[6B-212]
receiver
  appointment, [6B-195]-[6B-196]
  security, [6B-207]
rules, [6B-208], [6B-222]-[6B-223]
supplementary provisions, [6B-222]-[6B-225]
Visitors
  functions, [6B-201]-[6B-202]
  generally, [6B-199]-[6B-200]
  wills, [6B-192]-[6B-193]

Mistake in name of party
time limits, [8-87]

Mortgage claims
n.b. prior to 15th October 2001
and see now Mortgaged residential property
county court
  And see Mortgage claims (CCR)

generally, cc6.5-cc6.5A
court's powers
 extended, [3A-48]
 generally, [3A-31]-[3A-32]
particulars of claim
 Practice Direction, 16PD-006
statutory powers
 extended, [3A-48]
 generally, [3A-31]-[3A-32]

Mortgage claims (CCR)
n.b. prior to 15th October 2001
forms, cc6.5.3
particulars of claim
 dwelling-house, cc6.5A
 generally, cc6.5
service, cc7.15A

Mortgage claims (RSC)
n.b. prior to 15th October 2001

Mortgaged residential property, claims for possession of
n.b. from 15th October 2001
And see Possession claims
statutory powers
 extended, [3A-48]
 generally, [3A-31]-[3A-32]

Mortgages
persons under mental disorder, [6B-108]-[6B-109]

National Assistance Act 1948
asylum seekers, [3A-28.10]
local authorities, duty of, [3A-28.3]-[3A-28.8.1]

New tenancy claims
acknowledgment of service, 56PD-007
Practice Direction
 acknowledgment of service, 56PD-007

Nominated judge
appeal, [6B-204]-[6B-205]
definition, [6B-213]
functions, [6B-187]-[6B-189]
generally, [6B-186]
powers, [6B-190]-[6B-203]

Nominated officer
definition, [6B-213]

Non-payment of rent, forfeiture for
county court
 generally, [3A-290]-[3A-291]

Oral examination
n.b. from 25th March 2002
application, 71.2

Oral examination—*cont.*
contents of Part, 71.0.1
creditor's affidavit, 71.5
editorial introduction, 71.0.2
failure to comply, 71.8
hearing, 71.6-71.7
scope of Part, 71.1
service of order, 71.3
travelling expenses, 71.4

Oral examination (CCR)
n.b. prior to 25th March 2002
generally, cc25.3-cc25.3.3
non-money claims, cc25.4-cc25.4.1
procedural guide, D1-026
related sources, cc25.3.2

Oral examination (RSC)
n.b. prior to 25th March 2002
contents of Order, sc48.0.1
costs, sc48.3.12
editorial introduction, sc48.0.2
forms
 generally, sc48.0.4
 request, F4-004
 request for reissue, F4-012
generally, sc48.1-sc48.1.1
procedure
 conduct money, sc48.3.7
 costs, sc48.3.12
 further examination, sc48.3.11
 nature of examination, sc48.3.10
 nominated officers, sc48.3.9
 record of examination, sc48.3-sc48.3.4
 relevant debtors, sc48.3.5
 service, sc48.3.6-sc48.3.8
purpose, sc48.2, sc48.3.4
related sources, sc48.0.3

Orders
CCR
 certificate of judgment, cc22.8

Overseas principal, service on agent of
generally, 6.16

Particulars of claim
county court
 mortgage claims, cc6.5-cc6.5A
 possession of land actions, cc6.3
mortgage claims
 county court, cc6.5-cc6.5A
 Practice Direction, 16PD-006
possession of land claims
 Practice Directions, 16PD-006

Paternity tests, application for
county court, in
 editorial introduction, cc47.0.2
 generally, cc47.5

Patients
damages for
  benefit disregards, [6B-120]-[6B-122]
  generally, [6B-116]
  settlements, [6B-118]
  special needs trusts, [6B-123]-[6B-133]
  structured settlements, [6B-117]

Pending actions, time limits for
mistake in name of party, [8-87]

Periodic tenancy
assured tenancy
  succession, [3A-719]

Person under disability
mental disorder
  And see Person under mental disorder
  generally, [6B-12]-[6B-182]

Person under mental disorder
And see Patient
accounts
  fee, [6B-153], [6B-154]
  format, [6B-150]
  generally, [6B-149]
  lodgment, [6B-151]
  passing, [6B-152]
allowances, [6B-149]-[6B-154]
bankruptcy, [6B-114]
business, running of, [6B-101]
charging orders, [6B-113]
company meetings, voting at, [6B-103]
contracts, [6B-105]
costs
  agreed, [6B-172]
  estate agency, [6B-98], [6B-166]
  fixed, [6B-171]
  generally, [6B-155]-[6B-157]
  legal aid, [6B-158]-[6B-170]
  receivership management, [6B-163]
creditors, [6B-112]
damages
  benefit disregards, [6B-120]-[6B-122]
  generally, [6B-116]
  settlements, [2C-214], [6B-118]-[6B-119]
  special needs trusts, [6B-123]-[6B-133]
  structured settlements, [2C-214], [6B-117]
divorce, [6B-134]
exercise of power, [6B-106]
forms
  And see Court of Protection forms
  generally, [6B-173]-[6B-182]
grant of administration, [6B-107]
investment, [6B-85]-[6B-86]
management, [6B-83]
matrimonial causes, [6B-134]
mortgagee, [6B-108]
mortgagor, [6B-109]
partnership, dissolution of, [6B-102]

property
  charging order, [6B-113]
  estate agent's charges, [6B-98]
  generally, [6B-87]
  gift, [6B-135], [6B-137]-[6B-141], [6B-143]-[6B-144]
  improvements, [6B-110]
  jointly owned property, [6B-99]
  leases, [6B-104]
  preservation of interest, [6B-111]
  purchase, [6B-97]
  sale, [6B-88]-[6B-96]
  settlement, [6B-135], [6B-137]-[6B-141], [6B-145]
  tenancy for life, [6B-100]
receivers
  And see Receiver
  appointment, [6B-12]-[6B-34]
  discharge, [6B-35]-[6B-50]
receiver, appointment of
  first, [6B-12]-[6B-27]
  new, [6B-28]-[6B-34]
  vesting orders, [6B-59]-[6B-82]
receiver, discharge of
  death, on, [6B-41]-[6B-58]
  recovery, on, [6B-35]-[6B-40]
  vesting orders, [6B-59]-[6B-82]
settlements
  generally, [6B-118]-[6B-133]
  structured, [6B-117]
special needs trusts
  generally, [6B-123]-[6B-125]
  method, [6B-129]-[6B-132]
  relevant cases, [6B-126]-[6B-128]
  terms, [6B-133]
statutory wills, [6B-136]-[6B-142]
structured settlements, [6B-117]
taxation, [6B-51]-[6B-58]
testimony. perpetuation of, [6B-146]
trusts, variation of, [6B-147]
vesting orders
  And see Vesting orders
  generally, [6B-59]-[6B-63]
  receiver, [6B-64]-[6B-73]
  trustee, [6B-74]-[6B-82]
wills
  generally, [6B-148]
  statutory, [6B-136]-[6B-142]

Personal injury claims
discovery
  county court, [9A-589A]
time limits
  defective products, [8-18]-[8-19]
  fatal accidents, [8-26], [8-31]

Persons under mental disability
management of property and affairs
  And see Person under mental disorder
  Court of Protection Rules, [6B-227]-[6B-318]
  generally, [6B-1]-[6B-182]
  Mental Health Act 1983, [6B-184]-[6B-

225]
powers of attorney, [6B-319]-[6B-426]

Petition for leave to appeal to HoL
civil appeal
  admissibility, [4A-5]
  consideration on papers, [4A-19]
  costs, [4A-24]
  respondent's objections, [4A-20]
  title, [4A-13]
criminal appeal
  costs, [4B-20]
  extension of time, [4B-6]
  leave to appeal, [4B-1]
  preliminary procedure, [4B-15]-[4B-16]
  respondent's objections, [4B-16]
  time limits, [4B-6]
  title of appeal, [4B-9]

Petition of appeal to HoL
civil appeal
  anonymity, [4A-31.1]
  case statement, [4A-49]-[4A-52]
  costs, [4A-57]
  reporting restrictions, [4A-31.1]
  statement of case, [4A-49]-[4A-52]
  statement of facts and issues, [4A-38]
  title, [4A-30]
criminal appeal
  anonymity, [4B-26.1]
  appendix, [4B-33]-[4B-38]
  case statement, [4B-41]-[4B-44]
  costs, [4B-49]
  reporting restrictions, [4B-26.1]
  statement of case, [4B-41]-[4B-44]
  statement of facts and issues, [4B-32]
  title of appeal, [4B-25

Pilot schemes
generally, 51.2

Possession claims
n.b. from 15th October 2001
particulars of claim
  Practice Directions, 16PD-006
Practice Direction
  particulars of claim, 16PD-006
  starting proceedings, 55PD-001
starting proceedings
  Practice Direction, 55PD-001

Possession claims
n.b. prior to 15th October 2001
enforcement, sc45.3
forms, cc6.3.3
particulars of claim, cc6.3
service, cc7.15
venue of proceedings, cc4.3

Post Office Act 1969
applications

generally, cc49.15
postal packets, sc77.17

Postal packets, proceedings relating to
applications, sc77.17

Powers of attorney
And see Enduring powers of attorney
fees, [6B-321]
forms
  generally, [6B-320]
  prescribed, [6B-421]-[6B-426]
generally, [6B-319], [6B-322]-[6B-338]
rules, [6B-392]-[6B-420]
statutory basis, [6B-339]-[6B-391]

Practice Directions
admiralty proceedings
  generally, [2A-5]
anti-social behaviour, injunctions against
  bail, ccpd49-002
  medical examination and report, ccpd49-003
  warrant of arrest, ccpd49-001
arbitration proceedings
  applications, [2B-17]
  enforcement, [2B-67]
contentious probate proceedings
  counterclaim, [2G-17]
  editorial introduction, [2G-1]
county court, [9A-652]
default judgment
  evidence, 12PD-004
expert evidence
  questions to experts, 35PD-004
insolvency proceedings
  generally, B1-001
Insurance Companies Act 1982, applications under
  applications, [2F-1]
landlord and tenant claims
  Chancel Repairs Act 1932, 56PD-029
  definitions, 56PD-001
  LTA 1927 claims, 56PD-011-56PD-013
  LTA 1954 claims, 56PD-007-56PD-008
possession of land claims
  starting proceedings, 55PD-001

Prescribed forms
enduring power of attorney
  CoP direction, [6B-332]
  regulations, [6B-421]-[6B-404]

Privilege
self-incrimination, against
  High Court, [9A-337]

Prohibition
jurisdiction, [9A-81.1]

Second Cumulative Supplement

Property
  Court of Protection
    disposal, [6B-300]
    statement, [6B-298]
    stock, [6B-299]
  persons under mental disorder
    charging order, [6B-113]
    estate agent's charges, [6B-98]
    generally, [6B-87]
    gift, [6B-135], [6B-137]-[6B-141], [6B-143]-[6B-144]
    improvements, [6B-110]
    jointly owned property, [6B-99]
    leases, [6B-104]
    preservation of interest, [6B-111]
    purchase, [6B-97]
    sale, [6B-88]-[6B-96]
    settlement, [6B-135], [6B-137]-[6B-141], [6B-145]
    tenancy for life, [6B-100]

Protected tenancy
  grounds for possession
    effect, [3A-178]
    reasonableness, [3A-184]-[3A-184.2]
    post-Housing Act 1988, [3A-776]
    separate dwelling, [3A-89]

Provisional damages
  county court, [9A-581]

Public trustee
  address, [6D-88]

Public Trustee Rules 1912
  definitions, [6D-88]

Receivers, appointment of
  equitable execution, by way of
    And see Receivers (equitable execution)
    generally, sc51.A1-sc51.2
  Mental Health Act 1983, under
    And see Receivers (mental health)
    generally, [6B-12]-[6B-58]

Receivers (equitable execution)
  accounts, sc51.3.9
  criteria, sc51.1
  relevant Master, sc51.2

Receivers (mental health)
  accounts
    death of patient, discharge on, [6B-50]
    new appointment, [6B-34]
    recovery of patient, discharge on, [6B-40]
    tax, payment of, [6B-58]
  appointment of
    first, [6B-12]-[6B-27]
      Mental Health Act 1983, under, [6B-195]-[6B-196], [6B-207]
    new, [6B-28]-[6B-34]
    vesting orders, [6B-59]-[6B-82]
  Court of Protection Rules
    interim appointment, [6B-268]
    remuneration, [6B-269]
    security, [6B-282]-[6B-286]
    survivorship appointment, [6B-270]
  death of patient, discharge on
    application, [6B-44]-[6B-45]
    costs, [6B-46]
    documentation, [6B-45]
    final order, [6B-47]-[6B-49]
    generally, [6B-41]-[6B-43]
    passing final account of former receiver, [6B-50]
    vacation of security of receiver, [6B-49]
  discharge of
    death, on, [6B-41]-[6B-50]
    recovery, on, [6B-35]-[6B-40]
    vesting orders, [6B-59]-[6B-82]
  final order
    death of patient, discharge on, [6B-47]-[6B-49]
    entry, [6B-25]
    first appointment, [6B-22]-[6B-24]
    new appointment, [6B-30]-[6B-33]
    notification, [6B-26]
    objection, [6B-21]
    recovery of patient, discharge on, [6B-37]-[6B-39]
    sealing, [6B-25]
    security, lodgment of, [6B-27]
    tax, payment of, [6B-53]-[6B-57]
  first appointment of
    applicant, [6B-15]-[6B-16]
    application, [6B-13]-[6B-18]
    death of applicant, [6B-16]
    documentation, [6B-17]
    final order, [6B-20]-[6B-27]
    generally, [6B-12]
    interim order and direction, [6B-19]
    notification of application, [6B-18]
    objection, [6B-21]
    security, [6B-24]
    withdrawal of application, [6B-14]
  fees
    administration, [6B-304]
    commencement, [6B-303]
    detailed assessment, [6B-306]
    generally, [6B-302]
    introduction, [6B-11]
    postponement, [6B-309]
    receivership, [6B-307]
    remission, [6B-309]
    transactions, [6B-305]
    winding up, [6B-308]
  forms
    And see Court of Protection forms
    deeds and recitals, [6B-173]-[6B-182]
    introduction, [6B-10]
  interim order and direction, [6B-19]
  new appointment of
    application, [6B-28]-[6B-29]
    documentation, [6B-29]

final order, [6B-30]-[6B-33]
passing final account of former
  receiver, [6B-34]
security, [6B-32]
recovery of patient, discharge on
application, [6B-35]-[6B-36]
documentation, [6B-36]
final order, [6B-37]-[6B-38]
passing final account of former
  receiver, [6B-40]
vacation of security of receiver, [6B-39]
security
bond, [6B-286]
discharge of, [6B-285]
discharge by death, on, [6B-49]
discharge by recovery, on, [6B-39]
first appointment, on, [6B-24]
generally, [6B-282]
lodgment, [6B-284]
manner, [6B-283]
new appointment, on, [6B-32]
tax, payment of
application, [6B-51]-[6B-52]
documentation, [6B-52]
certificate of, [6B-54]
final order, [6B-53]-[6B-56]
passing final account of former
  receiver, [6B-58]
vacation of security of receiver, [6B-57]
vesting orders
And see Vesting orders
appointment of receiver, [6B-64]-[6B-69]
appointment of trustee, [6B-74]-[6B-82]
generally, [6B-59]-[6B-63]
retirement of receiver, [6B-70]-[6B-73]

Recovery of possession of land, claims for
n.b. from 15th October 2001
particulars of claim
  Practice Directions, 16PD-006
Practice Direction
  particulars of claim, 16PD-006
  starting proceedings, 55PD-001
starting proceedings
  Practice Direction, 55PD-001
statutory basis
  statutory tenancy, [3A-232]

Recovery of possession of land, claims for
n.b. prior to 15th October 2001
enforcement, sc45.3
forms, cc6.3.3
particulars of claim, cc6.3
service, cc7.15
venue of proceedings, cc4.3

References
Court of Protection proceedings, of
  judge, to, [6B-266]
  Master, to, [6B-267]

Rent Act 1977, claims under
Case 1
  breach of obligation, [3A-264]
  grounds for possession
    effect, [3A-178]
    reasonableness, [3A-184]-[3A-184.2]
  protected tenancy
    grounds for possession, [3A-176]-[3A-184.2]
    separate dwelling, [3A-89]
  security for tenure
    reasonableness, [3A-184]-[3A-184.2]
  statutory tenancy
    change of tenant, [3A-232]
    grounds for possession, [3A-176]-[3A-184.2]

Reopening credit agreements
restrictions, [3B-261]

Repairing obligation
criteria
  relevant repair, [3A-487]
relevant repair, [3A-487]

Reporting restrictions
House of Lords civil appeal, [4A-31.1]
House of Lords criminal appeal, [4B-26.1]

Representation orders
derivative claims
  generally, 19.9

Respondent's objection
House of Lords civil appeal, [4A-20]
House of Lords criminal appeal, [4B-16]

Restricted contract
post-Housing Act 1988, [3A-783.1]

Reviews
Court of Protection, [6B-280]

Rights of audience
county court
  generally, [9A-607]-[9A-608]
  Lord Chancellor, by direction of, [9A-612]

Rules of court
county court
  application of RSC, [9A-655]
  generally, [9A-653]

Sale of seized goods
third party claims, [9A-695]

Scientific tests, application for
county court, in
  editorial introduction, cc47.0.2

generally, cc47.5

Secure tenancy
assignment
  exchange, by, [3A-381]
forms of order, [3A-343]
grounds for possession
  reasonableness, [3A-342]-[3A-342.2]
notice
  dispensation, [3A-331]
possession
  discretion of court, [3A-348]
reasonableness
  appeals, [3A-342.1]
  ECHR, and, [3A-342.2]
  generally, [3A-342]
security of tenure
  generally, [3A-326]
succession
  qualifying persons, [3A-357]
tenant condition, [3A-322]

Security by receivers
Mental Health Act, appointed under
  bond, [6B-286]
  discharge, [6B-285]
  generally, [6B-282]
  lodgment, [6B-284]
  manner, [6B-283]

Seized goods
sale of
  third party claims, [9A-695]

Self-incrimination, privilege against
High Court, [9A-337]

Service
application of Rule, 6.1
agent of overseas principal, on
  generally, 6.16
claim form, of
  agent of overseas principal, on, 6.16
  Court of Protection
    certificate of, [6B-252]
    generally, [6B-245]
    method, [6B-246]
    next of kin, on, [6B-251]
    patient, on, [6B-250]
    person under disability, on, [6B-249]
    solicitor, on, [6B-247]
    substituted, [6B-248]
  out of the jurisdiction
    EC Council Regulation, 6.33-6.57
summary possession, proceedings
  for(CCR)
  generally, cc24.3

Service out of the jurisdiction
Commercial Court Guide
  generally, [2C-46]
  procedure, [2C-265]

EC Council Regulation
  extrajudicial documents, 6.48
  final provisions, 6.49-6.57
  general provisions, 6.33-6.35
  judicial documents, 6.36-6.47

Setting aside
summary possession, proceedings for
  (CCR)
  generally, cc24.7

Settlements
patients
  commentary, [6B-118]-[6B-133]
  Queen's Bench Guide, [1A-37]
  structured, [6B-117]
structured
  persons under mental disorder, [6B-117]

Sittings of court
Court of Appeal, [9A-288]-[9A-289]

Small claims track
appeals
  Practice Direction, 52PD-015A
Practice Direction
  appeals, 52PD-015A

Solicitors
costs
  wasted costs order, 48.7
jurisdiction of courts
  undertakings, enforcement of, [7C-213]
liens
  types, [7C-227]
wasted costs, order for
  generally, 48.7

Special needs trusts
generally, [6B-123]-[6B-125]
method, [6B-129]-[6B-132]
relevant cases, [6B-126]-[6B-128]
terms, [6B-133]

Specific performance, claims for
damages, and
  generally, [9A-261]

Starting proceedings
Commercial Court Guide
  service out of the jurisdiction, [2C-46]
possession of land claims
  Practice Direction, 55PD-001

Statements of case
court's powers
  dispensing with statements, 16.8
  House of Lords civil appeal

exchange, [4A-52]
generally, [4A-49]
lodgment, [4A-52]
House of Lords criminal appeal
exchange, [4B-44]
generally, [4B-41]
lodgment, [4B-44]

Statements of facts and issues
House of Lords civil appeal
generally, [4A-38]
House of Lords criminal appeal
generally, [4B-32]

Statutory receipt
persons under mental disorder, [6B-177]

Statutory tenancy
change of tenant, [3A-232]
grounds for possession
effect, [3A-178]
reasonableness, [3A-184]-[3A-184.2]

Statutory wills
form, [6B-181]
generally, [6B-136]-[6B-142]

Stay of proceedings
abuse of process, [9A-166]
changes in law, pending, [9A-167]
concurrent actions
actions, [9A-168]
criminal and civil actions, [9A-169]
county court
declaratory relief, [9A-665]
execution, [9A-674]-[9A-675]
equitable jurisdiction
change of law, pending, [9A-167]
concurrent proceedings, [9A-168]-[9A-169]
costs payment, pending, [9A-166]
CPR, under, [9A-163]
effect, [9A-165]
generally, [9A-161]
nature, [9A-165]
statute, under, [9A-162]
generally, [9A-161]
legislation pending, [9A-167]
methods
court's own motion, under, [9A-164]-[9A-165]
CPR, under, [9A-163]
particular statutes, under, [9A-162]

Stop notices
n.b. from 25th March 2002
amendment, 73.19
contents of Part, 73.0.1
definition, 73.16
discharge, 73.21
editorial introduction, 73.0.2
effect, 73.18

request, 73.17
scope of Part, 73.1
variation, 73.21
withdrawal, 73.20

Stop notices
n.b. prior to 25th March 2002
amendment, sc50.13-sc50.13.1
Attorney-General's holding, sc50.14.3
contents of Order, sc50.0.1
disharge, sc50.14, sc50.14.6
editorial introduction, sc50.0.2
effect, sc50.12-sc50.12.1, sc50.14.5
forms, sc50.0.4
generally, sc50.11-sc50.11.1
procedure, sc50.14.2
related sources, sc50.0.3
statutory basis, [9B-222]-[9B-223]
withdrawal, sc50.14, sc50.14.6

Stop orders
n.b. from 25th March 2002
application, 73.12
contents of Part, 73.0.1
definition, 73.11
discharge, 73.15
editorial introduction, 73.0.2
funds in court, for, 73.13
scope of Part, 73.1
securities, for, 73.14
variation, 73.15

Stop orders
n.b. prior to 25th March 2002
contents of Order, sc50.0.1
editorial introduction, sc50.0.2
forms, sc50.0.4
generally, sc50.10-sc50.10.12
related sources, sc50.0.3
starting proceedings, 8BPD-002
statutory basis, [9B-222]-[9B-223]

Structured settlements
persons under mental disorder, [6B-117]

Success fee, recovery of
introduction, [7A-32.1]-[7A-33.1]
Order
prescribed requirements, [7A-18.1]

Succession
assured tenancy, [3A-719]
secure tenancy
qualifying persons, [3A-357]

Summary possession, proceedings for (CCR)
claim form
evidence, cc24.2
generally, cc24.1
service, cc24.3

hearing
  generally, cc24.5
joinder, cc24.4
service
  generally, cc24.3
setting aside
  generally, cc24.7

Supreme Court Act 1981
constitution
  High Court, [9A-16]
costs
  generally, [9A-265]
Crown Court
  appeals, [9A-77]
damages, [9A-261]
documents, production of, [9A-441]-[9A-443]
equity
  generally, [9A-155]-[9A-169]
High Court
  constitution, [9A-16]
  jurisdiction, [9A-55]-[9A-85]
  powers, [9A-95]-[9A-152]
interpretation, [9A-3]
introductory note, [9A-2]
judges
  liability, [9A-38]
  rates and tax cases, [9A-44.1]
jurisdiction
  Court of Appeal, [9A-47]-[9A-50.1]
  Crown Court, [9A-152]
  equitable, [9A-155]-[9A-169]
  High Court, [9A-55]-[9A-85]

Tenancy
assured
  generally, [3A-607]
  notice of possession, [3A-841]-[3A-848]
  security of tenure, [3A-633]-[3A-672]
  succession, [3A-719]
assured shorthold
  generally, [3A-738]
  possession, [3A-748]-[3A-748.1]
protected
  generally, [3A-89]
secure
  assignment, [3A-381]
  generally, [3A-322]-[3A-331]
  possession, [3A-342]-[3A-348]
  succession, [3A-357]
statutory
  change of tenant, [3A-232]

Testimony, perpetuation of
persons under mental disorder, [6B-146]

Third party debt orders
n.b. from 25th March 2002
and see Garnishee proceedings
application, 72.3
consideration of application, 72.8
contents of Part, 72.0.1
costs, 72.11
debtors in hardship, 72.7
editorial introduction, 72.0.2
effect of order, 72.9
interim orders, 72.4-72.6
money in court, 72.10
scope of Part, 72.1
types of order, 72.2

Time limits
Court of Protection
  generally, [6B-230]
  variation, [6B-231]
date of knowledge
  generally, [8-26], [8-31]
defective products, [8-19]
generally, [8-3]
House of Lords criminal appeal
  petition for leave, [4B-6]
mistake in name of party, [8-87]
pending actions
  mistake in name of party, [8-87]
personal injury
  defective products, [8-19]

Title of proceedings
House of Lords civil appeal
  petition for leave, [4A-13]
  petition of appeal, [4A-30]
House of Lords criminal appeal
  petition for leave, [4B-9]
  petition of appeal, [4B-25]

Tort, actions in
generally, [9A-513]

Total charge for credit
included items
  generally, [3B-331]

Transfer of land
persons under mental disability, [6B-178]

Transfer of proceedings
county court, to
  generally, [9A-553]
High Court,. to
  order of county court, by, [9A-560]
statutory basis
  county court, from, [9A-553]
  county court, to, [9A-560]
  High Court, to, [9A-560]

Transitional arrangements
pilot schemes, 51.2

Trial
jury, by
  county court, in, [9A-627]
  High Court, in, [9A-326.1]

INDEX

Trial by jury
  county court, in
    generally, [9A-627]
  High Court, in
    generally, [9A-326.1]

Trustees
  representation by, sc15.14

Trusts
  variation of
    persons under mental disorder, [6B-147]
    statutory basis, [6D-147]-[6D-153]

Undertakings
  admiralty proceedings
    generally, [2A-123]-[2A-124]

Unfair contract terms
  consumer contracts, in
    enforcement, [3B-455]

Vacation business
  Court of Appeal, [9A-288]-[9A-289]

Variation of sentence
  statutory basis, [9A-138]

Venue for commencement
  possession claims (prior to 15th October 2001), cc4.3

Vesting orders
  appointment of receiver
    application, [6B-65]
    documentation, [6B-66]
    generally, [6B-64]
    order, [6B-67]-[6B-69]
  appointment of trustee (s.36 TA 1925)
    application, [6B-79]
    documentation, [6B-80]
    generally, [6B-78]
    order, [6B-81]-[6B-82]
  appointment of trustee (s.54 TA 1925)
    application, [6B-75]
    documentation, [6B-76]
    generally, [6B-74]
    order, [6B-77]
  generally, [6B-59]
  retirement of receiver, [6B-71]-[6B-73]
  retirement of receiver
    application, [6B-71]
    documentation, [6B-72]
    generally, [6B-70]
    order, [6B-73]
  types, [6B-60]-[6B-62]

Vexatious litigation
  statutory basis
    procedure, [9A-134]-[9A-135]

Visitors
  functions, [6B-201]-[6B-202]
  generally, [6B-199]-[6B-200]

Wasted costs order
  generally, 48.7

Wills
  patients, [6B-192]-[6B-193]
  persons under mental disorder
    generally, [6B-148]
    statutory, [6B-136]-[6B-142]

Witness statements
  summary possession, proceedings for, cc24.2

Witness summons
  Court of Protection, [6B-274]-[6B-276]
  enduring powers of attorney, [6B-411]

Written questions for experts
  Practice Direction, 35PD-004